WHY LEADERS FAIL AND PLUNGE THE INNOCENT INTO A SEA OF AGONIES

THE DANGER OF ABNORMAL POLITICS

VOLUME ONE

AGOLA AUMA-OSOLO

Political Scientist and Jurist, School of Deveopment and
Strategic Studies (SDSS)
Maseno University
Maseno, Kenya
0721-597402
auma_osolo@yahoo.com
agolaaumaosolo@gmail.com

Order this book online at www.trafford.com
or email orders@trafford.com

Most Trafford titles are also available at major online book retailers.

Scripture quotations marked KJV are from the Holy Bible, King James Version (Authorized Version).
First published in 1611. Quoted from the KJV Classic Reference Bible, Copyright © 1983
by The HYPERLINK "http://www.zondervan.com/" Zondervan Corporation.

Printed in the United States of America.

ISBN: 978-1-4907-1490-5 (sc)
ISBN: 978-1-4907-1491-2 (e)

Trafford rev. 07/17/2014

 www.trafford.com

North America & international
toll-free: 1 888 232 4444 (USA & Canada)
fax: 812 355 4082

TABLE OF CONTENTS

DEDICATION

THIS BOOK IS IN memory of my most beloved adoreable father Zakaria O. Osolo and mother Raheli Auma Osolo whose divine love and exemplary spirit of a just leadership and judgement in and outside their nuclear family homestead nurtured and moulded my whole being into/with wisdom and knowledge; and thus laid down for me: (1) the foundation of my firm commitment to sincerity; scientific truth; hard workmanship; courage; obedience to the rule of law and justice; and total war against every form of injustice, dishonesty, deceits, envy and malice, false accusations, and all other symptoms of evil against Holiness and Perfection of our Humanity; and (2) the conviction that only a life with a loving, honest, just, prudent, righteous and caring parents is the best teacher and, therefore, the only life worthy remembering, adoring, emulating and caressing.

Therefore, to both of you, Thank You so much since all that you taught me to do and not to do if I were to earn a caressing from nature, I have empirically confirmed it true!

Professor Agola Auma-Osolo
2013

PREFACE

I. A GREATEST SHAME TO MANKIND

It IS A COMMON sense and knowledge to us all in that according to our <u>Holy Bible</u> under Genesis Chapter 1 verses 24 through 30, the Everlasting Truth, since the Creation of our Universe to the Present, is that of all living creatures on our Earth Planet, it is only man and man alone who is blessed and endowed by The Creator with a Dominion Responsibility over all other living and non-living creatures found in the seas, air and dry land according to their kinds. Thus, at the onset of life, man was mandated by God to exploit this universe in his capacity as its leader for the purpose of his own <u>summum bonum</u>, i.e. his Greatest Happiness and all other forms of well-being.

In view of this obvious truth, the paradoxical nagging questions which, therefore, put mankind to the Greatest Shame are:-

1. Has mankind actually done so?

2. If not, why? And if so, to what extent?

3. <u>As scientists who</u>, by virtue of our being a special unique class in Society because of our unique advantage in abundant Knowledge and Wisdom gained from Higher Education, Research and Training which the overwhelming Masses of Society does not have, *are expected to come to the aid of total society* against each insecurity as Bio-scientists have superbly demonstrated against polio and other health menaces; and as physicists have also done against transport, telecommunication and other various human insecurities, what have we Social and Behavioural Scientists done vis-à-vis various society insecurities most particularly against Society Leadership Poverty and Ineptitude which has always plunged the innocent in Society to a sea of various untold agonies due to its own recurrent failures globally?

4. How can such menaces be eradicated or prevented just as polio has been done as a result of scientific intervention by Bio-scientists?

5. And, from Theological Science, the fact is that in order for one to be deemed a worthy leader of a people who have selected him out of themselves with a purpoe of granting him with a public responsibility of serving them with what one prominent political scientist, Professor Harold D. Lasswell, calls "Goods" and "Services", one must, <u>apriori</u>, recognize and adhere at all times to this Heavenly Sovereign Lord's commandment in his leadership: *"He that rules over men must be just, ruling in the fear of God. And he shall be as the light of the morning, when the sun rises, even a morning without clouds; as a tender grass springing out of the earth by clear shining after rain". ("Samuel 23:3-4, THE HOLY BIBLE).* The critical nagging question to both scientists and Total Humanity is: Is this being done? If so, to what extent? And if not, what has been the causes and effects to Humanity and the Environment since the times of our Patriarch Adam and Matriarch Eve to our own times (2013)?

Hence, the object of this book is to unlock these underlying mysteries surrounding the actual root causes of recurrent leadership failures that have always evaded recognition of other social and behavioural research since Antiquity. With this as its ultimate goal, the book will drive deep into the various horizons of dark jungles in search of those actual root-causes:—(1) which became responsible for leading our Patriarch Adam and Matriarch Eve to the confusion that made them lose their expected rational direction and their blessed endowment in The Garden of Eden freely given to them by the grace of God as so confirmed by the Holy Bible under Chapter 2 verses 15-17 of The Genesis; and (2) which have continued over time to lead our past and present generations into recurrent conflicts; infrastructure destruction and mutual genocide; and massive explosions of refugee flights in various confused directions in search of safe havens.

In this regard, it is here hoped that this book shall be able to serve as a break-through regarding these mysteries and as a prerequisite to our getting closer to a possible solution to this perennially evasive menace of leadership poverty and ineptitude which has always plunged the innocent general public into a sea of agonies from GENERATION TO GENERATION effective the Time of our Patriarch Adam to the Present.

ACKNOWLEDGEMENT

IN THIS REGARD, I sincerely thank our Almighty God whose abundant Mercies, Love and Grace has touched my heart and soul to indulge myself in this most diffuclt task in order to unlock these evasive mysteries for the good of our Humanity. Also, my gratitude is due to all those colleagues, friends and relatives alike for their assistance in various ways. This includes also those who were with the responsibility to assist but could not for unknown reasons. In all, my appreciations are due to Mrs. Leonora Manuya, formerly of Maseno University, before moving to USA; and many others for their devotion in typing the manuscript before being finalized to go to the Press; and all members of my family for their love and prayers: Mary and Sarah Leah, Rispah, Esita, Rael, Zakaria, Munywalo, Okomba, Faith and Jemima.

CHAPTER 1

INTRODUCTION

1. A Parable of a Hunting Partner Who Denied His Partner the Spoils Of A Hunting Expedition

A FACTUAL LESSON TO EVERY Leader Globally

"Once upon a time, there were two hunting partners who mutually agreed and planned to go together on a hunting expedition.

On their return home from hunting, the partners decided to harvest honey from a tree. One of the two decided to scale the tree as the other fetched fire to smoke the bees out. On his return with the fire, the fire fetcher found the other partner already helping himself to the honey.

But when he asked for some of the honey, he was told he could not be understood clearly for the honey harvester said he was deaf!

On realizing that his partner had now turned dishonest and gluttonous, the fire fetcher, with the fire, lit a huge bonfire below the tree and threatened to burn the one harvesting honey whom he now wanted to perish altogether with the damn honey.

When this dishonest partner now complained of the fierce fire below, he was also told of the story of a deaf man below who, like him, could not hear his cries"

By:
Former Prime Minister, Hon. Raila Odinga,
The Republic of Kenya.
Saturday, 31st January, 2004.

2. The Substance of the Book

This book is succinctly a clinical diagnosis of a mis-leadership agony in Africa which has been haunting the Continent and her peoples not only during her post-Colonial era but also in the Colonial era. It treats this agony as a serious pathological problem which must, therefore, be thoroughly and meticulously examined now with a view to establishing its actual root-cause and possible curative and preventive remedies for Humanity.

With this in mind as a corner stone for the foundation of this study, the book will attempt to establish answers to various questions whether the problem is just a recent or perennial one; whether it is limited to a country, like Kenya or a universal problem, etc.

But, as it will be noted in the details of this book, the study establishes that from The Holy Bible, it is self-evident that this pathological agony has been with man and mankind immediately after the creation time. It shows that it was the actual root cause of the fall of our Patriarch Adam and Matriarch Eve as a result of the latter's dishonesty to their <u>pacta</u> <u>sunt</u> <u>servanda</u> with their Creator, God i.e., their dishonesty to their mutual agreement with God when Eve foolishly availed herself to be fooled and used by Satan as a conduit for the latter to also penetrate bringing down Adam as a prelude of bringing down Adam's seed (our Humanity).

Thus, Satan's ulterior motive was not just to bring down Adam and the latter's seed. It sought to destroy Adam's sacred leadership potentials which had been endowed to him by The Creator at the time of Adam's creation, meant to be a prerequisite for a role leadership model for not only him (Adam) but also to be passed over as a heredity right to his seed.

But in order for one to establish and appreciate the truth of this phenomenon, one may need to ask oneself the reason(s) why Adam had to be given these sacred potentials.

From the same Holy Bible, we gather from Prophet Moses, author of The Book of Genesis, that these leadership potentials became a necessary additional asset to Adam's potentials given to him by his Creator on the understanding that Adam would use them to wisely conduct, manage, administer, govern or simply lead himself and all his welfare activities in The Garden of Eden to distinguish or judge for himself what was right or wrong; what was right for him to do or not to do, etc.

In this regard, The Creator's sole purpose by giving Adam these potentials as an additional potential prerequisite for Adam's meticulous use was not just a waste of God's time nor was it to be a luxury to Adam. As an Omniscient and Omnipresent God, The Creator definitely had a good purpose for Adam and Adam's generation. God's sincere intention was not to create a foolish man or a man with foolish leadership potentials. To God, this would be a zero-sum effort, a hopeless thing worth not doing especially by God, The Sole Creator of everything good not only in Heaven but also on earth, in its capacity as His foot-stool, which must also be good enough for His Feet to rest on.

Thus, inasmuch as the Creator's immaculate capabilities including His Leadership capability are inherently good, so did He also deem it inherently good to give a similar good leadership quality to Humanity by first implanting it in our Patriarch Adam who He saw it fit to make in His own good Image as empirically supported by The Creator's own Gracious Decision full of Joy as follows:

"Let us make man in Our image, after Our likeness; and let them have dominion over the fish of the sea, and over the fowl of the air, and over the cattle, and over all the earth, and over every creeping thing that creepeth upon the earth"[1]

And, by the same Gracious Decision, The Creator commanded mankind through our patriarch Adam to the effect that he was to use that good leadership potential to see to it that:

"Of every tree of the garden thou mayest freely eat: But of the tree of knowledge of good and evil, thou shalt not eat of it: for in the day that thou eatest thereof thou shalt surely die".

In this regard, it is clearly self-evident that unlike all other living creatures in the waters, air and on the dry land, man was definitely annointed with a pretty good quality leadership potential positively related to that of his own Maker, God, The Creator and expected to use that potential in his dominion or leadership over all those other creatures.

A corollary of this revelation obviously leads one to another revelation, that man was not left empty, stupid or foolish. He was also anointed with the necessary intellect or wisdom to enable him to have a good conceptualization (grasp) of this unique responsibility by clearly understanding and knowing what is around him; what to do, how, when and why, etc.

Accordingly, by virtue of this wisdom, he was also trusted that he was going to strictly adhere to that command from his own Maker. And also that he would know and believe the fact that if he ever failed to do so, he would definitely perish, as also confirmed by the following warning that ". . . thou shalt not eat of it: for in the day that thou eatest thereof thou shall surely die." (Genesis 2:17).

Succinctly, Patriarch Adam and Matriarch Eve fully knew this pacta sunt servanda (mutual agreement) with their Maker, and the consequences, if they ever failed to honour it. Their failure would not be tolerated by their Maker since the latter had accorded them with all necessary wisdom to know what to do and what not to do and why. They were given all potentials.

But, no sooner had they been forewarned by The Maker, than they landed themselves into the same problem as so confirmed by Prophet Moses under Genesis 3:1-24.

But the nagging question at issue is: How and why did our Patriarch Adam and Matriarch Eve break their pacta sunt servanda with their Maker knowing beforehand the serious results thereof? Why did they fail to utilize the intellect which they had been given by their Maker? Why did they foolishly succumb to a misleading advice from the serpent, the Devil? Was it simply because the serpent was more subtle than any beast of the field which the Lord God had made, as the Prophet Moses thus contends under Genesis 3:1? Or was there any reason other than that?

According to The First Book of Adam and Eve, also called The Conflict of Adam and Eve with Satan, translated from the Ethiopic version to English by Dr. S.C. Malan, Vicar of Broadwindsor, with the assistance of Dr. E. Trumpp, the then Professor at the University of Munich[3], we unearth the following revelations constituting reasons why our Patriarch Adam and Matriarch Eve succumbed to the deceitful dictate of the serpent and thus put mankind and its superb leadership qualities to ridicule up to this day (2004):-

Mankind had been inherently endowed, by the Grace of God, with an infinite first class mode of leadership second to none among all members of the Animal Kingdom, and, was thus placed in The Garden of Eden that contained each and everything security needs, sacrosanct to mankind's daily survival.

Enriched with this unique natural endowment by his Maker, mankind was always fully satisfied in all respects and other needs. And thus, he had no reason to toil for his needs as all was freely available to him whenever he ever needed them.

But because of this stupendous endowment, obviously the serpent became neither pleased nor amused. Obviously, he became acutely envious against Patriarch Adam and Matriarch Eve. He sought to topple them and make them lose the endowment.

Being the most subtle above all creatures of the field, he exploited that potential to cripple and incapacitate the two most beloved members of the Animal Kingdom (Adam and Eve) by cunningly deceiving them by misadvising them with a view to luring them to break their pacta sunt servanda with their Creator so that the Creator would consequently be enraged to disqualify and then remove them from the Garden of Eden; so that the two would also lose their endowment; and so that mankind and Satan would equally have to suffer as a result of disobedience to God.

Obviously, this is exactly what happened to Mankind in terms of the actual circumstances that eventually culminated into Mankind's loss of his endowment. Mankind dishonoured The Maker ignoring His command; by not hearkening and exploiting his intellect that was superior to that of all other members of the Animal Kingdom, so that he could have easily known what the serpent was actually up to as far as the Maker's advice was concerned; and by carelessly hearkening to a deceitful source of advice which, in turn, led him and his innocent seed (Mankind) into this on-going sea of perpetual agony.

Accordingly, the aim of this study is to use every tool available to slash and plough through every thick jungle regardless of its dangerous darkness, caves, cobwebs, and other numerous varieties of enemies of man, which have for ages hindered man's intellectual research efforts from understanding the genesis, scope, dynamics and remedy of this particular problem in its capacity as indeed man's perpetual pathological problem that has always been poised at hindering man's all concerted efforts to live a descent life that had initially been endowed to him by the grace of own Maker. Even among good friends who happen to be together in a business for having survived a mutual threat such as King Saul and the young valiant boy David son of Jesse, the <u>pacta</u> <u>sunt</u> <u>servanda</u> of their togetherness hardly endured that long simply because of this very perpetual pathological disease that has always haunted Humanity since the Antiquity.

Empirical evidence confirm that, influenced by this disease, King Saul was misguided by the spirit of dishonesty to see that he uses all his security machinery available to him to kill the young valiant boy David for a mistaken ill feelings against the boy that the latter was a potential threat to his leadership. And, therefore, that the only remedy was to kill him so that the King's leadership would be securely assured.[4]

The same example of the dangers of this pathological disease holds true with respect to the most famous of all cases regarding King Herod's paranoia against the most innocent Little Infant Jesus Christ because of whom Herod could neither eat well nor sleep soundly immediately he learnt that the Infant had been born in Bethlehem. Madly obsessed with this Jesusphobia (a fear of Jesus' presence), the King instituted an en mass infant genocide of every newly born boy child below the age of three years, with the mistaken view that the Infant was poised to usurp his kingship and that by so killing all infants, he would eliminate this potential threat; and then give himself a sigh of relief and a comfortable sound sleep.

But as will be noted in details in this book, this disease is not limited to those numerous sad cases documented in The Holy Bible. Because of man's failure to attempt seriously to discover a possible remedy, the disease also haunts the entire mankind. It has proved a perennial devastating disease from one generation to another against man's efforts to forge out good ways and means of leading himself to a hybrid culture that would enable him to easily subdue all his socio-economic obstacles to societal prosperity.

As a result of this continuous negligence by Mankind, numerous cases of leadership failures and latter's agonizing consequences to the innocent general public abound from generation to generation. For example, because of King Louis XVI's disobedience to his contractual obligation with his French general public in 1789 by denying them their natural justice, this fuelled the rise of the French Revolution in 1789; led the

Revolution to declare France a Republic thereby abolishing the monarch cult culture and system in France up to this day (2013) and finally put that King to execution on 21ˢᵗ day of January, 1793, with the hope that the action would become a good learning lesson to future leadership in France. And, before that tragedy, a similar tragedy had just taken place in England in 1649 during the English Revolution whereby King Charles I was beheaded in public by his own English subjects because of his own disobedience to honour the oath of office he had taken on becoming King of England to the effect that he was going to serve but not to be served by his subjects. His failure to honour this <u>pacta</u> <u>sunt servanda</u> with an arrogant claim that he was only subject to the divine Law of God but above the human law of the land, obviously led to an automatic leadership failure, and eventually he was sentenced to a summary execution, and England declared herself a parliamentary nation by devolving the powers of the monarch from a full executive chief to a ceremonial status; and transferring the executive powers to the Parliament under a Prime Minister who was at that point in time Oliver Cromwell (1599-1658). He, it was who initiated and led the Revolution; and then served first as Lord Protector (1653-1658) before his son Richard Cromwell inherited the father in the same capacity (1658-1659) before the title was later changed to 'Prime Minister'.

In these two tragic cases, Humanity hoped that such lessons could help to bring every leader to his/her senses and now understand that the virtue of leadership was to serve the general public that one is leading but not to be served by them; and also the severity of action that the general public would obviously take against that leader if he or she ever failed to honour his terms of reference inherent in his Oath of Office i.e. his or her <u>pacta</u> <u>sunt</u> <u>servanda</u> with his/her general public.

But, did such drastic actions in England and France ever prove a lesson to Mankind? If so, where, and to what degree?

A scrutiny of African leadership, for example, shows a shocking contradiction. The two lessons have never meant anything of a significant value to most African leaders. The lessons and their seriousness have simply fallen on a deaf ear in African leadership. And, this disease is not limited to Africa. It holds true all over the world particularly to less developed nations of Asia and Latin America and the West Indies. In Africa in particular, the disease is so rampant and devastating that one wonders where the continent is heading to and how to save it from the disease. In Kenya, for example, the overwhelming majority of Kenyans and non-Kenyans alike are today curiously wondering the reasons why President Daniel T. arap Moi officially initiated and operated the Goldenberg International Company's scandal to suffocate the country by looting and transferring all its assets in billions of Kenya currency without due respect to his obligation to the Terms of Reference under Oath of Office that, by virtue of that Oath, he was to be a chief custodian of the country's Assets and Its total Security, with total impunity. Also, everyone must be asking themselves what the President was up to when he engaged in various acts of atrocities against everyone that he found to be critical against his deviant acts. And, when President Moi was doing all this to his critics such as Dr. Robert Ouko, who had proved so much a defender of the President's Foreign Policy in his capacity as Moi's Foreign Minister, whom he had to silence so that Ouko may not leak the President's scandal to foreigners, everyone was obviously curious about the level of the President's sanity and commitment to his Oath of Office. And, further, when he was all this phobic to devour, even his own arch-policy supporters such as Dr. Ouko, the nagging question is did Moi ever know a solution to his acts of misrule and ineptitude? Did he have any? If so, which one? And, how is he now likely to escape a similar drastic action by Kenyans similar to the English and French actions against their own useless leaders due to their misrule during their tenures?

This book will prove that the President did not only fail to honour his Oath of Office as President of Kenya, but also failed to show any evidence that he ever had a clue of any remedy requisite for the dying Kenya because the disease was no any other but Moi himself. He was its actual root cause. He was the one who was looting the country's assets to a point of the country's death. Therefore, looking for a remedy was none of his business. It was not required to be on his agenda. To include it on the agenda would be tantamount to putting Moi on the agenda for trial.

Therefore, whereas the former President may now be held responsible for all the scandals, that will not be all. It is the belief of this book that Humanity needs more than trials and appropriate action against him for his evil acts. Humanity deserves assistance towards an ultimate remedy against this perennial disease which has always haunted mankind over the ages without a remedy. It has left Humanity in rampant abject poverty and various sicknesses, and without Humanity persevering to take time and search their souls as to what actually went wrong with his inherent leadership potentially endowed to him by his own Maker through his Patriarch Adam and Matriarch Eve; and to therefore do all necessary actions to rectify the situation.

In fact this is what leaders of the highly industrialized world are also interested in seeing happen in Kenya and the rest of Africa if socio-economic recovery is to be realized and if the continent is to move closer to an industrialization level of those countries which are now already industrialized.

This is the heart of the International Donor Community's concern which can no longer afford to stomach the nauseating Kenyan mode of leadership during President Moi's tenure. Applauding the new good mode of Kenyan leadership under President Mwai Kibaki which came into effect beginning 1st January 2003 (after the end of 40 years period of misrule by mainly President Moi effective 1978 on the death of President Jomo Kenyatta in August of the same year), the German, Chancellor Gerhard Schroeder who landed in Kenya in the night of Monday, 19th January, 2004, for a 3-day state visit, and quadrupled German development aid to Kenya to Kshs.4.8 billion for the fiscal year 2004 and 2005 from Kshs.1.2 billion aid for the year 2003. He also expanded the co-operation between the two countries in the areas of police and security agencies against terrorism, as a collective new good sign of German appreciation and recognition of President Kibaki's Government, which launched a recommendable drive against corruption and other symptoms and root-causes of bad governance and socio-economic stagnation in Kenya and other countries whose leaders sustained and thrived on.[5] Again, like every one that cherishes good quality of leadership as a prerequisite for any developing country to grow socio-economically, the German Chancellor encouraged Kenyan leadership to not only engage into desiring this and that as a matter of national prestige or other reasons, but to also emphasize their concept of quality and quantity. The two have to go hand in hand if a country is to succeed. But all this can only come about by the good quality of leadership akin to the new quality of leadership Kenya has now adopted and shown the World Community by the efforts of President Kibaki and his National Alliance of Rainbow Coalition (NARC) political party. Finally like other sympathetic persons interested in seeing Kenya and all African countries succeed in their socio-economic endeavours, the German Chancellor called on the countries of East African Community to speed up integration in order for them to attract more foreign investment—an effort that cannot and will never come about unless first, the East African Community forge out a sound mode of leadership characterized and governed by the rule of law, their consent to this conditions, and their mutual respect to their ideals. Hence, the ultimate aim of this book to assist not only the Academia in its advancement of Science and Technology but also political leaders in their capacity as real beneficiaries of a wisdom needed for their success in the art of leadership.

CHAPTER II

LEADERSHIP IN FAUNA AND FLORA

1. Leadership Problem in General

LEADERSHIP IS A NATURAL and indispensable biological ingredient found in all forms of life due to its strategic usefulness and capacity as a tool to each entity for the latter's management of itself and its all business or affairs requisite for its survival in life. However, whereas this is the strategic usefulness of leadership to every living entity without which that entity cannot live at all, the most amazing and embarrassing paradox is that its true identity in terms of its nature, scope, role, dynamics and limitations in life still remains blurred. Both scientists and laymen alike such as political leaders who do use it as their trade and, therefore, do scramble for it as their main source of income do not even understand it properly; and that this is the reason why most fail in their tenure as leaders.

But as will be noted in-depth in this book, leadership is not only an important tool in political life per se simply because of its strategic usefulness for management of political affairs nor is it only limited to that life alone as generally believed globally.

Contrary to such belief, this study will scientifically prove beyond any reasonable doubt that there exists lots of unknown wisdom and knowledge about the nature and character of this phenomenon called leadership which is still totally a mystery to mankind, and which, therefore, make most people fail whenever they are in such position.

Further, this study will show that leadership is a natural biological ingredient inherent in each and every living organism or entity by virtue of its strategic role and usefulness as both a managerial and administrative tool.

Its biological universalism and universality is manifested in the fact that it is governed by the law of nature which is also a foundation from which political morality way of life is also derived and rests.

Political morality way of life is succinctly a normal political life. It is a peaceful political life free from thuggery and all symptoms of anarchy in society/country. It is governed by the law of nature in the sense that it is biological. It is biological in that it is innate; it is innate in that it is a bio-chemical component or constituent part of the whole biological compound inherent in that whole compound found in every living organism which, in turn, biologically constitutes or makes up the total anatomical and physical component of that total being or organism.

Because of this universal functional role of leadership phenomenon to every living entity in life bestowed upon it by the law of nature to assist and enhance that entity's survival and quest for that survival, leadership is, therefore, second to none in terms of its strategic role to every member in both the Plant kingdom and Animal kingdom. This reality is explicitly manifested by the manner in which each member of the two kingdoms actually manages and administers itself and its total affairs amongst its other members of the community in terms of its various senses of self-preservation, self-love and self-respect on the one hand; and also in terms of its perceptions of its other fellows or counterparts in the community and relations with those other counterparts, on the other.

But, how and why does leadership as a biological ingredient in every living organism enhance the latter's sense of self-preservation, self-respect and self-love?

In life, it is common sense that each entity loves itself at all costs and at all times. It does so because it has to live/exist just like every other entity does. And, because it must exist like every one else, competition between and among the same entities or different entities abound. Trees of the same species/community/kind resort to competition for sunlight, water or minerals, all depending on what they must need and compete for with each other. Whenever they are located too close to each other, each may want to overgrow and overshadow the other with its branches and leaves so that the other dies off and leaves the whole monopoly of sunlight to it. Also, this selfish tree may want to grab all the water and minerals from the other so that the other may die off from starvation.

But, the other plant may not be that stupid or foolish. Because it has also to exist, this other one may also do the same against its opponent. In fact, it may try to outwit the other and using all ingenuity it can develop and use for the same purpose of its survival in this scarce and competitive life—a life which according to Charles Darwin is a life of the survival of the fittest.

The other manner in which each entity does strive to enhance self-preservation, self-love and self-respect is to develop certain biological mechanism by which to defend itself against its enemy in life. Some may develop horns, claws; poison; epidermis and dermis (a skin) kind, e.g. a crocodile's tough skin not easily cut through; frightening voice/sound aimed at frightening an enemy, e.g. hyenas, etc; and even witchcraft as in the case of human beings who resort to such methods of hurting their opponents.

But in each and every case cited above, each entity must also have ways and means of utilizing its weapon for self-preservation. To fight against hunger, each species must develop and know how to utilize its strategies of suppressing or fighting this hunger. It must organise its efforts; and it must know how to do so. Failure of doing so renders its weapon automatically useless to it.

But why does each species strive to do so? Why must it organize itself against its enemy? And, what is the meaning of all that effort?

Each species does strive to do so simply because it loves itself and it respects itself as a living entity with all rights to life as any other member of its community; it does, and has to organize itself and its efforts because it has to naturally do so if it is to exist just as every other species; and by so doing, it is, in the final analysis, not doing anything else other than responding to the law of nature requiring every living entity to manage and administer its own affairs needed for its existence. Hence the origin, essence and role of the concept 'self-leadership' in life.

But this self-leadership which we have proved to be innate is just one side of the coin of "leadership" concept in general. Therefore, leadership in general is also innate and universal to all living organisms for their survival purpose defined in terms of self-preservation, self-love and self-respect as explicitly explicated in-depth here below with specific nature and strategic role and importance in both the Plant Kingdom and Animal Kingdom, respectively.

2. Leadership in the Plant Kingdom

In the plant Kingdom, a botanical diagnosis shows that each plant or member of each species naturally directs itself and its total acts in a manner which is sacrosanct to those requirements sacred to the needs of its livelihood or well-being.

These needs include, for instance, respiratory security, food security, health security, etc. In the respiratory security needs for example, each plant or member of each species must conduct, direct, manage, or simply lead itself in a strategic manner that will definitely enable it to easily and properly breathe in and out as it is biologically or naturally constitutioned to do in order to enhance its metabolism.

To do so, it has to lead its branches and leaves into a suitable position essential for it to easily and properly get the needed sunlight. Also, in the case of getting its food security, each plant or member of each species has to lead its roots to position(s) it deems most appropriate for getting mineral water, etc from the soil. If the entity is a parasite which must depend on its host for food, the same strategy still applies in that the parasite has to lead its roots into the host and absorb what has already been obtained from the soil by the host. And in the case of health security, each member of each plant species has to lead itself in a manner it deems quite sacrosanct to its health needs/security.

In the final analysis, the concept and role of leadership in the Plant Kingdom is very important indeed. Without its presence, no member of each plant species can survive/live. It is a sine qua non/element for the survival of every member of the Plant Kingdom. It is enhanced and promoted by the concepts of self-preservation, self-love and self-respect.

3. Leadership in the Animal Kingdom

a) A Morphological Angle

Unlike the Plant Kingdom wherein the male and female (gender) morphological characteristics are inherent in the same entity, in the Animal Kingdom, this phenomenon (arrangement) is almost non-existent[1]. Each male and female has its own unique morphological potentials totally restricted to itself. For example, the male entity is endowed with much more physical power above that of its female counterpart.

And, another comparative scrutiny of their respective roles in society/community further shows that the male is, by virtue of its behaviour, a leader of all others. This is manifested in various societal needs such as in community territorial security where in the male usually plays the role of "defender" or "protector" as is the case in each nuclear family organizational arrangement.

Although a female individual may also play a leadership role particularly in a case where she is the sole bread-earner for a family because of a broken-up marriage, death of a husband, or because of marital problems, this is normally a rare case. It comes or happens as an accident. It is not a normally accepted phenomenon, in which each gender comfortably and rationally enjoys its role without contempt.

Similarly, although among the lion community (herd), a lioness (female) is the habitual bread earner for the family (her cubs and the lion) in her capacity as the only one which does the hunting for a prey, this is naturally arranged for her to do so because of her lean/slim body advantage or monopoly she has over her husband (the lion) which therefore enables her to run faster/ or much more swifter than the lion can possibly do due to the latter's heavy body and mane (too much hair around his neck) that cannot allow him to do a swift run like a lioness.

In all, unlike in all other species of the Animal Kingdom such as lions, elephants, monkeys, chimpanzees, etc, in which nuclear family social organization is not distinctly arranged, in the human nuclear family social organization, this arrangement is very distinct. This arrangement is universal from country to country, and community to community. It is an inter-subjective given globally. It is not a superiority inferiority complex syndrome between man and woman but purely and simply, a well-accepted cultural arrangement free from any negative ulterior motive or connotation.

b) From a Physiological Angle

Like in the Plant Kingdom, in the Animal Kingdom, no single species can possibly live without the presence of self-leadership coated with the tri-concepts of self-preservation, self-love and self-respect.

In the absence of self-leadership, obviously death is the automatic answer.

Like in the role of self-leadership in the Plant Kingdom noted above, the role of self-leadership in the animal Kingdom is also essential indeed. It is enhanced by the concepts of self-preservation, self-love and self-respect. From non-vertebrate living entities such as snails, locusts, centipedes, bees, butterflies, safari ants, etc. to vertebrate living entities such as human beings, birds, fish, etc., self-preservation, self-love and self-respect concepts play a significant role. They enhance and promote every member of each species to direct or lead itself to do what is sacrosanct to its survival, e.g. not only to be able to breathe in and out but also, and very important of all, to be able to get and breathe in good fresh air.

In other words, each entity usually strives to obtain an air which it deems sacred for its existence. If it happens to be in an environment which is not able to provide it with air which is sacred for its good health, then that entity is subject to abandon the place and seek an alternative.

This behaviour is strictly unique to members of the Animal Kingdom. It is not part and parcel of the members of the Plant Kingdom because all members of the Plant Kingdom are stationary. This limitation in the Plant Kingdom restricts all members of the Plant Kingdom to be unable to enjoy the freedom that members of the Animal Kingdom do enjoy because of their ability to lead themselves away from one hostile environment to a more desirably conducive environment able to provide what a member of the Animal Kingdom species needs.

Accordingly, whereas self-leadership element exists in all members of both Plant Kingdom and Animal Kingdom, degree of their self-leadership element differs in the nature of its use.

For example, whereas in the plant kingdom its usefulness is only relevant and instrumental by allowing/enabling the entity to relate parts of its body viz branches, leaves and roots, while the whole body is permanently fixed (is constant) in its original position of habitation, in the Animal Kingdom, self-leadership's usefulness is much more diverse. It is diverse in that it can enable an entity to change/or relate part(s) of its whole body only from one direction or place to another (as in the case of changing one's head position from one to another in order to either see well or avoid a problem) without moving one's whole body; also it can enable that entity to change position/location from one place to a totally new place altogether. This capability is totally absent in all members of the Plant Kingdom. It is not part and parcel of the self-leadership, ability inherent in the Plant Kingdom.

A very excellent empirical example to clarify this variance in the two kingdoms is their different behaviour during harsh conditions such as winter weather. Among the Plant Kingdom members, none of them has a self-leadership capability to enable them to move away from one hostile area to a more conducive (safe haven) area to avoid that condition. They may shed off their leaves (as in the case of pine trees) during fall period (a pre-winter time) with a view to remaining a bare trunk alone and fight through the hostile winter season in that same permanent position without moving away to find a safe haven. It has to remain as such till spring season (a pre-summer period) when the weather begins to warm up once again thereby giving a sign of good hope for the end of a hostile weather (called winter) and the beginning of a friendly weather (called summer).

In all, all members of the Plant Kingdom have to endure all this weather hardship every year; and cannot move away from one place to another because of their lack of diverse/more powerful self-leadership/capability that members of the Animal Kingdom do have and enjoy in event of a hostile situation not conducive to their lives.

Specifically, unlike the afore-documented case of the members of the Plant Kingdom and how they are thus limited to do this and that (all that they would want to do using their self-leadership element) in the Animal Kingdom, a human being would use his diverse self-leadership capability to do a lot of things to fight against hostility of a winter season to man. The latter can design warm clothing, boots, gloves and headgears. He can also design warm shelters by way of heating them using electricity, gas, charcoal, firewood, coal, etc. in order to enable him feel comfortable and, therefore, unthreatened by the natural threat of the chilly winter weather. In addition, man has also a capability inherent in his self-leadership element to move from one hostile place to another place, or environment. In the case of an American living in one of the northern chilly states of Wisconsin, Washington, Alaska, Illinois, or Minnesota, may wish to move away to a lesser hostile state in the southern states of Florida, Georgia or in the western states of California using his diverse/more powerful element of self-leadership that all members of the Animal Kingdom have but which all members of the Plant Kingdom do not have at all.

This diverse self-leadership element is not just unique to human beings in the Animal Kingdom per se. In the same temperate zone region that have to encounter or suffer the winter threat every year, all other members of the Animal Kingdom such as squirrels, lizards, cheetahs, monkeys, rabbits, deers, etc. also are endowed with the same biological element of self-leadership found in human-beings. Like human beings, they are able to use the same quality of self-leadership to move from one location to another in search for a safe-haven. Birds in North America, for example, do fly away from northern states and Canada to away south at the advent of pre-winter season called Fall; and then come back during the advent of pre-summer season called Spring.

But all those patterns of self-leadership behaviour in the Animal Kingdom are non-evident in all members of the Plant Kingdom. Therefore whereas self-leadership element is an innate attribute endowed to all members of the two kingdoms, the degree of that element in the Plant kingdom is much less powerful and less diverse compared to that of the members of Animal kingdom.

The other element of significant difference between self leadership in the Plant kingdom and another one in the Animal kingdom is manifested in the role and scope of their function. Whereas in the Plant kingdom self-leadership is biologically constant from youth to adulthood of the member of each species, in the Animal kingdom, it is not constant. In the Plant kingdom, each member of the species comes into being with that element already at maturity. It does not constitutionally grow in direct proportion with the physiological and anatomical growth of that member. A prima facie empirical evidence of this phenomenon is borne out by the behaviour of green plants called photosynthesis, by which a plant that happens to find itself growing in a dark environment without presence of any light naturally grows yellowish for lack of this sunlight and eventually dies off as it does not need help from its parents or any other member of its community. But, should there be any source of some light that it seriously needs for its photosynthesis, which is one of the source of its survival, that young plant/entity will automatically direct itself towards that source with a view to capturing that light for its survival.

The key point here worth underscoring about this phenomenon is that the process is not limited to only young plants. It also holds true to adult plants. In this regard, the process is biologically constituted constant in every member of each species of the Plant kingdom beginning from the algae which is the most primitive species of the

Plant kingdom to plants, shrubs and trees which are the most advanced species of the kingdom.

But, the nagging question for a scientist to explain is not only why each member of the species of the Plant kingdom behaves the way it does. The multi-million fundamental question also is how does each species manage to do so?

A meticulous analysis of this behaviour shows that obviously none of the species can manage to do so without having an innate element of self-help biologically constituted in each species to enable it direct/lead itself from the point of darkness or no light to the point of light (or presence of light).

But what is this self-help element? Is this element different from the element we call self-leadership?

Obviously, the two processes are synonymous. Both constitute two sides of the same coin in that each means the other.

Accordingly, self-help or self-leadership in all species of the Plant kingdom is constant. But is the process in the Plant kingdom the same as that in the Animal kingdom? Either way, how and why?

As already noted above, the process in the Plant kingdom is biologically constant in the sense that what is found in mature member of a species is also found in a young member of the same species and vice versa. However, in the Animal Kingdom the process is significantly different. It is different in that what is found in a mature member of each species cannot be found in a young member of the same species. A younger member has to be very much dependent on the goodwill of its parent(s) for its upkeep until it is mature enough to lead itself in respect of satisfying its needs. When young, a human entity (baby) depends totally on its parents or guardian, etc. for its basic needs ranging from food, shelter, protection, etc. Thus, the young cannot help itself or self-leadership ingredient in its biological capabilities. Although it may be having these capabilities, they are only potentials. They are yet to develop to maturity before they can be of any use to this human being. Accordingly, they have to develop in direct proportion to that being's physiological and anatomical development. By the time the baby reaches maturity as an adult able to take care of its own basic needs, the individual is said to be already mature, self-reliant and therefore able to lead and manage its affairs without much ado about its parents or guardian.

This gradual self-leadership development from youth to adulthood in human beings holds true in all other members of the species of the Animal kingdom, a process or phenomenon unique only to members of the Animal kingdom but totally absent in members of the Plant kingdom.

However, in spite of this significant difference between the two kingdoms on the nature, role and scope of the dynamics of self-leadership element, in both kingdoms share a crucial commonality. Each species member of each kingdom naturally knows and understands well enough its own natural rights on how to make its ends meet regardless of the presence or absence of various harsh natural or non-natural conditions or constraints such as chilly winters, war, etc. respectively. Their common awareness of such situations and how to tackle the situations is indeed a reliable acid test of their commonality in self-leadership.

This test manifests itself in the manner in which each species rationally organizes itself toward the object or goal it seeks to get or achieve. The goal could be shelter, food, love, security from an enemy, health, knowledge, happiness, etc.

This behaviour is governed entirely by the presence and degree of leadership in each species which enables this species to achieve its intended purpose on the one hand, and which also serves as an acid test with regard to the presence, function (role); and, more so, the efficacy of this leadership ingredient in each species of the Animal kingdom.

Now that we have been able to unlock and forced the door wide open to the mystery of this leadership ingredient in life, what can we see regarding the ingredient? How does it function in the human life? And, how far does its presence and role differ from or resemble its presence and role in other species of the same kingdom?

A.   Leadership in Human Life

In as much as the presence and role of leadership in all members of the Animal kingdom are congruent by virtue of their mutual purpose, the most significant variance of this ingredient in the human life is simply that this ingredient is much more vivid than it is in other members of the Animal kingdom. This variance may be better understood in the manner it functions between the two genders of the same species. For example, *inasmuch as each man loves and respects himself, he also knows how to govern himself and all his masculine affairs for his livelihood. Similarly, each woman also does the same in fulfilment of those natural acts, which are peculiar and sacrosanct to her own feminine gender.* Inasmuch as each man and woman naturally behaves this way by virtue of their biological difference from each other, their behavioural variance phenomenon is a significant acid test in our effort to understand better this mystery of the presence and role of the leadership ingredient in these two genders.

In this regard, we are now satisfied that each man and woman clearly knows how to conduct, organize, or guide oneself all depending on the constitutional dictates biologically bestowed upon its respective gender by law of nature. But in matters which are solely universal to both genders, e.g. eating or taking bath, again each gender also knows how to lead, conduct, organize or guide itself in pursuit of the objectives it seeks.

a) Leadership in Human Organization at Nuclear Family Level.

In each nuclear family, a man naturally knows that it is his duty to lead, conduct, organize or guide each member of his family and how. He is naturally knowledgeable and quite conscious of his multi-roles as a man, a husband of his wife, a father of his children or child, a security officer of his family; a teacher of his family, a spiritual guide of his family, and more so, a spokesman and judge of his family in all matters requiring such roles to be manifested as our Patriarch Adam was so commanded by God from the beginning of life.

Similarly, a woman in her family also naturally knows very well her multi-roles as a wife of her husband, a mother of her children in that family, and more so a helper of her husband, as Matriarch Eve was thus commanded by God to be to her husband, our Patriarch Adam. Failure of each party to observe and act within the framework of this norm, which is sacrosanct to one's success in self-leadership role, is automatically a failure.

But, naturally, nobody likes being a failure or to look a fool, ignorant, foolish or embarrassed before others. Inasmuch as one loves oneself more than they love another or others, it is equally evident that every one including drunkards, mad persons, prostitutes, etc., is also the best leader of oneself and one's affairs in life.

However, all this depends on one's ability and level of sanity to be able to properly lead, govern, guide, conduct or organize oneself and one's own affairs believed to be sacrosanct to and for his or her survival. If one is either critically disabled or incapacitated due to illness or other causes, such a person is obviously incapable of leading, managing or governing one's affairs and oneself. One is not able to be capable and physically normal or mature.

But besides nuclear family, how does leadership feature in other human organizations? What role does it play? And, how can the phenomenon be explained better than it now appears in the Academia?

b)   Leadership in Human Organizations above Nuclear Family Level

Above the level of human nuclear family, there exists six exhaustive and mutually exclusive categories of human organizations. These include:

(1)   Social organizations, which include clubs, fraternities, co-operatives, etc. whose ultimate purpose is essentially social (or entertainment).

(2)   Economic organizations such as companies, corporations, etc. whose ultimate purpose is essentially economic and specifically profit-making.

(3)   Political organizations such as nation-states, international organizations, political parties, etc. whose ultimate purpose is essentially acquisition and sustention of political power using every means ranging from politically democratic elections to political violence or war as is the present case of war between the United States of America and Afghanistan in defence and pursuit of political power.

(4)   Religious organizations, such as churches, mosques, etc. whose ultimate purpose is essentially salvation.

(5) Scientific and Technological organizations such as academic, training and research organizations whose ultimate purpose is to enhance all those four other organizations with appropriate skills on their efforts to sustain Mankind and the latter's civilization.

(6) Health organizations such as hospitals, clinics, dispensaries, etc. whose ultimate purpose is essentially to sustain life in support of those other organizations indicated in (1)-(5)) above.

But, in each of these six functional categories, none of them can surely survive at all in the absence of a leadership ingredient. As also living organisms, each type depends on the presence of this ingredient to lead it to such behaviour, conduct, objective(s) or goal(s) that are sacrosanct to its survival; or to lead it away from those acts, objectives or goals that could be antithetical to its survival.

B.   Leadership in Non-Human Life

A further study of other members of the Animal kingdom also shows that this ingredient is definitely much more explicit developed and complex in its nature and function in the human life than it is in these other members of the Animal kingdom. However, the study also shows that this ingredient is in some significant degree, equally and richly explicit to the naked eye in many of these members such as chimpanzees, elephants, lions, hyenas, caribou of the north most of the North American region, monkeys, etc.

The Caribou behaviour is most fascinating in this respect by the way the females do time the exact time they must organize themselves into a *mulolongo* safari (Indian file) and travel to their rightful destination point where they habitually go to give birth. The most striking aspect in this behaviour of greatest interest for this study is their most amazing accuracy in timing for their group mobilization for the journey in terms of the exact time of the season in the year they must do so, their most amazing ability to recognize and follow the same habitual trail they always follow to and from their point of delivery which is no less than one hundred kilometres (or a week's time-walk), their amazing ability to wisely sense and judge which ice carpets covering the trail may not be that safe enough for them to pass over and in this case quickly and prudently decide to avoid that spot and take a new alternative spot altogether for security purpose, and above all, the speed they must use to reach their maternity wards, the period they all must remain in their maternity wards in order to enable their young ones get sufficient maturity and strength to be able to travel that very lengthy journey with their mothers back to meet with their fathers at their habitual habitat; and finally their amazing ability to organize themselves and their young ones on the safari back home!!!

Obviously, this Caribou's organizational behaviour is not just an end into itself. To a scientist, it means a lot. It is more than just being an intriguing behaviour of a non-human animal worth hearing about. It is an empirical ramification of the presence of some explicit leadership ingredient inherent in the natural behaviour of these lovely creatures. Although this leadership ingredient may not be as much developed and complex to the level of that of man, their ability to mobilize themselves to and from their maternity ward point of delivery and their good judgement ability as to when to travel and reach the maternity ward point in good time for this natural delivery business begins is pretty flabbergasting. Thus their good judgement must be worth appreciation.

Shifting our observatory telescope from the larger species of non-human members of the Animal kingdom such as the Caribou of the north-most region of North America, let us also examine the behavioural pattern of the Safari Ants.

A study of safari ants also reveals a very intriguing phenomenon pretty rich in leadership. Their leadership ingredient is also as very articulate and meticulous as that of the Caribou deers in the manner they do manage to organize and lead themselves on a journey from one point or area to another in pursuit of food, shelter, and other needs which they know and believe to be very sacrosanct to and for their survival.

The most amazingly interesting unique phenomenon inherent in their behaviour, which pretty well serves as a reliable acid test of the reality and degree of the presence and dynamics of leadership ingredient in safari ants is borne out by the following facts:

1) During their *mulolongo* safari, for example, the leaders of these ants are systematically duty-stationed in accordance to their strategic duties that each is expected to perform for the survival of its total community.

2) Whereas some of these leaders are duty-stationed at the front-end of the *mulolongo*, others are also duty-stationed at the back-end of that *mulolongo*.

3) Those in the front line end are duty mandated to examine, monitor, sense and then promptly signal back to its community in the _mulolongo_ every security problem for the community's appropriate action against that problem.

4) Those which are duty-stationed at the back line-end also are duty mandated to also do the same by signalling forward to the community members in the _mulolongo_ for their appropriate action against any potential danger sensed to be following their _Mulolongo_ against their security and total survival.

5) And, in addition to those two contingents at the front-end and at the back end of the _mulolongo_, in-between the two are many other ants whose mandate is also to protect security and total survival of the community.

6) In all, this behaviour is none other than leadership which has always been a mystery to man.

In view of these prima facie empirical evidences confirming scientifically that leadership is also indeed present in this safari ants in as much as it is in the human beings, it is self-evident that leadership is a natural biological ingredient universally present in all members of the Animal kingdom as well as in the Plant kingdom.

Further, whereas leadership has always been generally misconceptualized and therefore misunderstood in the context of political leadership, from these evidences, it is now self-evident that leadership is much more complex and universal than the way it had been erroneously assumed to be before by other researchers using low power lenses that could not detect this reality, i.e., its actual nature and universalism in life.

Such myopic assumptions should now be no more a hindrance to man from this truth and satisfactory understanding of this phenomenon in-depth.

In this regard, the sole purpose of this book is to unlock this cumbersome mystery regarding the actual nature, scope and efficacy of this strange phenomenon in life we call "leadership" which has always been evading recognition in the Academia due to the latter's reliance on a low power lens. And to this end, to liberate Behavioural and Social Sciences in general and Political Science in particular from those various idols so that this Discipline may equally be able to freely glide into those prestigious horizons of Wisdom and Knowledge where both Bio-Science and Physical Science have already managed to reach and enjoy due to their courage and sacrifice manifested in their extremely impressive achievements in discoveries and innovation for the well-being of Humanity.

CHAPTER III

THEO-PSYCHIARTRY OF LEADERSHIP FAILURE

A Preamble:

UNDER GENESIS 1:26, OUR Lord God said

"Let us make man in our image, after our likeness; and let them have dominion over the fish of the sea and over the fowl of the air, and over the cattle, and over all the earth, and over every creeping thing that creeps upon the earth"

And so, The Most Excellent Lord God did just that!

But the pending nagging Question at issue now is: Has man actually done so? Has he put in place a viable leadership as a requisite means or tool to that end as so commanded and mandated by The Creator?

An amazing findings

Drawing from the knowledge and wisdom of <u>his</u> teachers who taught at The African Mysteries System of the Grand Lodge of Luxor now known as Alexandria in North Africa (Egypt) in the mid-400 BC, Socrates insisted that a good leader must be a Philosopher-king in the sense that one must be first trained on the art of leadership particularly on the theory of Good Governance or Leadership such as Theocentric Humanism (characterized by holiness and perfection) and the doctrine of <u>Summum Bonum</u> (characterized by the Greatest Good/Happiness for all the governed) so that the leader may be conversant with the fabrics of good Governance which include the virtues of Justice, Prudence, Temperance and Courage. In addition to that reality, our Clinical Diagnosis findings on all tasks in human life also shows that of all these tasks, leadership is the simplest and easiest. It is the simplest and easiest in that even a shepherd is also a very good leader in his own rights; and is naturally expected to be so at all times in that he takes care of all members of his flock or herd on a totally equal footing without any favoritism at all. Similarly, a parent of a nuclear family is naturally also a very good leader in his own rights and is expected to also be so at all times in that he takes care of the needs of all members of his or her nuclear family on a totally equal footing without favoritism at all. Neither of the two requires any formal education or training in the art of leadership in order for them to prove a good leader. In other words, both are, by nature, very good leaders. They are naturally born so. In this regard, then, by nature, man is born a good leader in all sectors of life including politics regardless of space and time. One's formal education in the art of Governance/Leadership is simply a reinforcement to one's innate qualities of leadership potentials. But unlike leadership, all other tasks do require a formal school education or training. For example, in order for one to become a teacher, doctor, lawyer, judge, preacher, scientist, musician, secretary, athlete, journalist, etc., empirical evidence show that one must first be formally taught or trained in that art. Hence, the difference between the art of leadership and other arts in life. Whereas the former partially relies on formal training in order to become a good leader, the latter totally relies on the formal training.

In this regard, then leadership must, therefore, be an inborn attribute. To be a good leader, one must be naturally born a good leader while a bad leader must be born so. With this in mind, then existence of or presence of a constitution, laws, rule, policies, codes of conduct and various other norms alone, no matter how excellent they may sound, may not in themselves be a reliable cure to socio-economic ills of any country without the presence of a leader of a sound leadership governed by that leader's own free will and love to honour and accept to live with and practically utilize these norms in his art of leadership for the good of those that he is expected to lead in his capacity as not only their leader but also as their philosopher King who is supposed to set up a good example for them to appreciate and emulate. By virtue of these dual roles, a good leader is expected to be fully cognizant of those norms and the goals they are expected to gain for the greatest satisfaction and happiness of those that he is expected to lead; the problems or constraints; the strategies to be applied; etc. Finally, by virtue of the two roles, he is equally expected to be cognizant of the serious consequences of nasty agony his innocent general public of his country are likely to suffer including his own profession in case of his failure to recognize and embrace those norms and goals inherent in his art of leadership and which are, therefore, sacrosanct for the survival of both his governed lot and his own office.

But, in our inquiry into the natural dynamics of the leadership phenomenon in both fauna and flora species above, our findings show that of all man's tasks in life, leadership is in-born and therefore the simplest and easiest. We have also proved that it is because of this natural fact that both shepherds and parents are naturally good leaders, and that this is the actual reason why they do not, therefore, need any prior formal schooling or training in their respective leadership duties in order for them to prove good leaders.

In view of this fact, then it must also be true that one does not need to have a chain of degrees in the art of leadership in order for him to prove a good leader in political life. But should this be true, why then do parents and shepherds alike always prove good leaders while their counterparts in politics always prove failures?

From our clinical Diagnosis of this question, the findings show the following:

That whereas man is naturally born a good leader man has failed to prove so in political life.

That this is so because the Spirit of Honesty (SOH) which is the single most essential ingredient common in theory and practice of both a shepherd and a parent alike which makes each to be strictly transparent and accountable to his duty is unfortunately marginal and lukewarm among leaders in political life.

That like the shepherd's SOH which is naturally enshrined in the security and total welfare of his herd or flock because of the shepherd's total commitment to this Spirit, the parent's SOH is also naturally enshrined in the security and total welfare of the parent's nuclear family because of his commitment to this Spirit.

That because of this natural Universal Spirit whatever affects the security of the herd or flock is automatically seen as affecting the security of the shepherd; and whatever affects the security of the family is also seen as affecting the security of the parents.

That unfortunately, this SOH ingredient that exists in theory and practice among the shepherds and parents alike does of course exist in theory but does not exist in the actual performance or practice of political leaders—a mystery which is the object of this Research to unlock and get its cure or solution for the future benefit of our Humanity.

That whatever and whenever it appears at all in political leadership, it is too lukewarm in practice to enhance or generate good leadership.

That whereas in nuclear families, each parent naturally loves to know who of his/her family members gets what, how, when and why, and whereas among the shepherds, each shepherd also naturally loves to know where, when, how and why he should take his herd or flock for a good green pasture, a good drink, night, rest, treatment, this reality does not hold true among political leaders as most of them are not equally bothered by the welfare of all peoples under their leadership—a mystery which is the fundamental object of this Research to understand its roots and dynamics in political life.

That the increasingly looming abject poverty, diseases, robbery, murder, corruption, strikes, world-wide, confirms this truth that the SOH among political leaders is definitely abundant in theory but is unfortunately too mild and lukewarm practice—another mystery which is also an object of this Research to understand.

That it is because of the presence of a significant degree of this unique natural spirit of good leadership qualities founded upon SOH in both the shepherds and parents that makes the two to be more successful leaders and to therefore last longer in their tenure than their counterparts are in political life—another phenomenon which this Research seeks to understand is why it is non-existing in political life.

That if this SOH were also naturally observed and practiced as much as it is done by both shepherds and parents in their respective roles as leaders also, then no one would fail to become a good leader in political life.

That it is because of the lukewarmness of this SOH in political life which in turn leads political leadership to decay and malfunctions thereby plunging their Innocent General Public into a sea of agony.

And that this decay and malfunction normally manifests itself in a myriad of abnormal symptoms such as massive corruption, public discontent, rebellion and revolution leading to the political death of the leadership as evidenced in most countries in Africa and total World, e.g. in France in 1792 whereby the French people became so disillusioned with the intolerable leadership of their King Louis XVI that they had to dethrone him in August of that year and then guillotined him and his misleading wife (Marie Antoinette) on 21 January 1793; and also in the Thirteen North American Colonies, India and Africa where the Colonial Masters were forced to surrender leadership to the nationalists in 1774; 1949 and in the 1950s-1960s respectively due to their own undemocratic leadership which was not sensitive to the virtues and goals of Summum Bonum which calls the Greatest Good or Happiness of all the governed. The same disease and its horrifying outcome has similarly proved prevalent throughout all post-colonial Africa, e.g. in Kenya during the Jomo Kenyatta leadership (1963-1978) and more serious of all, during the Daniel Toroitich arap Moi's leadership (1978-2002). The latter's horrors of massive corruption by the Goldenberg International as means had to force all Kenyans to rise up and drive the Moi Leadership out of office in the unprecedented General Election victory of 2002, and to set up a Commission of Inquiry to investigate and report to their new leader, president Mwai Kibaki and his National Alliance Rainbow Coalition (NARC) Government the amount of public assets that may have been stolen by Moi regime, their whereabouts, and appropriate action that the new Government should take against him and all others who collaborated with him in stealing these assets. By now (2013), the Commission of Inquiry has already established close to KShs. 100 billion stolen and their whereabouts in European banks. The outcome of the investigation has yet to be awaited.

A Nagging Concern

If such catastrophe is the obvious consequence of bad leadership then why has this simplest and easiest task proved totally difficult and impossible for most political leaders? If Science and Technology have been able to prove prolific in understanding the most complicated mysteries of life such as how to put man in space orbit, how to prevent or cure serious diseases such as polio, and how to communicate from one corner of the earth to another in a matter of minutes or seconds, why has this simplest and easiest mystery evaded or defeated social sciences to understand how one may become a good leader in political life?

Because of the perpetual negative effect on humanity by this notorious mystery which has always evaded man's recognition for ages since the time of Patriarch Adam, the fundamental aim of this Study is to attempt to unlock this mystery with a view to paving a way for Good Leadership in our political life globally.

Thus, we need to, first and foremost, understand very well what this mystery is in our life as a prerequisite for our knowing how to contain it as also a stepping stone to how to create and sustain a good and successful leadership which has always been difficult to do since the time of our Patriarch Adam.

But since both Behavioural and Social Sciences alone have already proved an ineffective tool with which to understand this mystery, this Research will now turn to a Psychiartric Approach using a mixture of the two approaches plus Theology as a reliable tool beginning first and foremost with what we all know about leadership in our life in general as a prelude to what we need to know most about this mystery in political life, sui generis. As also used in my previous research published work with an immense results flavour in depth understanding of the dynamics of one's behaviour in theory and practice, a Psychiartric Approach is not a treatment of mental disorder as so, understood in Traditional/Conventional Academic. Unlike the latter's approach, this Approach is succinctly an in-depth clinical diagnosis of the root-causes of one's behaviour in terms of one's decisions and execution of such decisions. It dives deep into one's decisions and execution of such decisions. It dives deep into one's total historical experiences since birth to the time of the decision or act with a view of unearthing contributing factors to the decision or act that a researcher would not have otherwise been able to discover using only those other approaches whose low power cannot possibly permit/allow that. For further details on this Approach see also Agola Auma—Osolo, Cause-Effects of Modern African Nationalism on the World Market, University Press of America, London, 1983, Chap.7 and 8.; and Auma-Osolo,". "A Retrospective Analysis of the UN Activity in the Congo and Its Significance for Contemporary Africa" Vanderbilt Journal of Transnational Law. Spring, 1975, Vol.8, No.2., pp.468-474; and _____, Psycho-Dynamics of African Nationalism: The Quest for National Self-Love and Self-Respect.

Also, this Approach is necessary for us if we are to successfully and meaningfully compete with our counterparts in Natural and Physical Sciences particularly in Chemistry, Physics, Astronomy, Computer Science, etc. who, by now, have already exceedingly advanced in amazing spectacular scientific and technological discoveries and innovations using high power lenses.

In this regard, with the aid of this New Approach, the following is a comprehensive in-depth Autopsy of the empirical conduct of select leaders effective the time of our Patriarch Adam to The Flood Time and to our own generation in order for us to shed sufficient light on this evasive cumbersome mystery as a pre-requisite to our thorough understanding of this mystery; and to our ability to save our generation and future generations from the existing scourge of the Honesty Deficiency Syndrome (HDS) in political life which has always scourged our Planet so much that our planet is now not only in a miserable wretched condition but also in an Intensive Care Unit (ICU)

1   Findings

From the Failure of our Patriarch Adam to the Failure of Israel Leadership under King Zedekiah (587 BC).

Name	Succeeded or Failed	Reasons Why	Outcome & Lessons (Meaning)
1. Adam (Patriarch)	Failed	Total disobedience to God. Ignoring or being indifferent to the bilateral Memorundum of Understanding (MOU) and the spirit of pacta Sunt Servanda between him and God, and Foolishly accepting Satan's deceits through his wife (Eve) to do what he perfectly knew from God was dangerous to do (Gen.3:1-13). A too lukewarm manleader without a proper and reliable vision to reject and contain what was/is dangerous to the self and one's innocent subjects and descendants from external enemy (satan). Too bankrupt in the virtues, spirit and concept of self-love, self-respect, self esteem and self-reliance by:	Received an everlasting punishment in a form of a curse and then thrown out of The Garden of Eden by God for his disobedience and dishonesty. (Gen.3:23-24) Was stripped of all unique rights and privileges of a dominion originally bestowed upon him and his wife (Eve) and all descendants over all creatures and all sources of food, health, shelter, and other securities for greatest happiness in life in that he will now henceforth have to work to get those securities (Gen.1;26-30). Consequently, became a habitual destitute fugitive subject to diseases, accidents, hunger, and death under the power of Satan as a pay-off (Gen.3:17-19).

| | | Forgetting his responsibility bestowed upon him by God under Oath, to do only Good but not Evil likely to plunge the Innocent into a sea of agonies;

Turning about-turn to lay his blame to a third party (his wife Eva) as one who had misled him (Adam) into a wrong-doing; and also

Pointing fingers to the same God as one who had brought him (Adam) the woman to mess him up. | Put all his descendants into the same perpetual suffering.

Exhibits an exemplary model of the on-going mode of Poor Leadership and Governance that always lead the Innocent Subjects into a sea of Agonies simply because of its deliberate disobedience to its own Oath of Office and Pledges contained in its Policies and Declarations.

Reveals and Conforms the fact that, it is indeed this act of disobedience by both leaders and all those in public offices vis-à-vis their Oath of Office that is the actual primary root-cause of all human tragedies and catastrophes agonizing Humanity globally.

Further reveals and confirms the real genesis of Leadership failure in Humanity and a possible need for an immediate repentance as the only available rational way forward. |
| 2. Cain (Patriarch) | Failed | Total disobedience to God's Authority by murdering his own follower brother, (Abel) on jealousy grounds (Gen.4:6-7)

Became a destitute wondering man bankrupt of fatherly and motherly love and blessings (Gen.4:11-4)

Became a first victim of death and hell as a punishment of sin. (Gen.4:23-24) | Exhibits an exemplary model of an evil spirit of every and homicide haunting mankind daily globally |

		Became a first victim of death and hell as a punishment of sin. (Gen.4:23-24) Descendants wiped out by the Flood (Gen.6:1-7)	
3. Abel (Patriarch)	Succeeded	Total obedience to God's Authority, Glory and Honour for being a martyr of his innocence. Received abundant blessings from the LORD (Gen.4:4). Became the first Hero of Martyrdom (Gen.4:10)	Exhibits an exemplary model of an Innocent, Just and God—fearing being that God wants from each person in the latter's capacity as a typical image and representative of God on Earth. Exhibits a right path toward a Hybrid Culture Society.
4. Noah (Patriarch)	Succeeded In the early part; but later failed due to drunkenness and disorderliness	Total obedience to God's Authority, Glory and Honour by virtue of being a perfect, honest, faithful, obedient and righteous man worthy of God's abundant Grace (Gen.6:9-10). Found favour in the eyes of the Lord (Gen.6:8). Was chosen the Blessed Head of the chosen remnant of humanity during the Flood and the God's seed of our present Humanity after the flood (Gen.&:1). Got drunk and exposed his nakedness to his children thereby making one of his children (Ham) cursed.	Exhibits an exemplary model of Good Leadership requisite for Good Governance. Exhibits a bad model of leadership to children. If one leaves one self to become a hostage of drunkardiness whose goal is to mislead every leader and non-leader alike into foolish awkward behaviour and utterances. Because we have been given leadership, we should not just ignore accepted morals. Like the case of Adam who despised God and became conceited so did Noah also misuse God's gift to him to do the irrelevant that caused his downfall just as Adam did fall. Depicts human weakness of growing too proud and doing what plunges the innocent masses into an agony of suffering.

| 5. Abram or Abraham (Patriarch) 2000-1825 BC | Succeeded | - Total obedience to God's Authority, Glory and Honour solely by virtue of his both Amazing Faith and obedience but not because of his works and deeds alone in order to please the law giver. Tried several times to plead to the angels sent by God not to destroy Sodom and Gomorra cities so that they may spare the two cities; but all pleadings proved fruitless due to the obvious intolerable rotten conduct of both cities confirmed to Lot and his family by those angels on the night of their arrival at Lot's Home. | Justified his faith and works by obeying to offer his only son (Isaac) as a burnt sacrifice to God (Gen. 22:2-12) Received Amazing Grace of God and was found justified as a chosen blessed father of humanity (Gen. 18: 17-19; & 22:16-18), (Rom. 4:1-25). Exhibits an exemplary model of Good leadership highly requisite for emulation by every man and leader. In spite of God's infinite love, grace and mercies, no true servant or child of God must ever overlook or doubt God's omniscience and omnipotence, by trying to plead or expect God to alter what He has already chosen for salvation or blessings; or has rejected for condemnation or destruction, e.g. Sodom and Gomorrah. Each man and woman has an infinite duty to trust God's Word |
| 6. Sarai or Sarah (Patriarch) | Succeeded | Total obedience to God's Authority Glory and Honour by virtue of her amazing faith and humbleness to God's promise to her that, inspite of her exceeding age, she was able to conceive and beget a baby boy and name him "Isaac". A total humbleness to her husband, Abraham, whom he addressed as "my lord". | Received amazing Grace of God for her exemplary model of a righteous woman (Gen.20:6; 1 Peter 3:6). Exhibits Exemplary model of patience and obedience to her husband for every woman to emulate in her matrimonial life. |

7. Joseph (Patriarch) 1720-1550 BC	Succeeded	Total obedience and faith in the True Living God even while he was in slavery in Egypt Totally refused to be swayed into idolatry. Totally refused to be swayed into great wickedness of adultery by his master's unrighteous wife.	Found favour in the eyes of God because of his extraordinary steadfastness, and honesty Was consequently made overseer of all prisoners in the King's prison. Was blessed with an amazing wisdom by God with which he was able to interpret Pharaoh's dream which all Egyptian wise men could not. Was consequently honoured with a Pharaoh's signet ring, garments of fine linen and neck gold chain; and elevated to the post of governor in charge of entire Egypt on the Pharaoh's behalf. Exhibits an exemplary model of Amazing success through Amazing suffering.
8. Moses (Patriarch) 1290-1240 BC	-Succeeded at the beginning -Later failed for rebelling against God's commandments. -And was only allowed to see Canaan from beyond the Jordan River but not to reach there (Numbers 27:12-14; 18-21 and Deuteronomy 3:23-27; 32:48-52)	- Rejected everything in Egypt inconsistent with his faith in the True Living God of His Fathers in Israel. - Was blessed with most difficult task of exodus from bondage in Egypt, to the promised land in Canaan (Exodus 3:7-22, 4: 1-26). - Total obedience to God by carrying out God's command to lead the children of Israel out of Egypt; and by receiving and communicating God's Ten Commandments to them during the Exodus.	Exhibits an extraordinary exemplary model of Good Governance for every wise and honest leader to learn from and emulate it. His disqualification to enter Canaan is a lesson which each leader ought to meditate over seriously.

		- Was commanded by God to go up the Psganeboh mountain and only see the beauty of Canaan land beyond Jordan River now that he was no longer permitted to step in Canaan due to his disobedience to God. - For this reason, was commanded to relinquish his responsibility of the Exodus to Aaron who was now commanded to lead the children of Israel to Canaan across the Jordan River.	
9. Aaron The High Priest	Succeeded at the beginning of the Exodus but failed at the end and was made unable to reach the promised land of Canaan. (numbers 4:14-16, 18:1-7, 20:23-29, Ex.4:16)	- At first, faithfully executed his duties without any deviation from his Terms of Reference and oath of Office administered to him and his sons by prophet Moses in keeping with the Sovereign Lord's command. (Exodus 40:13-15) - Yet inside his heart he was so jealous of Moses that he double crossed Moses by making a golden calf and lured all Israel children on exodus to worship this calf while Moses was on Mt. Sinai to receive further instructions from God. - Both he and his sister (Miriam) spoke against their brother Moses because of the Ethiopian woman Moses had married.	First exhibits an extraordinary exemplary model of excellent spiritual leadership and a Good model of mutual working relationship with political leadership in life worth emulation by every prudent leader in life. At the end, he depicts a model of jealousy inciting devil worship manifested in nuclear family, large organizations and states as is also witnessed in Kenya and other African countries.

		- Also, both spoke ill of Moses by doubting how God could have possibly spoken to Israelite children by Moses but not by them as well. - This sinful act put God to so much wrath that He summoned and talked face-to-face to three of them as He had once done before Abraham's time (Joshua 14:1-33) - Consequently Miriam became leprous though recovered after seven days due to Moses intervention calling on God to forgive her for her sins (Numbers 12:1-16)	
10. Joshua (Patriarch) 1240 BC	Succeeded	- Total obedience to God's command to rise and take over from Moses as a new Leader of Exodus now that Moses was dead. (Joshua 1:1-11) - Successfully completed the objective of the Exodus by leading the children of Israel from the bondage in Egypt to freedom in Canaan. - To confirm this completion, he made a covenant with them all on their arrival in Shechem to always obey God's Word by making for them statutes, ordinances and a great stone as a sign of their commitment to God on oath that they would never again serve foreign false gods as their fathers clean of any corruption, injustice, etc.	- Was so blessed by God for his obedient excellent leadership that even the Sun and the Moon had to obey him and stay still over Gibeon and Ajalon Valley respectively without going down until Joshua won the war (Joshua 10:12-14). - Exhibits an exemplary model of good leadership success for every wise leader to emulate. - Exhibits a good model of a leader's obedience and honesty to the objective of the organization or a people he is expected to lead and serve. - Exhibits a good lesson to every leader by strictly adhering to the rules without turning left or right for one's

			personal gains through lootings and torturing whoever criticizes him and his evil deeds with a mistaken myth that one is above the law forever (or untouchable).
11. Eli (The High Priest) 1160-1120 BC	Succeeded at first due to reasons (1)-(2) But later on failed as a spiritual leader due to to his carelessness he exihibited on his song misconduct.	Was anointed servant of The Lord God in capacity of a Priest and Judge over Israel Presided over all sacrificial services in The House of The Lord God of Israel and Judged Israel for 40 years. But unfortunately had 2 sons (Hophnin and Phinehas) who freely and arrogantly messed up with sacrificial meats to God by grabing the best meat to fatten themselves at God's expense without their father's intervention to restrain them. Because of this parental leadership poverty and negligence, God sent His servant to warn Eli against this ugly conduct of his sons and his own hands-off attitude by giving a preferential treatment to his two sons over God (1 Sam. 2:27-36) The same warning was also communicated to the young Samuel so that the latter may also be aware of Eli's sins and God's forth coming pay off to Eli's negligence (1 Sam. 3:10-14). In fulfillment of God's warning	- Exhibits an exemplary good lesson model of disjointed leadership critically enslaved by: (a) A Hyper-cowardice disability unable to boldly face and restrain his own arrogant and corrupt sons from their evil acts they were publicly doing with his own clear knowledge. A Hyper-Timidity and Inferiority Complex giving an unwarranted leeway to his corrupt sons to do as they so wished thereby allowing them to mess up with his sacred culture that had distinguished him an Israel as a good Priest and Judge over the children of God. Is a valid and most reliable lesson for one wishing to become a good leader to learn from. - Exhibits an exemplary good lesson to humanity of what the Sovereign Lord is able to do to His servants who do not stand on their TWO FEET in their services. - Exhibits an exemplary model of Poor Corrupt

		Eli's two sons got murdered in a battle by Israel habitual Philistines enemy Eli also collapsed and died instantly on hearing the news of his sons' death (1 Sam. 4:10-27) - Hence the end of Eli, the Priest and Judge of Israel, together with his sons for marginalizing God and His Glory. Succinctly Eli: Proved too weak to contain and properly guide his corrupt sons. Was consequently overpowered by his corrupt sons who induced him into sinful acts which, in turn, provoked God to give him and his total family a punishment commensurate to his highest leadership post of "High Priest" (1Sam.22:22-25) He and all his sons were wiped out by God due to their unforgivable sins and as a good lesson to all spiritual leaders from Generations to Generations. In His Word to Prophet Samuel against Eli, The Sovereign Lord warned: *"Behold, I am about to do a thing in Israel, at which the two ears of every one that hears it will tingle. On that day, I will fulfil against Eli all*	Leadership and Obvious Consequences to those who have ears but cannot listen and learn from such harsh punishment on Eli, The High Priest and Family.

		that I have spoken concerning his house, from beginning to end. And, I tell him that I am about to punish his house for ever, for the iniquity which he knew, because his sons were blaspheming God and he did not restrain them. Therefore I swear to the house of Eli that the iniquity of Eli's house shall not be expiated by sacrifice or offering for ever" (1Sam.3:10-14).	
12. Samuel (The High Priest, Political Leader and Judge) 1075-1035 BC	Succeeded	Another anointed servant of The Lord God of Israel also in capacity of a Priest and Judge in place of Eli after the latter's death. Born of a long-time barren mother (Hannah) and father Elkanah whose other fertile wife (Peninnah) had been blessed with some children (of unknown number). Presided over all sacred functions in The House of The Lord God of Israel; and also judged Israel all his life from his homestead in Ramah. Correctly and wisely advised Israel to return to The Lord their God with all their hearts and to put away all strange gods and then serve The Lord God only so that The Lord God may deliver them out of the hand of their habitual Philistine enemies.	Exhibits an exemplary model of Good Leadership but critically besieged by Nepotism. Had he learnt from the lesson of Eli's sons' corrupt behaviour influenced by these son's feeling that after all their father was the Boss of Israel, (a) He could have prevented this ugly behaviour of his sons by not appointing them as Judges. (b) He could have appointed non-family members and non-relatives who could have behaved with better caution to give him glory. - Exhibits a very useful lesson to leaders to avoid Nepotism and to rely totally on Merits as a key to success and glory to The Rule of Law and Justice.

		His wise advice was welcomed by Israel and put away their Baalim and Ashtaroth gods and began to serve God only. Then gathered all Israel together at Mizpah and prayed to the Lord God to assist them against their Philistine enemies. Was heard by God who thundered to these Philistine enemies and destroyed them all for Israel's victory. In recognition of this victory by God's intervention, puts up a stone called EBENEZER between Mizpah and shen (meaning "Thus far has The Lord God helped us against the enemy") (1 Sam. 7:1-12). After this victory and throughout his life, permanent peace and security prevailed between Israel and all their enemies (Amorites and Philistines) and all cities and Coasts previously taken by enemies were restored to Israel. But like Eli's sons, had also Samwel's sons (Joel and Abiah) who did not walk in their father's ways, for they turned aside from God's ways after money and bribes thereby selling Justice and perverting judgement against God's commandment (1 Sam 8:1-3).	- Exhibits a leadership culture typical of all leadership cultures globally most particularly in the Developing Countries, e.g, Kenya where appointments are all governed by: - Nepotism - Political Affiliation, etc at the expense of merits and productivity. - This action of putting up EBENEZER in recognition and appreciations of God's divine intervention must be a mandatory lesson to mankind to give Glory to our Creator and Source of life if we are to succeed against all forms of insecurities, e.g Health, Famine, etc. - Kenya deserves the right to do the same for her victiory against the 40 years of Dictatorship by KANU. - Exhibits an exemplary model of wise leadership that every one should emulate if one's to lead a successful life. - Former President Julius K. Nyerere of Tanzania and Nelson Mandela of South Africa fit this model.

		Consequently, when too old to serve Israel any more and sought Israel to accept his sons to judge over them, Israel rejected the sons and demanded to be given a King to rule over them like all other nations (1 Sam. 8:4-5).	
		But on enquiring to God for a directive on this Israel demand, was commanded by God to honour the demand (1 Sam. 8:7-22).	
		And, in this regard, he is directed by God to Saul, the son of Kish from the tribe of Benjamin, as one that he (Saul) may save God's people (Israel) from the hand of the Philistines (I Sam 9:15-17)	
		Faithfully executed his duties as a High Priest, Political Leader and Judge without any corruptive motive to enrich himself as we see it today among our leaders in spiritual, political and judiciary life.	
		- Although his sons whom he had entrusted his responsibility to judge over Israel did not honour their work as their father did, he did not succumb to their corrupt ways (1Sam.8:1-3).	
		- All Israel confessed that he was totally clean (1 Sam. 12:1-25)	

13. Saul (King of the United Kingdom of Israel) 1050-1010 BC	Initially succeeded but later failed.	A Son of Kish from the Israel tribe of Benjamin with a tall handsome mighty body structure next to none among all Israelites of his generation. In a process of searching for a man of God (Samuel) to prophecy to then (Saul and his father's lost asses, Samuel was commanded by God to anoint him (Saul) as Israel's King (1 Sam. 9:15-17). Correctly and diligently followed instructions given to him by Prophet Samuel immediately after being anointed by doing exactly as so commanded to do. Was forewarned by Prophet Samuel to know and remember at all times that the Hand of The Sovereign Lord God which had picked him from nothing and made him into a mighty person was equally ready to be against him and all Israel as it was against their forefathers whenever they did not hearken to God's commandment and instead turned to witchcrafts and other ungodly practices. (1 Sam 12:14-250. After reigning for only one year as Israel King, Saul began behaving strange. Contrary to Samuel's warning, began deviating from God's commandments given to him	Exhibits an exemplary model of good leadership selection because of the divine intervention. Exhibits an unfortunate role of human nature characterized by Disobedience to one/s Oath of Office to do the irrelevant contrary to what one is mandated under Oath to do. This human element is the root-cause of man's habitual failure in leadership as it pollutes the divine elements on the strength of human greed and other lists which drive one to salivate for another human's blood as Saul did to David for no honourable cause at all. Exhibits the danger of human greed and envy instinct that drives certain leaders away from Transparency and Accountability on the assumption that he/she is above the law or that he/she is not going to be caught. Also shows a lesson that whenever a leader sees that he/she is unable to satisfy those that he/she governs, he/she automatically develops a psychological disease of insecuritophobia propelling him/her to arrest and detain or kill whoever he/she detects to be a real or potential threat (competitor) to his/her leadership.

| | | through Prophet Samuel, by indulging himself in a sacrificial role he was not mandated to do (1 Sam. 13:9-15).

Such disobedience became a nucleus of his Kingdom failure in Israel (1 Sam. 13:13-14)

This nucleus is manifested in these symptoms:-

Seeks death for his innocent son Jonathan, but this is vehemently opposed by all Israel public calling on God to disallow the King's wishes (1 Sam. 14:44-45)

When commanded by God to exterminate all Amalek and all their possessions (ox, sheep, camel, and ass) but decides to loot these possessions for himself against God's will.

Because of this disobedience and lust for wealth at the expense of God's commandment and Glory, is informed by Prophet Samuel that God has now rejected him from being King over Israel (1 Sam 15:23)

And because of his evil heart of envy,

Seeks to murder his own valiant servant David (also his own son-in-law) in order to stop David from succeeding him as King over Israel; but | Exhibits a lesson to every leader and society as a whole that inspite of this discomfort and intimidation to real and potential competitor(s),

(a) Whoever God has willed to become a leader will not fail.

(b) The wages of envy, greed and all other symptoms of sin against the righteous is definitely one's own death.

The suicide of King Saul and the murder of all his three sons by the enemy (Philistines) thereby leaving David to majestically inherit the leadership and all wealth left behind by King Saul is a confirmation of this cardinal truth in life. |

		his own son Jonathan sees this as evil and therefore decides to save David. (1 Sam 19:1-7) Again-seeks to kill David while at a dinner table using a javelin but by the Grace of God, the Javalin misses David and lands in a wall and David escapes outside into the darkness (1 Sam. 19:10) Continues his efforts to search and kill the innocent David in order to satisfy his phobic lust for power using messengers, etc without success (1 Sam. 19:11-21) But the innocent David continues to spare Saul's life at all costs by restraining both himself and his own young men from slaying Saul whom he (David) strongly recognized as an anointed servant of God who must therefore not be slayed by any one (1 Sam. 24:6) This David's stand amazed Saul so much that Saul broke down into tears and prophesied right there:- that David was good but he (Saul) was indeed evil; and that David was definitely going to become the next King over Israel after him (Saul) (1 Sam. 24:16-20) - But on being denied by God a better way forward for Israel victory against their Philistines	

		enemy, turned to a medium woman to assist him (Saul) hear from the now already dead and buried Prophet Samuel on what to do now,	
		- Saul is terribly shocked by the dead Samuel's voice telling him (Saul) through this woman	
		(a) that Saul's Kingdom over Israel was already taken from him and given to David (1 Sam.28: 16-17); and	
		(b) that Israel was to be soon conquered on the next day by the Philistines and that his (Saul's) sons and himself were scheduled to die on the same day and follow Prophet Samuel in grave (1 Sam. 28:19)	
		- As as the medium woman's witchcraft had revealed to King Saul,	
		The Philistines emerged on the morrow and killed as many Israel men of war as they could catch up with.	
		They also killed all Saul's sons beginning with Jonathan and then Abinadab, and Melchishua.	
		On seeing this horrow, King Saul commited suicide by falling on his own sword and died including his armour bearer	

		Thus, the end of King and all his three sons because of his own disobedience to God and his abnormal envy to shed innocent blood contrary to his Vow of Office under Oath.	
14. David (King of the United Kingdom of Israel) 1000-970 BC	succeeded	- Total obedience to God - Brought back the Ark of the Lord from the House of Obed to the City of David with mighty rejoicing even at the displeasure of his own wife, Michal, daughter of Saul (2 Samuel 6:12-22) - Could not stand living in a house of cedar while the Ark of the Sovereign Lord dwelt in a tent (2 Samuel 7:1-3) - Unlike his Predecessor (King Saul), never consulted mediums. - Remained steadfast in God's Worship inspite of his sinful acts of murder of Uriah and taking the diseased's (Uriah's) wife (2 Samuel 11:1-27, 12:1-34) for which he received untold subsequent punishments from God. - On realizing that God sees and knows all whether in light or dark and that God does not spare anyone whether he be King, free or slave in the sense that one must reap what one sows, - went down on his knees repenting for his sins.	- Was blessed with abundant grace and favour to the extent:—that he became God's chosen successor of King Saul's reign instead of one of his seven older brothers in the house of Jesse; - That he escaped from various death attempts by King Saul; and - That he was victorious in various battles against the Philistines, and even killed their undefeatable commander, Goliath - Exhibits an exemplary lesson of a Repenting, Humble Leader worth emulation by every leader. - Left behind an exemplary legacy for Mankind that each man who seeks to be an anointed servant of God must hearken to in his leadership tenure: - Leader is actually a servant of the people but not vice versa - A leader is a provider of his people but not a beneficiary of their sweat through looting, usurpation,

		- died still a true devoted servant of God	theft, robbery, assassination, detention, or harassment of oppositions. - A leader should be like a good caring and loving parent that would rather go hungry or thirsty so long as every child is able to eat and drink. - A leader should be one who is readily able to repent and lead all his followers to do the same but not to remain unconcerned - A leader must not engage in DEVIL WORSHIP
15.Solomon (King of The United Kingdom of Israel) 970-930 BC	Started very well but later failed	- Though blessed by God with amazing wisdom and wealth above all other kings of his generation that many of them flocked to Jerusalem to pay tribute to him and though blessed to build the Temple on behalf of his father (King David), he flabbergastingly became so much lust fitted for foreign women:- - That he acquired 700 wives and 300 concubines; - And that he became a victim of these foreign women who induced him to abandon his True Living God of Israel and turn to their gods contrary to his own original faith reflected in his own confession (The Proverbs 4:3-27).	- God was put to anger by: - Solomon's turn to Devil worship, - And in-human hard labour (1Kings 11:1-14) - God tore the United Kingdom into 2 small weak kingdoms of Judah and Israel due to King Solomon's failure to keep his covenant with God enshrined in his oath of office (1Kings 11:9-13 and 29-40) - Since then, the United Kingdom of Israel and its glory has never been resuscitated to this day. - Is an exemplary model of a misguided Leader who uses his abundant resources to do wrong non-positive things.

		- Instituted so much inhumane hard labour on his subjects that many lamented they were better off in slavery back in Egypt; and revolted after his death	- <u>Also exhibits a model</u> of a leader without gratitude to God who made him a leader.
16. Rehoboam (King of Judah) 930-931 BC	Failed	- Instituted inhuman hard labour policy on his subjects which proved worse than that of his father, King Solomon (1Kings 12:3-11)	- <u>All people in Israel revolted, disowned him</u> and stoned to death his forced labour task master forcing the King to flee to Jerusalem. - <u>Because of this rebellion:</u> - Jeroboam became King of Israel; and - Rehoboam King of Judah (1Kings 12:20).
17. Jeroboam (King of Israel 930-909 BC	Failed	- While he became King of Israel by abundant Grace of God arising from God's wrath against King Solomon's disrespect of God's blessings and commandments thus causing God to tear the United Kingdom of Israel into two little and weak Kingdoms of Israel and Judah (1Kings 11:29-40), Jeroboam: - Despised God by turning to Devil worship in total disregard to God's command conveyed to him by Prophet Ahijah: (1) To rule over the 10tribes of Israel in the new Israel; and (2) To do so diligently in keeping with God's statutes and commandments as the United Kingdom of Israel had done during the reign of King David (1Kings 11:35-39)	- God warned Jeroboam to stop defiling God's Temple with sacrifices to idol altars; and to pour out all ashes upon it (1Kings 13:1-3) - On refusing to do so, all house of Jeroboam was condemned to total destruction - Apart from his son (Abijah) who was buried, all others belonging to Jeroboam who died in the countryside, their bodies were to be eaten by birds and those who died in the city, they were to eaten by dogs (1Kings 14:7-14) - <u>Israel was disowned by God</u> for the sin of their King Jeroboam (1Kings 14:15-16) - The innocent children of Israel suffered for a sin

		- Despised God by <u>appointing non-Levites</u> to priesthood and performed sacrifices to idol gods on the God's Temple altar in violation of Israel's faith since King David's reign (1Kings 2:26-33) - <u>And, did evil above all</u> that were before him forgetting that God had exalted him from among all people and made him leader over Israel (1Kings 14:7-9)	initiated and enforced by their leader (King Jeroboam) - Is another exemplary model of ungrateful Leader who became a Leader out of no where (i.e., without proper qualifications but by the Grace of the Sovereign Lord) and then become a TOTAL DISGRACE to the Sovereign Lord through DEVIL WORSHIP and VIOLATIONS OF HUMAN RIGHTS
18. Nadab (King of Israel) 909-908 BC	Failed	- Like his father, King Jeroboam, <u>also despised God</u> by doing what was evil in the sight of God and made Israel to sin through DEVIL WORSHIP	- His reign lasted for only 2 years (910-908 BC) - Exhibits a good example of a leadership without vision.
19. Abijah (King of Judah) 913-910 BC	Failed	- Like his father (King Rehoboam), also despised God by doing what was evil in the sight of God and made Judah also to sin through DEVIL WORSHIP	- His reign only lasted for 3 years (913-911 BC)
20. Baasha (King of Israel) 909-985 BC	Failed	- Prophet Jehu was directed by God with the following warning to King Baasha; "Since I exalted you out of the dust and made you leader over my people Israel, and you have walked in the way of Jeroboam and have made my people Israel to sin, provoking me to anger with their sins, behold, <u>I will utterly sweep away Baasha and his house</u>; and I will make your house like the house of Jeroboam. Anyone who dies in the city,	- An exemplary model of ungrateful man who becomes a significant person in life from nowhere solely by the Grace of the Sovereign Lord but then turns around to boast and insult his Master through DEVIL WORSHIP AND VIOLATION OF HUMAN RIGHTS as we see it globally today!

		the dogs shall eat; and anyone of his who dies in the field the birds of the air shall eat". (1Kings 16:2-4) - This warning through Prophet Jehu was fulfilled in the reign of King Zimri who killed all house of Baasha according to the Word the LORD (1Kings 16:8-13).	
21. Asa (King of Judah) 910-869 BC	Succeeded	- Like King David, - Did what was right in the eyes of the Lord, e.g., - Expelled all male prostitutes out of Judah - Removed all idols that his fathers (Abijah, and Rehoboam) had made. - Removed his grandmother (Maacah) from being queen mother because she had an abominable image made for Asherah - Cut down and burnt this image - His heart was wholly true to the Lord - Brought into the Temple of the Lord the silver and gold and all articles that he and his father (Abijah) had dedicated. (1Kings 15:11-15)	- <u>Was so much blessed</u> by God that his reign lasted 41 years (911-870 BC). - Like King David, <u>proved</u> another exemplary model of Good Leadership for Good Governance!
22. Elah (King of Isael) 885-884 BC	Failed	- Like his father (Baasha) walked in sin and also made Israel to sin through DEVIL WORSHIP	- His reign lasted for only 2 years (906-904 BC) as he was assassinated by army commander, Zimri

23. Zimri (King of Israel) 884 BC	Failed	- Like King Jeroboam, - Committed sin by doing evil in the eyes of the LORD. - Usurped leadership over Israel through a military coup d'etat after assassinating King Elah.	- His reign lasted for only 7 days. - Committed suicide on realizing that Jerusalem had been taken over by King Omri, army commander in total support of Israel. (1Kings 16:15-19) - Left Israel divided into 2 factions between those who supported <u>Omri</u> and those who supported <u>Timni.</u>
24. Omri (King of Israel) 884-87 BC	Failed	- More than all other Kings, <u>Committed exceeding sin</u> and made Israel also to do the same through DEVIL WORSHIP	- <u>Provoked the Lord</u> to anger because of DEVIL WORSHIP and IDOLATRY.
25. Ahab (King of Israel) 873-853 BC	Failed	- Did more evil than all his predecessors. - Married Jezebel, daughter of Ethbaal (King of Sidonians) <u>by whom he began to worship Baal</u> - Made Israel also to sin by ordering them;- - To recognize and worship Baal; - To reject God's covenant; - To break down their altars; and to put all their prophets to death with a sword thereby forcing Prophet Elijah to flee and become a lone refugee in caves. - Murdered the innocent like Naboth in order to grab Naboth's vineyard which Naboth had refused to sell to him (Ahab).	- <u>Prophet Elijah was sent by God</u> to declare to the King: - That as God had done to Kings Jeroboam, Nebat and Baasha, God was going to consume Ahab's house and all descendants, including every last male in Israel. - That Ahab's wife (Jezebel), who had misled him to kill Naboth, was to die and not to be buried but to be eaten by dogs. - And that all others who die in the city were to be eaten by dogs while those who die in the country-side were to be eaten by birds - <u>To fulfil this Prophesy, Ahab ignored Prophet Micaiah's council</u> not to go to war against the enemy (Ramoth Gilead) and

		- Extensified and intensified DEVIL WORSHIP in Israel due to his obsession with IDOLATRY AND WITCHCRAFT through his wife JEZEBEL (now the chief witch). (2 Kings 9:22) - Angered God so much that rain was immediately shut off for over three years thus putting Israel to a famine tragedy. (1 Kings 16:33, 17:1) - Continued to kill so many prophets of God in Israel that his own household governor and servant of God (Obadiah) had, through compassion, to secretly hide other prophets by fifties in each care feeding them on only bread and water throughout this genocide. (1 Kings 18:13) - Forced prophet Elijah by this genocide fear to flee and hide in the wilderness where he survived by hiding in caves and being fed by ravens, before he fled to Sidon where he was rescued and hidden by Sidonian widow for three years, before returning to Samaria on God's command to show himself to King Ahab and tell him that God will now send rain on earth (1 Kings 18:1) - On accidentally meeting prophet Elijah while searching for grass for his (Ahab's) horses, etc., accepted	preferred to follow lies from false prophets which misled him to go to war and get killed there. - As a result of the Honduras nature of her death, <u>Jesebel's dead spirit culminated into a killer evil spirit.</u> From this extra-ordinary empirical experiment by prophet Elijah, there is no doubt: 1. That his experiment was also scientific <u>sui generis</u> as it was purposively intended to <u>empirically</u> prove to both unbelieving King Ahab and his 450 prophets of Baal, who, between Baal and Prophet Elijah's God was a true living God. 2. That it was scientific in that it was a follow-up to other scientific experiments performed/demonstrated earlier by prophet Moses almost six centuries ago (144 BC) in pharaoh's palace in Egypt, whose aim was to <u>empirically</u> prove to pharaoh that prophet Moses had truly been sent by a True Living God to rescue and lead the children of Israel out of bondage in Egypt, to freedom in their promised land in Canaan.

| | | Elijah's request to participate as a principal witness in Elijah's scientific experiment on Mount Carmel designed to scientifically prove who of the two gods was a true Living God: (1) Baal or (2) Elijah's God.

- Agreed to provide two bulls for this scientific experiment: one for a burnt offering by Baal's prophets and the other for a burnt offering by prophet Elijah.

- Practically witnessed no fire coming down from heaven to consume the Baal's prophets' offering as expected by those prophets through supplications from 9 A.M to 3 PM.

- Practically witnessed fire coming down from heaven to consume prophet Elijah's offering immediately prophet Elijah begun to call on his God after 3 PM to bring fir down and consume his offering.

- Having empirically witnessed this truth,

- Immediately believed in Elijah's God.

- And immediately reported the same to his wife (Jezebel) upon returning, home, confirming that Elijah's God was The True Living God. | 3. Also that it was scientific in that it was further reinforced later, (after almost nine centuries) by our Lord Jesus Christ in numerous miracles e.g., the changing of pure water into wine in Cana John 2:1-1 and the raising of Lazarus from the dead (John 11:1-57), whose meaning and significance was to empirically prove to the unbelieving world whether or not his teaching had any truth or validity, and whether or not he was a begotten Son of our Creator sent by him to redeem this world. (John 11:41-42).

4. and that as a study of the relations between man and God, Theology is, therefore, also a science Sui generis aimed at discovering truth about God, using both scientific (empirical) and other relevant means as prophets Moses and Elijah and then Jesus Christ demonstrated publicly |

		- Having received this truth from her husband, Jezebel became so terribly ashamed that she desperately sought to immediately kill Prophet Elijah, in order for her to conceal this scientific truth from the public in Israel (1Kings 17:1-24; 1Kings18:2)	
26. Jehoshaphat (King of Judah) 869-848 BC	Succeeded	- Walked in the ways of his father (King Asa) and did what was right in the eyes of the LORD, - Initiated and maintained Judah and Israel Kingdoms. - Expelled all remaining male cult prostitutes in Judah	- Because of his exemplary leadership, on his death, he was brought and buried with his fathers in the city of David, his grandfather. - Like Kings David and Asa, he exhibits an exemplary model of Good Leadership for Good Governance!
27. Ahaziah (King of Israel) 853-852 BC	Failed	- Like the deeds of his father (King Ahab), all his were evil in the eyes of the LORD. - Like his father (Ahab), he:- —Caused Israel to sin through DEVIL WORSHIP; —Served and worshipped Baal there by also provoking God to anger as his father (Ahab) had done; —Invested all faith in Baal Zebub (god of Ekron), for wisdom to guide him on his leadership and health. —Unsuccessfully sought on three occasions to arrest prophet Elijah by sending a 50—man battalion on each occasion, but to his dismay two battalions were consumed by fire from heaven (vs.9-14)	- Exhibits an exemplary model of foolish leadership; always too blind and too deaf to learn from past experiences e.g. of his own mother Jezebel who had been wiped out by God due to their devil worship practice. - Also, is a good example of foolish leaders always interested in releasing their evil tempers on innocent persons as a scapegoat for their own leadership failures - Prophet Elijah was sent by God to tell King Ahaziah that because he had provoked God of Israel to anger, he was definitely going to die from accident injuries received at his

			place in Samaria albeit he would have survived had he honoured the God of Israel as his grandfather, King David, had done. Therefore like Elijah, every true servant of God must faithfully; honour God's omniscience and omnipotence; and never deviate from that faith by trying to question or plead to God to have mercies and alter his will or plan against what He has already rejected and condemned for destruction or death, as in the cases of the unrepeatable Ahaziah and Sodom and Gomorrah people; Or Against what He has already accepted for redemption or blessing as in the case of the repeatable Ninevch wicked people.
28. Joram (King of Judah) 849 BC and Israel 841 BC	Failed		- Married daughter of King Ahab - Due to this marriage, all he did was evil in the eyes of The Lord as he also believed and practiced DEVIL WORSHIP and believed in BAAL (Satan) as his god. - Initiated war against Edom (Arabs or descendants of Esau and Ishmael) as opposed to Israel (Jews or descendants of Jacob and Isaac). - Since then, Edom remains a rebellious people against Judah.	- In view of this REVELATION, the on-going perennial ARABISRAEL CONFLICT must be a function of this old cancer initiated by King Joram of Judah in 849 BC

29. Ahaziah (King of Judah) 847 BC	Failed	- Related to King Ahab's family by marriage - Consequently also believed in and practiced DEVIL WORSHIP as King Ahab's family had always done thus making Israel to provoke the LORD to anger	- His leadership did not please the LORD
30. Jehu (King of Israel) 841-813 BC	Succeeded	- Wired out both King Ahaziah of Judah in fulfillment of the Lord's word spoken to prophet Elijah as a pay off for King Ahab's murder of Naboth and grabbing of Naboth's vineyard. - Wiped out Jezebel in fulfillment of God's Word spoken through Prophet Elijah for her role in the murder of Naboth and for misleading Israel into idolatry and witch craft (2Kings 9:22; 30-37) - Completely wiped out all the 70 sons of the house of Ahab residing in Samaria in fulfillment of God's word spoken to Prophet Elijah (2Kings 10:1-17) - Completely wiped out DEVIL WORSHIP in Israel by killing all ministers of Baal established by King Ahab (2Kings 10:18-28)	- Pleased God so much that God told him:—"Because you have done well in accomplishing what is right in my eyes and have done to the house of Ahab all I had in mind to do, your descendants will sit in the throne of Israel to the fourth generation". 2Kings 10:28-30 - But because King Jehu did not prove fully committed as he failed to turn away from King Jeroboam's sins by which he also caused Israel to sin. The Lord reduced the size of Israel through the occupation of Israel by the Eastern Kingdom of King Hazel of Aram, East of Jordan (2Kings 10:31-33) - Another exemplary model of Good Leadership requisite for Good Governance.
31. Athalia (Queen of Judah) 841-835 BC	Failed	- Assassinated because of her jealousy and wickedness to annihilate all royal families on seeing that her son (Ahaziah) had been wiped out by King Jehu	- As a result of her elimination:—Israel destroyed all paraphernalia of BAAL WORSHIP including the temple and the altars

			- Israel killed Mattan, the priest of Baal (2Kings 11:18).
32. Joash (King of Judah) 835-796	Succeeded	- Repaired the Temple - Instituted so honest managers to manage finances brought in as offerings for the repair that:- —All people were fully satisfied with their work that they had no need for an auditor of the money entrusted to them. —Also priests were satisfied with the payment allocated to them by these managers. (1Kings 12:15-16)	- <u>Received</u> God's blessings - <u>Due to his success</u> and fame, two of his officers conspired and assassinated him - Another exemplary model of Martyrdom similar to that of Abel.
33. Jehoahaz (King of Israel) 813-798 BC	<u>Partially</u> failed	- Did evil in the eyes of the LORD by following the sins of Jeroboam which he had made Israel also to sin (2Kings 13:2-3) - <u>However</u>, the King Sought the Lord's favour (Forgiveness) for this sin. (2Kings 13:4)	- Due to this anger, <u>God subjected Israel</u> to occupation by Hazael, King of Aram (2Kings 13:3). - <u>God listened</u> to Jehoahaz's repentance and rescued Israel from Aram's occupation (2Kings 13:5)
34. Jehoash (King of Israel) 798-781 BC	Failed	- Did evil in the eyes of the LORD as he did not turn away from the sins of Jeroboam. - But demonstrated so much affection and compassion for Prophet Elisha during Elisha's illness and death that he found favour in God against Aram's Domination. - <u>Captured</u> King Amaziah of Judah; went to Jerusalem; broke down its wall from	

		Ephraim gate; and plundered all treasures in the Temple and in Royal Palace (2Kings 14:13-14).	
35. Amaziah (King of Judah) 796-767 BC	Succeeded	- Did what was right in the eyes of the LORD but less than King David - Executed all the officials responsible for the death of his father, but did not kill their fathers also (2Kings 14:3-5)	- Obedient to the law of Moses. "Fathers shall not be put to death for their children; nor children put to death for their fathers; each is to die for his own sin". (2Kings 14:6).
36. Jeroboam (King of Israel) 781-753 BC	Failed	- Did evil in the eyes of the LORD and committed Israel to sin, though he recovered for Israel both Damascus and Hamath, which had initially belonged to Judah	
37. Azariah (King of Judah) 767-739 BC	Failed	- Did what was evil in the eyes of the Lord just like his father (Amaziah) had done. (2Kings 15:3)	- Was afflicted with leprosy until the day of his death. - Was consequently secluded in a separate house where he died. (2Kings 15:5)
38. Zachariah (King of Israel) 753-752 BC	Failed	- Did evil in the eyes of the LORD through DEVIL WORSHIP and made Israel also to sin. (2Kings 15:9)	- was assassinated and succeeded by his assassin (Shallum) - was deposed through assassinated in fulfillment of the Lord's promise to King Jehu: "Your descendants will sit on the throne of Israel to the fourth generation" (2Kings 15:12)
39. Shallum (King of Israel) 752 BC	Failed	- Became King of Israel through a bloody coup d'etat in which he assassinated King Zacharia and succeeded him.	Was also deposed through a bloody coup d'etat and assassination by Menahem (Kings 15:14).

40 Menahem (King of Israel) 752-741 BC	Failed	- Came to power through a bloody coup d'etat and assassination of King Shallum. Flabbergastingly ripped open all pregnant women in Israel (2 King 15:16) Did what was evil in the eyes of the lord through DEVIL WORSHIP thus made Israel to sin (2Kings 15:18)	- Used funds levied from Israel population to buy a treaty with King Pul of Assyria to strengthen his leadership over Israel (2 Kings 15:19-20)
41 Pekahiah (King of Israel) 741-739 BC	Failed	Did evil in the eyes of the LORD and also caused Israel to sin through DEVIL WORSHIP (2 Kings 15:24)	Was assassinated in a bloody coup d'etat and succeeded by the assassin, Pekah as King of Israel.
42 Pekah (King of Judah) 739-731 BC	Failed	- Did evil in the eyes of the LORD and also caused Israel to sin through DEVIL WORSHIP (2 Kings 15:28)	- Was assassinated in a bloody coup d'etat and succeeded by the assassin, Jothan, as King of Judah
43 Jothan (king of Judah 739-731 BC	Succeeded	- Did what was right in eyes of the LORD (2 Kings 15:34). - Rebuilt the upper gate of the temple of the LORD.(Kings 15:35)	
44 Ahaz (king of Judah) 731-715 BC	Failed	- Did what was wrong in the eyes of the LORD. - Sacrificed his own son by passing him through fire as a ritual sacrifice in DEVIL WORSHIP	
45. Hoshea (King of Israel) 731-722 BC	Failed	- Did evil in the eyes of the LORD	- Was invaded by King Shalmaneser of Assyria. - All Israelites deported to Assyria. - This was the end of Israel Kingdom.

46 Hezekiah (king of Judah) 715-685 BC	Succeeded	- Did what was right in the eyes of the LORD just as his father, King David had done:— —Removed high places —Smashed sacred stones —Cut down Asherah poles —Destroyed bronze snake made by Israelites who were making burnt incense on it. - Trusted God fully ABOVE all other Kings before and after him e.g. —Kept the LORD'S commandments given to Moses. However, he made a dangerous blunder by revealing all confidential treasure of his Kingdom to the King of Babylon (Baladan), thereby opening the door for Judah conquest and blunder by Babylon (2Kings 20:13-18)	- Because of his abundant faith and obedience to God. —The LORD was with him all times —Was successful in whatever he undertook, e.g. —Successfully rebelled against Assyrian King Defeated the Philistines up to Gaza include its territory. —Conquered and occupied Samaria —Received a miraculous victory over undefeatable King of Assyria in fulfillment of the word of God through Prophet Isaiah (2Kings 19:20-34). NB: At night, all Assyrian army and its commander were annihilated by the Lord's angel; and the King himself was ambushed and murdered by his own sons while in the temple worshipping!! (2 Kings 19:35-37) —Was added 15 years to his life as per his prayers (2 Kings 20:1-6) Another exemplary model of Good leadership very much essential for Good Governance to be emulated by a very wise leader who needs success and praise in his or her leadership.

47 Manasseh (King of Judah) 686-641	Failed	- Did most evil in the eyes of the LORD because:— —Rebuilt high places of DEVIL WORSHIP, which his father (King Hezekiah) had destroyed. —Erected altars of Baal as King Ahab had also done in the temple of the lord contrary to the word of the LORD:—'In Jerusalem, I will put my Name'. —Sacrificed his own son in fire to please Baal. —Practiced sorcery, divination and all sorts of DEVIL WORSHIP. —Consulted mediums and spiritists.(2Kings 20:2-8) Made all people of Israel to support and join him in this DEVIL PRACTICES AND WORSHIP (2 Kings 20:9) —Shed so much innocent blood that Jerusalem was bloody all over!!	- His sins provoked God so much that Jerusalem and Judah were punished with such a devastating disaster that the ears of everyone who heard it tingled! E.g. —Jerusalem was completely wiped out; —Remnants of Israel in Judah were taken and handed over to their enemies; All treasures in Judah were looted and plundered by these enemies. An exemplary model of Killer leader who enjoys blood letting of his innocent subjects for his master 'THE DEVIL'. Similar to this model Are the cases of Apartheid Regime in South Africa and the Nazi Regime in Germany. In our own generation, tribal mutual genocide in Rwanda and Burundi, Bosnia, Liberia sierra Leon, and Arab-Israel endless war since 1949 to now (2004)
48. Amon (King of Judah) 641-639 BC	Failed	-Did evil in the eyes of the LORD Like his father (King Manasseh), —Worshipped Idols —Made Judah to sin against the LORD.	- Was assassinated in the 2nd year of his reign. (2Kings 21:23) - His violent death as an exemplary LESSON to Devil Worship Leaders.
49. Josiah (King of Judah) 639-609 BC	Succeeded	- Did what was right in the sight of the LORD:- —Discovered the BOOK OF THE LAW in the Temple	- Neither before nor after Josiah, was there any king like him who turned to the LORD with this Zeal. (2Kings 23:25)

		of the LORD containing the Lord's commandments, statutes and ordinances —Honored those commandments and statutes of the LORD found in that Book. —Removed all Idols, gods and altars in Judah —Removed Judah from DEVIL WORSHIP endowed by his father (Amon), and his grandfather (Manasseh). —Ordered all Judah to celebrate the Passover to the LORD as written in the BOOK OF THE LAW which had never been observed ever since the days of all kings of Israel and Judah —Banned all mediums and spirits and idols in Judah and Jerusalem in keeping with the Law of Moses.	- Because of irreparable sins of King Manasseh and King Amon which had kindled a heat of fierce anger in the LORD —Judah was conquered by the Egyptian Pharaoh (King Necho) —And King Josiah killed by King Necho. - Is another extraordinary model of good leadership though his performance failed to save Judah from the curse left behind by King Manasseh's extreme DEVIL WORSHIP and BLOOD letting for the benefit of his master, Baal, the devil.
50 (King Jehoahaz of Judah) 609 BC	Failed	- Did evil in the eyes of the LORD. - Was put in chains at Riblah in the land of Hamath by Pharaoh Necho so that Jehoahaz may not reign in Jerusalem (2 Kings 23:31-34)	Was deposed by Pharaoh Necho and replaced with Jehoahaz's other brother, Eliakim, whose name was changed to 'Jehoiakim' (2 Kings 23:34) - Was taken to captivity in Egypt by Pharaoh Necho where he died.
51 Jehoiakim (King of Judah) 605-597 BC	Failed	- Installed by Egyptian Pharaoh (King necho) to replace his deposed brother (Jehoahaz) now exiled in Egypt.	- The Lord sent Babylonian, Aramaean, Moabite and Ammonite raiders against Judah in fulillment of God's wrath against Judah due

		- In addition to agreeing to the Pharaoh's wish to replace his own brother as King of Judah, —Also did evil in the eyes of the LORD —Accepted to become a vessel to Nebuchadnezzar of Babylon for three years though he later changed his mind and rebelled against Babylon.	to the bloody sins Judah had committed during the reign of Mannasseh (2Kings 24:2-4) NB: King Necho (Pharaoh of Egypt) no more pursued invasion of Judah as it was now occupied by Nebuchadnezzar of Babylon
52. Jehoiachin (King of Judah) 597 BC	Failed	- did evil in the eyes of the LORD	
53. Zedekiah (King of Judah) 597-587 BC	Failed	- Agreed to be used by King Nebuchadnezzar of Babylon to depose his nephew and take his leadership as new King of Judah.	- Jerusalem was hit by so severe famine that:- —There was no food for Zedekiah, his royal family and the army. -When they tried to flee Jerusalem from the famine, all were caught by the Babylonian powerful army surrounding Jerusalem. —Zedekiah's sons were killed in front of Zedekiah —After witnessing the killings of his sons, Zedekiah's eyes were gorged out. —He was then bound with shackles and taken to Babylon for execution. - On Zedekiah's arrival in Babylon, Nebuzaradan commander of the Imperial guard and Nebuchadnezzar's chief official, was ordered

			back to destroy all Judah. Therefore, Nabuzaradan;
			—<u>Set fire on</u> the Temple of the LORD of the royal Palace; and on all houses in Jerusalem.
			—<u>Captured and took</u> to exile in Babylon all those poorest Israelites who had remained in Jerusalem and Judah; and
			- left behind only a few poorest Israelites to take care of the vineyards and fields.
			- While Zedekiah died of his own malice by which he colluded with Nebuchadnezzar to depose his nephew (JEHOIACHIN) so that he (Zedekiah) may be made King of Judah,
			—Zedekiah was later on executed by his own co-conspirator (Nebuchanezzar).
			—After the death of Nebuchadnezzar, the new King of Babylon (Evil-Merodach) released Jehoiachin from prison; gave him a seat of honour above all other kings also in captivity in Babylon; allowed him to eat on the high table with the King of Babylon; and gave him regular allowances for life. (2Kings 25:1-30)
			- <u>Exhibits</u> an exemplary lesson to conspirators and the Payoff of conspiracy in Life. AMEN!

****

A quantitative Analysis

The Old Testament exposes to us an amazingly striking answer to our curiosity on why and how each leadership fails. The Old Testament shows that most leaders fail simply because they despise God's Glory and Commandments by turning their faith to Satan through devil worship, deceits, dishonesty, false accusations of others, sale of justice, terrorism, vandalism, and grabbing what belongs to others, etc

Out of a total of 42 leaders (41 kings and 1 queen, Athalia) of both kingdoms of Israel and Judah beginning with king Saul during the United Kingdom of Israel in 1050 BC up to the break up of the kingdom after the reign of King Solomon in 971 BC into two small Kingdoms of Israel and Judah and so right up to the reign of King Zedekiah of Judah in 587 BC. When the kingdom of Judah was finally destroyed by Babylon, only the following nine leaders or (21%) proved successful: <u>King David</u> of the United Kingdom of Israel and Judah (1000-970BC); Asa(King of Judah, 910-869 BC);Jehoshaphat (King of Judah,869-848); Jehu (King of Israel,841-813 BC); Joash(King of Judah,835-796 BC);Amaziah (King of Judah 796-767 BC) Jothan (King of Judah 739-731 BC); Hezekiah (King of Judah 715-685 BC); and Josia (King of Judah 639-609 BC).

But all others totaling to 37 or 79%(or 36 Kings and 1 Queen, Athalia) proved a failure in their political leadership!

The most outstanding failures in their leadership include King Saul of the United Kingdom of Israel and Judah (1050 BC); King Solomon of the united Kingdom of Israel and Judah (971BC); King Rehoboam of Judah (931BC); King Jeroboam of Israel (931BC); King Baasha of Israel (908BC.).

King Ahab of Israel (874 BC); King Jehu of Israel (814BC); King Manasseh of Israel (697 BC); and King Zedekiah also of (587 BC) Their failure was explicitly a function of their despise and insult to the LORD God who had saved their forefathers from the bondage of slavery in Egypt, under the most powerful leadership of Pharaoh, King of Egypt, by turning to DEVIL WORSHIP in contravention of their covenant with the same God who had rescued him from this bondage and given them, through their leader, Moses, Ten Commandments also popularly known as THE LAWS OF MOSES to assist them as a guide in their daily social and spiritual life. This despise and insult resulted into a total leadership failure in both Israel and Judah and all leaders and population being taken captive to Babylon.

Nowhere in the Old Testament or other primary source do we find that all these leaders failed because of their ill-education or training in the art of leadership. This source shows us that:

They all failed mainly because of their obsession in devil worship and the leadership disease of self—pride, greed and failure to appreciate the fact that leadership is not one's right but a privilege gift from the Lord God Almighty for which one is expected by God to serve those who are under him.

Each leader is expected to know that while he is their leader, he is also under the leadership of him above who gave him a life as a free gift and also anointed him as a leader of those under him.

In the simplest terms, the leaders who usualy fail ignore or marginalize the fact that one is not anointed by God to serve one's selfish ends but to serve the ends of those children of God under whom both the political leader and all the people whom he leads fall. A vivid evidence of the tragedy of this egoistic obsession disease to one's leadership success is:

a. The failure of King Solomon's leadership in the United Kingdom of Israel.

b. King Solomon, who had been so much blessed and endowed with such enormous wisdom and wealth above all other leaders of his generation which no one had ever seen before in life and which made even the Queen of Sheba in Ethiopia to come and visit him in Jerusalem, did not only fail but also caused the United Kingdom of Israel to be destroyed from the same leadership cancer.

c. The Kingdom broke into two separate little kingdoms of Israel and Judah in 931 BC which, infact, turned out to act <u>as a first stage of its decay and final death.</u>

d. The autopsy shows that it was his misguided wisdom and egoism which misled King Solomon into various abnormal lusts and deeds.

e. The most dangerous one was his lust to acquire 700 wives and 300 concubines who, in turn, fooled and coaxed him into the practice of devil worship and a harsh forced labour on his subjects in Israel in total contravention of the commandments, statutes and ordinances of the true living God of Israel whom his own father, King David, had always worshipped and adored throughout his life; and the God who king Solomon was also taught to reverence and worship from his youth by his own father (King David) as King Solomon himself reveals it to us in the Holy Bible as follows:

When I was a son with my father, tender, the only one in the side of my mother, he taught me, and said to me,

O let your heart hold fast my words; keep my commandments and do not forget and do not turn away from the words of my mouth. Get wisdom; get insight.

'Trust in the Lord with all your heart, and do not rely on your own insight.

(iii) In all your own eyes; fear the Lord, and turn away from evil. It will be healing to your flesh and refreshment to your bones."(The proverbs of Solomon).

f. A further autopsy of other cases of leadership failure, using the Holy scripture, our foremost key primary source, also reveals to us that in as much as King Solomon's leadership had to fail because of the same natural root—cause of leadership failures in all generations, our findings from the same source also reveal that even King David who was more blessed than King Solomon was, and who was so much endowed with an extraordinary power, valour and wealth by God that all other kings of his time were not a match to him, was not an exemption to God's wrath when king David was caught red-handed by God with deeds which were not in keeping with the oath of his office as a King of the United Kingdom of Israel.!

g. In order for each of us to appreciate the Grace and love of God to us all even at the time when we may not actually deserve it; and also God's wrath against us whenever we do not appreciate this Grace and love, let us first of all briefly examine the case of King David—how he got this wonderful leadership; what he did contrary to his oath of office; and God's response to the King's deeds.

(c)   <u>A Psychiatric Analysis of King David's leadership as a unit of analysis</u>

David became king of the United Kingdom of Israel by a slim chance. He was the last born of the 8 sons of Jesse of Bethlehem. He was away in the field grazing his father's flock when Samuel, the priest, came to his parents' home on God's command to anoint one of his brothers as a successor to king Saul. But it was not until the anointing oil failed to come out from Samuel's anointing oil horn each time Samuel tried to pour the oil on every head of the other brothers that the little David was then (finally) called to come from the field and also undergo this anointing test. Unlike all his brothers, the anointing oil came out of the anointing oil horn to David's head when Samuel tried to pour it onto his head. Consequently, the little David was declared the anointed successor to the throne of the United Kingdom of Israel from King Saul. Although King Saul had sons who could have automatically succeeded him, according to the custom, unfortunately all of them summarily perished together with their father (King Saul) because of King Saul's inexcusable abominations and God's wrath against these deeds.

Otherwise, David could not have become king of the United Kingdom of Israel had it not been solely because of the abundant Grace and love of God the almighty preferring him above all his 7 elder brothers for this Kingship.

But as if this slimmest chance were too little, and insignificant to King David during his leadership, unfortunately, king David expropriated and misused his office to the extent that God could not hold back his wrath against him.

Nauseated and angry with King David's misuse of his office, God sent prophet Nathan first to test on the King's level of <u>justice</u> using a parable of a case between a rich man and a poor man. 'The rich man owned a large herd of cattle and a flock of goats and sheep while this poor man only owned one little lamb. Instead of using one of his own herd and flock, this rich man usurped that little lamb from the poor man from which he prepared a meal for his own guests.

Flabbergastingly, as if this was not enough for him, the rich man further killed this poor man in order to silence him from raising an alarm to the public to embarrass the rich man because of this little lamb'.

On hearing this, King David was extremely charged with anger against this man saying that the man deserved a penalty of summary death plus a fine of fourfold lambs to the deceased.

But no sooner had the King uttered this than Prophet Nathan jumped up in the air and exclaimed: 'you are the man'! 'Thus says the lord God of Israel: 'I anointed you king over Israel and I delivered you out of the hand of Saul; and I gave you your master's house and your master's wives into your bosom; and gave you the house of Israel and of Judah; and if these were too little, I would add to you as much more'. Further, prophet Nathan revealed to king David that because of all these sinful acts contrary to the king's oath of office, it was God's wrath that;

The sword with which the king had killed Uriah in order to take Uriah's wife would never depart from the king's house.

God was going to raise up an evil against the king out of the king's own house neighbour.

God was going to take the king's wives before his own eyes and give them to the king's neighbour.

This neighbour was going to lie with the king's wives in the daylight.

Although the king had committed this sin secretly, but now God was going to do this thing before all people of Israel, and in daylight.

While the king was not going to die because of this sin, his despise to God's glory and the leadership gift God had given to the king was enough and, therefore, the child who had been born to king David with Uriah's wife, must surely die.

But what exactly had King David done that was so critical as to put God to anger against his beloved and adored servant?

From 2 Samuel 12: 9 of <u>The Holy Bible</u>, we come across the following question to the king which seems to constitute the actual root—cause: 'why have you despised the word of the Lord, to do what is evil in his sight? You have smitten Uriah the Hittite with the sword, and have taken his wife to be your wife . . . .' also, from 2 Samuel 12:15, we further discover the following harsh punishment to King David because of the above abomination:

The Lord struck the child whom King David had begotten with Uriah wife (Bathsheba) sick.

For seven days, King David fasted and prayed to God for Him to spare the child but all in vain.

The child died on the seventh day.

Soon after the child's funeral, the king's family life deteriorated into the following irreparable sorrows:

One of his sons, Amnon, raped his half-sister, Tamar;

His other son, (Absalom), a brother to Tamar, became so much enraged by this rape act that he killed Amnon, and then fled home to a foreign country leaving behind his father (David) in a psychological turmoil because of the circulating rumour that Absalom had actually killed, not only Amnon but also all other brothers before fleeing.

When Absalom later returned home after two or so years, he staged a coup and deposed his father (King David) forcing the king to flee from the palace in Jerusalem to the Mount of Olives where he lived till Absalom's death and the death of Abner.

Even after his return and restoration to the throne in Jerusalem, King David did not recover from the hysteria and restlessness caused by Absalom's coup d'etat.

Because of this unstable psyche, arising from attempted coup, King David also did to his long-term most reliable chief military commander, (Joab) another sinful act, to carry out census that consequently put God to anger against the king.

Because of this new sin, God sent Gad, the seer, to warn king David on what was now going to befall Israel: 'and so, God sent pestilence upon Israel from the morning till the appointed time; and there died seventy thousand men'

Although King David's son, Solomon, managed to succeed king David to the throne, this succession cost him very heavily. (See (h) below).

In as much as king David had a burning desire to build for the Lord a temple of cedar so that the ark of the covenant of the lord would no longer remain under a tent, the king was categorically denied this sacred right because the king's hands were already too bloody (defiled) to handle such holy task. This is the reason why the king had to leave the task for his son, Solomon.

2   Lessons synthesized

But what useful lessons do we learn from this clinical diagnosis of leadership success world-wide?

(A)   From King Kavid's Leadership Case

The useful lessons gleaned (synthesized) from the case of King David are as follows:

1) Like a Sheperd and a parent in life, every leader ought to know and always remember these cardinal principles: (a) that he is not a servant of the self but a humble servant of those he is appointed or elected to lead in conformity with the terms and conditions of his oath of office: (b) that to be a leader is not to be a beneficiary of the goods and services of those that one leads; (c) that to lead is not to be served by the public but to serve the public with a total dedication, humility and humbleness in the spirit of transparency and accountability in the same manner a shepherd and a parent are God's anointed servants of their flock, herd or nuclear family respectively; and (d) that, in view of these facts, a leader is indeed an anointed public servant of God.

2) As a God's anointed public servant by virtue of one's oath of office on a Bible or other book of God, a leader is naturally required and expected at all times to be keenly mindful of the needs of all, regardless of their status, place of origin or ethnicity and gender. Thus, in order for a leader to easily succeed in his leadership career, his service must always be for all but not for only a few privileged classes based on and guided by the leader's nepotism, racism, regionalism, religiosity, political partisanism, and other elements of corruption totally antithetical to good leadership and good governance.

    This is exactly the sole reason why Socrates always taught and echoed to/in his home community of Greece and Macedonia that 'man know thyself' and that none should be allowed at all to become a leader unless and until that person is first certified as a philosopher king, i.e., one is first educated on the art of governance particularly on the philosophy of Theocentric Humanism embracing the belief in the holiness and perfection of one's conduct or character and the doctrine of <u>Summum Bonum</u> meaning the Greatest Good or Happiness for all the governed—a philosophy and doctrine he learnt during his studentship at Grand Lodge of Luxor from the African Mysteries System. According to this philosophy and doctrine, a leader's conduct is expected to be holy, perfect and godly in the sense that, as a God's anointed servant of the people he rules, he is perceived as being half god and half human being. Thus he is between God his creator on one hand, and the people he governes on the other. Accordingly, his conduct is expected to be holy and perfect as God is holy and perfect but not corrupt, unjust, dogmatic, partial, autocratic etc as our leaders always are globally. Because of this excellent quality, a leader is always assured of an easy entry into paradise. This is exactly the reason why pyramids were constructed and kings' bodies mummified in Egypt with a view to preserving the bodies in those pyramids awaiting the return of the soul at a later date. In this regard, a leader's virtous conduct is needed so as to set a good example for all the governed to emulate in their daily life.

This is also the reason why one had to be trained into a "philosopher king" before he could be deemed qualified for the leadership. One was expected to thoroughly master the philosophy of Theocentric Humanism characterized by the virtues of Perfection and Holiness plus the doctrine of <u>Summum Bonum</u> and its cardinal virtues namely Justice, Wisdom, Temperance, Concord and Courage—the virtues totally non-existent in our leaders globally today—before one could be recognized and allowed to hold and practise a position of leadership in society.

(3) On the strength of these requirements a good leader should be able to show no interest in expropriating his office to steal or usurp property of those whom he leads and or to harass and silence them through murder, arrests, detention, threats, bribery and the like as both king David did to Uriah, and also king Ahab did to Naboth. He should be meticulous, scrupulous and righteous in thoughts and deeds in keeping with those cardinal virtues of Summum

Bonum and the Theory of Theocentric Humanism. Thus, he must practise what he preaches and expects his followers to do.

(4) Any leader who boasts about good policies, which are simply a mirage to him, commits a blasphemy against the name of God. And by grabbing the assets of his country for the purpose of dishing them out as a bribe to his friends, relatives, political party, in search for political support in the form of votes, etc,:

(a The Leader, by doing so, commits an abomination not only to the people he leads but also to God since such evil deeds are not in keeping with the oath of the leader's office.

(b His pay off is the same as those in the cases of king David and other kings such as Ahab, Baasha, Jeroboam, who received severe punishments from God due to their sinful deeds against what was expected of them according to the terms and conditions of their oath of leadership.

(5) If a most blessed and loved of all leaders of his time such as King David could also be put to such painful punishment by God for misusing his most powerful office as King of The United Kingdom of Israel to do a grave injustice to his servant Uriah and Joab, it is self-evident that no leader is an exemption to God's wrath.

(6) Although in Uriah's case, God's wrath against King David was limited to the King's family, in the case of Joab, God's wrath against King David affected all people of Israel. All Israel suffered terrible pestilence to the extent that seventy thousand (70,000) people died as a pay-off for King David's leadership blunders—an explicit lesson to the governed that they would be equally regarded as partakers of their leader's transgression if they foolishly sit down condoning the leader's evil without stopping him or advising to do the right thing.

(B) **From all other Cases**

(1) We also learn from the case of King Solomon that when his deeds proved a demeaning act to the glory of God and all gifts that God had given to him on becoming King of the United Kingdom of Israel, the entire Kingdom suffered a fatal punishment from God's wrath for it was broken into two antagonistic

Kingdoms of Israel headed by King Jeroboam (as head of 10 tribes of Jacob who rebelled against Solomon's hard labour policy); and Judah headed by king Rehoboam (son of king Solomon) as head of two other tribes of Jacob who continued with his father's policy of hard labour and devil worship.

(2) We further learn from the case of the old Egypt during the pharaoh's leadership, that all people of Egypt suffered the agony of various types of pestilence e.g. locusts, frogs, etc. not because of the mistakes of the people of Egypt but simply because of Pharaoh's disobedience to God's commandment by not allowing the children of Israel to go to Canaan as commanded by God.

(3) But we again further learn that bad leadership is not only a disgrace but also a killer disease to the country as a whole. For example:—

As in the reigns of King David, King Manasseh and King Ahab of Israel and the pharaoh's in Egypt where all people of Israel and Egypt suffered various types of pestilence as a punishment to their respective countries because of their leader's disobedience to God's commandments, the on—going world—wide pestilence of recurrent civil wars, famine, floods, droughts, air and road tragedies, terrorism, earthquakes, hurricanes, genocide, etc. could also be due to our leaders' disobedience to God's commandments in their capacity as both chief political leaders and chief partakers in various abnormalities e.g. the on—going increase in devil worship, homo-sexualism, lesbianism, sodomy, oral sex, falsehood and wizards male cult prostitution, etc, not only in political life but also and very flabbergastingly, in the religious life! Which, have, in turn, caused God's wrath against our humanity.

And as also predicted by David Reagan in his recently published masterpiece because of these on going evil deeds, we could possibly be heading towards another catastrophe similar to that of Sodom and Gomorrah—a lesson that may already be dead or regarded as foolish old child tale to many of us not worth wasting time to think about.

(4) This amazing revelation on the actual root-causes of leadership failure in political life in the old time Israel should not be misconstrued as being limited to Israel of that time. The same also holds true with regard to the leadership

of today's Israel whereby the leadership ability to live in peace with her neighbours remains a thick darkness to all Israel leadership.

(5) A further clinical diagnosis of leadership eufunction in other countries during the same time bracket such as Babylon also shows similar results. Like all those political leaders in the old time Israel who failed in their leadership because of their failure to use their common sense to learn from the lessons of their predecessors' political leadership failure, all leaders in those other countries who also ignored to learn from the lessons of their predecessors' political failures similarly failed. And, their failure was equally as serious as that of their predecessors as follows:-

A vivid example of this failure is that of King Nebuchadnezzar of Babylon and his son, King Belshazzar, who succeeded Nebuchadnezzar on the later's death (in 586B.C)

Although king Nebuchadnezzar was so powerful during his reign (605-586 B.C) that he did not only conquer Israel but also took all children of Israel as captives to exile in Babylon and looted all their treasures to Babylon, God did not spare Nebuchadnezzar, when Nebuchadnezzar attempted to exalt himself to the level of God by demanding his subject (citizens) to worship him by way of songs, dances, as a way of humbling them to accept him as one above the law in a despisement to God's glory who had given him all gifts of life and the leadership out of all people in Babylon.

As a good lesson to Nebuchadnezzar and his Babylonian people, God made Nebuchadnezzar look and behave like a wild beast and to eat grass like an ox-a lesson all other leaders who are sane enough ought to pay heed to and check on their conduct to those they govern and to God who anoints leaders from dust to such prominent positions in life.

It was not until Nebuchadnezzar realized his blasphemy and remembered to repent and humble himself before God that he was restored to his original human status and throne as King of Babylon by God.

But, as if such lesson to king Nebuchadnezzar's punishment was not good enough to his son, King Belshazzar, who succeeded his father, King Belshazzar saw no need to pay heed to this lesson.

He despised God much more than his own father had done. During a royal banquet at his father's palace, king Belshazzar sought to show off his god-like glory to his guests, wives and concubines-a common character to leaders in our own generation too!!!

To do this, he ordered his banquet attendants to bring in before him sacred vessels which his father had looted from the God's House in Jerusalem during the conquest of Israel; and then begun using them to drink wine with his guests, wives and concubines a wonderful life in deed for lucky men and women in life.

This act of blasphemy provoked God to so much wrath that:

God gave king Belshazzar such a harsh punishment that Babylon was unable to recover from it;

Its magnitude was beyond that of his own father's punishment;

For example, while proudly showing off at the banquet with those vessels in his hands, the king suddenly begun seeing a hand of an invisible person writing the following on the wall of the banquet room "MENE MENE TEKEL PARSIN" Whose interpretation proved totally difficult for every one at the banquet including all Babylonian wise men in that country.

(i) Because of this mystery, King Belshazzar could neither sleep nor eat! He was permanently restless and trembled day and night. It was not until Prophet Daniel was brought in and gave the needed interpretation that he king realised the magnitude of his blasphemy and its consequence, namely:

   (i) that because of his blasphemy, his leadership was now no more and,

   (ii) that his kingdom had now been taken from him and given away to the kingdom of the Medes and Persians under Cyrus (Darius).

   (iii) In the night, immediately after receiving this interpretation from Prophet Daniel, King Belshazzar was slain and Darius took his Babylonian Kingdom in 612 BC as exactly as Prophet Daniel had told the King regarding the meaning of those strange words.

(6)   Important lessons gleaned from this case of King Belshazzar are as follows:—

The King lost his own life due to his disobedience to God and his pride by refusing to learn from the lesson of his own father's punishment.

His innocent Babylonian people who had no case to answer for their king's blasphemy also suffered though on a second degree scale.

Although they did not die like their blasphemous king, they lost their kingdom to the Medes and Persians.

This tragedy could have been avoided had their political leader (King Belshazzar) not been so foolish to ignore the harsh lessons of his father's failure—what a pity to those who never learn from previous lessons especially leaders who feel that they are too important and too big to be reminded of previous lessons!

(7)   But the case of King Belshazzar is not the only one. Many similar cases abound even in our own generation. For example, between 1900 to now (2013), the following astonishing cases come to mind:—

(a)   The case of the colonial ruler; Mussolini in Ethiopia, the: Nazi Germany; the former apartheid white regime in South Africa; the cannibal Bokasa; the president Ferdinand Marcosa; the homosexual President Banana case, the murderer General Sani Abacha; The autocratic president Danile. T. Arap Moi of Kenya; etc.

(b)   This list is endless especially of those who despise and abuse God by various other ways such as devil worship, mass blood—letting, human rights violations, perpetuation of poverty by making the poor poorer than before through deceits and looting of state wealth by and for the politically correct persons at the expense of these poor, contrary to their own oath of office and terms of reference.

(c)   This man—made flabbergasting tragedy is normally a function of leader who actually do zero work for the welfare of their people whom they had initially promised to help during their swearing in ceremony (inauguration), but whose efforts are focused to lootings of public liquid and fixed assets without any concept of shame, e.g., the former Zairean president Joseph Mobutu Sese Seko, the former Indonesian President—Suharto, the former Philippine President Marcos, the former Central African Republic Emperor Jean Bedel Bokassa. And the former Kenyan President Daniel T Arap Moi

(d)   Their Behaviuor is manifested as follows:

(i)   "Like King Luois XVI of France who foolishly angered his French citizens so much by claiming to them that he was the state of France and vice versa to the extent that his France citizen resolved to guillotined him in 1793, they also foolishly angered their citizens by claiming that they were the state and the state was them. Thus, as a state is immortal, they also claimed immortal, by forcing their citizens to accept them as <u>LIFE PRESIDENTS</u> and also <u>ABOVE THE LAW!</u>

(ii)   Like the Philippine President Marcos, they looted their state coffers bare like a wild fire miraculously races a dry bushy field bare to the ground—into what the Nigerian novelist Chinua Achebe satirically calls a 'wretched world'!

Leaders such as Bokassa and former Zimbabian ceremonial or honorary president Banana became so intocicagated from/with their official powers and ignorance of the meaning and use of that power that they consequently

Lost control of their sanity and

Fell into political suicide tragedy by turning into 'super cannibals'—a curriculture of the on-going 'wretched world culture! against these creator's original aim of humanity and political leadership enshrined in the creator's commandment and also reflected in the Theocentric Humanism philosophy and <u>Summum Bonum</u> doctrine of the African Mysteries System of the Grand Lodge of Luxor as far back as 7000-5000 BC

3   RECOMMNENDED REMEDY TO LEADERSHIP FAILURE

(A)   *From the Biblical Wisdom/Theological Science Efforts above:*

In view of these lessons gleaned particularly from king David's leadership and all other leaderships from our patriarch Adam to king Zedekiah in 587 BC leaderships and

Belshazzar of Babylon, it is now apparent that in order for us to save our endangered humanity from God's wrath, the solution is sevenfold.

(1) Weed out and avoid all wicked and unjust persons from leadership as per Apostle Paul's verdict envisaged in his letter to the Corinthians.

(2) Emulate the exemplary leadership model of king David, king Asa, king Hezekiah, king Jehosphat and king Josiah whose deeds and policies during their reigns proved right in the eyes of the Lord our God,

    (a) By worshipping the true living God instead of hypocritically cheating the general public that one is worshipping the sovereign Lord while he is actually worshipping Baal, Satan, the devil, and

    (b) By eliminating and refraining from all other practices of bad governance akin to those of king Ahab against Naboth's vineyard likely to cause God to anger—an excellent leadership model which, in turn, enabled

        (i) King David to receive God's Forgiveness and Mercy in Uriah's case; and;

        (ii) the leadership of all those five(5) Kings named above to shine and enhance an amazing amount of love, peace, unity and prosperity for all people in Israel never enjoyed during the reigns of other leaders such as King Saul, King Jeroboam, King Ahab, King Baasha, because of these leader's involvement in foreign gods and other insults against the Leadership and Glory of our True Living Lord God Almighty.

(3) As a protection mechanism,

        (i) It should be a natural duty of every leader to always remember that in as much as it is punishable to a child who despises, marginalizes, ridicules and disobeys his father and mother; and as it is also punishable to a citizen who despises or disrespects the laws of his country and government, so is it also punishable to a leader including every ordinary person who despises, marginalizes, ridicules, and disobeys the commandments, statutes and ordinances of God as also witnessed in the cases of King Saul, King David, King Solomon, King Ahab, King

Baasha, King Jeroboam and all other disobedient leaders in Israel and Judah—most particularly Kings Saul, Ahab, and Baasha who received the worst payoffs from God's wrath against their disobedience.

(ii) To call a spade a spade, except our SOVEREIGN LORD GOD ALMIGHTY no single human being is above the law!

(iii) Therefore whoever dares to boast that he is above the law is no better than Nebuchadnezzar and his son (Belshazzar) who tried to do so and got the fruits of boast. And that is not all.

(iv) The same applies to King Louis XVI of France who also harvested what he had sown (1792-1793) and finally Jean-Bedel Bokassa (Central African Republic); Moise Tsombe (Congo); Sani Abacha (Nigeria); Hastings Kamuzu Banda (Malawi); Mobutu SeseSeko (DRC former Zaire Congo); and finally Daniel T. Arap Moi (2002) who was terribly humiliated in a landslide victory by the opposition under National Alliance Rainbow Coalition (NARC) party thereby leaving him totally bare for legal prosecution for all the lootings and other crimes committed while in office (1978-2002).

4) In the same candid spirit of Prophets Samuel, Nathan and Elijah who never hesitated to reveal to their respective leaders (King Saul, King David and King Ahab) about God's wrath against these leaders because of the later's deeds which were seen as a despisement and an insult to God's glory in the eyes of God, similarly, it is also our duty as scientists to be vigilant and candid to our political and other leaders in all walks of life who are engaged in these on-going practice of devil and idol worship and other abominations which are also a despise and an insult to God's Glory in the eyes of God by apprising them:-

That enough is already enough for it is their support and direct participation in rampant practice of devil worship and other behavioural abnormalities today such as homosexuality, sodomy, lesbianism, massive corruption, falsehood, insecurity, self glorification akin to that of Nebuchadnezzar and his son, (Belshazzar), which <u>are the actual root-cause</u> of the on-going agonies of various pestilence such as world-wide

Aids, floods, civil wars, droughts, famine refugee exodus, poverty, ethnic and religious clashes, genocide, drug addiction and drug trafficking, terrorism.

That they should no longer be limping from one opinion, faith, or god to another thereby causing our True Living Lord God Almighty to anger. Let each take a stand!. If he chooses to follow the Lord as his God, let him do so sincerely day and night. But if he chooses to follow Baal or any other false gods, let him sincerely do so day and night! Let him not mix the two!

And, that, whoever has ears, let him hear this loud and clear because God is not a fool! God is tired of being played around with by devil worshippers who hypocritically go to God's Sacred House of Worship during the day especially on Sundays on false pretence that they are going to worship our Living God, while at night they secretly sneak into secret dark rooms and strip themselves naked to worship Baal, or Satan the devil. They also use innocent blood of their relatives or subjects or citizens to feed Baal, the devil, in the form of human sacrifices thereby provoking The Lord God our Creator to anger not only against those leaders who are the culprits of these heinous deeds but also against all the innocent under those leaders' jurisdiction.

Now that by the Grace and Love of God conveyed to us through Prophet Isaiah under 60:1-5, it is apparent that we, scientists, now have this revelation on the actual root-causes of the on-going world-wide perennial agonies of pestilence; and that in this regard, we must no longer remain timid or be afraid and silent. Any attempt for us to do so could be contempt of God; and would thus cost us heavily as an accomplice party to our political leaders' evil policies and deeds. As a special class in our respective societies, we have a scientific, moral and Spiritual Duty to God to reject what is suicide to our Humanity.

As a best way forward, we have to emulate the exemplary model of Prophets Abel, Seth, Enoch, Noah, Abraham, Jacob, Joseph, Moses, Joshua, Aaron, Samuel, Nathan, Elijah, Elisha, Jehu, Daniel, Isaiah, Jeremiah, Nehemiah, Ezra, Micaiah, in the manner they boldly told their respective leaders what was expected of them by God and the fruits of these leaders' obedience or disobedience.

If our leaders fail to pay heed to this revelation as King Ahab arrogantly refused to listen to Prophet Elijah and also to prophet Micaiah, then let them do so on condition that they fully accept all risks involved caused by their own disobedience to Him who anointed them. Thus, they should be willing to perish alone as King Ahab and King Baasha did including the people of Sodom and Gomorrah for it is written: "Only the obedient will enjoy the Glory of God as King Asa, King Hezekiah, King Jehosphat and King Josiah did after King David". Also, as Jesus Christ explicitly warned us on His Ascension "He who believes and is baptized will be saved; but he who does not believe will be condemned.[21]

In summary, what each leader ought to know and always pay heed to at all times for the normal functioning and success of his leadership is as follows:

(a)   Whereas in a locomotive train, the engine is the head and leader while all wagons are the followers; and, whereas in a nuclear family and a flock of sheep, the father and the shepherd are the leaders while the mother and children and the flock are simply the followers at the mercy, love and grace of the father and the shepherd respectively, however, in a political life, although the leader is the engine of all those under him who include all parents of all nuclear families and all shepherds of all flocks and herds while the latter are simply wagons under the mercy, love and grace of his government and laws, the same leader is also simply a wagon under the Mercy, Love and Grace of the Commandments, Statutes and Ordinances of our Lord God the Almighty who is the Overall Supreme Engine of Humanity and Total Universe!

(b)   Like our patriarch Abraham and his wife, Sarah, and also Kings David, Asa, Hezekiah, Jehosphat and Josiah who received abundant grace, love and success from our True Living God because of God's satisfaction with their faith, humbleness and adherence of God's commandments, statues and ordinances, it is also self-evident that every leader who does the same in his leadership tenure will never fail. His accelerated leadership success is automatically assured in abundance.[22]

(c)   Any leader whose deeds are contrary to this model, the fruits of his deeds is the agony of disobedience i.e. God's rejection akin to that of our patriarch Adam and his wife Eve and also of Kings Saul, Solomon, Ahab, Baasha and many others who chose to walk and do things not befitting their anointing (oath of office) and the Glory of God, who gave them a free gift of life and anointing them as political leaders (politico).

(d) From the above, it is self-evident that

  (i) Our leaders always fail in their leadership not because of their wish but mainly because, according to Prophet Isaiah's revelation (Isaiah 60:2), they are still in a thick darkness.

  (ii) As a result of this in (d) (i) above, they are still ignorant of the existence of this natural truth which is also clearly reiterated by Apostle Paul in his Apostolic Letter to the Romans as follows:

  "For the scripture says to Pharaoh, I have raised you up for the very purpose of showing my power in you, so that my name may be proclaimed in all the earth"[23].

(e) Like the Pharaoh, all our political leaders as well as most spiritual leaders have not yet woken up to recognize that their power and responsibilities are a true manifestation of the glory of God on earth through them. Hence, the root-cause of this continued leadership decay and failures world-wide over generations as empirically evidenced recently in Kenya during the Memorial Service Preparation for the 7 August, 1998 Bomb Victims whereby religious heads were found locked in a fierce schism on who should be the chief convener of the service.

(f) Whereas this truth in 8(d) and (e) above is real and natural, not many people globally know it. From our clinical diagnosis of the role of a shepherd and that of a parent,

  (i) It is obvious that this truth is naturally abundant and universal.

  (ii) It manifests itself in the Spirit of Honesty and Accountability (STA).

  (iii) But, as we have also confirmed above it is deliberately ignored or marginalized by leaders in political life.

(iv)   Its lukewarmness in political leadership usually breeds a Honesty Deficiency Syndrome (HDS) which, in turn, breeds leadership decay and death in political life as in the cases of the leadership of Kings Saul, Jeroboam, Ahab, Baasha and many others confirmed by the autopsy findings of those several leaders, enumerated and detailed in The Old Testament particularly in the 1 and 2 Chronicles.

(B)   Gleaned from Behavioural and Social Sciences Efforts above.

(1)   As Jesus Christ assures us in his teachings under Mathew 12:35 in the Holy Bible, that: "The good man out of his good treasures brings forth good, and the evil man out of his evil treasures brings forth evil", it is equally true and correct:

That a good leader, (out of his good treasures of obedience and humbleness to God who anointed him during his oath of office to do justice to all those under his leadership on equal footing as a parent and a shepherd naturally do to their children and flock respectively), naturally brings forth peace, love, unity and prosperity to his country during his leadership; and

And that an evil or bad leader, (out of his arrogance, self-exaltations and disobedience to God), naturally brings forth corruption and other signs of Bad Governance followed by God's wrath manifested in public revolts, strikes, revolutions, civil wars, genocide and other forms of public disobedience against that leader putting his leadership to death, as in the cases of King Solomon, King Rehoboam, King Ahab, King Baasha, etc., over two thousand years ago; and also as in the cases of the late Presidents Mobutu Sese Seko, General Sani Abacha of Nigeria and many other Heads of State in our own generation world-wide such as Adolf Hitler in Germany (the architect of World War II, 1939-45)

(2)   In view of these revelations on why and how the most powerful United Kingdom of Israel failed and got broken into two little and weak Kingdoms of Judah and Israel which also failed thereby subjecting all children of Israel to the bondage of captivity in Babylon, it is here hoped that the present State of Israel which was created by the Allied Powers (USA, UK, Soviet Union and France) in 1948 at the end of World War II, shall now be enlightened by the nasty experience of their fathers caused by the blunders of the political leaders during their fathers

generation such as King Solomon, King Jeroboam and King Baasha et al. Succinctly, it is self evident from these revelations above:-

That by no means can the present state of Israel succeed as stable nation-state unless and until its leadership takes time to seriously reflect on those past experiences, i.e. where, why and how their forefathers' leaderships failed.

And, that unless and until this step is taken,

(i) The present on-going war between Israel and her neighbours (Palestine, Lebanon, Jordan, Syria etc) is bound to continue unabated;

(ii) A durable peace and security in Israel is bound to remain a difficult up hill task for Israel Leadership;

(iii) No one in Israel will be able to prove a good leader until these past lessons are hearkened to and experiences used.

(iv) And, the on-going concerted efforts from the International Community to bring peace and security in Israel and her neighbours is also bound to remain a chronic headache and a failure or simply, a zero sum game! As it has always been ever since that state was created in 1948 due to man's persistent disobedience to the following obvious which must be under*stood and used as a way to the needed solution.*

3.   A re-test of the validity of this striking phenomenon using other sources gained from the experience of the Greek city-states generation to the experience of our own generation, the truth proves the same. The findings re-confirm that the root-cause of <u>our leaders' perennial failure has always been the same contagion of leadership dishonesty and disobedience to vivid lessons from previous leader's failures and professional advices by political thinkers shown below:</u>

On Previous Leaders: Misconduct and Consequences e.g.

(i) King Charles I of England was publicly beheaded by his own English subjects in 1649 during the English Revolution because of his own dishonesty to his

Oath of office characterized by mistreatment and marginalization of his subjects on the foolish assumption that <u>he was above the law</u> and that in this regard, he was only subject to and guided by <u>divine law but not human law.</u>

(ii) King Louis XVI of France was guillotined by his own French subjects (French commune) on 21 January, 1793 during the French War of Revolution also for a similar reason of dishonesty and self-pride.

Professional advices from the following numerous political philosophers novelists, and poets were never well received in spite of their good intentions to the leadership of the time if it ever bothered to listen, and make use of the counsel, as the Old Egyptian Leadership used to do that enabled them to develop into an amazing hybrid culture society second to none in Antiquity.[24]

1. Prominent of these political philosophers included:-

(i) John Locke (1632-1704) in England whose advice in his famous book, <u>Two Treatises of Government</u> (1689), was that every individual is naturally entitled to total human and civil rights which must be respected and protected at all times and at all costs by every leader and government in power; and that nobody should, therefore, be taxed by government or leader without his or her full participation in that government—an advice which so much enlightened the British North American colonies about their rights and how to defend it that they organized and revolted in the American War of independence against their British Colonial Master on the grounds that their rebellion was rational and just under the principle and law of "No taxation without representation".

Because of his failure to listen to Locke's advice and the cries of his American Colonies, King George III lost both the war and the colonies which became an independent nation-state which is now The United States of America. And, because of the same spirit of leadership disobedience to the American lesson, Britain continued to lose more colonies for example, in India in 1947 and in Africa beginning with the Gold Coast which is now Ghana in 1955 and finally 1957.

(ii)   Jean Jacques Rousseau (1712-1778), a French political philosopher whose advice in his book, The Social Contract (1962), called for the French Government to respect and protect the rights of every French citizen on the grounds that it was an inherent contractual duty of every government and leader to do so.

Rousseu's prescription was that if a government or leader in power proved unable to fulfil that contractual obligation, then the citizens had all the rights under the law of natural justice, to remove it and replace it with a new one which is deemed able—a powerful advice which, because of King Louis XVI's disobedience to it, also fuelled the French Revolution in France in 1789 and put that King to execution on 21 January, 1793; led France to be declared a Republic thereby abolishing the monarch cult in France up to today (2013); and became a lesson in our civilization which should therefore be paid leed to keenly by both the leaders and those being led as an indispensable exemplary lesson for their leadership success/failure of which their leadership is subject to commit a political suicide a kin to the case of Minority white Regime in South Africa indicated in (iii) below.

(iii) And, this author whose advice in his book[25] Cause-Effects of Modern African Nationalism on the World Market (1983) calling for the minority White Regime in South Africa to pay heed and uphold the essence and significant utility of those noble lessons and professional advice from not only Locke, Rousseau, Dickens, but also the Utilitarians such as Jeremy Bentham (1748-1832), John Stuart Mill (1806-1873); and the Scientific Communists such as Karl Marx (1818-1883) and Friedrich Engels (1820-1895) etc and immediately rescede from its prevailing unjust treatment of majority Black people in South Africa was also marginalized by its leadership thereby landing the Regime into a political suicide.

It is a terrible pity! Had this Regime respected this goodwill advice, it would not have lost power to the African National Congress (ANC)! It would still be in power! It is a terrible shame to the disobedient Botha and his unthinking compromising lieutenants of the now ghost white regime!

2.   And prominent of the novelists included, for example William Makepeace Thackery (1811-1863), Charles Dickens (1812-1870), Mathew Arnold (1822-1888), Thomas Carlyle (1795-1881), John Ruskin (1819-1900) etc.[26]

From the novelist's example, we note the following flabbergasting vehement resentments against their Mid-Victoria leadership in Europe:-

In his <u>Vanity Fair</u> (1848) Thackery ridiculed the emerging middle class and their unscrupulous behaviour.

In his <u>The Pickwick Papers</u>, <u>Oliver Twist</u>, <u>Dombey and Son</u>, <u>Bleak House</u>, <u>David Coperfield</u>, and other novels, Charles Dickens also ridiculed the new establishment's obsession with riches at the expense of the poor without human regard for miseries of the condition of the poor slums and prisons.

Bitterness against the establishment because according to Mathew Arnold,

(i) The materialistic standards of its industrialized society of his time in Europe were completely incompatible with the great humanistic values inherited from Greece and the Renaissance.

(ii) Its mid-Victorian culture was beset by personal self-seeking and lack of social purpose and moral strength by aristocrats,

(iii) Its new rich class individuals who had just emerged in Europe arising from the Industrial Revolution, were essentially "barbarians" because they lacked social consciousness about the prevailing inhumane socio-economic conditions of the "Populace" even though in contradiction, they knew how to maximize profits at the expense of the poor,

These persons were no better than "Philistines" on the grounds that they neither understood nor cared about their *culture in its humanistic terms.*

They were an industrial bourgeoisie who thought only of power and riches and saw in the external signs of change proof of spiritual advancement.[27]

And, according to Carlyle,[28]

(i) The prevailing to democracy's problems were so diverse and critical that they could not be settled merely by extending the ballot.

(ii)   Like Socrates in Plato's Republic, and Edmund Burke in his Reflections on the Revolution in France (1790), Carlyle argued that because "one wise man is stronger than all men unwise, the few wise ought to lead the innumerable Foolish—an advice akin to the fact that a country can only survive when it respects the principle of "Philosopher King" initiated by the African Mysteries System of The Grand Lodge of Luxor in the Antiquity but later crippled by the Greek Sophists' leadership and general public on the grounds that this principle was against their corrupt interests and gods. Hence their decision to eliminate all their fellow Greek philosophers such as Thales, Pathogras, Plato, and Aristotle who had learnt this from North Africa (Egypt to be exact) and tried to also transfer it back home in their mother countries of Greece and Mecadonia. The chief of all these philosophers (Socrates) was tried and Finally executed in 399 BC by his own Athenian government and people on the already said ground[29]. Also, when their own King Alexander the Great who accepted this doctrine and authorized it also to be taught to his subjects in Greece and Mecedonia, his dead body could not be welcomed back home for burial when he was pronounced dead in his Babylonian Captial in 323 BC. Because of this rejection by his own home subjects, his body had to be taken and buried in The Grand Lodge of Luxor whose name he had now changed to "Alexanderia"[30] after his own name after conquering North Africa in 332 BC and plundering all those unique wealth of knowledge and wisdom on the Art of Governance which was totally alien to his mother country of Greece Mecedonia and other foreign countries in Asia Minor. And, after Alexander the Great was buried in 323 BC, his own tutor, Aristotle, was summarily arrested and sent into a forced exile by the new regime in Athens with a view to totally eradicating that intolerable foreign philosophy of Theocentric Humanism and the Doctrine of <u>Summum Bonum</u> which had been transferred from North Africa to Greece. This action is solid proof or a prima facie acid test proving that all Greek Philosophers ranging from Thales to Aristotle learnt their Philosophy and Science from North Africa; that it was because of its foreignity that their doctrine was rejected by Greece and Macedonia. Consequently, they are not and cannot be the real. Founding Fathers of Philosophy and Science in our civilization as they have always been falsely claimed to be in the Western World, but the people of North Africa commonly called Egyptians[31].

(e) And, finally according to Ruskin,

  (i) The only cure to the existing social ills in the 18th-19th century Europe was an immediate comprehensive overhaul of the existing society and a wide aesthetic revolt.

  (ii) This action was found noble and an emergency so as to free his age from the ugly consequences of an increasing industrialism in Europe to reform the arts and handcrafts, many of which were being destroyed by cheap mass production.[32]

4   CONCLUSION

This Study brings us to the following wisdom:-

1.   It confirms our original working hypothesis gained from Prophet Isaiah's prophesy that the whole earth is indeed a perpetual hostage to a thick darkness ever since the time of our Patriarch Adam and Matriarch Eve. (Isaiah 60:2); and that this is the reason why all leaders are also a perpetual hostage to the Honesty Deficiency Syndrome (HDS) also called Dishonesty Positive Syndrome (DPS) compelling us to remain perpetual/natural failure in political life.

2.   Because of this perennial bondage:-

Most leaders from the Antiquity to the present are rebels against their own Maker—The Sovereign Lord to whom they all depend for security, successful tenure in their leadership by virtue of their Oath of Office and Terms of Reference. In which they call on Him for Anointing and Success in their leadership undertakings.

Like these leaders, total Humanity is also a rebel and yet it depends totally on Him for Anointing and Success of their respective leaders.

Unlike an ox or dog that knows, honours and sincerely loves its master; and, unlike an ass which know and honours its master's crib, <u>our conduct, effective our Patriarch Adam's and Matriarch generation to our own generation confirms that whereas we verbally claim to be true children of God and that we definitely</u>

know and love Him very much, we actually do not as per empirical evidence in (d) below.

In as much we are the offspring of evil leaders and sons of corruption, our behaviour also confirms that we are also the fathers and architects of the same evil against our Maker to whom we all run to seeking Him to anoint our leaders to their respective positions in our political life; and Who, therefore, through His own Divine Grace, Love and Mercies, natures and enhances continued mutual peaceful co-existence between us and our leaders in this hostile life of multi-needs and multi-insecurities which none is able to manage on his own short of these leaders in their capacity as our political machine (engine) mandated to identify and provide us with these multi-needs and to protect us against these multi-insecurities.

By virtue of our own daily acts, we are indeed a people so laden with a culture of corruption, injustice, murder, self-glorification, self-justification, self-seeking and all other manifestations of iniquity and Bad Governance that we are not well qualified enough to be a worth homage or clean vessel for our Creator in which He may wish to live and manifest His Glory on earth.

3.   The above two complex and complicated constraints in (1) and (2), constitute the backbone root-causes of the perpetual Bad Governance and leadership failures from Adam's generation to our own generation. Also, they are prima facie grounds or reasons:-

Why inept leaders in our generation are always intolerant and hostile to criticisms whenever they are told that what they are doing is non-productive to the nation;

Why they automatically become paranoid and ready to kill every innocent critic whenever they hear or see such a person wishing to stand against them in elections—a paranoid positively similar to that of the Chief Ruler and other rulers in Israel documented by St. John in his Clinical Diagnosis of their confused and conflicting attitude and behaviour toward Jesus Christ whom they believed to have something of greatest value to them and yet they eagerly sought to kill:

(i)   "Nevertheless among (these) chief rulers, also many believed on Him (Jesus Christ)[33]

But because of the Pharisees' (hostile threat on everyone that believes on Him), they did not confess <u>Him</u>, lest they should be put out of the synagogue.[34]

<u>"For they love the praise of men more than the praise of God"</u>[35] (emphasis added).

Why the enlightened few whom Socrates called the "Philosopher King", have always encountered serious difficulties including tortures to death from their leaders as it did happen to the same Socrates, all Prophets, Jesus Christ, St. Simon Peter, Martin Luther, Abraham Lincoln, Patrice Lumumba, J.M. Kariuki, Malcolm X, Dr. Martin Luther King, Dr. Kwame Nkrumah, Sekou Toure, Nelson Mandela, Samora Machel, Steve Bikko, Dedan Kimathi, Zakaria O. Osolo, Mukudi Namwonja, Sir Thomas More, Dr. Robert Ouko, Jaramogi Oginga Odinga, etc. when they sought to enlighten the leaders on the virtues of Good Leadership and Good Governance enshrined in the Doctrine of <u>Summum Bonum</u> and the Philosop*hy* of Theocentric Humanism, (on the virtues of Justice, Wisdom, compassion and courage).

4. The above constraints also constitute the root-causes of not only leadership failure in political life but also of the seed to the looming world-wide poverty, diseases, wars, refugee agony, floods, hurricanes, tornadoes, genocide, massacres, and the present AIDS disease which have not only proved an impossible mystery to man's science but also a major proof to humanity that our iniquity to God is obviously so much that we definitely do not deserve any iota of Grace and Love from Him. This must be the reason why He has locked up that mystery from our possible comprehension. Otherwise, one must wonder the reason why, with all this most sophisticated science we now have humanity has totally failed to understand this mystery of AIDS and its cure!

5. A solution or cure to this darkness is succinctly the aim and justification of the recommended remedies.

6. However, all these remedies should not be misconstrued as strictly meant for political leaders only. They are universally useful to Humanity in all aspects of life, viz:—in our individual life and positions and rights given to us as a free gift by our Almighty Lord God for it is natural that not all of us have the same position(s) and talents.

And, in that they had also been fortunately conceived and initiated for our humanity as far back as the Antiquity (300BC) by the African Mysteries Systems of the Grand Lodge of Luxor as so manifested in the latter's Philosophy of Theocentric Humanism calling on each of us to cloth ourselves with Perfection, Holiness and Godliness virtues in our daily conduct, work and total life; and in the Doctrine of Summum Bonum also calling on every individual to be guided by Justice, Wisdom, Temperance and Courage virtues at all times in our diverse positions although these Philosophy and Doctrine were later unfortunately disrupted and totally eliminated prematurely by the rise of the Greek opposition using their Philosophy of Anthropocentric Humanism and Doctrine of Summum Malum which was deliberately initiated and promoted by the Sophists in Greece and Macedonia for this particular goal, (eradication of foreign ideals).

These Greek philosophy and Doctrine are the actual root-cause of our existing cultures of Man-Eat-Man Society, Survival of the Fittest, Power to accumulate power, etc advocated by Charles Darwin, Niccollo Machiaveli, John Locke, Hans Morgenthau right to our own generation (2004-AD).

Condoning these vices of Anthropocentric Humanism and Summum Malum as the real essence of Science, Morgenthau calls it Realism defined in terms of power but St. Auguste calls it a human madness defined in terms of Sodom and Gomorrah consequences.

7. Accordingly, it is up to each individual to recognize and remember at all times that whatever one does is supposed to be a manifestation of God's Glory through him or her.

8. In-as-much-as Noah's self-adherence to his Spirit of Honesty (SoH) to Pacta sunt servanda between him and his Maker God automatically qualified him before God's abundant Grace to become head of God's chosen remnant of Humanity during the Flood and then God's chosen remnant of Humanity after the flood, so must it also be equally true that a similar God's Grace to each of us is fully assured provided that we also emulate Noah's paradigm of exemplary leadership in both theory and practice in our life, from both spiritual and political to all other walks of life.

9. As God did not compel Noah to believe and carry out evils, no more should a leader attempt to assume that by compelling his followers to do what he knows is not right, if he so seeks to triumph and prosper in his tenure, on grounds that whatever he does, he is doing it on the interest of God but to the Lord God Himself who gave him the right to life and anointed him to the position he holds; and, by detaining or killing an innocent person for advocating a just cause of human or civil rights, all that is succinctly evil to The Sovereign Lord and not to that visible person.

10. Similarly all these lessons bring us to this wisdom:—that by doing good to others in one's position, one is ultimately pleasing nobody but God; and that by doing evil to others, a leader is ultimately aggravating nobody but God who gave him a free gift of life and the position in which he is thus acting as a parent, teacher, doctor, professor, fisherman, preacher, lawyer, judge, etc.

11. Our leaders and entire Humanity have always failed in leadership simply because of their failure to recognize and appreciate the fact:—that God has a Covenant with each of us from conception to birth and throughout our life as a covenant of life, peace and success but not as a covenant of death, chaos and failures. And, that chaos and failures are our own making due to our own foolishness and spirit of dishonesty called Honesty Deficiency syndrome (HDS) or Dishonesty Positive (DP) disease.

12. Our actual Covenant with God is akin to that between God and Adam, Seth, Noah, Abraham, Isaac, Jacob, Moses, Joshua, and other Saints This covenant is entrusted to each of us in good faith with a view and good hope that we will utilize it well, with dignity, humbleness, loyalty, God-fearing and in keeping with the good judgement of our God-given gifts in our individual capacities in order to enable our Holy Heavenly Father to gladly manifest on earth the Glory and Power of His Mysteries through us so long as we make ourselves qualified for that noble duty. But, in reality, are we really qualified as vessels for this Glory?

13. The covenant is not meant to let our Heavenly Holy Father down but to exalt His Glory through our various individual gifts of status and talents. Consequently, our failure in our individual acts to make ourselves justified for these gifts is solely our own making.

14. It is due to our marginalization of this reality and our arrogance and self-pride by trying to exalt ourselves to God's level as both our Patriarch Adam and Matriarch Eve tried to do in the Garden of Eden and also as Noah's off-springs tried to do at Shinar after the Flood by building the Tower of Babel to reach Heaven, which, in turn, provoked God:—to cast out both Adam and Eve from the enjoying the Glory and Joy of The Garden of Eden because of Adam's HDS/DP.

To confuse Noah's off-springs by giving them different languages with a view to making it impossible for them to understand each other and to further continue finding ways and means of exalting themselves to God's level, by building that Tower; and

To teach Nebuchadnezzar a terrible lesson un-heard of in the history of mankind by reducing him to a status of wild animal living in wilderness and eating grass.

15. It is a pity that even religious leaders who are expected to be experts of this hidden truth to apprise and edifice Humanity regarding this truth, are also major partakers of this disease of self-exaltation:-

They betray their anointed responsibilities enshrined in <u>The Holy Bible</u> under which are: to <u>teach</u>, <u>guide</u> and even <u>rebuke</u> political leaders and Humanity at large whenever the latter appear to be going astray from God's commandments and expectations of a country.

As also envisaged under Jeremiah 23, most of them have proved to be a "chameleon" servants of God by falsely pretending during the day that they are serving Him while at night they cunningly put all that aside and bend their knees to Baal and idols for a bribe and other wealth thereby destroying instead of building the Church. This is why they are "men of cloth"

16. This conduct in religious leadership:-

Is the main root-cause of the failure of most religious leaders in their capacity as preachers, teachers and a guide to Humanity and political leaders?

Has made them totally confused and too incapacitated to properly position the hearts of our political leaders into a direction of perfection, righteousness, justice and peace akin to that position of Kings David, Hezekiah, Asa, Jehoshaphat and Josiah-a direction humble and designed to attract God's Blessings, Peace and Success for our political leaders and total humanity.

17. As a result,

Our political leaders remain empty with hardened hearts.

Most Religious Leaders and Scientists alike have betrayed our God in their anointed capacities as Scribes purposively trained for this purpose[36]

Both, therefore, should endeavour to reflect on and emulate the exemplary model of the original servants of our True Living God such as Samuel, Zadok, Nathan, Zachariah, Ahijah, Jehu, Elijah, Elisha, Micaiah, Daniel and other Biblical Think Tanks other than foolishly playing the role of a rubber stamp to evil policies and deeds of evil-minded leaders in exchange of a bribe and seats on high table in palaces and statehouses against their annointed oath of office and God's commandments well known to them. It is a pity!

18. Instead of depending on the role of these Religious Leaders and Scientists for wisdom which they have actually proved defiant of, it is not too late for our political leaders to rectify their mistakes as King David also did in order for him to earn God's forgiveness and continued blessings throughout his reign as King of The United Kingdom of Israel.; and by which he was able to save The Kingdom from falling apart as it later did after his son, King Solomon.

19. It is, therefore, hoped that each leader will take time to pay heed and learn the following advice from King Solomon who failed in his leadership due to his failure to pay heed to the same advice: "The fear of the Lord is the beginning of knowledge; fools despise wisdom and instruction". (Proverb 1:7, the Holy Bible).

20. Like King Jehoshaphat, we have nothing to fear or lose! The battle is not ours. Ours is a free victory and all riches plundered from this prince of darkness which has been tormenting our Humanity ever since the time of our Patriarch Adam and Matriarch Eve to the present[37]

21. In order for us to do so, the following call and counsel to our Patriarch Joshua by God noted under Joshua 1:1-9 of the <u>Holy Scripture</u> should be indispensable lesson for each of us to learn from if we seek success:-

"JOSHUA!": <u>Moses my servant is dead; now therefore arise, go over this Jordan, thou, and all this people, unto the land which I do give them, . . ."</u> (Vs.2)

"<u>Be strong and of good courage</u>" (Vs.6)

"<u>Only be thou strong and very courageous, that thou mayest observe to do according to all the laws which Moses My servant commanded thee: turn not from it to the right or to the left that though mayest prosper whithersoever (wherever) though goest</u>". (Vs.7)

"<u>This book of the law shall not depart out of thy mouth; but thou shall meditate therein day and night, that thou mayest observe to do according to all that is written therein: for then though shalt make thy way prosperous, and then thou shalt have good success</u>" (Vs.8).

22. What this call and counsel to Joshua also means to us is succinctly that: in as much as Joshua proved an obedient and successful leader when he was called by God to take over from Moses who had just died, every leader whether chosen through elections or other means must also recognize first and foremost the following cardinal principles:-

(i)   whereas the past normally melts and flows away with the wind, it is always a useful natural lesson for ones' good beginning and performance; and a road map to one's future success;

(ii)   guided by this principle in 22 (i) above, it is therefore, upto each leader to now rise up; have faith and courage; and use one's past lessons in order for one to do better for the benefit of the peoples or nation as a whole but not for just one's self or few people.

(iii) Finally in order for a leader to do this, that leader's faith and national constitution must be simultaneously observed and applied at all times by that leader as Joshua did throughout his leadership in order for him to give

<u>dignity</u> and <u>glory</u> to God who called him out of all others in the Exodus and mandated him with this unique honourable responsibility which Joshua had never dreamt of or expected before since his birth!.

23. Leadership is not any one's natural right. It is a God's gift which must, in turn, be respected and translated into good fruits to all God's children by each leader without prejudice or favouritism if a leader is to prove successful in his leadership as the following leaders did during their tenures:-

(i) As Joshua did in Canaan; by strictly adhering onto his <u>pacta sunt servanda</u> with God who had called him to do so.

(ii) As Mahatma Gandhi also did in India in his efforts to eradicate the man-made human oppression and sufferings called "untouchability" deliberately instutionalized and promoted by the doctrine of the Hindu Religion through a caste belief system effective 6th century BC and which still exists up today—a critical situation against humanity and God's glory in India which should have warranted immediate intervention long time ago by the Christian Church leadership as well as the United Nations Leadership in order to eradicate that evil had there been such a sound leadership in order to eradicate that evil had there been such a sound leadership quality in them worth of doing that.

(iii) As Nelson Mandela successfully, persevered in all those 27 years of imprisonment but in the end managed to rescue his oppressed majority Africans in South Africa from the agony of apartheid.

(iv) As Mwai Kibaki and his Cabinet Ministerial team is now so far demonstrating in Kenya through his National Alliance Rainbow Coalition (NARC) Government to resuscitate Kenya whose socio-economic life had already been paralyzed into a comma by the out-going KANU Government under President Daniel T. Moi before NARC took over in January 2003.

(v) And as Alfred the Great (849-899 AD) did demonstrate during his leadership in England from 871 to 899 with such a stupendous taste and love for the Rule of Law, justice and mutual peace between England and her neighbouring archi-enemies such as Guthrum's Danish terrorizing army which he had to convincingly coerce into signing the famous peace of Wedmore in 878 that he was successfully able to free England from further foreign invasions and all other forms of terrorisms; and then to resuscitate that country and his subjects from the already existing catastrophic wretched condition caused by those terrorisms. To achieve this goal, Alfred The Great instituted and promoted a Dynamic Emergency Resuscitation plan for his English subjects which included initiating and promoting literacy using foreign experts and teachers codifying select good laws from already existing ones, eradicating lawlessness and all other symptoms of anarchy and Bad Governance, and teaching his subjects good examples by directly participating in the exercise as a leader with a view to using himself as a role model for the subjects to emulate.

Last but not least to reckon, Alfred the Great's leadership was indeed a role model that our world community leadership today obviously needs in that he was bright, emulative, creative, imaginative and a justice loving leader with a striking burning desire to learn from within and without his own country but not as that parochially paranoid as most African leaders such as the former President Daniel Troitich Arap Moi loved to be arguing and dismissing every useful advice as being a foreign mentality and, therefore, of no use to him and Kenya during his tenure as a Kenyan leader (1978-2002).

24. Definitely, these exemplary leadership examples (in 23 above) are a representative of the type of leadership that our increasingly deteriorating wretched planet Earth now desperately needs in order for her to resuscitate her innocent Humanity from the latter's perennial agony of misrule and ineptitude also witnessed by the London-based Nation correspondent (Paul Redfern) in his lamentation titled "BABIES GIVEN AIDS IN TEST"[37]

CHAPTER IV

THEORY AND PRACTICE CONTRADICTION AND CONSEQUENCES TO THE INNOCENT

INTRODUCTION

OUR MODERN WORLD COMMUNITY is a human organism composed of a network or constellation of numerous various human organized entities ranging from multi-nuclear families to multi-nation-states, multi-international and multinational entities and many other organizations explicitly or implicitly, mutually or non-mutually co-existing in various ways. In spite of this significant variance among them, a striking common denominator of all of them is that each has its own unique identity or name, membership, goals and objectives, actual and potential resources, strategies and good hope; constraints and concerns; and above all, also having someone or some sort of a mechanism at the helm formally or informally charged with an explicit responsibility or role of co-ordinating the activities of this very entity towards those common set-goals and objectives. Be it the least in size, strength, etc to all other entities around it, and that it is as very informal and less sophisticated in operation as a nuclear family organization normally is another significant common denominator to and for all these multi-organizational entities is that each entity's ultimate aim and daily functions are succinctly to seek and achieve its set-goals and objectives it deems essential and sacrosanct for its survival.

But, in order for each of these entities to succeed, it has to co-ordinate its daily aims and activities in its own unique or peculiar ways sacrosanct to its own survival. And, in order to co-ordinate them, it must first and foremost have someone or some sort of a mechanism or arrangement within its own internal system explicitly responsible for this co-ordination. Hence, the universal and natural need in every human organization for the presence of a leadership for its own survival, without which it would not manage to do so.

In this regard, each of these multi-human entities in our modern World is neither an island to itself nor totally peculiar from the rest. Each is succinctly an explicit miniature of the whole world system resembling and representing the latter in those various needs and behaviour. Thus, whatever the system has in terms of membership, goals and objectives, capabilities, strategies, and constraints, and its methodology of overcoming those constraints in order for it to survive, is exactly what each of its multi-mini organizations or entities also does for its own survival. Therefore, although the two may not be anatomically (i.e., in size, capabilities, etc.), they are physiologically congruent in the sense that they both share one common ultimate goal which is "survival." No matter what each is in terms of its *size, strength, constraints, etc, survival is its ultimate goal for which it has to strive at all costs and all times to achieve.*

Hence, the flavour of this study which, in turn, constitutes the purpose and rationale of the study, and which has, therefore, attracted and stimulated every iota of energy or efforts of this study so that we may be in a better position to unlock open this mystery for our satisfactory understanding and appreciation.

This flavour, for instance, is borne out by the following questions:

- How does one who is accorded this co-ordination role treat this responsibility in order to satisfy the needs of his corporate body?

- How does he relate himself and his total concept of the self to others and their concepts of themselves and the goal(s) of their organization?

- How does he view himself and his personal needs on one hand and those of the body corporate governed by the latter's norms?

- How does he as a leader help to identify and mobilize efforts of those others that he and his body corporate adjust their individual values and weaknesses or deficiencies?

- What would happen whenever their values do not match or agree?

- How and when does a leader and those he leads adjust their attitudes vis a vis the competition and harassment from other organizations, lack of appropriate technology, lack of other assets requisites for effective functioning of the whole organization, and lack of ability of both the leader and the followers to adjust their strategies so as to bring in requisite innovation to meet the existing challenges and other deficiencies?

- And, finally how does one deemed to be a leader adjust his philosophy, ideology, and personal concept of reality with the goals and objectives of the whole? and

- How does a leader's theory rhyme, relate or function hand in hand with his own actions?

Hence the fundamental momentum of this study with particular focus on the African leadership as a unit of analysis. We will drive right deep into the subcutenous worlds of these individuals whose future stars fell on lucky days to be accorded a leadership responsibility out of all other millions whose stars fell on unlucky days; expose the factors that contributed to their being; examine these factors in terms of their role in these persons, management and execution of this responsibility; the extent to which they proved an asset or a liability to their leadership responsibility; and finally the consequences of these end-results to the innocent general public across the country. Thus, we will seek to meticulously and exhaustively clinically examine these factors with a view to establishing for our in-depth understanding whether they were of any significant service or a disservice to the countries and peoples they were expected, by their Terms of Reference on Oath to serve; and to measure the degree of that service or disservice. And, if each was expected to utilize that rare opportunity to facilitate his country and peoples to excel in their way forward toward a better living standard as so explicitly documented under Genesis 1: 26-30 that mankind was thus endowed with an everlasting leadership potential to dominate over every living and non-living entities in waters, air and on the dry-land for his own satisfactorily happy life, the nagging question we shall, therefore, seek to address ourselves in this study is whether man ever recognized, honoured and actually took appropriate time to make use of this sacred endowment for the benefit of his country and people entrusted to him in his capacity as their leader. And, if so or not, how and why?

(i)   Specific Problem of Leadership: <u>The Case of Kenyan Leadership</u>.

1.   PROBLEM

In all organizations ranging from a nuclear family to a nation-state such as Kenya which is our centre of focus as a unit of analysis, the chances and degree of peace(stability), progress and achievement of the set—goals and objectives in that organization individually and collectively rely totally on the nature and <u>degree of the followers' trust and confidence in their leadership</u>. And as will be noted in this study, this degree of trust and confidence also depends completely on the degree of <u>consistency between their leader's ideals and deeds</u>, i.e., what their leader says and promises them through various media and what he/she actually does.

Thus, the low the consistency between these two variables, the greater the chances that the degree of the followers' trust and confidence in their leadership will also be low; and the more this holds true among the majority of the followers, the greater the chances that both overt and covert actions (criticisms and campaigns) will begin to emerge and to multiply against that leadership with specific and clear intentions to either totally remove it from the decision-making machinery or to simply ignore whatever it says or requests them to do.

Failure to honour and maintain this consistency. Even those who claim they encourage the ballot, their ballot is not a ballot in the strict sense of the concept in Political Science. Some of them publicly announce to their followers that they are anti-corruption campaigners of various forms. They announce general elections dates but they rig-elections in order to maintain their positions. By so doing, they leave their level of honesty and consistency between their ideals and deeds wide open to question by the critics and the general public. Concomitantly, they become open to attacks and possible removal from their offices by the gun.

Absence of this consistency is succinctly a product of a low level of leadership rationality—its inability to prudently identify populous cost-effective developmental projects, i.e. inability (a) to meticulously analyse each project's gains and constraints; (b) to seek and prescribe sound solutions to such constraints; and (c) to do all this with a high degree of consistency and without any favourism.

This is precisely the reason why the Father of Philosophy, Socrates, concluded 20 centuries ago that an effective leadership is only possible from a philosopher king. Similarly, this is also the reason why Machiavelli chose to write his book, <u>The Prince</u>, to become a guide for this head of whose leadership he believed definitely needed the guide, short of which disintegration of that leadership was eminent.

Unfortunately, this problem has continued to evade recognition of scientists inspite of recurrent instability in all nation-states from generations to generations. Instead of addressing ourselves to this specific problem, some of us such as Robert Dahl tend to be concerned with petty issues such as Who governs.

Inspite of its strategic relevancy to the study of politics, it is submitted that Dahl's concern is too myopic. It neither evokes fundamental questions related to why such governors fail in their leadership from time to time and from one country to another. Consequently, such studies tend to leave all of us dangling on a cliff of ignorance and despair—in a mist of confusions.

2.   PURPOSE

It is due to this total omission in the study of Politics that this study seeks to meticulously examine the leadership problem in Kenya as a unit of analysis using the Late Mzee Jomo Kenyatta's leadership in its capacity as the <u>pioneer</u> of Kenya national leadership, i.e., as the first Chief Executive of that Nation, and as a paradigm for our understanding of not necessarily the dynamics of political leadership in the emerging nation-states but of the consequences of such type of leadership in every organization.

3.   METHODOLOGY

To do this, this study examines and critically analyzes the relationship between Jomo Kenyatta's political theory and his political practices in Kenya since he entered politics as an example. It will be concerned with (a) the logical consistency between the political promises which Kenyatta outlines to his fellow oppressed Africans during the period of colonial rule and which he was determined to fulfil the period of colonial rule and which he was determined to fulfil upon Kenya's rise to independence on one hand and (b) the policies and actions he put into real practice at that time on the other. When this is done, the Paper will then examine the implications of the consistency or inconsistency that exist between the two, in terms of their consequences on the level of progress in the national development in Kenya.

In order to achieve these objectives, the study is divided into three parts. Part I examines the theoretical aspect of Kenyatta's politics; Part II first examines the practical aspect of Kenyatta's politics in post-indepencence Kenya and then probes into the logical consistency between theory (Kenyatta's promises as seen in Part II) and practice (Kenyatta's actual policies and actions, as envisaged in the first section of Part III; and finally, Part IV compares and summarizes Parts II and III in terms of their interrelationship and consistency, and then studies the implications of the degree of consistency that has been observed, as a paradigm, i.e., a breakthrough to our understanding of real factors responsible for (a) the existing mounting problems of under-development in the emerging nation-states, and (b) inevitable poor progress in every organization with a low level of rationality at the leadership point.

Thereafter, the study will also examine succeeding leaderships of Daniel Toroitich arap Moi and Mwai Kibaki which assumed management of Kenya in 1978 to 2002 and 2003 to the present respectively with a view to identifying and analyzing their contributions; failures; and root—causes of such failures.

4.   RATIONALE

This Study is very critical for both scientists and non-scientists mainly peace-keeping administrators and enthusiastic in that it is aimed at unearthing most fundamental reasons why in various organizations (ranging from nuclear families to supra—organizations such as nation-states and World bodies) intra-organizational morale and stability become a problem; why and how rebellions or strikes often develop against the leadership, and above all, the impact of rebellions and or strikes on the Innocent General Public including the same Leadership in its capacity as the source of the situation. To call a spade a spade, the study selected Kenyan leadership as a spacimen in order to understand the reasons why there continues to be massive discontents in Kenya, effective Kenyatta's leadership and yet without this leadership's efforts to successfully mobilize Mau Mau uprising against the British colonial rule in Kenya, Kenya might not have achieved her independence at that time (1963); and (2) to use these findings as a paradigm for our understanding properly the real reasons why, similar discontents against the leadership and leadership circulation abound in various organizations and their impact on the Innocent General Public.

(A) JOMO KENYATTA'S POLITICAL THEORY AS A UNIT OF ANALYSIS

i. His Birth

Jomo Kenyatta was born and raised at Ngenda, Kenya, about ten miles northwest of what is now Nairobi. His father was Muigai, and his mother Wambui. Although the actual date of his birth remains a mystery, for official purposes, the Kenya records place it at approximately 1898. His name was Kamau and in August of 1914, he was baptized as Johstone Kamau in the Scottish Church Mission at Thogoto, in Kenya.

ii. His Political Theory

(a) At Early Childhood

Kenyatta's political theory was first manifested neither verbally nor in writing, but in his observable activism and rebellion in childhood. In <u>Kenyatta</u> for example Jeremy Murray-Brown clearly shows that Kenyatta was a rebellious child who would stand firmly committed on his course of action despite external pressures. He adds that when Kenyatta was to be baptized, he refused to abide by the conventional dictates of the Church of Scotland Mission. Every child to be baptized was free to choose either a Biblical or colonial master's name, but only one Biblical name was allowed.

Contrary to this dictatum, Kenyatta stubbornly demanded to be baptized "John Peter Kamau". He choose John Peter over other Biblical names because both Peter and John were the leading figures among Jesus' apostles. When the Mission refused his request, Kenyatta decided to fool them in order to get his own way. He realized that Peter meant "stone" and so he married the name John to the meaning of the name Peter, and, by-passing Mission regulations, he was finally baptized as "Johnstone Kamau". The Mission was indignant at the young boy's stubbornness and it took him many petitions and requests, but the future "Kenyatta" was eventually baptized according to his demands.

(b) Adult Stage

As the young boy began to reach maturity, Kenyatta's activism and stubbornness began to crystallize into mature, concrete political attitudes, beliefs and systems. It was not until he was old enough to understand and critically evaluate the British colonial political system under which he lived that his political theory finally began to assume a concrete shape. This reality is borne out in this early writings, such as <u>Facing Mt. Kenya</u>, which clearly demonstrates the evolution of his political thoughts.

(i)   Conservatism and Anti-colonialism

In <u>Facing Mt. Kenya</u>, Kenyatta's political theory is seen to revolve around two fused fundamental concepts: (a) <u>conservatism</u> and (b) <u>anti-colonialism</u>. Kenyatta bitterly accused the British colonial rulers in Kenya of using oppression and slavery on Africans, of usurping African Lands and mineral wealth, or disrupting traditional African cultures and values, and of practicing discrimination in all public sectors, including education, employment, recreation, and all the other facilities and opportunities that, in the 20th century, are essential for man's basic needs. He also criticized the British colonial rule for its spontaneous alienation of Africans from their lands, and the subsequent loss of dignity and the sense of identity. The deprivation of the African people extended even to denying them rights to equal due process of law, which would have allowed them to fight the mistreatment received at the hands of the colonial regime. Karl Marx and Friedrich Engels would have labeled such attacks on the African ego as "swindlerism" or an organized attempt by the colonial powers to dehumanize the African and the latter's ego into a commodity.

The bitterness against colonialism and imperialism and the strong conservatism, particularly with regard to African traditions, are also evident in Kenyatta's pre-independence overland covert political behaviours. His pre-independence activism is recorded by Jeremy Murray-Brown in <u>Kenyatta</u>. Kenyatta's political acts after his return from Britain in 1946 show that he was not only a political theorist, but also a practitioner. His enemy was colonialism and he aimed to destroy it as soon as possible and at all costs. It was this intense anti-colonialism/conservatism tension which eventually lead to and characterized Kenyatta's charismatic leadership from the late 1940's to the time of his arrest and imprisonment by the colonial rule in 1952.

(ii)   Kenyattaism and Leninism

Kenyatta's political theory between 1946 and 1952 shows a fundamental positive co-relation between Kenyattaism and Leninism. At that time, Kenyatta emulated Vladimir Lenin's leap-over theory which suggests that one does not need to wait for the natural suicide of capitalism and the latter's evils before one resorts to a revolution against capitalism. Because Lenin had successfully used it in Russia in the 1919 Peasant Revolution, Kenyatta decided to also use it against the British colonialism and imperialism in Kenya. This is mirrored in all of Kenyatta's political conduct in Kenya before he was arrested. For example, applying Lenin's theory, he subjected both the proletariat and the peasantry in Kenya to an oath taking ritual so that he could be certain of their full individual political commitment to his strategy of immediate destruction of colonialism at all costs.

Another indication of the Marxist origins of many of Kenyatta's ideas is the fact that Kenyatta rationalized the legitimacy of using Leninian strategy of force against force and evil against evil or any other methods necessary to eliminate British capitalism and imperialism which were making life in Kenya increasingly intolerable for Africans.

(iii) <u>Kenyattaism and Peterism</u>

In <u>Kenyatta</u>, Murray-Brown reports that Kenyatta vehemently denied leading the MAU MAU or even taking part in any oath-taking ceremonies. However, anyone who knows the Biblical story of how St. Peter denied his knowledge of Jesus to Pilate's security forces could not fail to understand and appreciate why Kenyatta denied his knowledge of the MAU MAU and the oath-taking to the colonial security. Kenyatta's denial was spurred by the motive of self-preservation vis a vis the existing forces around him. It was a psychological defense mechanism but not a sign of cowardice. Otherwise, he could not have boldly fought to be christened "Johnstone" against the Mission's will.

(iv) <u>Kenyattaism and Democracy and Pluralism</u>

Did Kenyatta's arrest and imprisonment by the British colonial rulers in 1952 have any significant effect on his "leap-over" theory, which he had taken from the writings of Lenin? This theory, which had been under development in his mind, did not weaken while he was in prison, and even though he was not permitted to utter any sensitive statements following his probation and release from prison in 1962, his political activism is still evident in most of his speeches, delivered immediately before and after independence was on December 12, 1963. For instance, in his inaugural speech to mark the beginning of self-government in Kenya on June 1, 1963, Kenyatta emphasized that, <u>unlike the previous colonial government, the new one was going to be a government</u>

of and for everybody in Kenya. It would not be a government for the few privileged individuals, groups or classes, but one for all Kenyans. Kenyatta made it clear that even the opposition was part of the government according to the Constitution and, as such, was entitled to an unbiased application of the due process of law.

Unlike the outgoing colonialists, Kenyatta made it clear that in spite of criticisms and disagreements between parties in a government concerning policies and action, the opposition party (which by that time was the Kenya African Democratic Union or KADU) was formerly recognized by the Constitution, which not merely tolerated the second party, but actually encouraged it as an essential element for a healthy political process and a sound programme of nation-building. Thus whereas the colonialists did not tolerate criticism, Kenyatta allowed it. According to him, both his ruling KANU party and the Opposition (KADU) party had a mutual responsibility in building Kenya. He argued that neither KANU nor KADU alone could successfully lead Kenya. It was only through their mutual efforts that Ujamaa (socialism) could be achieved in independent Kenya. Contradictory efforts were not only undesirable but practically suicidal. They were not in the best interest of their party of the entire nation.

(v)   Kenyattaism and the Genesis of "Harambee" Concept

Kenyatta's subsequent speeches in Parliament between internal self-government day (June 1, 1963) and final independence day (December 12, 1963) show that his political theory began to develop from anti-colonialism and pro-conservatism into a more broad and complex scope. For instance, his attention and emphasis began to shift from anti-colonialism and pro-African tradition to a concern for the dangerous, divisive forces that might be generated by "tribalism" and racism. These were also viewed as diseases which would impede progress. In order to avoid this political blunder in the new nation, Kenyatta appealed to all Kenyans to stand "shoulder-to-shoulder" in the spirit of "Harambee" a united struggle against the common enemies of "poverty, ignorance and disease.

The same sentiment is also reflected in three other Kenyatta speeches, one in Mombasa approximately one month after independence (February, 1964), one to the Meru Cooperative Union in August, 1964, and one in Githunguri, in September of 1964. In all these speeches for instance, Kenyatta promised his audience and the rest of the nation that as long as he had the mandate to rule Kenya, he was willing to accept and exercise

<u>his duties diligently</u>. He then <u>warned</u> that there might be certain people or groups who perceived him as a Kikuyu Prime Minister, but that he was not prepared to accept any such label. Personally, he did not care whether a leader was a Kikuyu or a member of any other ethnic group; all that mattered was that the leader be a Kenyan. Thus, Kenyatta's objectives was not to favour any one single individual, ethnic group or class. The divisive and oppressive colonial rule then defeated and now no single individual, group, class or ethnic group was to be permitted to dominate the others politically, economically or in any other way. Every Kenyan was legitimately entitled to participate equally in the political process and to enjoy equal distribution of public goods and services without any discrimination or favoritism. In Kenyatta's own words he promised the nation that:

It is my wish to demonstrate to you that Africans of this country are now free. The period of European rule is past. We are now all citizens of this country. Since we Africans are (now) ruling our country, all of us should rule it together.

(vi) <u>Kenyattaism and the Concept and Value of "Unity" in Kenya</u>

Another fundamental precept of Kenyatta's political theory that was demonstrated in the three speeches mentioned above is his firm commitment to equal participatory rights and freedom for every Kenyan in the political process. By emphasizing unity as a pre-requisite ingredient in Kenya's nation-building, Kenyatta showed himself to be aware of the inherent dangers of divisiveness. His assumption was simply that, without unity, there was no way Kenya or any other country would be strong. To him, it was immaterial whether or not each ethnic group retained its traditional culture and values as the Masai have done, for example. All that mattered was that everyone must be willing to work with one another in spirit of Harambee (socialism) for the sake of building the new nation of Kenya. From another perspective, Kenyatta's political theory at the twilight of self-rule in Kenya was that Kenya would definitely collapse and again be in a vulnerable position, in which colonialism and imperialism could grow, unless every Kenyan (individual and tribe alike) waived some of their differences and ethnocentricisms and began consolidating

> Whether waking or sleeping—only think of
> ruling Africa. And when they sleep, a dream
> comes to them urging them to divide Africa,
> divide and then rule[11].

Also he warned that only through unity could Africa contain the attempts by foreigners to dominate their continent. He made it clear that this unity was to begin in Kenya. If Kenyans could unite, the new nation would provide a model that the rest of Africa could follow.

If we (Kenyans) achieved unity the whole world would respect us. We shall be the foundation and the Shield of mother Africa[12].

Thus, Kenyatta did not perceive Kenya's rise to independence solely as an end for the Kenyans; he saw it as the nucleus of African Unity. Kenya was to be the stepping stone towards a united Africa and the more powerful the thrust of unity was in Kenya, the greater the chances were that the message would spill over the borders to all of Africa. Every living organism's growth must start from somewhere; in every life there is a beginning, a nucleus. So Kenya's unity was seen to be the starting point of African unity. If unity could not be achieved in the small nation of Kenya, how could one hope for continental unity?

(b) <u>On Racism or Apartheid: The Origin of His Suffering Without Bitterness Concept</u>

One of the fundamental theoretical points emphasized by Kenyatta in his Independence Day speech was his position on the racial question popularly known as apartheid in the South African politics. Because Kenya's independence came about as a function of the struggle between Black Africans and White British settlers in Kenya, Kenyatta resolved to ensure that independent Kenya's position on colonialism was free of racism. Arguing that his position against colonialism had nothing to do with racial discrimination, Kenyatta remarked:

> *Some people may say that—alas!—Kenyatta*
> *Now is advocating a colour-bar. This is not*
> *so: I have no colour feelings at all. What I*
> *want is for us to be united, so (that) we can*
> *go forward and co-operate with the rest of the world.*
> *This is our goal.*

In his speeches in Mombasa, Nairobi, Thika, Embu, and Githunguri, between February and September of 1964, Kenyatta frequently emphasized that he was not a racist. Addressing an audience in Nairobi in June of 1964, Kenyatta said:

> *Even though we were persecuted, we should not*
> *seek revenge. If people were unjust in their*
> *day, there is no reason why we should commit injustices.*

But, why did Kenyatta take such a stand vis-a-vis the enemy? Further, there was no doubt that Britain and other colonial powers in Africa were all against Africans and the latter's cultures and values, why didn't Kenyatta (and all Black Africans in Kenya) treat this enemy in the same manner the enemy had treated them? What was wrong with the "an eye for an eye" theory?

To Kenyatta, it was clear that this type of tit-for-tat theory would make a bad policy because it would indicate that those who were formerly persecuted were equally evils. If Kenyans were to mistreat the British nationals in Kenya, or hate Britain for her past colonial activities in Kenya, then Kenyans would not have brought in any positive change. They would have substituted an evil with another evil. As a result, Kenyatta resolved to make his fellow Kenyans to forget the past mistreatment they had unfortunately received at the hands of unthinking' colonial rulers. Also, they resolved to concentrate on building their new nation. Kenyatta maintained that the past was now no longer relevant to the present and the future Kenya. But if his "suffering without bitterness" concept is a fact of life which should become part of the basis of political realism vis-à-vis colonialism, in the entire colonial world politics, does this also hold true between Kenyatta's ruling party (KANU) and Oginga Odinga's Opposition party (Kenya Peoples Union, KPU) and other critics of the KANU party? And, if Kenyatta's Suffering Without Bitterness has been made into the fundamental philosophy underlying political actions in Kenya on matters concerning the colonialists, to what extent does this hold true with respect to his degree of tolerance he granted to his critics? This will be exhaustively examined in Part II of this Paper.

(c)   On Foreign Relations in Kenya

In the Swahili version of his Kenya Independence Day speech, Kenyatta emphasized that, under his leadership, Kenya would freely ally herself to either the East or the West all depending on her own will and wishes. Thus, Kenya was going to interact with any country that was willing.

He also emphasized that, although Kenya had now become independent, Britain's friendship was still welcome as he personally wanted good relationships between the two countries to prevail. The other important characteristic in his attitude toward foreign powers was that Kenyatta pledged that his Government would "never agree to friendship through any form of bribes". Of course, fine ideals; however, one now wonders the extent to which these ideals were put into practice. Further, Kenyatta maintained that "it is better to be poor and remain free than to be technically free but still tied on a string". A horse cannot choose to live according to its own dictates because it is fed by a master, whom it must obey. Kenyatta contended that Kenya was not prepared to live such a life and he promised that he was neither going to allow foreign nations, businesses or individuals to penetrate his young Kenyan government through the offers of foreign aid or other enticement not to allow himself to be induced to perform favours or provide certain incentives in exchange of bribes or other favours. One might now ask, to what extent did Kenyatta apply his ideals and live up to his promises?

iii.   Jomo Kenyatta's Political Theory In Practice

(1)   <u>Questioning Kenyatta's Political Theory</u>

In Part 1 of this Paper, we have noted a host of concepts, propositions and promises concerning Kenyatta and the emerging nation of Kenya. We have described Kenyatta's emphasis on unity as a prerequisite for successful nation building. Also, we have noted Kenyatta's deliberate down-playing of racial differences and his emphasis on the importance of a forgiveness to the British for whatever pains they might have inflicted on him personally and the rest of Africans in Kenya. However, certain nagging questions arise with regard to the consistency of Kenyatta's political theory and his political actions after becoming the first Chief Executive of the independent Kenya. Particularly, one wonders the degree to which he <u>actually</u> kept his activities within the promises he made to his people.

Thus, did Kenyatta keep his word in theory and practice, or was he just one of those men (leaders) whose words speak louder than their own actions?

From a behavioural level of analysis, it is submitted that, most African political practitioners are all a victim of <u>Europhilia</u> in thought, and deeds—a colonial psychosis arising from colonial classical conditioning among other various colonial mental tortures and brain-washing through schools, apprenticeship, etc. by the colonizers. This is explicitly borne out in Franz Fanon's book, <u>Black Skin, White Masks</u>, which places the blame for this phenomenon upon the type of education received by Black Africans. Further, as also noted by Leopold Sedar Senghor (First President of Senegal) African intellectuals and the intelligentsia, who are now national leaders in Africa, live in two conflicting worlds, "African" and "European". Most of them are strangers to their own (African) social settings. The more they deeply got involved in the Westernism (the Western way of life), the more they are now unable to understand their own people and the fundamental problems facing their predominantly black African citizenry. This reality is also confirmed by other African scholars such as Robert Muema Mbato (Kenyan African) and non-African writers such as Colin M. Turnbull (non-African).

(2)   <u>Findings: Kenyatta's political Behaviour in Kenya</u>

In his Kenya Independence Day speech on December 12, 1963, Kenyatta addressed the audience in English before he turned to Kiswahili. Having had the privilege of being one of the participants in that Uhuru (Independence) Day Celebration, I noticed that African outnumbered both Europeans and Asians together by 100:1, and yet Kenyatta chose to speak in a foreign language first, as though his own African culture had no language worth respect and worthy being used at that extremely historical occasion. A further examination of his speech on that "Uhuru" Day shows another intriguing phenomenon which reflects significantly on those allegations made by Fanon, Mbato and Turnbull. For instance, Kenyatta began his speech as follows:

> *Your Royal Highness, Your Excellency*
> *Distinguished guests, ladies and gentlemen.*

Who was this "Royal Highness"? Who was this "Your Excellency"? It is submitted that the "distinguished guests" at the celebration could have been Africans or other individuals from foreign countries who were invited as special guests. The "ladies and gentlemen" Kenyatta referred to could have been Africans or any other participants. The "Royal Highness" and the "Excellency" Kenyatta addressed could only have been the Duke of Edinburgh (husband of Britain's Queen Elizabeth) and Mr. MacDonald (Britain's Governor General in Kenya), both of who were there to represent the Queen of Britain at the Uhuru Day Celebration. In the entire opening speech there is absolutely no indication of Kenyatta's conduct at the Uhuru Celebration and the criticisms made by Fanon and the others, we can still look further into Kenyatta's activities in the search for evidence that may either refute or support such allegations!

A further examination of his Uhuru Day Speech unearths additional interesting phenomena. Kenyatta's speech focused primarily on the Queen's husband as if the latter was the only most visible key political figure at the occasion. In the Swahili version of the speech, Kenyatta repeated what he had done earlier in the English version. Thus, he was fully convinced that the first image worth addressing was the same colonial master who had initiated and baptized him with the Fanonian "white masks". The Swahili version of the speech began as follows:

We are all grateful for the greetings from Her Majesty the Queen which the Duke of Edinburgh has read to us today. We ask him—when he returns to Britain—to convey our greeting to the Queen: tell her that, although we have become independent, we shall still remain her friends.

Of course, it is nice to be polite to guests, both friend and enemy alike in your own home or yard. It was equally polite to show that, in spite of the hardships Kenya had been subjected to by Britain, Kenya had nothing significant to gain from seeking revenge.

However, the fact that Kenyatta's focal point in both the English and Swahili versions of his Uhuru Day Celebration were both the Queen and her husband raises questions. Did Kenyatta consider them the most superior characters in the Independence Celebration drama?

Does this attitude not render Kenyatta's perceptions and appreciation of African tradition, sovereignty and dignity also questionable? If the Kenya Independence Celebration was to mark the Restoration of the African Sovereignty and dignity, which had been side-tracked into a perpetual adolescence by the British colonial rule, why did Kenyatta begin addressing such a momentous occasion by addressing the oppressor over his own consituency, the oppressed Africans he was now to lead? Who was the Star of the Play?

It is submitted that on many occasions prior to December 12, 1963, the British colonial elites (including the Queen) had played the leading role in Kenya politics. They had been addressed with dignity and at times worshipped by Africans as though they were little gods. But the Uhuru Day Celebration was to be a turning point in the history of Kenya. It meant that African Sovereignty and Dignity were to be the first priority to which Kenyatta and every other African nationalist was, therefore, supposed to address Africans first, before addressing any other sovereignties.

The fact that Kenyatta chose to uphold the British sovereignty was not an oversight on the leader's part. Rather, it was due to Kenyatta's own attachment to the white man umbilical cord that he had to do so. Otherwise, he could have suffered acute dissonance. From a psychoanalytical perspective, such conduct is indicative of the conflict between Kenyatta's inherited black skin and culture on the one hand and his acquired white masks on the other, just as Fanon contends. It is also a function of the asymmetrical dialectic of two values in which masks dominated over his black skin in Kenyatta's political life.

It might further be said that Kenyatta's circulatory system was injected with more white doses than black ones and that, consequently, he had no alternative but to behave as he did in order to maintain his own psychic balance.

Any failure to do this, i.e., to recognize the image of the colonial elite as the superior character in the Uhuru Celebration Day ceremony, would definitely have been psychologically costly to Kenyatta. This reality holds true among all post-colonial African political leaders, e.g. Senghor, et.al.

But, to what extent do the above findings hold true in the remainder of Kenyatta's political life? As a political broker between Kenyan Africans on the one other, where did Kenyatta concentrate his attention and interests? We have noted in his political theory (see Part 1) that unity among the Kenyans was essential for both nation-building in Kenya and the unification of Africa, but to what degree did his political actions after independence contribute to African unity in and outside Kenya? How significant is the agreement between his theory and practice?

Data on Kenyatta politics from December 12, 1963 to the time of his death in August, 1978, shows that, apart from Nigeria, the Ivory Coast and Ghana in the West: Egypt, Libya, Tunisia, Algeria and Morocco in the North; and Azania (South Africa) and Zimbabwe in the South, Kenya was rated as the most socio-economically progressive country of all Africa nations as supported by her steady rise in her GNP and per capita income and by a higher level of urbanization in Kenya than one would find in her neighbouring countries of Ethiopia, Somalia, Tanzania and Uganda during that time. Also, it was alleged that Kenya's currency exchange rate at that time was far superior to those of Tanzania and Uganda, Kenyatta's Kenya was a capitalist country and, therefore, the only democracy in Eastern Africa.

On the other hand, serious questions arise with respect to Keyatta's political actions in Kenya between December 12, 1963 and his death (1978), regarding the promises he had made to the people of Kenya. In order to establish a clear correlation between Kenyatta's theory and practice, let us first examine the following: (a) Kenyatta's response to the call for African unity;

(b) his political actions with regard to who controlled various key institutions in the country; (c) his conduct in the economic sector; (d) his response to his African critics in and outside Kenya; and (e) his view of the relations between Africans and non-Africans in Kenya.

In his speeches at the dawn of Kenya's nationhood, Kenyatta gave the impression that internal unity in Kenya would kill two birds with one stone. Thus, he assumed that this would increase the chances for a rapid nation building and to this end, contributes to the future unification of Africa. Yet an examination of his perceptions of other ethnic groups in Kenya shows negative correlation between his promises and his actions. For instance, in most of the Government key positions throughout Kenya's major infrastructure, one finds members of Kenyatta's ethnic tribe (Kikuyu). What is perhaps most important to note is that, since independence nearly all key cabinet ministries (i.e., Finance, the Defense, Foreign Affairs, State, Attorney-General and Land Settlement Ministries) were held by a group of members of Kenyatta's ethnic tribe. The same phenomenon holds true with respect to all Kenya's Ambassadors to major world powers e.g., U.S.A., and U.K. to chairman and managing directors of major parastatal bodies and substantive committees and boards ambassadorial personnel overseas, and Kenyans working in foreign embassies in Kenya. Not withstanding, over 50% of foreign grants and scholarships given to Kenya were re-routed to students from Kenyatta's ethnic tribe most loans and grants for economic development, which were supposed to be open to every Kenyan interested in business, were given to people from Kenyatta's ethnic tribe; most Provincial Commissioners, and District Officers in Kenya were from Kenyatta's ethnic tribe; most key commanding officers in the armed forces (including the police) came from Kenyatta's ethnic tribe.

Finally the Central Bank Governor, the University of Nairobi, which was the only centre of higher learning in Kenya and the Commander of the General Service Unit (GSU, Kenya main security force) were all manned by men from Kenyatta's ethnic group. The same holds true with respect to developmental grants to Kenya from overseas which were diverted to Kenyatta's home district of Kiambu in particular and Central Province in general.

Another intriguing phenomenon in the above profile is that approximately 85% of all the individuals mentioned were from Kenyatta's home town, Gatundu-Kiambu, while the remaining ones came from the Gatundu-Kiambu periphery (Muranga, Forthall, Nyeri, and so on). Either way, the people from both areas belong to Kenyatta's tribe and related tribes, such as the Embu and Meru, which are culturally similar and easily communicate with no difficulty. These three tribes together represent one of the largest groups in Kenya, like the Abaluyia, Luo, Akamba, Nandi, Kipsigis and Masai.

A further examination of who is who in Kenyan economic sector during the reign of Kenyatta (1963-1978) reveals a host of other striking phenomena which, in turn, raise further questions about the consistency of Kenyatta's political theory and practice. For instance, the studies in the 1960's and 1970's show that in the Kenyan political economy, both political and economic sectors were controlled by the same individuals or families. In its study of the Kenyan economy after ten years of independence, To The Point[24] notes that there were ten African Millionares in Kenya: Kenyatta, Kenyatta's wife (Ngina), Mungai Njoroge (inlaw), Njonjo (Attorney-General from Kenyatta's home district), inter alias. The argument recurs in a slightly altered aspect in the Christian Science Monitor's study, Who Controls Industry in Kenya?, William A. Artwood's study, The Reds and the Blacks, and in Colin Leys' study, Under-Development in Kenya: The Political Economy of Neo-Colonialism, 1964-1971. How did Kenyatta, his wife, and their immediate associates become so wealthy in such a short time (1963-1968)?

The studies indicated above show that Kenyatta's ulterior motive in politics had always been to use his political position as a means through which to obtain economic benefits. Ali A. Mazrui notes that:

> *What is significant (in Kenyatta's politics) is (Kenyatta's) conviction that failure to prosper is an argument against a leader. As a socialist radical, (Bildad) Kaggia was urging a redistribution of land in Kenya to the poor. Kenyatta was suggesting that a person who had failed to prosper through his own exertion should not be advocating free things.*

Both Bildad Kaggia and Kenyatta had been in jail together during the colonial rule but because Kaggia later became disillusioned by the high degree of discrepancy between Kenyatta's political theory and practice, Kaggia demanded that Kenyatta honour his promises to the Kenyan people. For instance, since land issue had been the fundamental cause of the "MAU MAU" war against the British settlers in Kenya, and since in his <u>Facing Mt. Kenya</u>, and <u>Kenya, The Land of Conflict</u>, Kenyatta had indicated that African land and cultures were to be returned to, or left intact for their habitual African owners from whom the settlers usurped the land, Kaggia expected that after Kenya achieved her independence, those lands which had been taken by the European and Asian settlers would be returned to their rightful owners. However, to Kaggia's surprise, no one received his land back! Kenyatta demanded that whoever wanted his land back must first of all pay for it. The axiom was simple: <u>no money, no land</u>! Thus, the possession of money was the <u>sine qua non</u> for land restoration or acquisition.

Kenyatta ridiculed and disgraced his ex-inmate (Kaggia) by publicly saying,

(Kaggia), we were together with Paul Ngei in Jail. If you go to Ngei's home, he has planted a lot of coffee and other crops. What have you done for yourself? If you go to Kubai's (another ex-inmate) home, he has a big house and a nice shamba.

Kaggia, what have you done for yourself? We were together with Kungu Karumba in jail, now he is running his own buses. What have you done for yourself?

This argument between Kaggia and Kenyatta took place in 1965; but more recent studies on the land tenure question confirm that Kenyatta's objection to the distribution of land prevailed till his death in 1978. Land which belonged to x before independence could only be returned to x after independence if x had the money to buy back his own land. Otherwise, x had no right over it.

Another most amazing aspects of Kenyatta's political actions was his demand that Africans must buy lands that were/formerly lost to white settlers, since Kenyatta knew perfectly well (1) that most of his own people who lost land were too poor to buy the land without the benefit of loans, and also (2) that no one could get a loan without any substantial collateral or sound proof of ability to pay back the loan. Finally, numerous studies by scholars, the mass media and others collectively and individually show that Kenya's own possessions were considerable and that he had many avenues for getting them and the money. Another most intriguing finding by those studies is that Kenyatta was one of the CIA payroll—a major contradiction to his pledge that he would never allow himself to be exploited by foreigners with bribes or any such corruptive incentives.

Kenyatta's ambition to rapidly increase his own wealth can be juxtapost to his act of not allowing people to reclaim their lost land and property. This is a significant evidence to prove the existence of the contradiction between his political theory and practice. His criticism of Kaggia is yet another indication of this; otherwise, it is certain that Kaggia would not have challenged Kenyatta with the demand that the lands be restored to their respective rightful owners.

Those who dared to go further than Kaggia in their protestations against Kenyatta's political behaviour (e.g., Tom Mboya, oginga Odinga, J.M. Kariuki, Martin Shikuku, Ronald Ngala, Argwings Kodhek and others) have been silenced or eliminated. Roger Mann, The Washington Post Special Correspondent in Kenya noted in his analysis of Kenyatta's leadership in Kenya that Kenyatta's methods and motive were not only undemocratic and oligarchical, but also opportunistic.

Together with his Gikuyu clique (mainly from the Kiambu District), Kenyatta always shielded Kenya's leadership from non-Kikuyu tribesmen. For example, in his observation of the problem of succession (i.e., who was most likely to succeed Kenyatta to the presidency), Mann found that,

In the years that followed, the likely candidates to succeed Kenyatta were eliminated. Oginga Odinga, Kenya's first post-independence vice-president (but then resigned because of his disappointment with Kenyatta's policy) was jailed and his opposition party banned. Tom Mboya, Kenyatta's most likely successor, was shot dead in Nairobi by a Kikuyu (Kenyatta's tribe) gunman. Ronald Ngala, widely popular Cabinet Minister, died in a mysterious car accident. Finally, (J.M.) Kariuki, a politician with mass appeal and open presidential aspiration was murdered.

It is clear that the elimination of one's critics and possible successors was a significant contradiction to the promises that were made to the people of Kenya in Kenyatta's pre and post-Uhuru speeches. Kenyatta had promised the Kenya nation that his rule would be totally and completely different from the British rule which had excluded Africans from the political process of law. Unlike its outgoing British government, Kenyatta's government was to fling open all the doors to all Africans. He alleged that he would welcome criticism from the opposition party, and individuals and concentrate on a co-operative policy aimed at nation-building. He declared that without such criticisms, his single party government could not be effective. Thus, Kenyatta had initially viewed the existence of an opposition party as a <u>healthy input</u> to the political process in Kenya.

But one is led to wonder why Kenyatta had to depart from his political ideals given that he suffered so much at the hand of undemocratic colonial rule in Kenya.

The above analysis of Kenyatta's activities suggests that his departure from this earlier line of action to a different one must have been a function of his realization that he had already solidified his political leadership position well enough not to worry about. Thus, Kenyatta did not just become a revisionist.

Rather, the analysis shows that he became a <u>deviant political theoretician</u> highly obsessed with most attractive enormous economic gains and political prestige attached to the office of the Presidency.

Like his all counterpart throughout the developing world, Kenyatta became so flooded with riches coming from corrupt offers from inside and outside Kenya in return to his favours to the source of such riches and offers that he could not stomach criticisms from Kaggia, Odinga, Kariuki and other socialism advocates.

There is no doubt that this must have been the reason why his wife (Mama Ngina) and all other members of his family became millionaires within a very short time; why sharply observant leaders, such as Odinga and Joseph Murumbi, could not be allowed to continue as Vice-Presidents by Kenyatta; why he wanted the post of the President to remain within the Kikuyu tribe in order to protect the wealth he had already accumulated on a large scale; and why Kenyatta could not tolerate the existence and political ideals of his critics, e.g., Mboya and Odinga (Luo), Ngala (Giriama), Kodhek (Luo), Shikuku (Abaluyia), and even critics from his own tribe such as J.M. Kariuki. Kariuki became so disillusioned with Kenyatta's deviation from the promises that he at once began to strengthen his relationships with non-Gikuyu tribes against Kenyatta's leadership which, to them, was no longer intolerable and acceptable.

Worried of the future of his Presidency amid these mounting critics, Kenyatta adopted a double-edged sword strategy—an elimination strategy designed to completely clean out every potential critic whether or not such a critic was of his Gikuyu tribe, e.g., J.M. Kariuki or from outside Kenya e.g., Idi Amin in Uganda. Both cases are evidenced by the facts that he brutally eliminated J.M. Kariuki (his own tribe's man) and he privately collaborated with Israel in the Entebbe invasion on 4th July, 1976—an incident Kenyatta unsuccessfully tried to deny but which was finally confirmed by the media.

His main objectives in an overthrow of the colonial rule would have been the following: to restore the usurped land to the rightful owners; to eradicate all forms of class distinctions and their causes; to see to it that every one in Kenya had a right to the due process of law (a right previously denied to many by the colonial rulers); to eradicate all forms and causes of coercion which were being exercised by the colonial regime; to govern Kenya within the framework of Harambee, a socialistic principle of all against the common enemies, i.e., hunger, poverty, ignorance, disease, opportunism, bourgeois oppression and so on.

In the final analysis, it is evident that Kenyatta's political theory grew directly out of Leninism. Unlike Karl Marx and Friedrich Engels, whose political strategy against capitalist's oppression prescribed that primitive (pre-industrial) societies should accept imperialism first in order to give capitalism room to commit its inevitable, natural suicide, Kenyatta's judgement was that the Africans in Kenya had already suffered enough at the hands of the imperialists. Like Vladimir Lenin's attitude against the suffering mass proletariat Russians before 1917 Russian Peasant Revolution against the few filthy rich Russians, Kenyatta's attitude towards colonialism and imperialism was that the two were too oppressive to bear; and that Kenya was, therefore unable to await such a natural death. By so doing, Kenyatta argued that it was high time for the oppressed African to take another route altogether and apply the most direct means possible. Emulating the leap-over theory used by Lenin in Russia in 1917, by Mao Tse Tung in China in 1949, by Kwame Nkrumah in the Gold Coast now Ghana between 1952 and 1957, by Fidel Castro in Cuba in 1959 and Patrice Lumumba in the Congo now Zaire in 1960, Kenyatta decided to fight the evils of capitalism and imperialism right away by inflicting a heavy blow on the British colonial rulers in Kenya so that his fellow Africans would be free once again. Having succeeded against colonialism, Kenyatta's next step in his political strategy was to mobilize all Kenyans into a united front under the slogan of "Harambee", meaning togetherness in order: (a) to build their emerging new nation (b) to help him in unification of all Africa.

In Part III, we have attempted to examine the correlation between Kenyatta's political theory on the one hand, and his actions during and after independence on the other. In doing so, our fundamental goal was to measure the comparison between Kenyatta's theory and practice and to sue this finding as a paradigm for our understanding, explaining and predicting the ability of many key political leaders to initiate and enhance national development.

As a result of our investigations, we noted that significant degree of inconsistency abound between a political leader's theory and practice. This is borne out by our findings on Kenyatta who at the eve of independence gave several empty promises that he later on could not honour. These include his promise that he was going to welcome the Opposition and other government critics as an essential ingredient for a healthy political process; that he would respect and uphold the due process of law that he would not tolerate job distribution which was not based on merit or achievement; that he was not a Kikuyu leader but a national leader and therefore, all tribes were going to harvest equal shares of Kenya's independence (December 12, 1963). His other problems included his decision to eliminate those he perceived as his political threats; his deviance from Pan-Africanism and his alignment with Israel and other foreign powers against neighbouring sister countries are explicit ramifications of his significant degree of departure from his political theories. His boasts that during his Presidency in Kenya, Kenya had nothing of value to gain from both Tanzania and Uganda which caused the demise of the East African Community in 1977. As explained in Part II there is no doubt that these and other Kenyatta's political actions collectively demonstrate a clear practical departure from his political theory. This is also the reason why many people during Kenyata's leadership felt that Kenya was still "Not Yet Uhuru".

In the final analysis, Kenyattas practices, seen in Part II of this book, and the contradiction between those practices and Kenyattas theories as expressed in Part I suggest that not all political leaders adhere to their theories in practice.

Thus, Julius K. Nyerere's fourth assumption in "The Rational Choice", which suggests that African national leaders do not aim at replacing their "alien rulers by local privileged elites but to create societies which ensure human dignity and self-respect for all is definitely worth questioning. Our diagnosis of Kenyatta's political life in Part II of this Paper fails to support Nyerere's argument. It may hold true in Nyerere's Tanzania, but it definitely does not do so in Kenyatta's Kenya.

As the data in Parts I and II confirms, there is very little sense of respect for the concepts of human dignity and self-respect throughout the developing world. Elimination of political oppositions abound in this world though it is also evident in highly industrialized world. In his study of this phenomenon in Kenyatta's Kenya, Roger Man discovered that Kenyatta's opposition and critics were eliminated from the political scene by (1) assassination, (2) disqualification (3) or elections would be called off when it was predicted obvious that Kenyatta or one of his favoured politicians was going to lose the election. From a Marxist perspective, this contradiction between Kenyatta's promises and his actual political policy automatically suggests a fact that Kenyatta's revolution against colonialism had not yet reached maturity, i.e., it had not yet reached the quality of a genuine revolution of the proletariat. In Mao Tse Tung's words, it was simply "counter revolutionary front of world capitalism . . ." Another important phenomenon in Kenyatta's leadership in Kenya is that although Kenyatta strongly attacked colonialism and imperialism, Kenyatta's failure to focus his political activities in Kenya within his own political theory and promises to his people suggest that his behaviours were essentially of a "bourgeoisie—democratic nature" but not of a proletariat—socialist nature".

This reality is borne out by his engagement in opportunism, capitalism and the elimination of those who criticized him or demanded that Kenya be transformed into a socialist society.

According to his critics such as Odinga, in order to become a socialist state in which satisfaction and respect for the majority can be realized, Kenyatta's bourgeois—democratic revolution would first have to undergo a counter revolution; otherwise they argued that Kenyatta's Kenya was likely to remain a bourgeois democracy indefinitely. It is evident from the foregoing analysis that his rational choice was a contradiction of what he had promised his Kenyans at the eve of independence. However, the data clearly suggest that to Jomo Kenyatta, theory and practice meant two different things—a problem extremely antithetical to peace, populous trust and a high degree of progress.

As noted in my other paper "Objective African Military Control: A New Paradigm in Civil-Military Relation." Peace Research Vol.17 (1980) more than 60% of all independent African countries have already tested either a military or civilian coup. The same problem also holds true with respect to all countries in the Third World including USSR, China, etc.

An examination of the causal factor responsible for this problem shows that it is, by and large, this inconsistency between theory and practice that breeds coups and all other forms of political instability from country to country. Similarly, in each organization including nuclear families, the degree of this inconsistency between what a leader says and what he actually does is always a disease—a terminal cancer to the public trust and confidence in the leadership.

And as also noted in Mary P. Nicholas' recent inquiry into the actual essence of rhetoric, it is submitted that no single leadership is free from internal instability no matter how rhetorically powerful that leadership may be unless its ideals and deeds are consistent. In short, powerful rhetoric, military might, etc., at the disposal of any leadership are definitely not a reliable insurance against the fall of that leadership. The most reliable insurance for every leadership is succinctly a high degree of consistency between theory and practice of that leadership.

Kenyatta's decision to extend his double edged strategy of elimination from his domestic politics to regional Africa politics by seeking to destroy the leaders of his own African neighbouring states such as President Idi Amin Dada of Uganda by collaborating with foreigners such as Israel is not an end in itself. It strongly confirms that Kenyatta was interested in protecting his presidency and massive wealth he, his family and associates had accumulated.

Also, it suggests that he was a permanent hostage of "black skin"; "white masks" confusion—of which the latter seems to have been paramount to the former.

Otherwise, it is open to question why, in his capacity as one of the pioneers of Pan-Africanism (others being W.E.B du Bois, Kwame Nkurumah and Mackonen), Kenyatta could have encouraged the Entebbe invasion against his own sister African nation-state which, in conformity with the concept of Pan-Africanism, Kenyatta was expected to defend and protect against foreigners. And, the fact that he eliminated Mboya, Ngala and Kodhek in cold blood and put Odinga, Shikuku and others into detention throughout his presidency, it is obvious that Kenyatta's political action did not conform to his political theory. The two were significantly contradictory—a leadership problem prevalent in all nation-states though the problem is extremely acute in the developing countries.

iv. CONCLUSION

In Part II of this Study, we were concerned with the nature, scope and dimensions of Kenyatta's political theory before and immediately after the Africans of Kenya regained their sovereignty from the British colonial rule. In all, we noted that Kenyatta's political theory was vehemently anti-colonialism on the one hand and strongly conservative on the other. This duality is reflected in his two books, Facing Mt. Kenya and Kenya, The Land of Conflict, which he wrote while in exile in England. He was bitterly anti-colonial because of the usurpation of African land and the colonial attempts to disrupt African traditions, particularly with reference to the Kikuyu female circumcision.

In the final analysis, like all living organisms, all organizations ranging from minute nuclear family to supra-organizations states and both regional and universal international organizations, are also governed by concrete behavioural laws. Some of these laws are specifically related to organization leadership, e.g., (a) the manner in which that leadership must conduct itself if it is to maintain a high degree of trust and confidence among members of that organization; and (b) what would happen in the event that this degree of trust and confidence is lacking. From our afore findings on

Kenyatta's Kenya, it is submitted that the low degree of populous trust and confidence in Kenyatta's leadership must have been a function of high degree of inconsistency between Kenyatta's action in theory and in practice.

Otherwise, his own closest associates, e.g., Kaggia, Odinga, Mboya, Shikuku, Kariuki and many other outstanding pillars of the rebellion against the British colonial rule in Kenya such as Kaggia (who together with Kenyatta suffered bitterly in the British colonial detentions) could not have totally differed with Kenyatta short of this high degree of contradictions between Kenyatta's ideals and deeds and immediately after Kenya independence (1963).

7. Leadership Behavioural Laws Synthesized From Kenyatta's Theory and Practice In Political Life

The question as to who can prudently decide for whom with a high degree of satisfaction in any given organization be it a nuclear family, company, nation-state, etc, has been a critical area of concern and inquiry from the time immemorial, dating as far back as the time of Socrates (470-399 BC) before Christ's birth. Testing the question, this Study strongly confirms, and finally synthesizes the findings into the following Behavioural Laws, depicting the actual dynamics of the relations between theory and practice political life, and which may therefore be easily used to explain and predict that phenomenon with a significant degree of confidence for one's satisfactory understanding free of time and space limitation:

In every type of organization, the latter's degree of eufunction is totally dependent on the degree of its members' trust and confidence in its leadership;

Both these trust and confidence are also dependent on the degree of compatibility between that leadership's ideals and deeds;

This compatibility, in turn, totally relies on that leadership's rationality—its ability to prudently distinguish and analyze the difference between the two variables and the consequences thereof; and

That any leadership's failure to recognize and uphold this natural behavioural law will have no cure but self-deterioration and a possible total disintegration, leading the innocent general public into a sea of acute agony.

(B) THE DANIEL TROITICH ARAP MOI—LEADERSHIP CASE (1978-2002) AS A UNIT OF ANALYSIS

Immediately President Jomo Kenyatta died in August, 1978, Daniel Troitich Arap Moi ascended to power to succeed Kenyatta as President of the Republic of Kenya by virtue of the Kenyan constitutional provision under section 2(A) authorizing a Vice President to do so in event of death, and other reasons incapacitating a president to continue his or her duties as Head of State in the Republic.

However, no sooner had he assumed this responsibility than Moi realized that all was not well with his intention. He had a series of serious sleepless nights and restless day times arising particularly from anti-Moi efforts by a section of some senior politicians in the country who did not feel comfortable with him as president on the grounds that he was not, according to their rational evaluation and judgment of him throughout his tenure as vice President to president Jomo Kenyatta, as properly qualified enough to lead a country like Kenya which was still recuperating from the scourge of the Colonial misleadership (undemocraciphobia) as Mzee Kenyatta had effectively attempted to do ever since Kenyan independence in December, 1963.

In view of this serious reason, the anti-Moi group demanded for an immediate change of the constitution with a view to removing or altering a provision of the section authorizing a vice President to automatically take over the Presidency due to those stated reasons of disability.

But fortunately for Moi, this effort failed to materialize. It was nipped in the bud before it could go far. And, Moi therefore, ascended to power on the collective assistance of some Mt. Kenya mafia powers such as the then most powerful Attorney General Charles Njonjo and G.G. Kariuki on an assumed good hope that Njonjo would thereafter relinquish his post of Attorney General and join Moi to the State House as Vice President, and Kariuki as cabinet Minister in a most strategic Ministry—a portfolio Kariuki got as Minister of state in the office of the President in charge of Internal Security.

Although Moi succeeded to do so, and pledged to the Kenyans in his Nyayo philosophy that throughout his leadership, he was going to adhere and honour all that his predecessor Kenyatta had initially aimed at creating a Kenyan nation of Peace, Love and Unity, the fact is that all this did not deter further efforts to bring him down from power, with a strong view that he would definitely not manage to effectively lead Kenya to the expectations and satisfaction of most Kenyans as Kenyatta had tried to do and a totally another person could do.

As a result of this continued anti-Moi efforts, an abortive bloody military coup d'etat erupted in 1982 against him spearheaded by the Air Force junior officers who appeared to be the most enlightened among all other security officers and who therefore had a rare opportunity to know better of who Moi was and whether he could or could not lead Kenya well. Convinced that Moi lacked the requisite qualities, they resolved to root him out of the Presidency but failed to do so due to their own drunkenness (getting too much drunk ahead of the coup operation with moisten wishful thinking that their take-over was going to be a simple matter for them).

Because of this abortive military coup d'etat, Moi continued to rule Kenya. Moi put in place severe internal security apparatus which included units such as the Nyayo police Torture cells where arrested rebel politicians could be forced to undergo inhumane punishments which included drinking one's own urine and eating one's own feaces, with view of teaching that rebel a good lesson. All these were managed by the special Branch with the aid of the General security unit initially put in place by President Kenyatta during his tenure. In addition, these apparatus were aided by the forces of the ruling political party called Kenya African National Union (KANU) which had been legally declared as the only recognized political party in the country and to which each and every Kenyan was expected to become a member. However, whereas one was free to become an ordinary member, every one that sought to contest for a parliamentary or civic seat in an election, that person had to become a life member of KANU but not just an ordinary member. Secondly, it was not that easy for one to achieve that life membership. One had to go though strenuous means to get it; and to become a candidate particularly for a parliamentary seat, one had to use lots of bribe to get that candidature; and to get it, one had to first get clearance by the KANU Executive Committee comprising of the President, the KANU National Chairman, The Secretary General, The National Organizing Secretary, The Treasurer and Deputy of the Chairman, the Secretary General, the Organizing secretary and the Treasurer.

This KANU Executive Committee was the most vicious animal in Kenyan political life. Whatever they wished to be done, was done. The President listened to them and used them at will to bulldoze the Kenyans as they so wished. Together with the special Branch and the General security unit, they created a very tormenting political culture that no Kenyan had ever experienced during the colonial era although the latter was foreign and was therefore hated for being non-democratic by favouring the whites, Asians and Arabs above majority indigenous Africans.

Succinctly, it was a culture of the few against the majority Kenyans.

These few became popularly known as THE NYAYO-NYAYO HAND CLAPPING SQUAD because of their obnoxious, silly behaviour as though they were nursery and kindergarten children with undeveloped intellect just following the dictates of their teacher (s) aimlessly for either silly joy or just to pass time.

Whenever Moi arrived in any place (airport, stadium, school, etc,) the leader of this SQUAD could ignite the shouting motion "NYAYO-NYAYO!! Which eventually turns into an euphoria of public orchestra of hands clapping and singing of "NYAYO-NYAYO" Chorus. This obnoxious silly behaviour became incarnated into Kenyan political culture as a must to be done by each and every one in the audience whenever Moi arrives or passes by. Failure for one to blow by this current, made one to be marked as a rebel; followed and questioned why they did not do like all others. In the end, one's job or business may soon be messed up for that silly reason only.

A psychiatric analysis of this culture reveals a lot of intriguing findings. The culture fooled Moi so much that he always assumed that everyone in Kenya loved him and his mode of Democracy. Because of this foolery, Moi became so much obsessed with doing whatever he felt like doing regardless of its bad implications and danger to his future political life. Moi began to encourage the NYAYO-NYAYO HAND CLAPPING SQUAD by awarding to them various Kenyan public assets in the form of cash, land, buildings etc with the aim of using them as puppets to promote his wishes and those of KANU party to all corners of Kenya.

And, exactly as what the Nursery and Kindergarten children usually do, they also continued with joy accepting and enjoying whatever Moi gave them and wanted them to do for him in return.

As a result, Moi was always obsessively happy and pleased with everything that he was doing. And, he always had a mistaken assumption that the more these hand clapping maniac proved very happy with him and his deeds, the more the whole country must also be feeling the same. Similarly, his Nyayo-Nyayo Hand clapping maniacs also became so obsessively happy with Moi because of the bribery of goodies they were receiving from him that they equally landed into a mistaken assumption that this bribery leadership culture was to live with them permanently; and that this culture was normal and immortal. Hence, the mutual abnormal love for the evils that was going on in Kenya by these two at the expense of the total innocent Kenyans.

(b) The Consequences of the Moi Bribery Leadership Culture at the Expense of Majority Innocent Kenyans.

As a result of the Moi Bribery Leadership Culture the Hand Clapping Orchestra and the Nyayo-Nyayo Chorus was always characterized by a multitude of KANU maniacs comprising of cabinet Ministers, Assistant Ministers, Members of parliament without ministerial portofilios, youth wingers, civil servants and right up to the entire general public who totally constituted the audience at every rally or meeting president Moi attended. Immediately, his arrival was noticed, the whole audience busted into the Hand-Clapping Orchestra and Nyayo-Nyayo chorus to the extent that President Moi always felt as if he were a god of some kind in the country. And because of this practice, President Moi equally became maniacally obsessed with his leadership powers that whoever he noticed to be an expert in the Orchestra and chorus had to be rewarded immensely at the expense of the innocent general public. Such a person was awarded public assets in the form of cash money looted from the national coffer mainly Central Bank of Kenya, the Kenya Commercial Bank and other Banks to the extent that by the time he was pushed out of office by the voters in the 2002 General Elections most of these state owned banks has been rendered almost bankrupt. In addition to cash money, President Moi also awarded his favourites with fixed assets in terms of public plots and houses. Other goodies included appointments to public or parastatal jobs to the extent that one person may be found holding more than one public offices though he may not be qualified for any or both of them.

A scrutiny of such culture by the Daily Nation, Nairobi, of Tuesday Feb. 10, 2004, the following facts come handy as empirical evidences:-

1. Before the Air Force officers staged an attempted coup d'etat against President Moi in 1982 with an aim of saving Kenyans from this abnormal mode of leadership, General Mahamoud Mohamed who later became the Kenyan Army General and then Chief of General Staff (CGS) in May 1986, was first a senior officer in the Air Force. But when he played a critical role in crushing down the Air Force coup attempt on 1st August, 1982, President Moi quickly awarded him with the following goodies:-

    President Moi made General Mahamoud Mohamed's ordinary shop keeper brother in Garissa, Maalim Mohamed member of parliament and summarily elevated him to the post of cabinet Minister.

    In May, 1986, General Mohamed was promoted to a full general and made chief of staff with an assurance that he was to hold it for the next 10 years to his retirement in October 1996.

    Before then, President Moi had awarded him lots of public fixed assets which included a plot at the Kenyatta Market on which he constructed several massionates and quickly forced the Ministry of Health, to buy from him at an exorbitant price beyond the market value.

(2) President Moi also made sure that General Mahamoud Mohamed's other relatives also got awarded. Consequently, the following relatives were awarded various public assets at the expense of the innocent Kenyans:-

    Mohamed Yusuf Haji was made Provincial commissioner for Western Province though he had no sufficient standing for the office.

    Ali Korane, an in-law Mohamed Yusuf Haji, was made District Commissioner. He then served in Kisumu, Mombasa and Nyeri.

    Because of such abnormal patronage in the Moi Bribery leadership culture, Korane exploited his provincial administrative post to the Maximum and became the wealthiest provincial administrator with massive properties in Nairobi, Mombasa and other towns.

(c) Moi Elimination Leadership Culture in Kenya

Another very striking phenomenon in the Moi Leadership culture in Kenya is his elimination tendencies.

Like the Biblical Cain who resorted to killing his innocent brother Abel simply because of Cain's jealousy against the most blessed Abel; and like King Herod who also did the same by murdering thousands of innocent infants in Judea; and also like the British Colonial leadership in Kenya which Killed many Kenyans such as Dedan Kimathi for the same jealousy; and finally like president Kenyatta who committed similar sins by murdering Tom Mboya, JM Kariuki, Ronald NgaLa and others and also detained Jaramogi Oginga Odinga, Martin Shikuku, etc for leadership jealousy, President Moi's leadership also did the same. Those murdered include the Foreign Minister Robert Ouko as an example among political leaders eliminated during Moi leadership. Several innocent men, women and children who were also murded during tribal clashes organized by the state are an avid empirical example of the correlation between Moi leadership and that of King Herod in Judea and Galilee—in the carried out a genocide on innocent non-political persons most especially children.

(d) The Moi Pseudogodly Leadership Culture in Kenya

And another striking phenomenon in the Moi leadership culture is his pseudogodly leadership culture.

Whereas every worship day (Sunday) President Moi always attended church, the most flabbergasting thing is that when a country-wide outcry erupted in Kenya against the horrors of the Devil worship practice in the country with an accusation finger being pointed at the Freemasons sect in Kenya as one of the principal practitioner, and a report was made and submitted to President Moi, the latter prohibited it from being made public. But no sooner had the President done so than word went all out that he was one of the principal members among the Kenyans. And when the late Assistant Minister for Foreign Affairs Job Omino died in January 2004, and buried on the 26 January 2004, on the following day (27th January 2004) the local media in Kenya carried out a comprehensive report on the Freemasions religious culture showing all Kenyan members of whom President Moi was one of the top five member of the sect—a fact which makes it worse for any sane intelligible answer to the question why president Moi ever loved attending Christian churches and yet he was not a true Christian.

A scrutiny of the sad cases from Patriarch Adam to Matriarch Eve and right up to Kings Asa, Ahab, Jeroboam, and others who loved to worship other gods contrary to the commandment of the True God of Israel shows the catastrophe such leaderships suffered. King Solomon's ungodly tendencies resulted into the break down of the United Kingdom of Israel. And, it is not possible that President Moi Leadership ended the same way and his Goldensberg catastrophe may be a result of his indulgence in Devil Worship on the one hand, while on the other hand he, deceives the innocent Kenyans that he is a sincere and honest Christian by always being an active church Day observer in Kenya. Such hypocratic tendencies always made all kings of Israel end their leaderships in death of entire family and associates.

(e)   The Setting Down of Moi Leadership in Kenya (2003)

But, at the closing of the 1980s and the beginning of the 1990's, the forces against Moi autocratic mode of leadership increasingly intensified mainly due to the assassination of his Foreign Minister, Dr Robert Ouko in 1987. His assassination that was blamed on Moi and his closest political associates because of the latter's anger against Ouko's refusal to accept their corruption dealings in Kisumu molasses, etc.

But on realizing that their political life in Kenya was already turning too hot and red to rely on, Moi and his political associates began to heavily indulge in so much corruption that most donor aid that came in had to be looted and converted into personal asset. This now became such bee-hive order of daily leadership throughout the 1990s that by the end of the 1990s and the beginning of the 2000's, Kenyan socio-economic life was already chaotic.

But, Moi and his political associates were not that foolish. They were so clever, cunning and tactical that they immediately hatched out a multi-edged strategy of keeping most Kenyans in such thick darkness that no one was able to clearly see, understand and then question what they were doing. At times, they could cause tribal clashes; at another, election riggings, arbitrary arrest and detentions of critics in Nyayo Torture Cells; and retrench lots of civil servants on false pretense that donors had demanded Kenya to reduce the civil service before donor aid could be resumed; and further, throw the country into a panic on false allegation that there was no such and such essential foods, e.g., sugar and cereals so that they could gain an excuse to indulge in massive importation of foreign foods for their own selfish profits while these foods were actually lying and rotting in Kenyan silos and stores.

As a result of all these multi-edged tactics, Moi and his political associates drove the country and the opposition so crazy and confused that majority Kenyan general public never could tell what was going on. In fact, most Kenyans blindly began blaming all their miseries on the foreign donor community on a mistaken assumption that Kenya would not be suffering this way had these donors refused releasing the aid to Kenya.

In other words, by using this multi-edged tactics, to keep most Kenyans in a thick darkness from the reality, Moi's sole aim was to permanently mislead them into falsely believing that he was not to blame except his officers. For example, at the 2nd Economic Consultative Meeting held at the Kenya College of communication Technology (KCCT) in Mbagathi, Nairobi, on Friday, 12th September, 1998, the then President Daniel Toroitich Arap Moi of the Republic of Kenya bitterly exclaimed: "I am no longer prepared to be demonized locally and internationally for corruption epidemic in Kenya". Seeking to exonerate himself from this shame, he instead put the whole blame on his Government officials whom he vehemently accused as the actual root-cause of this epidemic and other viruses of Bad Governance in the country against his Government. To possibly contain this epidemic, he threatened that from then on, he was going to summarily arrest any officer coming to him with a complaint or issue for an advice that he himself is empowered to solve on his own.[42]

In his reaction to those who siphoned huge sums of cash from the National Bank of Kenya, thereby forcing the bank to fall in a coma, he vehemently made it also crystal clear to them during his Presidential Address to the Nation on the Jamhuri Day Celebrations (12th December 1998) that he was already too exhausted by defending the deaf corrupt; and therefore, insisted that each debtor must pay the debt and should no more come to him for assistance.[43]

And on 18th February 1999, he quickly made a drastic major reshuffle in his Government with the explanation that he wanted to re-organise the system to seal up the loopholes of existing corruption and other root causes of Bad Governance in his leadership.[44] Among the notable changes and introductions into his government, were the restoration of the former vice President, Professor George Saitoti and the replacement of Mr Simeon Nyachae with, Mr Francis V. Okoyada Masakhalia as Finance Minister.

This was followed later by another series of reshuffles by swapping or replacing Ministers and Permanent Secretaries as in the case of Minister Masakhalia swapping with Energy Minister, Chris Okemo, after Masakhalia had served for only six months as a Finance Minister! To crown it all, Dr. Richard Leakey was elevated from the post of Chief of Kenya Wild Life Services to the post of the Head of Civil Service and Secretary to the Cabinet as a sign of good hope to bring about a quick economic recovery to Kenya.

In the final analysis, what did all these vehement threats and reshuffles mean and yet he was expected to be one of the most experienced political leaders in Kenya? He was the longest-term serving Member of Parliament from 1955 to independence in 1963 and to 31st December 2002. First, he served as a Vice President for over a decade under President Jomo Kenyatta; and then as the President of the Republic of Kenya effective from Kenyatta's death in 1978 to December 2002 (the time he was ousted from power by the National Alliance Rainbow Coalition (NARC) under Hon. Mwai Kibaki. What could have gone wrong to his long-term leadership experience to easily govern effectively and efficiently without any huddle from his officers?

Why has he failed to steer all these officers into the Spirit of Honesty and Accountability (SHA) which is always extremely essential for the existence of Good Leadership and Good Governance instead of crying foul against them? Why is his leadership in a crisis? Is this crisis unique to Kenya or is it global?

But, this concern was not all. A clinical diagnosis of the role of the Parliament in these entire sagas is equally shocking. A critical siege against Moi Presidency also erupted in Parliament. In its capacity as Kenya's law-making organ, it became very furious with the President because of the injurious acts and culture of his key assistants ranging from the Cabinet Ministers to Assistant Ministers, Permanent Secretaries, Chairmen and Managing Directors of State Parastatal Bodies, etc., whom it vehemently accused and held squarely responsible as the actual root-cause of the financial mismanagement crisis in the country for embezzeling public funds and fixed assets such as government plots, buildings etc thereby rendering the country so bankrupt that most industries had already closed down and others were also following suit leading to critical revenue and unemployment crisis in the country. It even went to the extent of accusing of treason though this move did not get far in parliament due to Moi's strong influence over parliament using his cronies whom he had brought to the House without winning elections and who have therefore always enabled Moi to remain in power for all that long period (1978-2002) unperturbed.

Although the Foreign Aid Donors had eventually agreed in the year 2000-2001 to soften their three year old siege on the Aid by announcing that it would now release some of the aid to Kenya, a war of words between parliament and the President could not be over. The battle continued indefinitely calling for the Donors' demands as well as those of the opposition (who are the Watch Dog of the majority poor) to be satisfactorily met first.

Even in the Administration of Justice where one would have invested a good hope for protection and relief against the injustice of Bad Governance by Moi's KANU political leadership, the situation was no better either. In the "FACE THE FACTS" Column of The Sunday Standard, the findings were extremely flabbergasting. The situation was a total disaster and very scaring indeed. The advocates of Justice whom the general public expect with good hope in society to set up in motion the wheels of genuine Justice, were also bogged down in a morass of habitual malpractice and injustices thereby leaving the people and entire society into a total dilemma as to where and to whom to turn for assistance against political leadership injustices. Between 1996 to 31st March 1999 alone, the Complaints Commission in the Attorney General Chambers in Kenya received a total of 11,000 complaints against their advocates arising from "Failure to account or withholding funds payable to clients; failure to keep clients properly informed of progress or outcome of their cases; "case delay"; failure to render professional services to clients; and issuing cheques to clients which were dishonoured when presented to banks by clients

And when in April 2002, the then Kenyan Chief Justice Benerd Chunga sought to set up a corruption court—to handle corruption cases, he was vehemently challenged and questioned by the general public of his honesty and the integrity of that court since all past efforts against corruption cases had died a political death caused by political interference in Administration of Justice.

Immediately Moi's KANU party was ousted in the December 2002 General Elections by the National Alliance Rainbow Coalition (NARC) party headed by Mwai Kibaki, Raila Odinga, the late Michael Wamalwa, Charity Ngilu, and others, which officially began in state House business, lots of revelations against Moi's corruptive mode of governance began to surface to the amazement of every Kenyan and non-Kenyan in and outside Kenya. All that Moi had been denying about a year ago during his tenure as president of Kenya turned out to be not true.

The revelation from the Goldenberg Commission of Inquiry set up by his successor (President Mwai Kibaki) mandated to publicly examine and report the findings of the Moi Regime with respect to the reasons and manner in which the Country Assets disappeared and by which and through whom has found Moi himself fully responsible for the loss of over Kshs. 22 billion and plans of the loss.

The commission has established that as far as 1990, Moi and his political associates did actually initiate and institutionalized various complex dealings in export compensations and other questionable payments tactically aimed at robbing Kenya of her liquid and fixed assets using a businessman of an Indian origin called Kamlesh Pattni and a group of former Treasury and the Central Bank of Kenya officials.

The said businessman, Pattni exploited the existing political anxiety and confusion in Kenya to mislead both Moi and Moi's group that he actually owned a company called "Goldenberg International Ltd" somewhere outside Kenya (possibly in Dubai, Switzerland, etc) with a business mandate of exporting gold and diamonds to Dubai and European markets.

In this regard, and because of his hysterical state in which both Moi and his political associates were arising from the worrying wind of change now taking place in Kenya against Moi and his KANU political associates, obviously Moi opted for the Pattni's Goldenberg offer as the only option to hand on.

Whereas the normal export compensation rate was at 20% of value of goods, in the case of the Goldenberg, Moi increased it to 35% to please his errand boy, Pattni. Consequently, by the time Mwai Kibaki's NARC Government took over from Moi's KANU Regime effective 1st January, 2003, up to Kshs. 68 billion was said to have been looted out of Kenya through this Goldenberg and other associated scandals.

But, then, what has the Kibaki NARC leadership been able to discover using its Goldernberg Commission of Inquiry it set up in February, 2003? And, what was its mandate?

The Commission's mandate[46] was:

- To disentangle and get to the root of the complex web of transactions known as the Goldenberg affair.

- To identify detrimental effects the web had on the Kenyan economy and vital institutions of governances.

- To see to it that justice is seen to be done for the Kenyan people contrary to the mischievous game that had been going on in courts on the same matter by the Moi KANU government for its own selfish ends.

And to do this so as to enable the Kenyan people chose one of the most ignominious chapters in the Nation's economic history.

But to what extent, was Kibaki NARC's directive to the Commission expected to achieve these four amorphous goals?

Specifically, the Goldenberg Commission of Inquiry was to do the following:

To examine specific payments made so far by the Central Bank of Kenya to the Exchange Bank in respect of fictitious foreign exchange claims and other related matters.

To investigate the origins of the acceptance and implementation by the KANU government of the proposal to award export compensation for gold and diamond jewellery under the Local Manufacturers (Export Compensation) Act, Chapter 483 of the Laws of Kenya.

To inquire into allegations of irregular payments of export compensation to Goldenberg International with a view to establishing the following:-

- Whether any gold or diamond jewellery was ever exported at all from Kenya and if so, how much and to whom.

- Whether the amount of gold or diamond jewelry exported was processed through customs as required.

- Whether there was a declaration and remittance of foreign currency.

- Whether the alleged foreign currency earned was cleared and remitted to the CBK and if so, how much?

- The circumstances and grounds upon which the compensation was claimed and paid to Goldenberg International.

- The actual amount of export compensation paid to Goldenberg International, including but not limited to KShs. 5.8 billion and whether any of it was ever paid to third parties and if so, the identity of such people or companies and the amounts paid to them.

In addition to these specific duties, the commission was also mandated to further investigate the alleged payment of US $210 million (amounting to KShs. 13.5 billion) by the Central Bank of Kenya (CBK) to the Exchange Bank in respect or fictitious foreign exchange claims with a view to establishing:

- Whether the equivalent in Kenya shillings was ever paid to the Exchange Bank and/or Goldernberg International and if so, how it was paid and utilized.

- Whether any or all the money was ever paid to third parties and if so, the identity of such parties and the amounts so paid to them (Here the Commission was to establish all these persons whether public or private include in the alleged irregular claims and payments to the Goldernber International and/or Exchange Bank and the extent of their responsibility).

- And, to inquire into and investigate any other matter that is incidental to or connected with it.[47]

Whereas when Kibaki's NARC Regime took over from the Moi KANU Regime effective 1st January, 2003, it was rumored that only up to Kshs. 68 billion may have been looted out of the Kenya's Treasury coffer, the in-coming revelations is showing increasing amount daily, By December 17ᵗʰ, 2003, the Goldenberg Commission of Inquiry had already established the following shocking details:-

That "More than US $ 1 billion (equivalent of Kshs. 75 billion) looted from Kenya during the rule of President Moi has been traced by an international firm of finance detectives."

That "The money—Kshs. 75 billion—has been funded in recoverable assets and cash, some of it stashed in foreign bank accounts by big name politicians and civil servants."

That "it is believed to be only part of the huge illegal gains made by former and serving politicians and public officials uncovered over the past six months."

That "the total of illegal funds could be from US.$.3 billion-US $ 4 billion (KShs. 225 billion-Kshs.300 billion), equivalent to a third of Kenya's annual budget."

That "assets identified so far include expensive homes in European capitals, shares in two London hotels and cash generated partly through foreign exchange transactions at leading international banks."

That "The Justice and Constitutional Affairs Minister Kiraitu Murungi, who passed through London last week (8-14 December, 2003) confirmed that he held talks with senior executives from the finance detectives to review progress."

Also that "transfers from Kenya, dated October, 1992 have been linked by forensic accountants to Goldenberg International, the company at the center of the judiciary inquiry into alleged fictitious gold and diamond exports.

That "investigations are also seeking information from ABN Amro, Barclays, the former ANZ Grindlays, Indosuez—Sogem Aval, Middle East Bank, Standard Chartered and some other local Kenyan banks, . . .

And that "some of the banks involved require a minimum of US $2 million (Kshs. 150 million to open an account [48]

Another most flabbergasting revelations unearthed by the Goldenberg Commission of Inquiry on Moi and his mode of leadership and how this mode affected Kenya is from the face-to-face testimony of Moi's Head of Civil Service during the operations of the Godenberg scandals, Professor Philip Mbithi. At its 131st day of the Commission's sittings at Nairobi Kenyatta International Conference Center (KICC) on Thursday, 22nd January, 2004, this former Head of Civil Service who quit his service in 1996, on disagreeing with Moi over his transfer from the Head of Civil Service to work in Nairobi to serve as Executive Secretary of the East African Community based in Arusha, Tanzania, narrated to the Commission about Moi and the Goldenberg operation's effect on Kenya:-

That although he had severally refused to accept to come and testify to the Commission as per the latter's summons, he had now agreed to do so in keeping to God's command under Leviticus 5:1 of the Holy Bible: which stipulates that

"And if a soul (person) sin, and hear the voice of swearing, and is a witness, whether he has seen or known of it; if he do not utter it, then he shall bear his iniquity.

That the Goldenberg was established in 1990 by Kamlesh Pattni

That although, in his capacity as Head of Civil Service, he (Mbithi), he was expected to have full supervisory role over the operations of the Civil Service which included both Ministries and Parastatals, he was not allowed to do so to the operations of the Treasury, Police, the Central Bank, and some key parastatals.

That the Treasury was left to the full command of the Permanent Secretary; the police to the Commission of Police; the Central Bank to the Governor; and the Parastatals to their respective Managing Director.

That all these were, in turn, so directly under the Head of State, President Moi, that they communicated and worked directly with him without having to do so through him (Prof. Mbithi). Mbithi was only involved when he was needed by President Moi to also go and participate in their meetings with the President.

That in this regard, lots of Kenyan liquid assets in cash was looted out in his darkness though he was only able to know a total of Kshs. 5.8 billion which the President called him from Mombasa in 1992/93 instructing him to locate and tell the Treasury, Permanent Secretary, Dr. F. Koinange, to transfer it through the Central Bank to Mr. Pattni.

That this was not the only injurious way President Moi was to Kenya. Others included the following:

Whoever proved inquisitive and un-cooperative to the looting e.g. The Countroller and Auditor-General, D. G. Njoroge, automatically became a hot cake (center) for discussions to be removed from office. Mr. Njoroge asked too many questions in a corrupt system. Consequently, he became the subject of many cabinet meetings with attempts to remove him although he enjoyed security of tenure."[49]

Between 18 and 20% of the population now came to control 80% of Gross Domestic Product; the money, the structures, etc some people could now easily shop nowhere but in London, etc. We now came to have a Muthaiga/Mathare syndrome in Kenya.[50]

And by 2002, i.e. before the Moi Leadership was terminated by the Kibaki NARC's land slide victory in the December 2002 General Elections, the Moi Leadership and its looting operations had changed the social and cultural values and outlook (picture) particularly the infrastructure of Kenya to an intensive care conditions as follows:

All of a sudden, it was alright to loot in Kenya as one so pleased and desired.

Then there were people with so lots of wealth and power that some of them were no more than mad dogs in behaviour ready to devour any one that questions his deviant act(s).

The center of power was now no more with the professionals (the think tanks). It was subtly and suddenly moved from the professionals, the career Civil Servants discussion into the kitchen cabinets and others. One of them who hardly went beyond Standard Two in Primary School yet he would in this cabinets judge everything I did.[51]

d)   A Retrospective Analysis of the Moi Leadership vis a vis his concept and Practice of Democracy.

The above shocking account clearly reveals the true nature and character of not only Moi Leadership in Kenya, but also as a role model of African leadership across the continent—a leadership poverty beset with man-eat-man attitude. It is an explicit manifestation of an African leadership in true colours while in office; and a valuable test-factor of whether such a leader actually had any right attribute required for a leader, given the fact that, from his conduct so far, such a leader had no concept of the welfare of his Kenyan people at heart by looting cash meant to assist them against their various insecurity problems, e.g. hunger, diseases, water-borne diseases, depleted road net-works, illiteracy, shelter, clothing, etc.

From the data on Moi Leadership, and how he could officially sanction such filthy culture of lootings and unprofessional behaviour in the Civil Service, it must be self-evident that Moi was no leader at all. Leadership was imposed to him against its own will but unfortunately it could not say NO! as it could not speak. Therefore, Moi was a total failure!! He must have just been picked up from the blues (no where) and placed in leadership by President Kenyatta either without scrutiny or care of Moi's qualifications and what Moi was expected to do for President Kenyatta and for Kenya as a nation. Otherwise, one must wonder how on earth a normal (sane) leader of long standing such as Moi who first served as Vice President under President Kenyatta and as President (1978-2002) after Kenyatta's death could really have done what Moi has done to a nation he had taken an oath before God that he was going to lead and defend with all his heart and mind. One must further wonder why Moi had to turn his government into a den of thieves, liars, police torturers in Nyayo cells, murderers, devil worshippers, non-nationalists and non-patriotisms whose sole aim was to see to it that they look the country to point of its national death!!

But what must have been the actual root-cause of Moi's leadership failure? Is this problem unique to Moi or is it universal? If so, how and why? And, how has his successor, Mwai Kibaki faired during his one full year of leadership since he took over power from Moi effective January, 2003?

C) PRESIDENT MWAI KIBAKI LEADERSHIP (JANUARY-DECEMBER 2004) AS A UNIT OF ANALYSIS.

a) The Rise of Kibaki Leadership in Kenya

President Mwai Kibaki assumed the Presidency of the Republic of Kenya effective 1st January, 2003 after having won in the Presidential General Elections of Kenya on December 2002 with a land-slide majority vote on a National Alliance Rainbow Coalition (NARC) ticket against Moi's sponsored presidential candidate, Uhuru Kenyatta, on a Kenya African National Union (KANU) ticket. However, by that time (2003) President Kibaki had unsuccessfully tried several times for the same in his capacity as Chairman of the Democratic Party of Kenya (DP) in 1983, 1992 and 1997, because of the cunning tactics Moi's KANU had always used in every elections against the opposition in order to remain in power for the last 40 years, since independence in December 1963.

Therefore, Kibaki's victory in December 2002 over KANU was just a rare chance based on the grace of God as follows:

NARC was conceived and born in the same year of the Elections (2002).

It was a product Government of a political marriage between two major opposition political parties called National Alliance of Kenya (NAK) party headed by Hon Mwai Kibaki (who is now the President of Kenya effective 1st January), the late Hon. Michael Wamalwa (Wamalwa Kijana) and Hon. Charity Ngilu on the one hand; and the Liberal Democratic Party of Kenya (LDP) on the other, headed by the die hard KANU leaders who disapproved a hand-picked Uhuru Kenyatta as a viable KANU presidential candidate and then resolved to team up with the official opposition party (NAK) as the only rational way forward to remove KANU and its Moi hand-picked Uhuru Kenyatta myth from power in order to save Kenya from her on-going slow death.

Those die hard KANU leaders were headed by Former Prime Minister Hon.Raila Odinga, Hon. Kalonzo Musyoka, Hon. Moody Awori, The late Hon. Prof. George Saitoti, Hon. Joseph Kamotho and others but with Hon. Odinga as their chief strategists of this now rational way forward. Others included Hon. Musalia Mudavadi, Hon Katana Ngala and Hon. Francis Oyakoyada Musakhalia who later secretly opted to return to KANU for their hidden reasons; and Hon. Simeon Nyachae who chose not to return to KANU but to join Ford-people with an aim of using this party's flag to contest for the Predidency in 2002 immediately Hon. Nyachae realized that candidature on a NARC had been slapped against him in favour of Hon. Mwai Kibaki.

However, it should also be noted that by this time (2002), Hon. Mwai Kibaki had tried several times in his capacity as Chairman of the Democratic Party of Kenya (DP) to contest for the presidency without any success in 1983, 1988, 1992 and 1997.

So, because of the former Prime Minister Hon. Raila Odinga's rational way forward, NARC successfully managed to easily oust KANU from the latter's 40 year leadership monopoly and to host the NARC leadership Flag in Kenya effective January 2003. But

NARC scooped this overwhelming majority vote over KANU not because of any reason other than that most Kenyans were already too much fed up with KANU's poor mode of leadership which had failed Kenya in various sectors of life and forced Kenya to over bleed up to her last depot. By the time NARC rushed in to rescue her from KANU, she was already in ICU fighting for her last breath. This is the reason why Kenyans decided en mass to vote out KANU by all means inspite of KANU's overflowing cash money to buy votes as it had always done throughout its 40 years of misrule in Kenya.

Because of this existing countrywide euphoria in support of NARC against KANU, NARC exploited this euphoria by offering heavens of promises to Kenyans. These heavens included: (1) Free Primary Education; A New Constitution within six months from the date NARC was to take over power from KANU (3) Provision of New Jobs at the rate of 5000 jobs per year (4) Immediate Eradication of a Corruption Culture and Resuscitation of the Kenya socio-economic Life; (5) An Immediate Restoration of Kenyan Lost Glory in the Cities and Towns; etc.

Due to these and other heavens, almost all Kenyans went wild. All and sundry proclaimed total willingness to support NARC. And as such, they told KANU to go to hell and leave NARC alone to fulfill these heavens for them immediately NARC came to power in January 2003!!

b)   Its Positive and Negative Symptoms to Innocent Kenyans.

By all means, NARC has been honest to fulfill the Free Primary Education promise for which it has scooped a mark. Similarly, NARC has also scooped another A (plus) mark by providing that it was determined:-

To Eradicate the Existing Corruption Culture in Kenya by setting up Commissions of the inquiry to examine and report to the general public the nature of this disease in the Judiciary and the Executive Arm of Government of the previous KANU regime;

To Restore the Lost Kenyan's Glory by initiating an Immediate clean up of the cities and towns whose stinking odour had been driving people so much crazy that the odour had now become an acute threat to tourism; and

To provide a new mode of Governance of good hope to Kenyans as an obvious alternative to the out-going KANU regime whose mode of Governance was just a total disaster characterized by professional thieves, murderous and liars—a government that had subjected most Kenyans to terrible night mares and sleepless hick-ups due to its deliberately sponsored culture of tribal clashes; night armed robberies; abnormal inflation; abnormal retrenchment of civil servants due to lack of salaries as most state liquidity had been stolen and siphoned abroad into foreign banks; lack of government essential services without bribery; stolen justice in and outside the Judiciary by way of robbing Peter to pay Paul; false accusations as a way of punishing the critics of KANU's spirit of deceit; arbitrary arrests and detention in the Nyayo torture cells without a cause; vote-buying thereby forcing the Kenyans Legislatures to be composed of rotten thieve, liars, and corrupt parliamentarian without any honour, ability and other qualifications needed for every law-maker in parliament.

On the other hand, NARC has disappointed many Kenyans. It has proved wanting in various critical heavens it promised the Kenyans. With regard to the Constitution Review, NARC promised Kenyans that a new constitution would be out in not later than June 2003. Later, the dead-line was pushed to November, 2003. But when November arrives, all that Kenyans could receive was a shameful NARC Cabinet Ministers' internal quarrels and name callings between one group headed by two Hon. Kiraitu Murungi, Minister for Justice and Constitutional affairs; and Hon. Dr. Chris Murungaru, Minister for Internal Security calling for the on-going Review by the Bomas of Kenya Delegates to be scrapped off and another group headed by Hon. Raila Odinga, Minister for Roads and Public Works; and Hon. Kalonzo Musyoka, Minister for Foreign Affairs and supported by Prof. Yash Pal Ghai (Chairman of the constitutional Review Commission) opposing that call.

With regard to its promise to wipe out a Corruption Culture in Kenya, NARC has proved honest and therefore deserves a patting on the back for a work-well done by rooting out corrupt judges in the Judiciary in order to restore the Judiciary to its original glory which had been eroded by the KANU regime that never believed in true justice apart from a bribed Justice. But NARC has not yet clean swept the Judiciary. This is the reason why the Law Society of Kenya (LSK) had to re-do the sweeping of the Judiciary and submit a new list of the left over corrupt Judges to the Chief Justice for action. Also, whereas NARC has acted on the Judiciary, and the Goldenberg issues, it has not yet acted on its own corrupt officers mentioned in the Goldenberg inquiry who are now hiding behind the corridors of NARC powers with false pretense that they are clean.

With regard to restoration of Kenya's Lost Glory, NARC deserves another A (plus) mark for regaining the Foreign Donor Community Confidence which Kenya had already lost during the KANU regime. Also NARC deserves another good grade for cleaning up the decaying and stinking cities and towns in Kenya with the Hon. Karisa Maitha (Minister for Local Government) personally visiting all cities and towns and ordering their immediate clean-ups and rehabilitation to their original glory!!, for cleaning up and rehabilitating all jails by the efforts of the Vice President Moody Awori in his other portfolio as Minister for Home Affairs, for rehabilitating country-wide health care and doctors' remuneration by the efforts of Hon. Charity Ngilu; and for resuscitating Kenyans road net-work through the efforts of Hon. Raila Odinga so that motorists may now safely drive without worrying about their vehicles falling apart. Therefore, Bravo NARC Government!!

But given this superb job that NARC has so far demonstrated in response to its promises to Kenyans during its 2002 campaign, then what could be the root-cause of the on-going acute schism within the NARC Government? But if it was specifically former Prime Minister Hon. Raila Odinga who played a leading role in bringing NARC to the State House by virtue of his own personal ingenuity to hatch out a wining strategy for NARC by first joining KANU; second destabilizing KANU; third, creating a "RAINBOW" party (NARC) embracing all different ethnicities in Kenya; and fourth by influencing all other opposition leaders to accept Hon. Kibaki as their "satisfactory option" with the slogan "Kibaki TOSHA"; and given that this slogan angered other opposition so much that some such as Hon. Simeon Nyachae had to quit the NARC and join Ford-People instead, the puzzling question is why must he be fired by President Kibaki as so damaged by Mr. Mutahi Ngunyi in his article "Why Kibaki should Fire the LDP Brigade Now, "that appeared as a Special Report in the Sunday Nation of December 28, 2003 (P.15)? Is this not the same Raila who spent most of his campaign time and other resources campaigning not for himself in Langata but for Hon. Kibaki all over Kenya while Hon. Kibaki was in a London hospital?

In this regard, let us re-examine the reasons and whether they merit Mr. Ngunyi's demand?

In his response to this puzzling question, Hon. Kivutha Kibwana who is a Constitutional Lawyer and Assistant Minister in the office of the President, reveals in his article "Using to Paint Others Black"[52] that it is succinctly the "Spirit of Dishonesty" which is the actual root-cause. He reveals that in order for NARC to successfully take over power form KANU, the NARC leadership mutually agreed to share power as follows:

NAK was to take the Presidency, (Hon. Mwai Kibaki). Vice Presidency (Hon. Michael Wamalwa Kijana); the second Deputy Prime Minister (Charity Ngilu); and the Third Deputy Prime Minister docket (Kipruto arap Kirwa).

And the LDP was to take Vice Presidency on equal footing with the Vice Presidency docket of Hon. Michael Wamalwa Kijana (Hon. Stephen Kalonzo Musyoka); Executive Prime Minister docket (Hon. Raila Odinga); the First Deputy Prime Minister docket (Hon George Saitoti); and a Senior Co-ordinating Minister (Hon. Moody Awori).

This Memorandum of Understanding now popularly known as MoU was entered into by both NAK and LDP at the Hilton Hotel, Nairobi. And, the two ostensibly established a defacto NARC Transitional Leadership with all those signatories as dejure Member of the NARC Summit.

Apparently, this was the hidden reason why Hon. Raila Odinga had to spend all his time on campaign trails all over Kenya for Hon. Kibaki while the latter was unable to do so by himself.

But when the NARC Government sat to award ministerial posts, did this exercise conform to this MoU?

Unfortunately, NARC failed to honour this MoU. Instead NARC created and implemented a new ministerial post of Justice and Constitutional Affairs but forgot all those already collectively agreed on posts of Vice President, Prime Minister and Deputy Prime Minister for its mutual LDP friends.

Also, with regard to other significant posts of Assistant Minister, Permanent Secretary, Parastatal Chairman and Managing Diretor, NARC failed to honour equity.

Similarly on the Question of the Constitution of Kenya Review which became such a fovourite weapon for NARC's campaign against KANU for dishonesty that most Kenyans realized the need to hate and reject KANU in favour of NARC's victory, the NARC Leadership has equally proved dishonest. Both Justice and Constitutional Affairs Minister and the Internal Security Minister, for example, have characterized the Review as a secret effort to favour Hon. Raila Odinga, with a view to awarding him a post of Prime Minister. They therefore argue that the Review must either be scrapped off or be halted until further notice. Hence, the actual root-cause of the on-going disturbing schism in NARC Leadership.

But what is this schism leading NARC to?, And what remedy is necessary? The following scriptural warning to each of us is simple but loud and clear. "MSHAHARA WA DHAMBI NI MAUTI"! (i.e., the wage of sin is death). But in as much as the price of sin is death, and so is the price of dishonesty.

From the beginning of the Human Life, we note with sorrow from The Old Testament Bible that it was succinctly our patriarch Adam's dishonesty to his agreement with God that led him into confusion and death that also befell all Humanity till today. Similarly, we also note that it was Samson's dishonesty to his agreement with God that landed Samson to death. Another explicit prima facie empirical evidence of the danger of dishonesty is that of the wisest leader named King Solomon. Because of his dishonesty to his agreement with God during his lengthy appealing prayer to God for wisdom so that he maybe able to lead his subjects with justice, King Solomon later failed to honour all that. King Solomon assumed that God was such a fool, blind and sleeping being that would neither see nor mind what King Solomon was doing. Consequently, King Solomon ruled his subjects without justice and reverence to the same God he had received the unique wisdom that he had prayed for. Misusing this extraordinary wisdom he married 700 wives and also kept up to 700 concubines wheels for sex purpose. As a result of all this dishonesty, God decided to break the United Kingdom of Israel into two (Israel and Judah) which eventually withered away and all Israel people taken into captivity by Babylon. Another scientific evidence is that of King David who had also to suffer so much that he ended up, crying like a little child due to his own spirit of dishonesty by mischievously betraying his own honest loyal soldier called Uriah to death so that King David may grab this soldier's wife. And, from the New Testament of the Holy Bible, we also note the same price of dishonesty. Because of Judas Iscariot's dishonesty to his own Master, Jesus Christ, Judas Iscariot did not only lose his job as the Cabinet Minister for Finance but also lost his own dear life. His stomach burst open and all his bowels thrown out, due to his spirit of dishonesty.

In our own generation, we also note that death is a universal pay off to every case of dishonesty. This death may be physical, political, economic, professional, scientific or spiritual. The dishonesty of all Colonial Masters in Africa, Asia and North and South America did not allow them to prevail and prosper. Their dishonesty caused them to be ousted and forced out by their own colonial people into a political suicide. And all nationalist leaders that took over from the colonial power but proved dishonest to their subjects were equally ousted and forced into the same political suicide.

An interesting empirical evidence of this phenomenon in Kenya is the Moi KANU Regime which went the same way because of its love for "The Spirit of Dishonesty." Because of this spirit, the Moi KANU regime did not want to accept its exisiting well-seasoned leaders such as Prof. George Sitoti, Hon. Raila Odinga, Hon. Joseph Kamotho, Hon. Stephen Kalonzo Musyoka and many others as a qualified material for the Presidency later having used them for all those good years of loyal service. No matter what appeal these leaders put across to their KANU Party master Moi, the latter could not give a damn. Instead, the Moi KANU Regime decided to impose on them an infant politician whom these KANU leaders decided to radical as a "Moi Project" and reject it by all means. To make it worse they conspired with the Opposition (NAK) TO TEACH THEIR Moi Master a lesson equal to his own dishonesty that he would never forget throughout his life. This lesson was to subject Moi's KANU Project to a Political Suicide not because of their envy or malice against Moi as a person but because of their sincere objection to their KANU Master's Spirit of Dishonesty. Hence, the KANU Leadership loss to NARC leadership in December 2002 Elections leadership potentials, i.e. his/her productivity which the Kenyatta-and-Moi leadership failed to do.

Thus, Kibaki's leadership style is reminiscent of a leadership paradigm shift in Kenya and total Africa from the old parochial and paranoid character of leadership to a rational liberal character founded on the mutual trust between the President and his Cabinet Ministers (the latter serving him as Ministry's Managers on behalf of the president).

Therefore, this new leadership paradigm is not a sign of cowardice or paper tiger mode of leadership but a liberal leadership based on trust vested in each Minister's Oath of Office and Terms of Reference. Whereas each organ of a body is controlled by the head as a store of intellect, each organ must show its worthiness. In as much as a hand must do so, so is the leg, the eye, the ear, etc without depending on the head to come down and walk on behalf of the leg. c) <u>Its Spirits of Honesty In Accordance To Its Vow During Its Oath Of Office.</u>

One's Spirit of Honesty is measured in relations to one's theory, policy, promise or belief(s).

In this regard, the following is a retrospective analysis of NARC Government's performance so far, relative to the following opposition's critical assessment.

In the <u>Daily Nation</u> of Friday, Nairobi 20th February, 2004, the Leader of opposition, Hon. Uhuru Kenyatta contends that President Mwai Kibaki leadership has proved too weak and is therefore unable to synchronize a smooth functioning of the body policy. And, that it is too weak because of the Present's leadership style of hands-off-management of Ministries thus leaving the latter into the dangerous hands off multy-Ministers who may not be competent enough to run the Government smoothly.

But although Uhuru Kenyatta may be the Leader of Opposition, the fact is that he lacks a well balanced experience in both leadership and Policy management because he has no prior experience either as a civil servant or private business manager of any organization. It was not until the year 2001 when he was made a nominated member of Parliament by President Moi with an ulterior aim of using him in future as a KANU Presidential Project in the 2002 General Elections. Before then he had no prior experience as a politician. In this regard, he is still a too adolescent political leader, to stand independently.

The Hon. Mwai Kibaki decided to introduce a new leadership policy of hands-off in matter pertaining to management of Ministries in order to correct and erase the Jomo Kenyatta-Moi dictatorial/autocratic modes of leadership by which the two had terrorized Kenyans into mental and socio-economic breakdown. He did so to enable each of his cabinet ministers show his worthiness.

Unlike the Kibaki new paradigm, the Kenyatta-Moi paradigms were the same and characterized by dictatorship forcing ministers to do only what they were told but not to be creators of their own developmental ideas. Even if Moi could not understand an idea given to him in terms of its advantage or disadvantages to Kenyans, his response was to disallow it and called it foreign so long as it was not originated by him. Hence the failure of Kenya to grow socio-economically during the Kenyatta—Moi leadership eras. And this is the reason why Kibaki had to seek a new mode of leadership as a relief to Kenyans in keeping with the NARC Government vow during its Oath of Office and its Terms of Reference assigned to each Cabinet Minister, Assistant Minister and President Mwai Kibaki himself.

And, also in an article by the present Shadow Minister for Finance and Member of Parliament for Mandera Central, Mr. Billow Kerrow, titled "Total Man Murungi's Vindictive Ways" appearing in The Sunday Standard of February 8, 2004 at page 9, Mr. Kerrow bitterly castigates the Justice and Constitutional Affairs Minister Kiraitu Murungi and the entire National Alliance Rainbow Coalition (NARC) Government for what he feels to be sins against his Kenya African National Union (KANU) comrades, whom he feels to be totally innocent of the ills they did commit against Kenya and her children! He strongly feels that the Minister and the NARC Government's administrative way forward is of no positive resuscitation effect to the Country's socio-economic ailing health as most Kenyans seem to believe. To him, it is a total confusion and high-profile wrestling matches, which have consequently placed the Kenyan business community in a dilemma.

For this reason, Mr. Kerrow takes a very critical issue particularly with the Honourable Justice and Constitutional Affairs Minister Murungi who he bitterly accuses as the real man in this militia outfit with the potential to send our Mother Kenya into a destructive spin. And, derogatively, labels the Honourable Minister with nasty adjectives as an arrogant, vicious and angry man walking all round with a noose in his hands, looking for the next victim. What an unfortunate non-honourable language by an expected Member of Parliament of our Republic!

In summary, Mr. Kerrow hurls his bitterness against both the Justice and Constitutional Affairs Minister and the entire NARC Government with the following three bombshells:

1) That the NARC Government has no case against the former KANU Government criminals since "two-thirds of its (NARC's) Administration

including its (NARC's) serving senior public servants were all in the former KANU Government now being accused of human rights abuses and economic crimes",

2)   That NARC Government must emulate the South African model whereby the now ruling African National Congress (ANC) Government chose the path of reconciliation and amnesty rather than rulers for their inhumane crimes (sins) against Africans;

3)   And that Kenyatta Government also chose the same model to forgive but not to avenge the atrocities of the colonialists against Kenyans.

Yes, in my capacity as a born-again Christian and servant of my Lord Jesus Christ, I believe and agree that forgiveness is the only ultimate answer to all sins. However, it is also important that Mr. Kerrow gets edified right now on the following God's divine conditions clearly spelled out in our Holy Scripture before we come to the conclusion as to what the NARC Government must do or not do against the KANU Government's deliberate injuries already inflicted on the socio-economic health of our Mother Country and her Children:-

•   Under Exodus 20:20, 34:7; Daniel 9:9 and Mark 2:7, we are told that it is only God and God alone who can forgive every sinner. Therefore, it is now up to KANU Government individuals implicated in those various injurious act to Kenya and her Children to directly bend their knees before Him, the Creator of Heaven and Earth, and seek His forgiveness since the sins so committed were not directed against Kenyans as such but against God Himself who anointed KANU Government to lead His Kenyan children on His behalf, and a responsibility that KANU Government gladly prayed for under Oath that it was going to honour but instead cheated God for not doing so!! In this regard, NARC Government cannot also afford to repeat the same mistake of KANU Government by failing to honour its obligations to God contained in their Oath of Office.

•   Under 1 Kings 16:2, we must also know that God is always angered by sinful acts deliberately committed against the innocent as in the cases of Cain against his innocent brother Abel; King Ahab and Queen Jezebel against the innocent Prophet Elijah; King Herod against the Innocent Infant Jesus Christ and thousands of other infants he murdered; King David against innocent soldier Uriah; etc. Therefore, KANU Government has a serious case to answer to God's wrath. And for this very reason, the Justice and Constitutional Affairs Minister and the NARC Government fraternity cannot risk their Oath of Office by compromising with the KANU Government sinful acts in order to please Mr. Kerrow and KANU.

- Under Job 10:14; and Revelations 18:5, God always marks and remembers sin(s) till the sinner repents directly to Him for forgiveness. Therefore, it is now up to KANU Government to go before God but not to the innocent and divine less NARC Government which is only doing its job in fulfilment of its Terms of Reference under The Oath by unearthing all those sinful acts against Kenya and the Children deliberately initiated and carried out by the KANU Government without any regard to the health of the innocent Kenyans today and future generations.

- Under Job 31:33, one is always guilty of concealing sin as our patriarch Adam, King David, etc. did which, in turn, costed them very dearly in their whole lives. Therefore, for concealing all those sins of looting the Kenyan wealth thereby suffocating the country to death, and of the Nyayo Police cells tortures and murders thereby driving the families and friends of the victims to madness and endless gnashing of teeth, KANU Government is obviously guilty beyond any reasonable doubt because had all these not been unearthed by the Goldenberg Commission of Inquiry on the strength of Justice and Constitutional Affairs Minister Murungi who is now being called all sorts of nasty names by Mr. Kerrow on behalf of his KANU criminals, most Kenyans would have not known those sins; and how to recover them from those foreign banks where they were siphoned and hidden by the KANU Government looters.

- Under Psalms 4:4, one has a duty before God to guard himself or herself against sinful acts which KANU Government had the duty to do under Oath of Office but deliberately refused to do due to its obsessed appetite for looting, murder and police cells tortures. Therefore, Mr. Kerrow and his KANU Government criminals have a case against themselves but not the Honourable

Justice and Constitutional Minister and the entire NARC Government which is simply doing its mandated watchdog duty for all innocent Kenyans under its Oath of Office failure of which NARC Government may be either lynched or driven out of office by the dissatisfied angry innocent Kenyans.

- And, under Romans 6:23, we are explicitly warned that death is the wages of sin. Therefore, this must therefore be the succinct answer to Mr. Kerrow and all his KANU comrades with whom he willingly, comfortably and happily shared the loot of all Kenya's wealth at the expense of the overwhelming majority of innocent helpless Kenyans as Abacha was found doing against his Nigerians.

In this regard, it is self-evident that in as much as one must reap what one has sown, similarly, Mr. Kerrow and all his KANU comrades for whom he is campaigning for must also reap what they did sow. There is no any other way out at all. Secondly, what South Africa and President Jomo Kenyatta's KANU Government did, they did out of their own will but not out of the will of the responsible sinners. In fact, Kenyatta repeated doing the same sins the colonialists did to Kenyans. Immediately after independence right up to his death in 1978, he looted most Kenya's assets and siphoned them overseas. These are the same assets his family has used during the 2002 Presidential Election which they are lavishingly living on since his death! Like the colonialists, he murdered many Kenyans, e.g. Ronald Ngala, Tom Mboya, JM Kariuki, etc. And, like the colonialists, he also detained Kenyans, e.g. Jaramogi Oginga Odinga, etc. Impressed by the way Kenyatta had grown filthy wealthy through this looting method, obviously his predecessor declared a Nyayo Philosophy meaning that he was going to use the same looting method. Hence, the beginning of a looting culture in Kenya. But, in Mr. Kerrow's all bitter accusations against the Honourable Justice and Constitutional Affairs Minister Murungi and total NARC Government, it is obvious the accuser is not honest. If he were so, one then wonders why he is.

Besides the above, the truth about Mr. Kerrow's articles and accusations against the Honourable Justice and Constitutional Affairs Minister and total NARC government is openly abusing the Justice and Constitutional Minister Murungi by calling him all sorts of dirty names as if the Minister was the one who misled the KANU Government to indulge in such sins against God who anointed them (KANU

Government) to be in power all that long period from 1963 to 2003, in good faith that the Government would assist God in nursing His Kenyan children on His behalf.

Obviously, Mr. Kerrow seems to have lost direction. By so abusing the Honourable Minister who is just doing his job in keeping with his Terms of Reference under Oath before President Mwai Kibaki and all Kenyans in total, Mr. Kerrow is definitely an ignorant man! He is not yet intellectually grown up. He therefore seems to be very unfit for being in the Parliament of The Republic of Kenya since he even cannot tell well how to properly address his own Parliament comrades. His language is too primitive. It is unheard of in a Civilized Society!

But, from a psychiatric angle of analysis, it is self-evident from Mr. Kerrow's sentiments contained in his own article, that both the Justice and Constitutional Affairs Minister and the NARC Government must be doing a superb job in conformity with their Terms of Reference and Oath of Office they took before all Kenyans on taking over leadership from KANU in January 2003. For this reason, President Mwai Kibaki's NARC Government has a reason to be congratulated for a work well done since the impact is now being felt all over including by KANU folks such as Mr. Kerrow. Otherwise, Mr. Kerrow would not be feeling pain if the pot were not boiling!

As one of the major victims of KANU Government's hooliganism who was messed up several times through election riggings in 1979, 1983 and 1992; and through job deprivation simply because of my opposition stand together with other enlightened Kenyans against KANU's hooligan mode of governance that KANU was perpetuating in Kenya ever since the independence (1963), I am duty bound to throw all my full weight behind the Justice and Constitutional Affairs Minister Kiraitu Murungi and total NARC Government comrades with whom I bitterly suffered from 1979 to 2002 (December). And I hereby therefore appeal to the entire enlightened Kenyan fraternity to do the same so that NARC Government may clean up the existing dirty image that KANU hooligan regime had created and left behind for us to clean.

Yes, I fully agree with Minister Murungi's way forward. It is the only rational path to restoring our African Dignity we had lost in the International Community as a result of the hooligan culture of looting, murder and dishonesty created by KANU Government. What the Minister is doing is what I personally would have done. In fact I would have done more as the only best way that those merciless KANU hooligans and thieves who depleted our Kenya's socio-economic strength through looting deceits and other leadership ineptitude and poverty must and should be handled.

Mr. Kerrow needs to be re-educated to know that outside there including his own Mandera Central Constituency, exist hundreds of thousands of innocent sane Kenyans who are now gnashing their teeth in an agony of captivity of poverty and various sicknesses not because they are incapable of working but simply because of having been wrongfully laid off through a foolish retrenchment scheme on false pretence that Kenya had been denied donor aid by the Donor Community. While KANU Government fed them on this foolish lies, they also hatched out another lie to them that because of this aid denial, Kenya was no longer financially able to sustain their monthly salary.

Whereas these victims of KANU hooliganism and lies were misled to believe and accept to be paid their terminal benefits cleverly coated with attractively misleading name of "Golden-Hand-Shake", these innocent and ignorant victims did not get all their benefits. The same KANU Government hooligans with total impunity looted some of their benefits. What a mercilessly dishonest Government!!! Expected on Oath by God to be a faithfully honest guardian of God's children in Kenya but turned out to be a leopard in a sheep's skin!!

Due to all these hooligan methods, Mr. Kerrow needs to understand and appreciate that most Kenyans who were laid off were done so unceremoniously by his KANU Government comrades whom he seems to be bargaining for blindly. But if the Goldenberg Commission of Inquiry had not been formed by President Kibaki and placed under the same Honourable Minister for Justice and Constitutional Affairs whom he is now labelling as arrogant, vicious and angry man, how would majority of Kenyans have known the actual reason of retrenchment? From the Commission's findings, Kenyans are now able to understand the truth that it was not because of the donor aid issue other than that KANU Government has already depleted the whole Kenya's economy through looting.

In my capacity as former personal Aid to the late Honourable Masinde Muliro during his role as Vice Chairman of FORD in 1991/92 at the climax of Opposition Heat against KANU's Government mischiefs and hooliganism, all I can say in response to Mr. Kerrow's article is that ENOUGH IS ALREADY ENOUGH!! Cabinet Minister

Murungi and all others in The NARC Government, go ahead. Have courage and spare NONE including me of course!! All over Europe and America and elsewhere, Kenyan image is too poor because of the hooligan culture initiated and promoted by KANU hooligans, who thought that they were too wise thieves to be considered. Since they are that too clever then the NARC Government needs to be super-clever. Otherwise, all that was looted and hidden in foreign banks at the expense of all innocent poor Kenyans may not be expatriated. They will treat you as a joke and as a cow treats a singing frog but majestically advances and drink all the water it wants. Therefore, my advice to you the Justice Minister Murungi is that you should not only rely on a noose of sisal or synthetic rope. If necessary, also use a live electric wire noose so as to teach these most clever thieves a good lesson they deserve.

Mr. Justice and Constitutional Affairs Minister, look at the hooligan way the most Kenyan luxurious Grand Regency Hotel was financially acquired secretly using Kenya's public funds looted from the Central Bank of Kenya, which is the only granary of Kenya's liquid assets. Look at the way all-the innocent but helpless customers of the Kenya Power and Lighting Company have always been forced to pay for the loots made by the former Managing Director. Look at the most notorious woman of all times in Kenya who exploited her position as head of the National Aids Control Council and ripped off the Council to the tune of Kshs.26.9 million at the rate of about Kshs.2.3 million monthly salary so that she and her family may live a lavish life and eat and belch all day and night at the expense of the innocent but helpless aids victims without money to buy for their medicines. Look at the thousands of acres of fertile lands dished out by the KANU Government hooligans to sycophants while Kenya has thousands of landless men and women. Look at the notorious way jobs in Kenya were being forcefully or cunningly taken from the most suitably qualified Kenyans and given to KANU sycophants' relatives and friends without regard to qualification (as in my case whose international job was secretly taken away by a senior KANU member of Parliament and given to his relative simply because the MP was a Minister of East African Regional Affairs docket) etc. This list of shame is endless. The nagging question at hand now is, WHAT MUST NARC GOVERNMENT DO TO SUCH KANU CROOKS? Just speak to them? Take them to court that is still equally so corrupt that may set them Scot free through the backdoor? Or must NARC Government do exactly what it is currently doing through its Ministers such as the Justice and Constitutional Minister against the Goldenberg crooks and murderers? The candid answer is that NARC Government should even tighten the noose. It should be tougher than it is now. If I were the Justice and Constitutional Affairs Minister now, I would speak very softly but carry with me a number of live electric nooses ready for those most destructive hooligans that have messed up Kenya's economy and image internationally. One noose alone is not enough given the way revelations are now coming out with more and more new fat cats to catch. Kenya had already been turned into a den of international thieves by the KANU crooks to the extent that it also attached other crooks such as Sani Abacha who used Kenya as a conduit of his loot from Nigeria to the tune of US Dollars 100 million (Kshs.7.6 billion). What a shame to Mr. Kerrow and his KANU hooligans!! Is this what Mr. Kerrow is now abusing the Justice and Constitutional Affairs for, desiring the Minister to let these criminals go Scot free at the expense of the majority innocent but poor Kenyans? If the Minister accepts such primitive demand, then that would be the end of him because he is expected to be an honest servant of all Kenyans and of God in particular in accordance with his Oath of Office. The Vow he took is final. By this vow, he is duty bound to serve Kenyans but not to favour criminals at the expense of all Kenyans and the latter's God. Therefore Mr. Kerrow, leave the Justice Minister and NARC Government alone so that they may do their work in fulfilment of their vow!! And for NARC and the Minister for Justice and Constitutional Affairs, well done in your work. And please don't be cowed by singing frogs in the pond.

2. A BALANCE SHEET OF KENYAN LEADERSHIP CULTURE AND EFFECT ON INNOCENT KENYANS (1885-2004)

(a) Introduction

In order for us to establish an accurate and reliable Balance Sheet of the Kenyan Leadership Culture today in terms of its net-gains or net-losses to the well-beings (satisfaction and happiness) of the Kenyan people it is expected to serve in conformity with its Terms of Reference under Oath whenever each leader came into office with a solemn vow to them to the effect that one was indeed going to be their servant and provide them with all needed goods and services (such as food security, water security, health security, shelter security, etc), let us first and foremost drive deep into those various subcutaneous strata/regions of this culture, scoop out and identify its actual roots, and then meticulously examine and analyse these roots one by one with a view to understanding their actual contributions to these gains or losses to the Kenyans today. In this regard, the following longitudinal inquiry into its genesis and the trend of its growth and development over time before and up to its present status today (2013) is very necessary.

Administratively, Kenyan leadership culture today is anchored in the ex-British Colonial Culture which began in 1885 at the time Kenya was declared a de jure British sphere of influence by the Berlin Conference which resulted in the Scramble for Africa held in Berlin, Germany from November 1884 to March 1885 by European powers quarrelling for Africa's abundant natural wealth among themselves; viz: Britain, French, Germany, Holland, Spain, Portugal, Belgium and Italy. At the end of this Conference, a Berlin General Act was concluded in March 1885 partitioning the African Continent into colonies and protectorates by which these scrambling powers were now legally empowered to help themselves on these colonies and protectorates. In this case, Kenya fell to Britain.

Thus, by virtue of this Berlin General Act, Kenya legally became a subject of and for the British administrative concern. Hence, the genesis of the Kenyan leadership culture today (2013).

The British colonial administration in Kenya is the actual genesis in that, although Britain was always not welcome or liked by Kenyans throughout her colonial tenure as it was shown the door-out on 12th December 1963 by the rise of strong nationalism and patriotism, spearheaded by Jomo Kenyatta, Odinga Oginga, Tom Mboya, Masinde Muliro, W.W. Awori, Ronald Ngala, Argwings Kodhek, Arthur Ochwada, James Osogo, Peter Mbiyu Koinange, etc. Britain left behind all her colonial administrative legacies in Kenya which the independent Kenyan African leadership gladly inherited.

But what was the nature of this British colonial legacy? What was its actual contribution to today's leadership culture in Kenya?

To get an accurate answer to this question, a psychiatric approach on the leadership is necessary. And to get this done, one has to first get to the bottom of the ultimate objective and goal of the quarrel among these European colonial seekers in Africa in order to establish the roots of their administrative policies and behavioural patterns in Africa.

Each colonial power's goal was to get hold of Africa's abundant wealth. But this could not be easily forthcoming, as the actual owners in the Continent would not freely agree. But although they could not freely agree, they lacked as much sophisticated means of coercion with which to contain this foreign aggression. Because of the same on the one hand and the colonial powers' awareness of this weakness on the other, obviously these powers remained with all freedom of monopoly to bulldoze and force the colonized Africa into submission and subjection. And, the more the colonial powers did so, the more they also developed a lionism spirit of man-eat-man culture in its administration of each African colony and protectorate.

Hence, the British colonial leadership style in Kenya with clarity that all that Britain needed had to be looted at all cost and at all times and to discipline every Kenyan seemed to be either a real or potential threat to them and their goal. This is exactly why and how Deutential Law was introduced and instituted in Kenya, and also the reason why and how those African Nationalists in Kenya such as Jomo Kenyatta, Achieng' Oneko, Paul Ngei, Bildad Kaggia and many other members of MAU MAU were rounded up and herded into detentions in order for Britain to contain the sources of the viruses against her looting aim in Kenya. They were a nuisance to Britain.

But why were they regarded a virus? And, what was Britain looting in Kenya and for what purpose?

These nationalists and the MAU MAU movement were vehemently opposed to the looting of Kenyan wealth. This wealth included grabbed fertile lands particularly in the Central and Rift Valley regions of Kenya Britain had converted into a whites' personal property which they derogatively and cunningly christened as "White Highlands" as a way of containing African owners from coming back to claim them; mineral wealth such as gold, in Kakamega (Western Kenya); hard wood; lucrative agricultural produce such as cotton, pyrethrum, maize, beans for insecticides; and many other most valuable food and cash crops not available back home in Britain and total Europe.

In addition, Britain enjoyed a rare monopoly of free and forced labour in Kenya. Cheap and free labour was never obtained through a social consent of the Africans as the latter were always simply forced to do whatever the white man wanted them to do. Even one that was paid for the job, the payment was not equivalent to amount and nature of the labour. A graduate African with a high school certificate earned less than a primary school drop out white person earned, simply because of this colour difference. And, worst of all, an African woman would be put at the mercy of a white man who incited his dog to have a forced sexual intercourse with her!! In the final analysis, the whole British colonial leadership in Kenya was not only abnormal but also satanic.

But this colonial leadership culture was not limited to Kenya. It held true throughout all colonies and protectorates that Britain ever controlled and administered as her spheres of influence in Africa. In fact, this is the fundamental root-cause of the on-going bitterness in Zimbabwe where lots of stolen lands are now being demanded back by their legally African owners.

Also this is the secret reason why the British Prime Minister, Tony Blair, is vigorously fighting President Robert Mugabe and the latter's government policy on the issue of this stolen land. Tony Blair is not being honest. He is blindly fooling the World Community that Mugabe is to blame for not respecting the fundamental human rights of these British settlers in Zimbabwe clearly enshrined in the UN Charter and our Present World Civilization; and that by so doing President Mugabe is actually not only violating those settlers' right but also the rights of The UN Charter and our World civilization. Blair is obviously cunning and ill motivated against Mugabe's leadership not for any reason other than racism. His ulterior motive is to sustain and perpetuate the racial overtone spirit of survival of the white supremacy initiated and promoted throughout the British colonial era in Africa, which in turn became the root cause of its suicide in Africa, Asia and in all other areas Britain ever exercised colonial dominion.

An autopsy of this British colonial rule in Kenya shows very clearly that the rule was beset with acute contradictions. Whereas the rule was very emphatic to the Max Weber's bureaucratic rule which emphasised efficiency and honesty to one's professionalism and professionality, the same rule also very emphatic to the Charles Darwin's survival of the fittest rule which emphasized that every one was free to use his lionism (lion type of capability and style) to grab by force whatever one wanted with total impunity (without any regard to rule of law and justice).

This is exactly the double-edged nature of the British colonial culture in Kenya and other colonies which in turn became a womb of its own failure wherever it ever existed. Although it aimed at high quality of bureaucracy in civil service where the work was always <u>spick and span</u>, in political leadership, it killed whoever it saw fit to do so, e.g. Dedan Kimathi and many freedom fighters. Others such as Kenyatta etc. were put in detention.

(b) <u>From Colonial Rule to Kenyatta's Rule (1885-1963)</u>

In the final analysis this is the exact character of the legacy which Britain ever left behind in Kenyan administrative life when Kenya became independent on December 12, 1963. Mzee Jomo Kenyatta automatically inherited this legacy and used it also throughout his leadership tenure without knowing the actual implications and consequences of it to his own leadership. For instance,

1) Like the British colonial leadership which loved detention of its critics such as Kenyatta, Achieng Oneko, Paul Ngei, Bildad Kaggia, and others, Kenyatta's rule loved the same detention policy by which he rounded up all his arch-critics such as Oginga Odinga, Martin Shikuku, and others and put them into detention so that they may no longer bother him.

2) Like the British Colonial leadership, which behaved and used elimination e.g. of Dedan Kimathi, his leadership continued with the elimination policy by which he eliminated every one he needed done so e.g. J.M. Kariuki.

3) Like the British colonial leadership which was thirsty and hungry for looting Kenya's wealth, he too was also thirsty and hungry for looting the country's fixed and liquid wealth to the extent that he grabbed all neighbouring land to his home in Gatundu and forced all legal owners to vacate and look for other places to go without any compensation.

4) Like the British colonial rule which emphasized nepotism called "Britonization" by giving top civil service jobs to British persons only his rule emphasized nepotism called "Kikuyunization" by staffing most key government positions with his own ethnic group particularly from Gatundu. In 1966/67, he overhauled the Civil Service and Kikuyunized it: from Divisional Officers to District Commissioners, Provincial Commissioners, Permanent Secretaries, Heads of Parastatal Agencies, Governor of the Central

Bank, Commissioner of Police, Attorney General, Commissioner of Prisons, Chief of General Security Unit (GSU), Director of Criminal Investigation (CID), Director of Special Branch, Principal Immigration Officer, Air Force Commander, etc. Hence the Kenyan Leadership Tragedy of 1966/67.[53] This 1966/67 was the same period of Kenyatta leadership's acute conflict with his out-going Vice President Oginga Odinga who accused Kenyatta of corruption and claimed that because of Kenyatta's bad leadership, Kenya was not yet Uhuru (i.e. independent). Faced with this Odingaphobia, Kenyatta looted civil posts and replaced with his Kikuyus regardless of proper qualification. Most of them turned out to be mediocre. Kikuyu cohorts pushed in to serving Kenyatta personal political interest (personal peace from Odinganism and Odingaphobia). In the Sunday Nation of 1st February, 2004, we see a typical model of civil servants Kenyatta believed in for success of his leadership in Kenya:-

"He [Charles Njonjo] also criticized the All Saints Cathedral for refusing to conduct a requiem service for Kisumu Town West MP Joab Omino on the grounds that he was a Freemason".

"The head of Freemasons in the world (grandmaster), the Duke of Kent, is a cousin of Queen Elizabeth, the head of the Anglican Church".

Obviously, one must wonder why and how on earth being a cousin of Queen Elizabeth must be an automatic rite of passage for a Freemasons to be given a service reserved totally for non-Freemasons. Queen Elizabeth and her cousin (the Duke of Kent) are two independent human beings each with a different body and soul. It is questionable what Queen Elizabeth would/will say about such linkages. On the whole, these are a kind of persons that governed Kenya whose legacy is the root-cause of the present legacy of leadership chaos and ineptitude haunting Kenyans.

5) Like the British colonial rule which never allowed Democracy his rule could not also allow any mode of a true democratic process in Kenya as Kenyatta abolished all efforts to multi-party democracy by banning Oginga Odinga's efforts to launch his opposition party called Kenya Peoples Union in 1966 after having disagreed with Kenyatta's grabiosis policy (grabbing illness) and then

resigning from his post of Vice President with the good hope that he would be able to use his KPU to resuscitate Kenya from Kenyatta grabiosis policy likely to suffocate Kenya socio-economically and politically.

6) Like the British colonial rule which initiated and thrived on the looting spree of the Kenyan wealth without care of the feelings of Kenyans, his rule left Kenya in a maggot culture of corruption at all level of Kenya's life in which each officer thought of not the Kenyan general public's welfare but for his own self as a priority and a means and end of his office work—This is exactly the reason why in 1966 President Julius K. Nyerere of Tanzania lamented to the effect that Kenya was a "man-eat-man society".[54] Definitely in the mid-1960's up to the death of Kenyatta in August, 1978, Kenyatta was too abnormally obsessed with the Coffee Boom smuggled into Kenya from Uganda during the Idi Amin Dada's leadership that Kenya was culturally a total mess as everyone was so much a liar and a thief at the same time that Kenyatta had only a body without a soul. Kenyatta lost all her sanity to evil and could kill at any time whoever opposed such a culture. This is the reason why President Nyerere's echo cost him dearly as he was rebuked left and right by Kenyatta's leadership and the general public.

7) And, like the British colonial rule which enjoyed inciting inter-African leaders' conflict for their own good, Kenyatta's rule lavishly flourished on the same schism e.g. between Tom Mboya on the one hand and Oginga Odinga on the other, in which Mboya supported Capitalism on grounds that it was the most viable vehicle for a nation's socio-economic development while Odinga argued that Communism was the most viable vehicle since it was closely related to communalism and egalitarianism in traditional African communities. [56]

Thus the sum total of Kenyatta leadership legacy on the one hand and the British colonial leadership legacy on the other that was left in Kenya as at Kenyatta's death in October 1978.

c) <u>From Kenyatta's Rule to Moi's Rule (1963-1978)</u>

On Kenyatta's death in October 1978, the then Vice President Daniel Toroitich arap Moi took over the leadership with an explicit world-wide vow that he was going to sustain Kenyatta's policy left behind by Kenyatta. Accordingly, he boldly lounged a philosophy, which he titled s "Nyayo" meaning following Kenyatta's leadership footsteps. But no sooner had time passed than vehement accusations were levelled against him because of his questionable mode of leadership. For example, he was accused of preaching wine and yet drinking water. But what was the meaning of this metaphor?

Although he preached Nyayo philosophy of Peace, Love and Unit in the sense that like Kenyatta's tenure he also stood for Peace, Love and Unity, but in practice, was this true? Besides, did Kenyatta's leadership stand for Peace, Love and Unity? If so, did Kenyatta's policy of Kikuyunization of 1966/67 agree or support that argument. And, did Moi's Kalenjinization support it?

The above account on Kenyatta's leadership refutes all that. And the following account on Moi leadership has yet to establish whether or not Moi's leadership did honour Moi's own Nyayo Philosophy of Peace, Love and Unity during his leadership tenure:-

1) Like both ex-British colonial rule and Kenyatta's rule, Moi's rule also embarked on nepotism of "Kalenjinization" in which he also made sure that all key positions in the Kenyan Civil Service is manned by Kalenjins who are of his own ethnicity.

2) Like both the ex-British colonial rule and Kenyatta's rule which individually ensured that the Civil Service's outlook is of their own kind, similarly, Moi's rule was determined to see to it that the Kenyan Civil Service's outlook was none else but of his Kalenjin ethnicity.

3) Like his predecessors' leaderships which were fully determined that the Civil Service served none else but their British and Kikuyu community interests respectively; similarly, Moi leadership ensured that the Civil Service now put in place by him served none other than the interest of his Kalenjin Community—a total paradox of his philosophy of Peace, Love and Unity!

4) Like the two former leaderships, whose strategy was largely to satisfy their personal interests at the expense of the entire Kenyan general population through lootings, etc.

5) Like the two leadership again, which was totally opposed to Democracy in the truest sense of its meaning, by physically and practically keeping out all oppositions from direct participation in the electoral processes, and also by making sure that elections do not actually take place in a genuine manner, the Moi leadership also ensured that this policy prevailed at all costs.

6) Like the ex-British and the out-going Kenyatta leaderships which had to encounter various rebellions forces from within and without Kenya aimed at removing them due to their inherent injuries to the Kenyans and then replacing the two with a better mode of leadership, (e.g. the Mau Mau against the British Colonial rule and the mutiny against Kenyatta's rule in 19 **), the Moi leadership encountered a severe storm of attempted military coup in 1982 by the Air Force determined to root it out of power. But like the mutiny against Kenyatta's leadership, this military coup also failed.

7) Like the Kenyatta's leadership which rooted out all non-Kikuyus responsible for the mutiny and replaced them with his own Kikuyus, Moi leadership also rooted out all non-Kalenjin officers in the Air Force who had been either directly or indirectly implicated in the attempted abortive military coup d'etat of 1982 against his government and replaced them largely with his own Kalenjin ethnic officers.

8) Like the ex-British colonial rule and the Kenyatta leadership which resorted to un-democratic norms meant to tie down free and fair elections in order to keep out their critics so as to ensure continuity of their respective leadership, Moi leadership believed in the same approach. For example, in 1988 Moi leadership introduced an Amendment in the Constitution to the effect that whoever Moi wanted to be in Parliament to support his undemocratic mode of governance, he made sure that he enables the person to gain a 2/3 of the Nominations (called Primaries in USA election process) and then free that person from going through actual regular elections.

9) And, effective 1989, Moi leadership also introduced a method, akin to that of the ex-British colonial rule and Kenyatta leadership, of staffing Parliament with illiterates who knew the least regarding the art of governance provided that they were able to support continuity of his leadership both in and outside Parliament.[56]

10) Like the British colonial rule and Kenyatta's rule in Kenya which were determined to remain deaf to the general public's cries from within and without Kenya against undemocracy which never allowed participation[1] of majority Kenyans in the political processes of the country by using all sorts of dirty tricks of fooling the general public that their leaderships were for the welfare of all Kenyans, Moi used the same tricks as a means to his ends. For example, although he accepted the World demand in 1991 to repeal Section 2(A) of the Constitution by disbanding a one-party system of governance in Kenya and allow Kenya to adopt a multi-party system of governance in response to the worldwide demand, he did so only in theory but not in practice. Like his predecessors, he kept out opposition parties by refusing them to freely hold political rallies during campaigns. Such rallies had to receive a government licence to take place. But getting this licence was always a too frustrating experience for one to endure. Consequently, most opposition parties went to elections very unprepared. Also, like his predecessors, Moi leadership was so ruthless and cunning that most Kenyans could hardly understand what Moi was actually up to in his leadership particularly now that he had repealed Section 2(A) of the Constitution allowing these oppositions to freely participate in the political process of the country.

11) But, unlike both the British Colonial Rule and the Kenyatta leadership which did not engage in inciting inter-tribal clashes in the country, Moi leadership

---

[1] A good example of this about: (1) In his role as Member of Parliament, Hon. Kariuki Chotara observed that the University of Nairobi was too critical against Moi leadership simply because the University was saturated with Marxism and Communism. He, therefore, called on Kenyan and World leadership to arrest and prosecute this man called Karl Marx for spreading this ideology without knowing that Karl Marx died in 1883 i.e. over one hundred years ago. (ii) Another Member of Parliament nominated by Moi went to Germany on official duty and went on speaking his language to hotel attendants by assuming that Germans understood his language. (iii) And, another Member of Parliament nominated by Moi to support his leadership could not differentiate official mission from private mission. When appointed by Moi Leadership to head a Kenyan Women Delegation to Beijing's World Women Conference, the Member of Parliament went on mobilizing a team of personal assistants to her for various personal affairs such as who will be fixing hair, shoes, etc—a matter that turned out too embarrassing to Kenyan image when such things were discovered in Beijing.

became so fond of this tactics that lots of innocent Kenyans such as the Pokots and Marakwets lost their lives in their hostilities fanned by reckless utterances of politicians and provincial administration officers engineered by the Moi leadership, in order to confuse the direction of the 1992 general election and make it pave the way for continuity of Moi leadership. His goal was, by all these means, achieved and Moi leadership continued unperturbed till it was ousted in the Election of 2002.

12) Like the Kenyatta's leadership which loved frustration of those whom the leadership did not want any more as in the Oginga Odinga's case pf 1966 when Kenyatta created a deliberate havoc to antagonize him by cheating him that his Vice Presidency had been split into four branches in order to make him personally resign and thus gain an indirect way of driving him out of the government, Moi leadership loved the same dirty tricks. Toward the General Elections of the year 2002, he fooled and frustrated all those he did not want to succeed him by denying them a chance of being nominated by the Moi KANU ruling party. Vice President George Saitoti, who by virtue of his vast experience in his long tenure as Vice President was deliberately frustrated and the slot of Presidential Nomination given to a totally inexperienced young man called Uhuru Kenyatta instead—an act that angered Saitoti and all other senior members of KANU party to decamp from KANU and form their own opposition party called the Liberal Democratic Party (LDP) in 2002, which then united with the existing opposition party called National Alliance of Kenya (NAK) party forming the National Alliance Rainbow Coalition (NARC) party that managed to out-wit and defeat Moi in December 2002 and take over the Kenyan leadership.

13) And, like the British Colonial Leadership which looted most Kenya's fertile lands and turned them into personal "white highlands" thereby turning their natural owners into paupers, and destitutes, in Kenya today, the Commission of inquiry into illegal and irregular allocation of Public Land set up in June 2003 by the new NARC Government of President Mwai Kibaki, which came to power effective 1st January 2003, discovered that over 200,000 plots in the country had been irregularly allocated by the previous governments of Kenyatta and Moi dating as far back as the time of Independence in 1963. The

Commission was chaired by Lawyer Paul Ndung'u. The Commission reported that "The abuse of Public land for patronage in the past has undermined Kenya's economic development and democratic rule. It has also caused a major outcry for justice to be done with relation to the past as well as ensure that public assets are safeguarded for future generations."[57]

(d) <u>From Moi Rule to Kibaki Rule (1978-2002)</u>

After the defeat of the Moi leadership in the General Election of the year 2002 by Mwai Kibaki's National Alliance Rainbow Coalition (NARC) party, Kibaki leadership officially commenced effective 1st January 2003.

But although its only one year in office (January-December 2003) it is not enough time to warrant an objective evaluation of its performance, the data out of its one year tenure shows a balanced mode of governance bent on rectifying the ills left behind in Kenya by both the Colonial Rule, Kenyatta leadership and Moi leadership, respectively. Its drastic action to weed out corrupt judges from the Judiciary, followed by its action to sniff out those who actually wanted to suffocate Kenyan nation by looting most of its liquid and fixed assets and take them outside to foreign banks as also witnessed by the proceedings of the Goldenberg International Commission of Inquiry is very encouraging. It is a good hope of Kibaki leadership's aim to rectify the corrupt legacy of the three predecessors.

Notwithstanding this good hope, the data on ground of negative aspect of Kibaki leadership shows the following:

1) Like the British colonial rule, Kenyatta rule and also Moi rule, Kibaki rule is being accused of bending towards nepotism by trying to reiterate what those three leaderships tried to do during their tenures, e.g. by trying to staff his Administration with his cohorts hailing from Mt. Kenya Region whom are now being derogatively referred to as "Mt. Kenya Mafia" due to their <u>ruthless</u> behaviour they seem to display in their political dealings with their NARC party partners.

2) Also, like its three predecessors which did not believe much in <u>pacta sunt servanda</u> (i.e. faithfulness to agreement) with their partners as also witnessed

in Kenyatta's dishonesty to his friends particularly Odinga and Tom Mboya; and Moi's dishonesty to his friends such as Dr. Robert Ouko, George Saitoti, Raila Odinga, Kalonzo Musyoka, Joseph Kamotho and other KANU barons that had always saved Moi leadership from various public accusations of bad governance from within and outside Kenya, Kibaki leadership is also being vehemently accused by its own barons. For example, in his own words, one of these barons, Raila Odinga, lamented about Kibaki's leadership saying that:-

"if you are polygamous, you must love all—otherwise you create a situation you cannot handle.

"Again, when you show your love to only a section of your people, therein lies the problem as chaotic situations are inevitable.

"the problems that had beset the coalition could end if leaders were honest with each other.

"What is happening now is a situation where some leaders are playing their cards under the table".[58]

(e)   <u>A Conclusion</u>

As already noted above, the Kenyan leadership has moved on from the British colonial masters (1885-1963) to Kenyatta (1963-1978) and then to Moi (1978-2002). In the course of this trend, Kenyan leadership went on shedding off certain old values and acquiring on various new leadership cultural values, e.g. in the Administration of Justice in the Judiciary today.

On the whole, however, the main foundation of the leadership still remained the same as most barons of corruption in the country are yet to be brought to book and return all the assets that they had so far looted from the Kenya people.

But since the traditional formula of reward and punishment has never proved enough globally without a structured Dynamic Cultural Engineering of Society with a view to re-educating society in order to cleanse and rehabilitate it from its past dented attitude and desires, it is the ultimate aim to do just that so that Humanity be rescued from this perpetual pathological disease.

This action is necessary if sanity has to be restored to Humanity which had been lost due to man's disobedience and dishonesty to his own good leadership potentials graciously given to him by his own Maker as so witnessed by Prophet Moses in <u>The Holy Scripture</u> under Genesis 1:26. Because of this disobedience and dishonesty, man subjected humanity to leadership immorality, chaos and failures. And, because of these problems, obviously it is not always the man in leadership that suffers the most other than the innocent general public who cannot discern between what is in its left or right hand.

And because of their ignorance certain leaderships such as the Moi leadership do enjoy seeing the innocent suffer. A good case in mind is the Goldenberg International company scandal which forced thousands of innocent Kenyans to suffer through massive retrenchment on false excuse that since foreign donors had denied Kenyans foreign aid, Kenya did not have enough money from taxation alone to pay civil servants' salary. But from the Goldenberg Commission of Inquiry proceedings that investigated the scandal, the data revealed that the true excuse for the retrenchment is that Moi leadership had stolen Kenya's public funds in billions and hid them in foreign banks overseas. The data therefore refutes the Moi leadership's initially alleged excuse of donors withholding of aid to Kenya. Further, such dishonest and disobedient leaderships such as the Moi leadership will always put the innocent to a myriad of other agonies such as those arising from tribal clashes that claimed many Kenyan casualties in deaths and bodily injuries, particularly in the Rift Valley region on purpose to serve the Moi leadership's selfish interest!

CHAPTER V

LEADERSHIP ILLNESSES IN OTHER COUNTRIES

A. A Nagging Question

Bᴜᴛ ɪs ᴛʜɪs ᴀʟᴀʀᴍɪɴɢ disgrace arising from both Political Leadership and Justice Administration illness in Kenya noted in Chapter IV unique to Kenya or is it also universal to other countries globally?

In order to respond adequately to this question either in positive or negative, let us first and foremost turn our research lens from Kenya to other nations such as France and Britain by virtue of their significant role as ex-colonial countries whose leadership and justice administration preceded leadership and justice administration in all independent African countries; and which, therefore, are the sine qua non-foundation and paradigm for political leadership and administration of Justice in Kenya and entire African Continent.

1. LEADERSHIP ILLNESS IN FRANCE (Napoleon I, 1769-1821)

(1) A Striking Signal about Napoleon I

In order for a reader to understand and appreciate who and what Napoleon actually was and why he behaved as he did in political life as a leader, it is advisable that one takes time to first and foremost reflect on the following quotations from him (Napoleon) before he ever entered the leadership arena:

"When I see an empty throne, I feel the urge to sit on it!"

(2) His Birth and Political Development

Also nicknamed <u>Le Petit Caporal</u>, i.e. the little corporal because of his courage and short stature slightly below average height of all men, Napoleon was born on August 15, 1769 at Ajaccio, on the island of Corsica in the Mediterranean Sea which was at that time a French sphere of influence.

He was the second son of Carlo Maria de Bounaparte (re-named Bonaparte in English Language) and Letizia Ramolino, an Italian noble family. His father was a lawyer by profession.

In March 1796, he married a Creole from the West Indies named Josephine de Beauharnais whose husband had been guillotined two years earlier because of his opposition to the coup d'etat in France by Robespiere whose revolutionary government came to power through such means.

Though born in a French colony whose determination was to get rid of French colonialism and declare self-rule, Napoleon had a father whose vision was to stick to France whose policy would benefit himself and his family members. As such, Napoleon's father sent this little boy (Napoleon) to a French military school (at Brienne) where Napoleon spent a few months learning French before entering school at 10 years of age.

Thereafter, Napoleon transferred to the royal military school in Paris where he graduated. And, at 16 years of age, he was commissioned as a second lieutenant of artillery in January 1786.

He joined the artillery regiment and by three months, he had already gone through the ranks of <u>private</u>, <u>corporal</u>, and <u>sergeant</u>.

Napoleon was determined to master as much military <u>strategies</u> as he could manage in the shortest span possible for his future hidden agenda.

At first, he was bent on using these strategies to free his home island of Corsica from the French colonial rule. He then took many months of leave on Corsica Island where the nationalists, Pasquale Paoli, sought to lead a revolution for independence in 1789.

Although he took part in the revolt, Napoleon differed with its leader (Paoli) and then returned to Paris in the French Army in which he rose to the rank of Captain in the year 1792.

But all along, Napoleon was neither satisfied nor settled in his mind on what was actually going on in the French political leadership.

Although French monarchy had been toppled by the French revolution of 1792, in 1794, that revolutionary regime led by Robespierre fell from power. The French people who had been under the <u>Convention</u> form of government under Robespierre revolutionary regime now no longer wanted it. They again wanted the monarchy to come back.

With Napoleon's talented military skills, Royalism was defeated and Napoleon made his way up to the centre of power.

The Directory succeeded the Convention as the new government of France headed by Vicomte de Barras and Napoleon as Barras' assistant.

On 5th October 1795, a "Red Letter Date" was declared in the history of France.

In as much as it was the D-Day for Royalism to be put to an end in France so was it also the D-Day for Napoleon to rise to power. And as soon as the Directory succeeded the Convention as the government of France Napoleon gradually began to pave his way up by grabbing power from Barras.

Two days after his marriage, Napoleon left Paris for Italy to drive out Austrian Army which was occupying Italy.

In 1797, he arrived in Italy and drove out the Austrian army by the Peace Treaty of Campo Formio. Thereafter in 1798, he invaded Egypt, a Turkish province, to avenge insults to French merchants. With 35,000 man military expedition, Napoleon defeated the Mamelukes army.

But in the Battle of Aboukir Bay where Napoleon's French fleet had anchored, Lord Nelson's British fleet followed Napoleon and destroyed his fleet. Because of that defeat, Turkey, Britain, Russia and Austria formed an alliance and declared war on France but Napoleon escaped from Egypt and safely reached Paris.

After escaping Egypt and reaching Paris, Napoleon seized power from his boss in the <u>coup d'Etat</u> of Eighteenth Brumaire on 9th November 1799.

After grabbing power, Napoleon abolished the Directorate and set up a new government of three members called <u>The Consulate</u> with him as First Consul.

In other words, Napoleon did not only grab power through a coup d'etat but also abolished both royalism or monarchy and democracy of the Convention and Directory respectively and concentrated all power in himself.

Napoleon immediately embarked on various reforms in France. He codified the French law into what is known in France as La Code Napoleon and what is now the basis of the French law.

In 1800, Napoleon set up a Bank of France. In 1801, he negotiated the Concordat of 1801 with Pope Pius VII which ended the prevailing confusion of church-state relations caused by the French Revolution. And, in 1802, he founded the French Legion of Honour to honour soldiers and civilians alike for their impressive service to their motherland France.

But because Austria still occupied Northern Italy due to allied forces there from Britain, Russia, and Turkey, Napoleon sought ways of getting more funds for these wars of conquests.

In 1803, he sold Louisiana to USA.

In order to do all he sought to do unquestioned, Napoleon renounced the title of "First Consul for Life" which the French people had voted him for in 1802. And, in May 1804, the French Senate voted him to the title of <u>Emperor</u>.

And, on 2nd December 1804, the coronation ceremony was held at Notre Dame Cathedral. But as soon as the Pope took the crown to crown him, Napoleon grabbed the crown and placed it on his own head to show the people that he himself had won the right to wear it. Thereafter, he also crowned his wife, Josephine as his Empress.

Napoleon was a unique military leader in that he combined his training with his own zeal and uncontrollable urge for power.

However, he re-organized France in that he guided French internal affairs as he directed his army. He set up a strong central government and appointed prefects to head territorial areas, which he called Departments. He re-organized the education system and founded the Imperial University. His measures later resulted into a breakdown between the French government and the Roman Catholic Church.

(3) <u>Object of War, Victory and Conquest</u>

In all his military preoccupations, Napoleon believed in OCCUPATION as the ultimate goal of war. To him, the object of war was "victory"; the object of victory was "conquest" and the object of conquest was "occupation".

In this regard, Napoleon saw in 1805 the new alliance between Britain, Sweden, Prussia, Austria and Russia against France and Spain as a real threat to France and his own Empire which he must destroy. He therefore decided to concentrate on the mainland enemies: Russia, Austria, Sweden and Prussia.

He then crushed Russian and Austrian armies at the Battle of Austerlitz on 2/12/1805 and forced them to sign the Peace of Pressburg.

Believing that occupation was his real goal which he must achieve first in order for him to be safe in Europe of his enemies, Napoleon sought to occupy all Europe for France, e.g.

a.   He made his brother Joseph king of Naples.

b.   He made his brother Louis king of Holland.

c.   He also made his sisters sovereigns in Naples and Tuscany.

d.   He carved the provinces of Germany and Italy into principalities and dukedoms and awarded them to his favourite generals, marshals and other politically correct persons.

e.   He abolished the Holy Roman Empire.

f.   He created a confederation of the Rhine consisting of German western states under his own supervision.

g.   On 14/10/1806, he defeated the Prussian armies and entered Berlin en route to Russia.

h.   At the same time (14/10/1806), he forced Prussia into signing a Berlin Decree banning all British goods in Europe.

i.   Portugal which had been a good friend of Britain for hundred years, and which had refused to obey Napoleon's Berlin Decree on British goods ban was summarily occupied by French army in 1807.

j.   Spain was invaded and

  i. Spain's king Ferdinand VII was removed from the throne.

  ii. Napoleon appointed his own brother Joseph as king of Spain.

  iii.   Marshall Joachim Murat whose French army had invaded Spain, took Joseph's place as king of Naples.

(4)   <u>Beginning of Napoleon's Leadership Disasters and Failures</u>

First, Napoleon was faced with the psychological problem prompting marital life. He had not received any child with the empress Josephine, and Josephine was not faithful too. He, therefore, abandoned his empress to marry another woman who could give him a child to succeed him.

Secondly, in 1807, the British invaded Spain forcing Napoleon's brother king Joseph Bonaparte to flee from Madrid.

Thirdly, although Napoleon had now signed a treaty of alliance with Russia in 1807, but Czar Alexander I of Russia had not fully honoured the Berlin Decree banning British goods in all Russian posts.

Fourthly, when Napoleon army sought to teach Czar Alexander I a lesson for non-compliance, most Russian forces safely escaped eastwards and destroyed most of its valuables that French forces had little to gain from Russia as a punishment to the disobedient Russia.

Fifthly, all these disasters began to prove an explicit end of Napoleon's leadership in Europe.

Sixthly, as Napoleon's Grand Army tried to make it back home without enough food and energy as Russians had already set fire on everything including foodstuffs in Moscow, the French army of over 600,000 men, 500,000 or so died of hunger, snow storms, long journey and attacking enemy armies called the SWARMS OF COSSACKS.

Seventhly, when Napoleon struggled to rush back to Paris to organize for a new army before news reached Paris from Russia and Europe regarding all those Napoleon disasters, unfortunately this news got to Paris before Napoleon was able to put together a new army to go and reinforce the old one still on the way back home.

Eighthly, due to this news the already defeated countries were now able to raise army and collectively intercept the remnants of Napoleon's Grand Army and to finish it off on the way.

Ninthly, although Napoleon was able to raise a new army and defeat all allied armies of Russia, Britain, Prussia, Spain and Sweden in Lutzen, Bautzen, and Dresden, Napoleon was no longer able to match the growing strength of his enemies' armies.

Tenthly, in October 1813, he failed to defeat them in the Battle of the Nations.

And by the power of the Duke of Wellington's army from south against Paris, Napoleon was totally finished at the battle of Waterloo.

(5) Rise of European Nationalism

Napoleon's shocking aggression precipitated the rise of nationalism in Europe against future acts of aggression. Every country in Europe was angry at France. Prussia now sought to recover her Rhine from Napoleon's France.

(6) Death of Napoleon

Shocked and tired of such aggression, Napoleon's friends and allies began to leave him alone. Napoleon himself begun to realize his own faults; but already the damage had been done.

In April 1814, he acknowledged that reality. Consequently, the French Senate called for a return of their old Bourbon king to the French throne, which the French Military commanders pressed for Napoleon's resignation (abdication) from the throne.

On 11th April 1814, Napoleon consented and abdicated the throne at Fontainebleau. And, Louis XVIII was returned home to France and crowned King of France.

Napoleon was exiled to a small island of Elba off the coast of Italy in the Mediterranean Sea where he was allowed to act as its ruler. But in February 1815, he managed to escape and march back to Paris in a year's time forcing King Louis XVIII to flee from Paris calling on Allies to rescue him and Paris from the dreadful hand of Napoleon.

From that February 1815, Napoleon again ruled France as its Emperor for a total period of 100 days. Throughout those 100 days, Napoleon battled for his supremacy in France against the Allied forces of Britain, Prussia, Russia, Austria, Spain, Norway, etc. whose aim was to oust him from the French throne and reinstate King Louis XVIII.

Although Napoleon had shown much military strength in a number of battles, he was finally finished at the Battle of Waterloo.

Napoleon fled from Waterloo to Paris and wanted to escape to USA. But the British army caught him. He surrendered to the captain of the British warship at Rochefort on July 15, 1815.

The Allied forces took him to England as a prisoner of war and later exiled him to St. Helena Island in west coast of Africa where he died of cancer on 5 May 1821.

He was buried on that island but in 1840 the French government collected his remains and buried him in the dome called "Eglise du Dome" (or "Church of the Dome" in English).

7)   <u>Reactions of Nations to correct Napoleon's Leadership Errors</u>

Napoleon's defeat and death was of a great sigh of relief to entire Europe, including France, Napoleon's home country he sought to expand at all cost.

In 1814, Europeans diplomats met in the Congress of Vienna to correct most of Napoleon's mistakes. But this effort was disrupted by Napoleon's escape from Elba Island and renewal of fight for the throne in Paris. Even when Napoleon was finally defeated, Alsace and Lorraine districts were left to France. But all this caused Franco-Prussian war of 1870-71 in which Germany seized it in 1870 claiming that the two areas belonged to it. The same has been the cause of World War I (1914-18).

The Treaty of Versailles returned Alsace and Lorraine to France thereby enabling France to continue to extend its territory to the Rhine.

In 1936, Germany under Adolf Hitler repudiated this agreement and began to militarise the region arguing that the region had been its own till 30 years War when it was taken from it by France.

During World War II beginning in 1938, up to the end of that war in 1945, the area was the main battlefield between the Allies and the Axis.

After the war, the area is again a region of all in the area as well as their obvious root-cause of future war.

2.   LEADERSHIP PROBLEM IN ENGLAND

(a)   POPE LEO X (1475-1521)

Pope Leo X was born in Florence, Italy on 11th December, 1475 as Giovanni de Medici. He was a second son of Lorenzo the Magnificent. His father wanted him to join an ecclesiastical (church) career. Consequently, the father prevailed on Pope Innocent VIII to create him a cardinal, who also agreed and secretly did so on 9th March, 1489.

When the Medici was expelled from Florence, the young cardinal spent some years travelling to France, Germany, and Asia Minor.

He developed friendly terms with Pope Julius II because of the latter's anti-French policy; and used the Pope's victory over the French in Florence to restore the Medici there in 1512.

On Pope Julius' death, Cardinal Giovanni de Medici was elected Pope on 11th March 1513. But, it was not until after his election as pope that he was ordained a priest and consecrated a bishop.

Pope Leo X inherited two crucial roles viz: (1) the Fifth Lateran Council whose goal was to bring some reform in the church but failed to do so and then died off in 1517. (2) The Indulgence policy which Pope Julius II had used to raise funds for the construction of the new St. Peter's Basilica in Rome. In 1515, he authorized the preaching of this policy in the dioceses of Mainz and Magdeburg where such preaching by Johann Tetzel provoked Dr. Martin Luther so much that the latter decided to publish his 95 Theses in the late 1517 denouncing the essence of the Indulgence—an act which also provoked Pope Leo X so much that on 15th June 1520, the Pope issued his bull called "Exsurge Domine", condemning Luther on 41 counts. In turn, Dr. Luther retaliated by burning the bull on 10th December, 1520, followed by the Pope's counter-retaliation by excommunicating him from the Roman Catholic Communion.

In addition to this indulgence war with Dr. Luther, Pope Leo X found himself also engaged in another costly war in which he sought to forcefully remove Francesco Maria della Rovere as duke of Urbine and to instead install his own nephew called Lorenzo de Medici in his place—an act of nepotism which proved the Pope a man of bias leadership.

In 1520, Pope Leo X awarded King Henry VIII of England the title of "Fidei Defensor" (i.e. Defender of the Faith) for publication of the King's religious views expressed in the Statute of Six Articles contained in his pamphlet he had written in support of the Pope's condemnation of Lutheranism—a stand which King Henry VIII had taken while he was still in good accord.

But no sooner had the same King ran into a fierce discord with the Pope after the latter could not grant him leaf to divorce his brother's widow, Catherine of Aragon, and then marry his palace maid, Anne Beloyn, whom the King hoped could bear him a male heir that Catherine had proved unable to do, than the King turned tail against the Pope and his own Statute of Six Articles against Lutheranism.

a) <u>Root-cause of His Leadership Failures</u>

1. <u>Luther's "Tower Experience"</u>

While meditating on his study tower the issue of this Indulgence with a view of understanding what it is was all about in terms of its actual meaning and significance to man in spiritual life between Man and God, Dr. Luther remembered the warning of Apostle Paul to the Romans to the effect that "The just shall live by his faith" (Romans 1:17). From this warning, Luther came to realize the fallacy of the Pope in Rome since according to this Paul's stern warning, the sacraments and works of the church would not and cannot in and by themselves alone suffice one's salvation because by nature man is corrupt. Thus, he came to summarize that it is only abundant mercy and grace of God that can and would lead one to salvation. If so, then the Pope must be in error, and is therefore bent to exploit the church for his good at the expense of their ignorance of the truth.

(2) <u>Luther's Revolt against Indulgence</u>

This discovery automatically laid a solid foundation for Luther's excuse to revolt against the Pope over this Indulgence.

(a) <u>The Roman Catholic Doctrine of Indulgence</u>

To Roman Catholic dogma contends that if a sinner confesses his/her sin, that sinner would first receive partial forgiveness from God through the sacrament of penance while still alive on earth and the remainder through purgatory after death where one's soul is made fully pure to enter heaven.

Accordingly, according to this dogma, Indulgence was a true remission of part or all of both punishments (in penance and in purgatory).

To the Roman Catholic faith, the Indulgence was thus a justified spiritual exercise since Jesus Christ and His saints through their infinite eternal goodness built and left behind a treasury of merit to the Pope, in his capacity as successor of Jesus Christ and these saints, to dispense grace to sinners who accept to do indulgence in return.

In this regard, Indulgence came to be used by the Pope in specific ways:

(i)   to reward those who had fought in the Crusades to liberate the Holy Sepulchre in Jerusalem and The Holy Land in the entire Palestine from the Moslem and other enemies of The Christian Communion effective Pope Urban II's arousing sermon in November 1095 at The Council of Clermont calling for noble listeners to take up arms against those Moslem enemies right up to the surrender of the last crusader stronghold in the year 1291.

(ii)   And, to reward those who contributed money in lieu of participation in direct fighting.

(b)   <u>Indulgence as a Lucrative Source of Funds for The Church in Rome</u>

Through the stewardship of Pope Leo X, the Indulgence became a most lucrative source of funds for the Church in Rome, and to other ecclesiastical and secular centres throughout the Roman Empire in which the Roman Catholic Church was the centre of Christian faith and worship.

As a result, indulgences became an easiest way of purchasing forgiveness of sins or of shortening the time in purgatory for those on whose behalf indulgences were purchased either by the self or the third party.

And, in Germany in particular where the importance of ecclesiastical activities were second to those in Rome, sale of indulgences was intensified in Germany and the rest of Europe as part of the collections was retained to take care of the expenses in Germany, which served as the centre through which all collected proceedings passed before these proceedings reached Rome.

As Archbishop of Mainz, Albert of Brandenburg was the Pope's principal agent of the collections in Europe whose functions had to be financed by part of the collected indulgences in Europe.

c)   <u>Significant Factors/Forces Leading to Dr. Luther's Decisive Victory Against Indulgence and Pope Leo X's Destructive Mode of Church Leadership in Rome:</u>

(i)   Luther's Rebellion against Indulgence—Hawking in Europe

Dr. Martin Luther was no more amused by what appeared to him nonsensical Indulgence—Hawking in Europe under the umbrella of Pope Leo X in the centre of Christiandom. In Brandenburg, a Dominican friar called Johann Tetzel was the papal representative responsible for this hawking that kindled so much anger in Dr. Luther that on 31st October 1517, Dr. Luther posted a list of 95 Theses as a protest against Indulgences, on the north portal of the Castle Church in Wittenberg.

(ii)   Luther's 95 Theses against Indulgence

Although a protest, the Theses were initially a Latin-written document calling for a scholarly audience to debate on the spiritual merits of the Indulgence Hawking, which according to Luther was a total insult to the Christian Faith.

But, no sooner had these Theses been translated into German language than their knowledge spread all over Germany and the entire Roman Empire. And, when this occurred, the whole Roman Empire was in arms against the Papal Supremacy in Rome, and his obvious abuse of that supremacy.

(iii)   The Diet of Augsburg and Augustinian's
        (October 1518)

Before Pope Leo X could reply to Luther's 95 Theses, the Dominican Order quickly intervened to fiercely assail Luther and his Theses in support of their fellow Dominican Johann Tetzel, the papal agent for Indulgence Hawking in Germany. And, in October 1518, Luther was summoned by the Pope to appear for questioning before a general of the Dominican Order, Cardinal Cajetan, who tried to make Luther change his opposition against the exercise. <u>But Luther flatly refused to do so arguing that the Pope could also be wrong in matters of faith.</u>

(iv)   The Augustinians' Support to Luther against the Pope's Bad Mode of Church
        Leadership

The Augustinians, who were the rivals of the Dominican Order, came to Luther's support calling for a reform in the Christian Church in retaliation to the Pope's Bad Leadership in The Church of Christ.

Luther is Protected by Frederick The Wise of Saxony (1518-1519)

The failure of the interview between Luther and Cardinal Cajetan attracted certain significant political leaders such as Frederick the Wise, the elector of Saxony (i.e. one of the Germany prince qualified to participate in the election of an Emperor in the Roman Empire).

Obviously, Luther was very lucky for such intervention as the elector refused to banish Luther from his homeland under his political jurisdiction. Also, Luther was fortunate as the Pope could no longer put pressure for his banishing as the Pope did not wish to do so as this could have jeopardized the Pope's chance of obtaining Frederick's support against the election of the Basburg Charles of Spain as Holy Roman Emperor in the forthcoming election in 1519.

(vi) Luther's stand is sustained by Various Forces of The Time (1519)

By His Convincing Debate with ECK (July 1519)

In July 1519, Luther held a convincing debate with a German theologian Eck at Leipzig where he disproved beyond any reasonable doubt to the audience the divine origin of the Papacy; and strongly defended validity of the doctrines of Jan Hun (1369-1415), a Czeck within Bohemia, who had been sadly burnt at Stake jointly by Pope John XXIII and Emperor, Sigmund of Bohemia (1415) because of Hun's condemnation of Indulgences.

According to Luther, Huns' execution was evil since Hun's doctrines were spiritually and morally good for Humanity as they were inspired by the doctrines of John Wycliffe (1328-1384), an Oxford theologian, scholastic philosopher and popular preacher whose thread aims were:

- To dismantle distasteful corrupt practices inherent in the European medieval culture, e.g. clerics' venality (vulnerability to bribe and bribery), absenteeism, immunity from civil justice, and various other immoral behaviours, which, in turn, were the root-cause of the soulnessness of society;

- To reject and correct the existing Catholic dogma of transubstantiation which held that bread and wine of Eucharist were miraculously and entirely transformed into Christ body and blood, respectively; and

- To save the Church from those man-made impurities by abolishing confession, excommunication, pilgrimages, indulgences, and veneration of clerics.

Luther further argued that by excommunicating and executing Hun simply because of Hun's opposition to Indulgences, which the Pope desperately wanted to use in order to raise money for his war against the King of Naples, obviously both Pope John XXIII and Emperor Sigmund had done no good to themselves, their leaderships and the Church other than an irreversible sin against themselves, their leaderships and the church as a whole. The innocent blood of Jan Hun was now on their heads and that it was going to haunt them throughout their lives.

Drawing from the distinction between the following two treaties by John Wycliffe viz <u>On Civil Dominion</u> and <u>On Divine Dominion</u>, Luther consented with both Wycliffe and Hus that Medieval Church leadership had grossly errored by usurping the role Civil Dominion in having land and other property endowed to the church while this was not expected to be its role. Also, he further argued, that Church clerics had no business in temporal office-holding as this was solely a role of the Civil Dominion, in keeping with God's wish who granted earthly powers to the earthly state.

By Increasing Intervention by Luther's Fellow Monks in support of Luther's stand

Luther's inspiring debate with Eck at Leipzig attracted the attention of so many other monks who also now recognized the fallacy of Pope Leo X's leadership and Indulgence.

By Luther's Electrifying Pamphlets on the Doctrine of Justification by Faith but not by Indulgences

Between 1518 and 1520 alone, Luther published a great number of electrifying pamphlets in which he clearly refined his definition of salvation by one's Faith but not by one's purchases of Indulgences as so purported by The Pope in Rome, and called for an immediate reform in the Church leadership structure as a remedy to the existing anomalies in the Church.

By Luther's Reformation Treaties (1520)

In 1520, Luther published additional but much more specific line of action or way forward documents which he called Reformation Treaties e.g.

<u>The Address to The German Nobility</u> whose aim was to appeal to the German nobility to create their own reformed German Church in order to end the earthly conduct of the Church in Rome aimed at abusing its leadership role.

<u>The Babylonian Captivity</u> whose aim was to call for the reduction of the number of sacraments from the man-made seven to the original two as so commanded by God. In this Treatise, Luther accused the Roman Catholic Church Leadership of mischief because of having over-looked these two number of God-given sacraments by increasing the number to seven which included veneration of saints, indulgence practice, interdicts (denying a faithful spiritual services e.g. during burial, partaking of Holy Communion, etc. due to one's conceived misbehaviour or unethical act contrary to Church doctrine) and mandatory priestly celibacy.

<u>The Freedom of the Christian Man</u> whose aim was not only to spell out the value of good works but to also spell out the supremacy of one's faith as a mandatory basis of one's good works, but not vice versa. In this Treatise, Luther argued that only The Bible was the only supreme source of one's faith and good works but The Church Leadership as the latter may pollute God's Word and therefore mislead one to do what is not acceptable to God and hence disqualifying one from entering Heavenly Kingdom.

By Luther's Burning of The Papal Bull (1520)

In June 1520, Pope Leo X issued a papal bull giving Luther a period of sixty days by which he was to renounce his doctrines against Rome if he were to survive an excommunication.

In response, Luther also burnt the bull as his own publication had also been done so in Rome.

By Luther's Appeal to the Holy Roman Emperor Charles V

Convinced that he was in the right and that the Pope was in the wrong, Luther defied the Pope's bull and instead resolved to appeal to The Holy Roman Emperor Charles V, an uncle of Queen Catherine of Aragon, wife of King Henry VIII of England whom the latter had inherited from his deceased brother, Arthur, in 1509.

By Luther's Survival of The Diet of Worms' Martyrdom (1521)

Emperor Charles V consented to Luther's appeal and required this appeal hearing to take place at Worms in April of the following year (1521) before the Electors of the Diet of Worms.

Before the Diet of Worms, Luther stuck to his original stand in support of his view that Indulgence was a violation of the Teaching of Jesus Christ contained in The Holy Bible; and therefore, that it was not him but the Pope who was in error on the issue.

In his own words, Luther continued to re-affirm his stand to the Diet of Worms:

"Here I stand. I cannot do otherwise!" But because of the existing triangular relations between the Emperor and King Charles VIII by marriage (due to Queen Catherine of Aragon's blood relations with the Emperor and her marital relations with the King as his wife) on the one hand; and also good relations between the King and the Pope on the other, and the Pope and the Emperor in the latter's capacity as The Emperor of the Holy Roman Empire, Luther lost appeal and was therefore sentenced to a ban throughout the Empire by the Diet.

But, by divine grace of God to whom Luther was serving and was to serve in his future life, Luther miraculously escaped the Diet's martyrdom plan. He was fortunately kidnapped by Frederick's secretly arranged agents who hid him in their private premise at Wartburg Castle where Luther remained for approximately one year.

By Luther's divine Efforts of Translating The New Testament of The Holy Bible

During his hide out at Wartburg, Luther wisely spent his confinement time and translated the New Testament from Greek to the German vernacular so that the congregation may be able to discover for themselves the truth Luther was defending against The Pope's Indulgence policy vis-à-vis salvation qualifications.

By Killing Two Birds with One Stone

Whereas Luther's ultimate goal in translating the Bible was to enable the Germans and the rest of the World Christian Communion discover for themselves the truth against the Indulgence policy, Luther realized later that his translated German Bible became a sine qua non of the German vernacular—a serendipity that he had not dreamed of before.

By His efforts at University of Wittenberg (1521)

While still in a hide-out at Wartburg Castle, Luther learnt that his doctrine had been able to accelerate throughout Germany and the rest of Europe with the University of Wittenberg as its booster.

And, in the late 1521, Luther was able to get to that university and add more oil on his already burning doctrine against the Papal Church misrule.

By His Insistence on Justification by One's Faith as The Only Valid Qualification for Salvation

Unlike the Roman Catholic dogma that insisted on seven sacraments, including Indulgence, Luther argued that One's Faith was the only required qualification for one to receive Salvation, and that one's works were, only a function of One's Faith! First, one has to have faith as a base for one's good works. Then through this faith—good work—faith circulation (rotation) one's salvation is hereby assured. Otherwise, one good works such as the buying of Indulgences would in no way lead one into Salvation because such works would not be classified as good works, meriting God's salvation.

By his stern and Convincing Reason on The Meaning and Character of The Eucharist

Whereas according to the Roman Catholic Church leadership in Rome, the bread and wine are miraculously transformed during the Mass into the body and blood of Christ, and that this miracle of transubstantiation can only be performed by ordained priests, Luther, on the other hand, held that no such miracle does occur. To him, Christ is nonetheless present in the natural substance of the bread and wine. He called this process "consubstantiation".

Also, contrary to the Roman Catholic's policy emphasizing ordained priests as the only partakers of the wine, Luther allowed everyone in the congregation to partake both wine and bread during the Eucharist which Luther renamed "The Lord's Supper" or "The Holy Communion".

By his stern stand on The Concept of "Priesthood"

Whereas according to the Roman Catholic Church leadership, Priesthood is a special function strictly reserved for a certain class of elite trained and ordained for that service, to dispense sacraments and interpret the Bible to the congregation, Luther sternly objected to this idea arguing that each individual had the right and potentials to know God on his own and confront God for his own salvation.

Accordingly, he believed that "priesthood" was for every believer. In other words, Luther called this phenomenon a "Priesthood of All Believers". He also believed that there neither ought to be hearing of confessions by priests nor monasteries and a monasticism culture.

It was due to this last argument that made Luther abandon his monk's career in 1524 and in 1525 got married to Katherine von Bora, a one time nun, who, like Luther had also abandoned her nun career (vocation).

By His Stern Argument that the Bible is the sole Authority

Luther's bad experience with the Papal mis-interpretation of the Bible and insistence to retain the Bible and its interpretation as a monopoly thereby keeping the entire innocent congregation in a perpetual darkness, for the sole purpose of exploiting them with the fallacies of Indulgences and other policies, led Luther to argue that The Bible was the only sole Authority since it is the only document which contains God's Word. And, that because of its sole strategic importance to every person, each individual ought to have an access to a Bible. In this regard, Luther emphasized that in the manner he had translated it from Greek to German language, the same should be done in every Language in order to enable every community have a copy in its own language.

Finally, Luther argued that due to this cardinal truth, the Pope should no longer try to tie the congregation's hands from doing so, or try to force his own interpretation of the Bible down their throats. Either way, the Pope's decrees (papal bulls) conciliar decrees, writing of church fathers and other authorities should no longer be held too sacred to be questioned, now that the congregation has also witnessed the papal fallacies of Indulgence policy.

<u>By his Influence to the Creation of his Lutheran Church</u>

All these forces stated above collectively resulted into the creation of a reformed church called "Lutheran Church". Luther's battles with the Pope Leo X's church leadership in Rome and throughout the Roman Empire, collectively became a womb in which the Lutheran Church we witness today was born. Short of these battles and the ineptitude and misrule of Pope Leo X in Rome, nothing of this phenomenon could have occurred by chance alone.

2) POLITICAL CONSEQUENCES ARISING FROM LUTHER'S VICTORY OVER THE MISRULE & INEPTITUDE OF POPE LEO'S CHURCH LEADERSHIP (1521)

From December 1521 onwards, radical reformers at Wittenberg University and its environs incited the innocent common people to riot in protest against bad mode of church leadership under Pope Leo X.

In these riots, sacred religious images were destroyed. Also, innocent priests' personal security was in danger.

Although Luther personally began preaching a series of sermons effective 1522 aimed at watering down the use of violence as means of dismantling Roman Catholic dogmas and rites in Germany, Luther's initiative was not a contraceptive against violence, e.g.

(1) The German Knight's War

German Knights became the first group to exploit Luther's original revolutionary religious concepts and aims in their capacity as a minor among major noble land owners such as the German princes who held a monopoly of greatest influence on behalf of the Papal supremacy in Germany. The Knights vehemently resented this existing situation and therefore accepted Luther's concepts and aims as means of reversing this agonising situation and of seizing territories and wealth endowed to the Catholic Church.

In 1522, they joined with Franz von Sickingen to attack the archbishop of Trier whom they considered as the most powerful territorial prince in the country as a necessary stepping stone to capturing those endowments.

(2) The German Peasants' War

Two years later (in 1524), a bloody Peasants' War started throughout the southern region of Germany echoing Luther's doctrine that "Before God all human beings were equal", and that for that reason, they too needed equality, so that they could be liberated from their long lived suppression relative deprivation and frustration caused by the Roman Catholic Policy of forced taxation to subscribe to the Pope's Indulgence policy in Rome.

In 1525, for example, this revolt became evident in their publication of <u>Twelve Articles</u> containing a list of grievances calling for an overhaul of their existing socio-economic culture and structure which was beset with agonizing serfdom, excessive feudal dues and services aimed at servicing the Papal Indulgences in Rome through the archbishop of Trier who was the Pope's agent based in Germany for this very purpose, death tax, excessive church tithes, imposed church pastor able to preach to the congregation from his own view other than directly from the Bible. Succinctly, their <u>Twelve Articles</u> called for an immediate end of this serfdom; reduction of feudal dues and services; abolition of this death tax; reduction of church tithes,; and freedom of every community in Germany to choose its own church pastor who is able to preach directly from the Bible but who is not a puppet of the Pope seated in Rome only sent to Germany to dictate the wishes of the Pope such as the Indulgence policy.

The consequences of all these new developments in Germany resulting from the Papal leadership poverty in Rome were obviously too agonising to the innocent German masses in their country—a situation which could not have occurred at all had there not been this poverty mode of Leadership.

Beginning from Northern Germany, Lutherans began to replace Catholicism at a greatest speed. By 1525, Lutheranism had displaced Catholicism as a recognised national faith in most Germany principalities and later became also a recognized national religion throughout Denmark, Sweden, Norway, Iceland and Finland at a highly costly price in blood-letting.

Another political symptom of the adverse consequences of the Pope's leadership poverty was manifested in the loss of the Papal supremacy in Germany and all Scandinavian countries. In Germany, for instance, only a few German princes opted to embrace Lutheranism as a religion. According to most German princes, the new religion was seen as their good omen toward a miraculous God's manna to them. Damping Catholicism in favour of Lutheranism was a stupendous socio-economic and political gain for them, as this would automatically place them at the helm of their respective territories as political sovereigns, and also make them heads of their territorial Lutheran churches.

Another significant socio-economic and political gain from this dramatic change was that each was going to confiscate all monasteries and their respective endowment. By so doing, each prince was now going to be able to have absolute political control over all church revenues at the expense of the Pope and the Roman Empire Emperor since the latter's supremacy was no longer alive.

A third symptom of this dramatic socio-economic and political climate further manifested in a mood of a stupendous joy among the German town dwellers particularly the guild class who now also scrambled to embrace Lutheranism and use the same as their stepping stone to shake off their long-lived agonies of poverty.

The only community left behind in a messy situation of Catholicism was the rich bourgeoisie who perceived no gain other than a loss in Lutheranism and therefore resolved to remain in Catholicism as their only rational choice.

(3) The Pope-Emperor's Joint War against Lutheran Converts (1530)

This sweeping wind of change infuriated both the Pope and the Emperor Charles V so much that the two colluded to use military force against the peasants and their new Lutheran faith.

However, this failed to materialize due to the Emperor's more critical problem from France and Turkey.

But in 1546, Charles V used his powerful Spanish army to smash the Lutheran princes and their city allies who had in 1531 jointly formed a Schmalkaldic League as a containment mechanism to protect them from the Emperor and the Pope. And, in 1547, Charles V defeated the League. Whereas this had proved a decisive victory for both the Emperor and the Pope, the latter could no longer continue with the war as the

Emperor later realized that he was no longer financially able to sustain further wars with the Lutherans.

(4) The Peace of Ausburg (1555)

Because of this financial inadequacy on the emperor's part, the Emperor conceded to a dialogue with the Lutherans.

The Emperor called on the German Diet (a body consisting of eligible voters in Germany mandated to sit and participate in a body responsible for electing officials of the Empire, e.g. the Emperor, the Pope and Cardinals) to convene a peace dialogue and recommend to him a viable solution between the two conflicting parties.

This compromise culminated into what we know today as The Peace of Augsburg, in 1555.

The Peace of Augsburg recognized the individual right of each German territorial prince to choose its own religion of choice between Lutheranism and Catholicism as its national religion, gave the right to every German subject to move to one's territory of religious interest should one's residential territory choose a religion which is not of one's choice, awarded Lutherans legal right to assume titles to all endowments forcefully taken from the Catholic Church before 1552, and guaranteed the Lutheran Church a permanent security in the Roman Empire.

(5) The Amazing Contagious Efficacy of Lutheranism against Catholicism due to Papal Leadership Poverty*

Between 1530 and the year 1546 when the Emperor finally resolved to use his Spanish military might against Lutheran princes and their cities' partners (known as the Schmalkaldic League) and defeated them in 1547, the Emperor had repeatedly pressed on Pope Leo X to convene a church council and correct the existing Indulgence policy and other anomalies in the Church Leadership, without any success.

But no sooner had the Emperor now resolved to give up his Spanish military expeditions against Lutheranism in the Empire—a decision that had resulted into the Peace of Augsburg of 1555,—than the following various other intellectual forces mushroomed all over Europe to also benefit or take advantage of the new conducive weather at the expense of the dying Catholicism:-

(a) Ulrich Zwingli (1484-1531), a Swiss theologian and humanism philosopher, began to preach the need for a Catholic Church reform as far back as 1519. He embraced Luther's stance that only faith and the Bible alone are the true sources of religious truth; that only each individual other than church clerics has the sole right to interpret the Bible to one's understanding and to administer the sacraments for him, and finally that there are only two legitimate sacraments viz: Baptism and the Lord's Supper but not seven as so claimed by The Roman Catholic Church Leadership.

(b) John Calvin (1509-1564), a French theologian and reformer, added another oil on the already glowing fire of Protestantism against the Roman Catholicism because of the latter's crude Leadership. Calvin emphasized ritual simplicity and strict moral discipline by every one who seeks to enter and enjoy God's everlasting life. He called on each to play the role of an elect by policing over one's own acts as one's way forward "predestination" toward that needed eternal life. Calvin further called for State's subordination to the Church and that only the spiritually and morally eschewed clergy are fit to interpret the law and police over the acts of a state.

Calvin's work spread all over the continent like fire. Many flocked and gathered in Geneva to receive an amazing Calvinist doctrine from his newly founded Academy (1559) and then return back home to also spread around Protestantism. In Scotland where Calvinism had also reached, a revolt ensued against Catholicism and Queen Mary. And, a Presbyterian Church was soon established headed by John Knox, along the line of Calvinist doctrine. In England, Calvinist group of clerics and University professors formed a "Puritan" movement to displace the already existing Episcopal Church establishment with Presbyterianism. In France, the Calvinists called themselves Huguenots and became a formidable force to reckon with within a Catholic French state. In Spain, the Calvinists revolted against their Catholic Spanish leader, Philip II. In Holland, Calvinists created a Dutch Reformed Church and forced their fellow Dutch to revolt against their Spanish Catholic overload. And although unlike Lutheranism, Calvinism was not recognized by the Peace of Augsburg of 1555 as a state, it speedily spread all over Europe and won as many converts as Lutheranism had done particularly in Germany.

The other amazing phenomenon about Calvinism in contrast to Lutheranism in entire European continent is that unlike its Lutheranism counterpart, Calvinism believed that the church was supreme to state and therefore that Church Constitution should be the one to govern state behaviour.

In a nutshell, Calvinism turned the European continent into a hurricane of Religious Reform thus adding oil on fire already lit by Lutheranism against the Papal leadership's misrule and ineptitude in Rome. A list of symptoms of Calvinism's injuries on Catholicism include:

On Predestination, Calvin argued that no one is fit to know one's future fate but only God, who, in His omnipotence uniqueness, only knows who is who and whether what one is doing will be justified for one's admission into eternal life; and therefore believed in justification by faith alone.

On The Elect, Calvin argued that because of this existing great valley between man and God in knowledge, man's inherent imperfection cannot allow all to receive admission into eternal life but only a few, The Elect, who by the grace of God will be admitted; and that this admission will not be by one's good works manifested in one's active participation in Indulgences but solely by one's faith. BY faith a few are foreordained to eternal life; and by good works of Indulgence, etc. the majority of such acts are surely foreordained to damnation.

On Moral Duties, Calvin therefore advised that for one to receive this gift of God, it is one's duty to behave as if he were also already an Elect by doing what one believes it honours God's glory. For this reason, Calvin formulated strict moral/ethical conditions to be enforced by the community of the faithful who recognized this goal, e.g. regular church attendance; puritanical behaviour and appearance in life by way of one's clothing, hair style, etc., stern orthodox attitude against immoral acts involving sexy (ndombolo) dances, etc, (i.e. austere); swearing (which is always an easy habit of liars using it as a tool to convince and get away with one's crime), card playing and other forms of gambling (which was at that time of medieval Europe a natural habit promoted by the antiquity lawless culture headed by the Patricians in Italy and the Sophists in Greece and Macedonia who have now metamorphosed into a Mafia menace we witness today headquartered in that very region of Southern Europe), etc.

<u>On Leadership</u>: Calvin's doctrine attracted Europe so much that in 1536, he was invited by Protestant Reformers in Geneva headed by Guillaurme Farel to come and help them to reform the Swiss canton (constitution), a gesture he accepted and was made head of a theocratic state in Geneva throughout his life. During his leadership, Calvin relied on the Bible as his guide.

<u>On Church and State Relations</u>: By virtue of his experience in Geneva as head of a theocratic state from 1536 till his death in 1564, Calvin believed that in order for a country to be free from corruption and other unethical/immoral viruses, such as those of Indulgences promoted by the Papal Leadership poverty in Rome, a country ought to be governed by the Bible as a guide; and that the clergy of pastors, teachers, lay elders, deacons, etc. should be responsible in guiding good governance.

<u>On the Role of A consistory & State Morality</u>: Calvin argued that whereas in order for a country to be governed well, of course the Bible should be deemed as a primary source of law, there must also be a consistory (a body of ministers and lay elders carefully selected by the general public to enforce and instil moral discipline in the entire Country and those who govern it. He believed that this Consistory's other duties should include censorship of all publications so as to present a country from the virus of falsehood and other immoral tendencies; supervision of schools and other institutions of learning to ensure that they are indeed focussed to building a good moral standard in a country but not involved in immorality likely to tear the country apart. To him, the consistory should be mandated to punish every offender so found as in the case of the on-going Goldenberg scandal in Kenya. He argued that The Consistory should be mandated to punish the offender by using every means necessary including banishing one to exile, and putting him or her to death. He further argued that for even minor offences such as adultery, blasphemy and heresy, it should be the duty of the Consistory to decide what sort of penalty it should use, but the punishment must be good enough in order to prevent future acts of the same crime. This is exactly the reason why a Spanish doctor, Michael Servetus, who had escaped into exile in Geneva from Spain to escape the Inquisition on charges of his denunciation of the Trinity by abusing it as a mere falsehood, was not spared but accordingly burnt at stake in Geneva in 1553 for that blasphemy.

<u>On Calvinism Impact on Catholicism</u>: Calvinism, like its counterpart Lutheranism, made an irreparable damage on Catholicism throughout Europe and outside Europe. As also noted above on the impact of Lutheranism, Calvinism was an added injury onto the existing supremacy of Roman Catholicism as it destroyed and up-rooted most Catholic-strongholds in various parts and regions of Europe; and spread all over into the horizons of the New World we now see as the United States of America, Canada, etc. making it extremely difficult for Catholicism's original long-time claim for supremacy.

<u>On the Agonies of The Innocent Congregation</u>: The entire European Continent which by virtue of its being under the supremacy of the Catholic Roman Empire was also completely Catholic by religion, the main sufferer of this widespread animosity and bloodshed was the Innocent Congregation of both sides, due to their participation in the war in an effort to aid their respective faith leaders. Some were burnt at stake; some killed in combat, some banished into exile; while some were thrown into deep water of the oceans, seas, lakes and rivers to drown. And, as this will be also witnessed further in the succeeding account on the added inputs by King Henry VIII of England on the already burning huge fire of the demand for church Reform initiated by Luther, Europe became a theatre of blood-letting of the Congregation between the pro-Church Reform and the anti-Church Reform. It was a terrible catastrophe of mutual genocide simply because of Pope Leo X's Leadership Poverty.

(c) King Henry VIII (1491-1547), a second son of King Henry VII and Elizabeth of York, succeeded his father on the throne in 1509; and the same year married Catherine of Aragon, a widow of his late brother Arthur, who had passed away in 1502.

King Henry VIII's sudden political about-turn from his amazingly famous role as Pope Leo X's indispensable asset for the supremacy of the Roman Catholicism, to his role as a devastating killer-disease/virus against that supremacy. Like Lutheranism, Calvinism and Zwinglianism in Germany, France, Switzerland, Holland, Denmark, Sweden, Finland and almost all other parts of Western Europe, King Henry in England was an added petrol on the already blazing fire in Europe against the Roman Catholic Supremacy. Like the authors of those faiths against the Papal Leadership in The Holy Roman Empire, King Henry also inflicted a devastating blow to the Roman Catholicism in his home yard. Although some remnants managed to escape the King's poisonous blow and managed to remain in the British Isles, obviously the King's aim was to dismantle and sweep his home-yard totally clean, free of any elements of that Roman Catholic supremacy.

And, like Luther, Zwingli, and Calvin, King Henry VIII formed his own reformed church from the Papal Leadership based in Rome. But, unlike the three, King Henry VIII did not form Henrism, a denominational faith after his name such as Lutheranism, Calvinism and Zwinglianism. Instead, he established what we now know as the Anglican Church which, in turn, added to the efforts of all those other reformers to establish what we also now know as "Protestantism", meaning an objection, refusal, rejection, opposition of/to the Papal doctrines, policies, plans, aims and other unscriptural and anti-gospel tendencies bent on corrupting and thus condemning one's soul to hell other than saving it.

But what could have so far propelled King Henry to go to all these pains? And, what was the outcome of these pains?

A post-mortem of this death of the Roman Catholic Supremacy in the British Isles shows clearly that the following salient facts:

(1)   Throughout his life (1491-1547) King Henry was an indisputable stern Roman Catholic believer and supporter as also manifested in his publication titled a Defence of <u>The Seven Sacraments</u> (1521) in which his sole aim was:

    (a)   To defend the Roman Catholic dogma emphasizing seven sacraments (Baptism and The Eucharist, i.e. The Lord's Supper of The Holy Communion).

    (b)   To condemn Dr. Martin Luther and the latter's Lutheranism whose doctrine emphasized only those Two Biblical Sacraments.

(2)   Because of this powerful stand in support of Pope Leo X against Dr. Martin Luther and the latter's Lutheranism, the Pope loved the King so much that he awarded him a unique and outstanding title of "DEFENDER OF THE FAITH".

(3)   But later, in 1527, King Henry VIII came to be psychologically confronted by the following frustrations and dissonance:

(a)   That throughout his eighteen years of marriage with his later brother's widow (Catherine of Aragon), he had not gotten any male child (son) to serve him as an heir to his throne;

(b)   That in order to avoid his dissonance it was imperative that he gets other ways of getting a son;

(c)   That to do so, he had to get support and consent from his dear friend, Pope Clement VII in Rome, the new successor of Pope Leo X in 1521 and whom he (the King) had just defended against the contagious dangers of Lutheranism, on the one hand, and also the support and consent of his political counterpart and relative-in-law, The Holy Roman Emperor Charles V, Catherine's nephew, and both offsprings of the most powerful and famous King Ferdinand and Queen Isabel of Spain (to whom Catherine was a daughter);

That due to the existing orthodox dogmas of The Roman Catholic faith on the one hand, and the fame of Catherine's parents and nephew (The Holy Roman Emperor Charles V) on the other and the latter's political and religious ties with Pope Clement VII due to the Pope's significant role as Spiritual Leader of The Roman Catholic Church in the Emperor's Dominion, his desire for a divorce of Catherine to marry another wife (Anne Boleyn to whom he was already in love and ready to marry) would not be that easy;

That whereas this may not be that easy, this potential wife (Anne Boleyn) who in fact was already working for him in the Palace as a maid was now pregnant;

And, finally that due to this unfortunate development of pregnancy, which the King obviously did not wish to be exposed to his Queen while still in the Palace, and since the pregnancy may be a son whom the King now desperately needed at all costs, he resolved to totally ignore the Pope's veto to his two intentions (to divorce Catherine and marry Anne Boleyn), and do all those two intentions as he wanted by all means, in case Pope Clement VII ever dared to do so.

(4)   Armed with this weapon, in 1527, King Henry VIII deliberately submitted his request to Pope Clement VII to annul his marriage to Catherine whom he

now tacitly accused as being "barren" (unable to bear him a son) but explicitly accused to the Pope as being the root-cause of his sin against the canon law of the Church by marrying her, a widow of his own later brother, Arthur.

(5) In spite of the Pope's good regard for King Henry VIII due to the latter's outstanding support to the Pope in defence of The Roman Catholic supremacy in The Holy Roman Empire against Lutheranism, Pope Clement VII was equally confronted by the following frustrations and dissonance:

(a) To refuse permission to the King and then risk losing the King's support against Lutheranism contagion vis-à-vis Roman Catholicism in The Holy Roman Empire.

(b) To accept and grant permission to the King and automatically create (i) a heated animosity and his possible future downfall from Queen Catherine's powerful family members and other relatives such as The Holy Roman Emperor Charles V of Spain, who would obviously never want a divorce action against their relative (Queen Catherine); (ii) an acute embarrassment to the Roman Catholic Church which, under Pope Leo X in 1509, had dispensed the King's marriage to Catherine; and (iii) another possibility or reason for Emperor Charles V's renewed invasion and plunder of Rome using his most powerful victorious army that had once ransacked Rome in 1527 and made the same Clement Spain's political prisoner.

(6) As a result of the Pope's reluctance obviously because of these two crucial factors in (5)(ii) and (iii) above, King Henry VIII:

(a) Dismissed his Chancellor, Cardinal Wolsey, who had been carrying out intensive negotiations with Pope Clement VII in Rome on the King's behalf.

(b) Summoned Parliament of 1529 with a view of initiating his first revolutionary aim against the stubborn Roman Catholic Leadership in Rome.

(c) In 1531, he forced his English clergy to recognize and declare him their "Singular Protector" or "Supreme Lord", or "Supreme Head" of the Church of England on assumption that this would make the Pope change his mind and grant him an okay to divorce Catherine and marry Anne Boleyn.

(d) But on realizing in 1533 that the Pope was still adamant on his veto, King Henry resolved to secretly marry Anne Boleyn.

Thereafter King Henry convinced Parliament to pass a number of statutes formalizing legal barriers between England and the Pope in Rome, to the effect that no one would be allowed to seek any redress from the Pope.

Accordingly, King Henry VIII formally established his own Church of England and empowered it to also establish/create Church courts to adjudicate all cases pertaining to spiritual matters, such as his own case.

(h) These two actions were hurriedly effected because Anne Boleyn was now already pregnant, and the obviously because the King wanted to contain a royal family embarrassment.

(7) In his response to the King's act, Pope Clement VII retaliated against the King by excommunicating him from the Roman Catholic Communion and also declared his new marriage null and void and his old marriage still valid.

(8) In 1534, King Henry responded to the Pope's retaliation with his more pungent counter-retaliation by making Parliament adopt:

(a) <u>An Act of Supremacy</u> declaring King Henry VIII "Supreme Head of The Church of England".

(b) Other acts (i) granting the King powers to appoint ecclesiastical heads; (ii) terminating all financial obligations to Rome, e.g. remittal of sales of Indulgences, tithes, income or proceeds from Church holdings entrusted to various leases, etc.; (iii) recognizing Anne Boleyn as new Queen of England and her seed as heir of the throne; (iv) declaring treason every action means to reject, oppose or deny recognition of the King's authority as head of Church, and the legitimacy of this Church as a National Church of England; (v) Dissolving Roman Catholic Monasteries; (vi) confiscating all properties of these Monasteries and lands previously owned by The Roman Catholic Church authority in England which amounted to approximately 10% of the total land in the British Isles, etc.

(9) Confiscated lands from The Roman Catholic Authority was dispensed as follows: some was rewarded to those who sided with the King against Rome; and some was sold to some well-to-do families, who collectively formed a "landed gentry" class that continued to be loyal to the royal family (the then Tudor House) and assumed a financial responsibility to sustain the newly founded Church of England, and the Royal Family.

AGONIES TO THE INNOCENT CONGREGATION

The Papal Leadership Poverty in Rome from Pope Leo X to Pope Clement VII bred painful agonies to multitudes of the innocent in both the mainland Europe and British Isles, which the two had never experienced before.

In the British Isles, for example, a conflict of various personal interests between King Henry VIII and Pope Clement VII based in Rome precipitated untold sorrows of blood-letting wars of reformation.

Those dignitaries who were opposed to the King's personal burning desire to nullify his marriage with Catherine of Aragon, e.g. Sir Thomas More were executed on the order of the King. Also, Queen Anne Boleyn was executed in 1536 on charges of infidelity (her refusal to renounce Catholicism and bow to Protestantism).

A further post-mortem of the events during King Henry VIII and his successors such as Mary Tudor who reigned from 1533 to 1558, and who was a devout Catholic by virtue of her being a daughter of Queen Catherine of Aragon, and daughter of King Ferdinand and Queen Isabella of Spain (a devout Catholic family) and also blood relative to The Holy Roman Emperor Charles V, her nephew, Queen Mary Tudor revealed the following:

(a) Reversed Reform legislations passed by Parliament during the reign of the now deceased King Henry VIII and also King Edward VI.

(b) Persuaded Parliament to repeal its Act of Supremacy that had granted King Henry VIII to establish The Church of England as a national church and declared him supreme Head of that Church.

(c)   Ordered a wholesale persecution of Protestants whom she declared heretics against Catholicism—an act which put a total 273 to death as martyrs, e.g. Archbishop Thomas Cranmer.

(d)   Was consequently popularly abused as "Bloody Mary" by the general public because of this bloody attitude against Protestantism and everyone affiliated to it.

(e)   Ruthlessly exploited her marriage to King Philip II of Spain, also a Catholic, to make her religious intolerance extremely bloody against Protestantism, till her death in 1558.

In the final analysis, all these unfortunate agonies on innocent congregation on both mainland Europe and the British Isles were a function of none other than an unfortunate Papal Leadership Poverty in Rome. And, although this poverty had been initiated by Pope Julius II, it was nevertheless exacerbated by Pope Leo X and the latter's successor, Pope Clement VII.

Thus, in spite of the fact that Pope Leo X (1475-1521) was indeed instrumental in making Rome a centre of the artistic and literary world, in his capacity himself as an ardent scholar and patron of arts, who, through his own efforts, enabled scholars to obtain high posts in the Papal court in Rome, his unfortunate preaching and promotion of Indulgence in Germany with a view to using it to raise money to rebuild St. Peter's Basilica (Church) in Rome,

(1)   Precipitated Dr. Martin Luther's break from the Roman Catholic Church, and create The Reformation, a genesis of Protestantism; and

(2)   Exacerbated the untold sorrows of mutual genocide between the pro-Roman Catholic Congregation and the pro-Protestant congregation, at the expense of his leadership poverty characterized by ineptitude and misrule.

These two heinous situations were further accelerated by Pope Leo X's successor, Pope Clement VII, who was left with no other choice but to follow his predecessor's footsteps in order to sustain the security of his position in Rome. And, the more he did so, the more he added fuel on the already brazing fire of Reformation against the Roman Catholicism. Hence the root-cause of King Henry VIII's amazing irreversible about-turn decision against his life-time mutual friend in Rome and the latter's Catholicism; and the untold sorrows of mutual genocide imposed on the innocent pro-Protestantism on the one hand, and the innocent pro-Catholicism on the other, albeit its manna of political and religious independence and sovereignty it helped to breed for them in the British Isles, as Luther's similar about-turn had also done to Germany and other parts of mainland Europe.

(b) ALFRED THE GREAT (849-899)

Was born in Wantage in Berkshire in 849 AD and lived upto 899 AD. Was born a bright boy and was the youngest of a family of 5 brothers. By the age of 7 years, he had already travelled twice to Rome where he was confirmed by Pope Leo IV.

These travels impressed the young Alfred so much by the progressive advanced civilization in Rome compared to his backward English culture at home.

After the death of his fourth brother, Alfred became King of England in 871. But because of the pressures from the Danes headed by GUTHRUM, Alfred was only able to take charge of the western part of England while the Danish Guthrum continued to control most of the northern area comprising of East Anglia, Yorkshire and the Five Boroughs of the eastern Mercia.

All these Danish controlled areas came to be called and continued to be known as the DANELAW.[2] To this end, the Dane law adopted Danish customs and laws which in the end of Danish occupation, made a significant impact on the English culture.

At first, Alfred was invaded by surprise by Guthrum's Danish army forcing him to flee to the ISLE OF ATHELNEY in January 878. But by March 878, Alfred re-grouped his Britonian army against the Danes and defeated them in the BATTLE OF EDINGTON. And by virtue of that defeat, Guthrum was forced to sign the PEACE OF WEDMORE of 878 by which the Danes were forced to vacate WESSEX permanently and Guthrum to be converted to Christianity. And by the same Treaty, the Danish leadership was confined only to the North Area of The Thames (Yorkshire, East Anglia, etc.) which came to be known as the DANELAW.

But by 886, Alfred had already recaptured London and all other areas which had been under the lordship of the Danes. But because the Danish invasions had significantly reduced the number of people who knew Latin, Alfred decided to promote literacy in the OLD ENGLISH especially among the nobility and the clergy. By his initiative he imported scholars from Wales, Northern England and Europe into Wessex to transplant valuable Latin words into Old English, e.g. Pope Gregory's PASTORAL CARE and Boethius' CONSOLATION OF PHILOSOPHY.

Alfred's love for justice and creativity encouraged compilation of the code of laws by carefully selecting and rejecting the laws previously decreed by his predecessors. This accomplishment was noble and significant indeed to curb the existing lawless situation that existed in England during that period.

Alfred built fortresses along all English coasts to curb invaders. By the time of his death in 899, he had also introduced compilation of English current events in what he called ANGLO-SAXON CHRONICLE which is still considered today as the best source of Anglo-Saxonian history.

(b) LESSONS LEARNED FROM THE LEADERSHIP OF ALFRED THE GREAT

(1) Was bright, emulative, creative, imaginative and a justice-loving person. Therefore it is self-evident that in order for a nation/people to succeed against its insecurity forces, it must first and foremost have a bright, emulative, creative, imaginative and justice-loving leadership. It must not have a dull, ill-educated/ill-exposed, non-emulative, non-creative, unimaginative and justice-carefree leadership.

(2) Had a burning desire to learn from foreign cultures/civilization and compare that with his own for the good of his own (therefore, for a people to progress, it must have a leader who has a burning desire to learn from advanced, cultures/civilization and use it to advance his own.

(3) Ability to initiate and personally participate in leading that initiative. For example, Alfred, on realizing that his English people lacked intellectuals to educate his backward English people who were that backward to mainland Europe especially Rome because of recurrent Danish invasions which had already depopulated England and thus affected England's intellectuals, decided to import into Wessex learned people from Wales, Northern England,

Europe to educate Wessex and to translate books from Latin into Old English with a view to promoting and increasing literacy in England.

(c) OLIVER CROMWELL (1599-1658)

Oliver Cromwell was born in Huntingdon in the year 1599 to a family which had good relations and favours with the kings. As a young boy, he studied at Sidney Sussex College in Cambridge. He had a unique character of "Iron Will"[3] and the love for justice and fairness for all.

Cromwell was first elected member of the Short Parliament and then to the Long Parliament and ruled England during the period of the Commonwealth and Protectorate (1649-58).

When the Civil War broke out in 1642, Cromwell became the mobilizing force in Parliament. Though having no military training, Cromwell used all his in-born ingenuity to train his regiments against the King. In selection of members of his regiments, Cromwell relied on persons who had religious convictions of justice and humane attitude coupled with military interest and strength.

Although Parliament in 1645, did pass a SELF-DENYING ORDINANCE prohibiting members of parliament from participating in military Cromwell's case was excluded. As such, he formed and led his regiment called "IRONSIDES". But when the PURITANS in England broke into two factions called "PRESBYTERIANS" and "INDEPENDENTS", respectively, Cromwell decided to side with the latter on fear that the former could bring the deposed King Charles I to power. To make sure that the deposed King Charles I does not ever return to the throne, Cromwell endorsed the Independent's wish that Charles I be executed.

The Long Parliament lasted for 12 years. But it had so much perennial inherent problems, that it was unable to accomplish anything. For example, it neither went along with Cromwell nor wished to disband. As such, Cromwell had to use the army to disband this Parliament.

On disbanding this Parliament, Cromwell's army unilaterally drew up what they called the INSTRUMENT OF GOVERNMENT by which they sought to make Cromwell LORD PROTECTOR. Later, the new Parliament he constructed wanted to offer him the title of "King" but he rejected this offer. Due to the existing political disorder, Cromwell had to resort to austerity measures to reinforce law and order.

3. LEADERSHIP PROBLEM IN GERMANY

ADOLF HITLER: A Resurrection of a German Traditional Warrior

I: AN INTRODUCTION

Ever since World War II began in 1938/39 to this time (the year 2013), numerous nagging questions are still being asked from various quarters of Humanity without any satisfactory answer as to the actual reason why the War was fought at all or ever allowed to take place by the World Leadership of the time while the latter was pretty clear of both potential and actual dangers to Humanity and the Environment from the horrifying lesson of World War I which had just ended barely 20 years ago (in 1919) which had consequently forced the same Leadership to come up with The Brian-Kellogg Peace Pact (also known as The Pact of Paris or Paris Pact) in 1928 containing explicit protocols prohibiting every Nation-State and all other Subjects of International Law from use of war or any other means of force or violence as means of settling or solving international dispute(s).

Even among the scientists who are expected to be the only oasis of advanced learned wisdom and knowledge on how to find actual root-causes of diseases and conflicts using every appropriate formula such as Etiology, none of them has been convincing enough with regard to their findings on the real causes of World War II apart from being abundantly rich in speculations and more so accusative.

In view of this existing difficulty, the actual reason why the war erupted still remains a mystery. Even Adolf Hitler who is globally understood as being the real architect and, therefore, the principal culprit of the war, his real roots which collectively constituted his actual being and behaviour in leadership also still remains a mystery although he is obviously known to have been a German sue generic having been born of parents who were also Germans by jus solei (birth).

But the accusing finger to Hitler is not only against him because of the War. The case against him is multiple. It is too complex indeed. He is accused for being the architect of the War; the architect of Genocide of the Jewish Germans, the Gypsies, etc; the architect of racism; the architect of disobedience to the spiritual concept of Brotherhood and Sisterhood and, thus the architect of an insult to God's Creation and Wisdom manifested not only in different races, gender and sizes in Humanity but also in all members of the Animal Kingdom in conformity with His Own Formula that a simple product of His this Formula such as Adolf Hitler was not mandate to question. In fact, the same also holds true in the Plant Kingdom albeit smaller size species tends to suffer at the advantage of large ones as in the case of carnivorous species against their herbivorous counterpart. But all this behaviour is strictly biologically constitutional in that it is inherent only in non-Human Members of the Animal Kingdom, namely wild animals, fishes and birds of air, who must do so for their food failure of which they must perish. But, it is not inherent in Human Life at all!!

In view of this common sense fact which is also supported by the biological constitution, Hitler's reasons of designing World War II and the Genocide is, therefore, very perplexing indeed, deserving a thorough re-examination leaving no stone unturned in order to achieve this long-overdue sigh of relief as to why Hitler had to do what he did, given the fact that reasons which most writers to date have attempted to advance definitely fall too below those factors which were responsible of Hitler's role as the real architect of World War II and the Genocide that ravaged Europe in particular and the rest of the World in general. Such contentions and accusations as well are too superficial, and, therefore, too unsatisfactorily to the long-lived hunger and thirst for real root cause(s).

The world Book Encyclopedia's and other authorities' assumption that Hitler was odd, moody, easily angered, a racist, mad and so poor in his high school studies that he failed even a simple entrance examination to the Academy of Fine Arts he had desired to join in Vienna thus forcing him to spend most of his time day dreaming, drawing pictures and reading nonsensical books must, therefore, be open to question, given the fact that he, as a single person in the whole Country of Germany could not have been able to initiate and then fight the war alone and also carry out the Genocide without the support of his German people to his ideas. To manage to do so, everyone must have followed him fully in partnership in everything that he had set forth in his Government policy agenda to accomplish for them in Europe

But given that he was a mad man possibly suffering from schizophrenia or any other mental disorder problem(s) as so alleged, how and why did everyone in Germany agree with him? Why did they support him? Was Hitler the only one single man in the whole Government and Country? And, if he was that so dump and dummy, how was he able to influence the entire German population using electrifying speeches? Where did his electrifying speech quality come from if he were that foolish? How come he was not interested in advisors or using notes in his speeches and yet he always proved coherent and amazingly so factual and accurate in his speeches?

In other words, what actually was this man called "Adolf Hitler"? Has all about him been known? Or is there other hidden mysteries about him that one must also know in order to understand better those exogenous and endogenous facts about him that must have consequently led him into being the architect of World War II and the worst Genocide the World had never experienced before?

Above all, what lessons do we learn from Hitler's leadership? And of what significance can these lessons assist us with in our understanding the actual root-causes of the reasons why leaders fail and then plunge innocent civil society into a sea of agonies as displaced persons madly fleeing from their homes in search of safe havens? And, above all, what remedy can we glean from a synthesis of all these lessons in Hitler's leadership failure?

II. PURPOSE

In view of these numerous serious questions noted above, and many more as well, it is the purpose of this Chapter to resort to a much more powerful methodology such as Etiology as a solution with which to re-examine afresh the still perplexing Adolf Hitler's Leadership Failure Question using both high and low power lenses so that we may be able to succeed in identifying those hidden microscopic factors as answers to those various salient questions which conventional research had unfortunately overlooked on the Question.

For example, how can his mode of leadership be scientifically explained? Thus, why did he behave the way he did thereby plunging the innocent World Community, most particularly in Europe, into a sea of unbearable agonies? How can his leadership be explained compared with the massive kleptocracy of the most immediate former Kenyan President Daniel Toroitich arap Moi whose policy organized and exacerbated rampant institutionalized tribal clashes and blood-letting, deceit, dishonesty, and daily massive public looting by his cohorts as a bribe to them for their political support which, in turn, became such a terror to all Kenyans that by the end of his 24 years period of rule, when he was now forcefully ejected out of office in December, 2002 by a combined force of all opposition political parties under the umbrella of National Alliance Rainbow Coalition (NARC) headed by Honourable Mwai Kibaki, Moi had practically vandalized and reduced the Country's Socio-Economy to a stand-still (thus forcing many industries to close down and many employees in both the Civil Service and Private Sectors to be retrenched) in a total violation of pacta sunt servanda inherent in his own Oath of Office on succeeding the late President Jomo Kenyatta in October, 1978 vowing that he was going to protect and defend both the Constitution and Assets of Wananchi (Kenyan Citizens) at all time and costs? Or was his character and leadership akin to that of the scyzopherania King Herod of Judea who, because of his mental instability, exacerbated a massive Genocide of the Innocent Infants in Bethlehem with a devilish aim of using this method to also exterminate The Innocent Infant Jesus Christ whom he (Herod) terribly suspected that He was possibly going to grab the leadership from him; and who also not only did that but also annihilated all his brothers and sisters for the same phobia and even went so far and threatened all his subjects in Judea with death so that they could agree to weep bitterly for him when he dies? Or can Hitler's leadership be explained in the context of the character of another Herod-like leader in Africa called Chaka The Zulu who also not only annihilated his brothers and sisters for the same reason as Herod's but also put to death hundreds of select beauties of his Zulu Community in South Africa by ordering that the must be buried alive together with his already deceased mother on her burial in order for them to also suffer his mother's death and be able to continue serving her after death? And, if not, through what body of knowledge can Adolf Hitler's character and mode of leadership be well understood and explained succinctly with a high degree of parsimony and satisfaction to whoever that wishes to properly understand him and the real reason{s} why he plunged the innocent into a sea of unbearable agonies and devastated lots of property and environment particularly in Europe which was the real scene of the War thereby forcing lots of expensive intervention by the United States of America with Marshall Plan for The Reconstruction of Europe? Did Hitler emulate the leadership of his ancestor of the ancient Europe such as Charles The Great (popularly known as Charlemagne)? Or Napoleon Bonaparte? Or Alexander The Great? or Otto von Bismack? whose militaristic mode of leadership subjected Europe to so much terror of military conquests that each leader always left behind the horrors of bloody trails of genocide among the conquered peoples on the pretext of empire-building? Hence, our fundamental objective in this Chapter and the following etiological efforts.

III: Who and What was Adolf Hitler?: A Psychiatric

Approach

I: AN OVER VIEW (A Clinical Diagnosis)

Adolf Hitler was born on 20th April, 1889 in a small town, Braynau am Inn, on the border of Austro-Hungarian Empire, where his father, Alois Hitler, worked as a customs officer. He received his primary school education in this town. And, after five years of schooling, he later on moved to Vienna in 1907, where he made a living by selling paintings, drawings, posters, and advertisements made by himself.

He twice sought to join The Academy Graphic Arts but never succeeded. Thereafter, he left Vienna for Munich in 1913 in order to avoid a military service draft in Austria for a mysterious reason(s) only known to himself as the following detailed account of his extra-ordinary love for militarism and militarization during World War I and II in 1914-1918 and 1938-1945 respectively totally defeats every hypothesis that he did so because of cowardice or lack of interest in militarism and militarization.

Numerous prima facie evidences clearly show that although Hitler deserted or fled from Vienna in order to evade or avoid the draft, but no sooner had he later on learnt that his own Mother Country (Germany) was now on the verge of brinkermaniship of World War I having an attractive national goal for his Germany People akin to lucrative goals of previous intra- and inter-European cases of brinkermaniship, than he at once begun showing his true colours of militarism and militarization as proof of a resurrection of the German warrior tradition. Such cases, for example, include One Hundred Years' War (1337-1453); The War of Reformation also known as The Religious War (of the 16th Century beginning in 1517 with Dr. Martin Luther's unleashing retaliation against what he believed to be un Biblical and, therefore, ungodly Sale of Indulgence by Pope Leo X contrary to The Holy Scripture; The Thirty Years' War (1618-1648); The Seven Years' War (1757-1763); and finally the Franco-Prussian War (1870-1871) in which each initiator fought fiercely and decisively for the purpose of not only winning the war but also for using the victory as a vehicle for acquiring either more or totally new good/fertile land space for food production and settlement, plundering a foreign country's wealth and legacies, expanding one's empire, colonizing small and weaker nation(s) or people(s) with a view to using them as one's vassals or a buffer zone as an added security asset against external aggression, or simply for using them as one's supportive or defense mechanism vis a vis certain religious doctrine or philosophy as in the case of Luther against the Pope.

Because of the significance of the goal inherent in World War I for his Mother Germany, obviously Hitler had no minute to waste. He automatically became so extremely interested and eager in military service that he rushed to enlist in the Bavarian army when World War I broke out in 1914. And, the empirical evidence shows that he did not only go there to serve for the sake of serving but to definitely serve with such a distinction that, unlike others, he was consequently awarded an impressive recognition of "The Iron Cross" and not only once but twice; and thereafter promoted to a "Lace Corporal" rank in 1917, i.e, within a very short period of three years of service!

To him, such a service was extremely crucial in his life in that it was a "Kameraderie", i.e., a United Germans' cause against explicit foe—a sacrifice for his Fatherland that no other person or country would give them free of charge on a platter other than whole heartedly resorting to military conquest and sacrifice strategy. And although he was injured by the enemy's mustard poison gas attack; and was, therefore, still in hospital when World War I was brought to an end with Germany's defeat, he was, of course, physically not with his comrades on the battlefield but, he was certainly with them psychologically and spiritually.

On learning of this defeat and the degree of the humiliating terms of the Versailles Treaty of 1918 against his Germany nation, with particular regard to the colossal reparation debt of British Sterling Pound of 6, 000, 000, 000 that his Mother Germany was now expected to pay other European Countries that had suffered from the War plus a total loss of all territories Germany was claiming as a the root-cause of the War, obviously Hitler could hardly accept it. He took it as not only a clear stab-in-the Germany's back but also in his own back. Also, he strongly believed that this defeat was not a function of his German military colleagues' cowardice, incompetence or miscalculation at all but a function of the civil society and the latter's empty rhetoric of democracy and democratic rights manifested in the emergence of November 1918-1919 extremists' revolution against Germany's ultimate goal against the enemy.

After having been discharged from hospital, Hitler still worked for the army. At this time, his duty was no more on the battlefield but only to keep surveillance on the movements and acts of numerous extremist groupings that existed in the Country and mainly in Munich.

It was, therefore, during this time of his tenure as a spy on those wanted/undesirable/ disruptive elements that Hitler, developed a negative attitude towards democracy and its inherent rights arguing that democracy was no better than a dangerous virtue only good for leading one to vanities, failures and agonies of such failures; harboured such a hostility against democracy because of his belief that it was this democracy and its virtues which had led Germany to lose the war; and, therefore, saw it very necessary to resort to a granite love for dictatorship A kin to that of the Italian fascist leader, Benitto Mussolini, whose dictatorial mode of leadership had empowered him to successfully unite and defend Italy against her enemies

Further, it was also during this tenure that Hitler came into a direct contact with the German Workers' Party (DAP) of Anton Drexler, a German locksmith in Munich, who after some interactions with Hitler discovered in Hitler something of a unique value not common in most people, arising mainly from the Hubbub Beerhall Politics in Munich, where Hitler's electrifying political speeches showed sufficient proof of extra-ordinary brilliance and command able to convince and mobilize a majority of the audience. For example in his October 1919 electrifying address to the DAP, he stunned many, and hence became the DAP's spokesman.

And, on February 24, 1920, the DAP changed its name to the National Socialist German Workers' Party (NSDAP) (which came to be called "Nazi" in short) with a sole double-edged objective;

To call for not only the revision of the Versailles Treaty and the restoration of all German territories lost to the enemy e.g. Parts of Poland, Alsace-Lorraine, etc but also for the unification of all Aryan Germans (ethnic Germans) in all, parts of Europe into a single Reich; and

To exclude all non-Aryan-Germans such as the Jews, Gypsies, etc by way of denying or revoking their citizenship; and also by deporting them back to their country/countries of origin (in order to protect and preserve Aryan Germanic blood purity).

To introduce a selective socio-economic policy that was to nationalize major economic activities save small ones with a view to uplifting the majority poor and small business persons who were now faced with more serious hardships.

Because of this new NSDAP drastic policy compounded by the facts that Germany was now in a critical socio-economic problem arising from a major currency devaluation and military occupation of the Country's economic region of Ruhr Valley due to Germany's non-payment of the Versailles Treaty reparation debt, Hitler's NSDAP so easily won the Bavarian Government's attention that the latter was no longer ready to accept orders from the national Government from Berlin. The tension between the two Governments was so serious that the Bavarian Government was on the brim of secession from Berlin.

As a result of this tension, Hitler exploited the situation by proclaiming in his Munich beer hall speech of 8th November, 1923 a Nazi revolution. And, on 9th November, he staged an abortive coup d'etat against The Reich(the Central Government based in Berlin) by taking over the Bovarian Government as a beginning—a move which came to be known as the Beer Hall Putsch (i.e, revolution).

In this revolution, Hitler led a contingent of over 2,000 storm troopers against the Government that resulted into the death of 16 Nazi troopers and Hitler's arrest and five years imprisonment for treason.

But when he was in jail, he wrote a very striking book, Mein Kampf (ie. *My Struggle*) in which he detailed all his thoughts and what he actually wanted to achieve for Germany amid other nations in European political life. Succinctly, he made it crystal clear that for the sake of Germany's safe future, it was his right and mandatory duty:-

To conquer as much Europe as possible;

To restore all territories particularly Alsace, Lorraine, and all parts that Germany had lost in World War I and which had now subjected Germany to an irreparable and un acceptable ridicule and socio-economic hardship of reparation repayments;

And to conquer, annex and add to his German fatherland all parts of Austria and Czechoslovakia where Germans also lived so as to have one Pan-German nation (ein Volk) under one empire (ein Reich) in keeping with an original idea that their former German leader, Otto von Bismarck, wished to achieve during his military conquests but died in 1898 before doing so

To also seize a *lebensraum* (i.e., a secure and sufficient living space) for the already overcrowded but increasingly growing German nation in Europe in emulation of and appreciation to Otto von Bismarck's original good hope for Germans as also manifested in his series of war victories of 1866 and 1870/1 aimed at liberating Germans from overcrowdiness.

To do so particularly from Russia and other Countries in the Eastern European region which obviously had this potentials to satisfy Germany's doctrine of <u>*Blut*</u> <u>*and Boden*</u> (meaning "blood and soil").

To protect and preserve German blood purity from all other non-German nations' blood since his German nation was not only the highest but also the most superior above all others in Humanity such as the Jews, Slavs and Gypsies who, to him, were no better than "half way between man and ape" as compared to his Germans who, to him, were none other than "images of the Lord"!

To do so in order to liberate the already populous Germans who were already crowded but were being forced to live in a tiny area that could not meet its total needs against their wishes.

To do so at all costs since such pressure normally lead to political and socio-economic decay (unrest) most particularly in urban areas as opposed to rural areas which are normally peaceful because of being spacious and therefore comfortable for everyone.

To use dictatorship as the only rational leadership if one was to succeed in saving Germany from communists and the Jews who according to him (Hitler), were already too well known architects and partakers of all evils of the World under the disguise/ protection of Democracy and the latter's values of individual rights and freedom of self-expression.

To use as much big lies as possible without feeling shame for the sake of victory for his German people that were, to him, now endangered by the harsh conditions of the Versailles Treaty. Hence the genesis of Hitler's mode of leadership in his new Government which he called the "Third Reich".

(II) HITLER'S RELEASE FROM PRISON AND FORMATION OF HIS THIRD REICH (i.e., GOVERNMENT)

While still in prison (for his five years term sentence) two dramatic developments occurred:-

Hitler used the occasion to map out details of his next move/strategy after his release vividly manifested in his *Mein Kampf* book (meaning My Struggle) his political party (NSDAP) used it to strengthen itself against the Government in Berlin which Hitler's Beer Hall Putsch had attempted to dislodge on the evening of 8th November, 1923.

But before going to jail, Hitler had already captured most Germans through his electrifying Beer Hall speeches that had portrayed him as the kind of leadership material that Germany actually needed in order to bring to a solution, Germany's existing woes. The NSDAP used that reason and the reason of having been jailed to mobilize most Germans into NSDAP. And the more NSDAP did so, the more it managed to build up a formidable force in NSDAP by which the latter, in turn, successfully pressurized both the Bavarian Government and the national German Government in Berlin to immediately release Hitler. Hence, Hitler's immediate release in December 1924 after having served for only nine months out of five years.

But although Hitler's NSDAP party had officially been out-lawed, the movement remained explicit, real and unquenched.

Therefore, when Hitler came out of prison, he went ahead to vitalize it beyond Government's power and also to convince the Government to reinstate its original registration.

On the strength of its reinstatement,

Hitler re-built it further and also won numerous friends of various status and ranks in, for example, the labour unions, big businesses, big industries, including agriculture.

Hitler set up his own private army composed of elite guards called the <u>Schutzstaffel</u> in short meaning the "SS" who were totally different in composition from his earlier storm troopers who were simply armed hoodlums that he had used in his Beer Hall Putsch (attempted military coup d'etat) on 8th November, 1923 that landed him in prison.

Therefore, unlike these storm troopers, the newly formed SS was a de facto battle-ready army able to take on any conventional professional army.

Consequently, by 1929, Hitler's Nazis and the latter's NSDAP political party had obviously become such a most formidable opposition in Germany that both Baverian and national German Governments could hardly underestimate.

And by 1930, Hitler's fame now surpassed every other's fame in both Governments mainly as a result of Hitler's successful vehement opposition country-wide using protest marches, organized mass meetings, speedy etc against the Government's attempted intention to accept the Young Plan of 1929 to pay the Allies for the damages caused by Germany during the world War I.

In addition to exploiting this Young Plan of 1929, Hitler also added the Jews and the communists concern on his list of those national German nagging problems that he and his NSDAP political party were now ready to address as soon as possible should they be given the mandate to do so as a Government. These critical items on his list included:

- Disallowment of the harsh Versailles Treaty terms of reparation repayments.

- Restoration of all lost German areas during World War I

- Eradication or expulsion of all Jews and Communists from Germany.

- Unification of all parts of Europe inhabited by Germans and where their language was spoken

Because of this existing turmoil in the Country, five major elections were held in 1932 with a good hope that the newly elected Government would now restore sanity to Germany that was already chaotic.

But apart from the July 1932 Election, none of them had any encouraging or reliable result. In the July 1932 Election, on the other hand, Hitler's NSDAP party emerged one of the strongest with a 40% of the total vote.

And, on having refused to accept an offer of some cabinet posts for himself and other key pillars of his NSDAP party in exchange for his dropping of his NSDAP party, Hitler categorically refused the offer terming it a political bribe. As a result, he exploited this opportunity to convincingly bargain with the national Germany's Government President Paul von Hindenburg that he was not going to be as dangerous as he had proved during his Beer Hall Putsch of November 1923, if he were called on to form a new Government on the strength of his NSDAP party's 40% vote.

On the strength of this promise, the President willingly called on Hitler on 30th January, 1933 to form a new Government in his capacity as Chancellor.

(III) HITLER'S EVENTS LEADING TO WORLD WAR II RESURGENCY

Replacement of Democracy with Dictatorship

Convinced that nothing could be realized in and for Germany with Democracy as a mode of governance, Hitler opted to the following drastic actions as his rational choice:-

He chose dictatorship as a rational choice of his Road map to a New order in place of the Weimar Republic in order to effectively deal with an already unstable country.

To strengthen his rationale, Hitler also resorted to a Machiavellian strategy of lies and dishonesty in leadership. He organized an arsenal act on the Reichstag (or parliament) building and blamed the act on his enemy, the Communists, as a scapegoat, so that he may use this excuse to dismantle the existing Weimar Republic's Democracy and the latter's virtues in Germany; and then legitimize his intention to amass all powers onto himself which he needed very badly for pursuit of his chain of objectives.

Using such a cunning strategy, Hilter succeeded in hoodwinking President the aging President von Hindenburg to sign a law wiping out all democratic individual rights in the Country and to detain every suspect without trial.

And, by mid 1933 (July), Hitler's new Government had already outlawed all labour unions, press freedom, all political parties, save NSDAP party.

With such Presidential assent, the Reichstag had no reason to deny Hitler full law-making and financial powers.

Hitler quickly set up a secret police called "<u>Gestapo</u>" a ruthless agency that hunted down and either shot dead or jailed any real or suspected opponent to Hitler's policy.

After President von Hindenburg's death in August, 1934, Hitler assumed both his and the deceased President's powers, and thus changed his title of Chancellor to the title of Fuehrer (meaning "leader"). And began to propagate to all Germans The New Order or New Rule and its glories he was determined to bring.

He set up a Nazi-controlled press and radio to flood Germany with news about the glories of Germany and what the new socio-economic recovery that the New Order Planned to bring to the Country as proof of the New Order's good policy, e.g. state marriage loans for single parents, creation of new jobs, involving over 5.26 billion DM (Deutch marks) invested in Autobahnen (road building) and armament factories.

He forced all industries and professionals alike to lay off all Jews and every opposition to Hitler's New Order.

He mandated his Nazi's and the NSDAP party to be in charge of all employment throughout the Country in the sense that no one could be employed without going thorough NSDAP and the Nazis.

He set up a Hitler Youth organ and mandated it to act as a political socialization agent on the concept and significance of Nazism to Germany.

Every German boy and girl was required to join and be a significant member and participant of this Hitler Youth organization in the sense that each was required to march; exercise; learn the Nazi beliefs, goals and strategies; also work on farms or any other nation enterprise(s); spy on everyone suspected of opposing or talking ill of Hitler, whether or not one doing so is one's parent, relative, or friend.

The Parliament (Reichstag) existed but was always docile and speechless as it always met to listen to Hitler but not to be heard.

The Judiciary similarly existed but only at the whims of Hitler in his capacity as the Country's Fuehrer whose final word was essential in all critical cases whose verdict had national implication(s)

(3) World War II Preparedness

Cheerfully and happily convinced that President Paul von Hindenburg's death in August, 1934 must have been some sort of a good omen for him in order to use the vacuum to replace the deceased's Weimer Republic's Democracy with his own New Order's Dictatorship, Hitler sought to use the latter as a full green light for him to achieve his two far reaching dramatic goals of the Germany's needed additional living space (Lebensraum) and the Jewish questions.

In a nut-shell, in his capacity as The Fuehrer (i.e, leader), Hitler swiftly used the vacuum to fulfill those drastic goals with every means he could now hutch out guided by his motto that "conquest [was] not only a right, but [also] a duty!!"

Guided by this motto, Hitler did the following as evidence of his preparedness for a war with those he considered enemies of his Country's survival:-

By January 1933 (even before the ailing and too aged President Hindernburg's death in August 1934), the Fuehrer's Hitler Youth organization had already mobilized a total of 55,000 members; and by December, 1933, half of the total German youth population aged between 10 and 14 years.

And, by December 1935, its membership had reached the tune of 4 million

Similarly between January 1933 and December 1934, his NASDAP party had already enlisted a similar number of membership with an annual increase of 200%.

And by 1939, the NSDAP had an over 5 million membership to effect Hitler's double edged goal.

The free rush from the Civil Society to both organization for membership was an amazing proof of overwhelming national support to Hitler's goals.

Death penalty type of cases increased dramatically from three (3) to forty six(46) in order to enhance national cohesion needed for achieving this most costly double-edged goal.

In this regard,

The critical mandate of Germany's two intelligence monitoring and gathering organizations viz: The Gestapo and SPD (the latter being charged with the SOPADE reports production from outside Germany on Germans in exile), multiplied significantly since national unity building was very much dependent on their work so as to enable the New Order regime root out both real and potential divisive elements of the out-going Weimar democratic politics aimed at frustrating those two new goals needed by the Country by disrupting national unity building efforts;

And, also, the military expenditure; rearmament; and the demand for military conquest were also drastically multiplied in order to empower Germany to undo the Versailles' Treaty protocols and harsh treatment imposed on Germany and her People.

III. The War Catastrophe

Fully armed with his motto that "conquest is not only a right but [also] a duty", Hitler, in his new capacity as Germany's Fuehrer (meaning "The Leader"), was, by 1939, no more interested in speeches and words as to what he wanted to do for his besieged Germany and German people. By that time, he had already secretly and openly armed Germany fully and ready for war against the Versailles Treaty and the latter's architects against Germany as follows:-

Initially, he sent his troops in 1936 into Germany's Rhineland with a view to occupying and then using it as his granite base of his conquests of Western Europe—a move he easily succeeded without any significant resistance from France.

Thereafter, in March 1938, he also successfully annexed Austria to Germany, without any resistance from any one.

And, in September, same year (1938), he also did the same to Czechoslovakia by absorbing all areas of Czechoslovakia inhabited by Germans with the full support of both the United Kingdom of Britain and France.

And, no sooner had he seen no resistance from any one in Europe most especially from both the United Kingdom and France who were the leading super powers of the time, than he now swiftly moved into the remaining Czechoslovakia head and tail and grabbed it all, by March 1939.

After such successful victories in the Rhineland in 1936 followed by his grabbing of both Austria and Czechoslovakia in 1938 and 1939 respectively without any ado, Hitler was such a happy man that he began salivating for more victories, for his motherland, Germany, e.g,

Knowing that both the United Kingdom and France had a mutual agreement/ memorandum of understanding with Poland that the two would be ready to defend Poland in event of external aggression, Hitler cleverly dashed to Russia and signed a treaty of friendship with Premier Joseph Stalin in August, 1939 assuring Hitler that Russia would not challenge a German invasion of Poland.

And no sooner had Hitler finished this than he swiftly commissioned his troops to enter Poland effective 1st September, 1939, with a sole view of another conquest/ victory!!.

Unfortunately for Hitler and fortunately for Poland and the Polish people, both the United Kingdom of Britain and France honoured their Pacta Sunt Servanda with Poland and swiftly moved into Poland fully armed to defend their endangered friend against external aggressor, Hitler's Germany thus leading to the beginning of World War II.

But, in spite of this threatening move by both the United Kingdom and France in defence, of Poland, this did not bother Hitler's Germany's further move in pursuit of victories after victories, e.g.,

Hitler's Germany easily and quickly overran Poland;

And, by early 1940, he also quickly conquered Belgium, Luxembourg, The Netherlands, Denmark, and Norway.

Impressed and then influenced by such Hitler's Germany's consecutive victories after victories in such a short span of time, Italy's fascist leader, Benito Mussolini, also began salivating for the same. Emulating Hitler's military conquest, Mussolini swiftly invaded both the United Kingdom and France on 10th June, 1940.

Now more happy and encouraged by Mussolini's attack on the United Kingdom and France, on the grounds that this combined attack by Germany and Italy against those two enemies was now an assured easy catch and Victory by Germany, Hitler swiftly:-

Overran France forcing France to surrender on 22nd June, 1940; and also overran both Yugoslavia and Greece.

Impressed by such swift Victories, Hitler wrongly gambled on the question of the United Kingdom by erroneously assuming that the United Kingdom would simply be frightened by such victories and raise up her hands to Hitler without actual military invasion and conquest by Hitler. As a result, Hitler decided to concentrate on others save the United Kingdom where he only commissioned in air raids aimed at forcing that Country to surrender due to German bombers that devastated most London City with heavy air raid bombardment day and night. In stead of swiftly invading the Country as he had already done to all others that he had now gained victories over, Hitler directed that strategy to Russia where he expected to gain more living space (Lebensraum) for his Germany people whom he claimed to be already too overcrowded in Germany and, therefore, needed this Lebensraum not in the United Kingdom but in Russia and other Eastern European countries.

Because of this crucial purpose, Hitler commissioned in a German army of three million men against Russia with the hope that these men would definitely humble down Russia and allow Germany to acquire the Lebensraum for her Germans.

Unfortunately, this hope fell on an evil day in the sense that;

Russia's military resistance proved too much unbeatable by German military capability.

The most bitter cold weather of the Russia winter added more oil on fire in defence of Russia against Hitler's Germany's army men.

By 1942, the War was already against Hitler's Germany as the United States also entered the War in support of both Russia and the United Kingdom, which were, by then, the only surviving countries against Hitler's Germany's conquest aim.

By 1944, the Russians were already driving away the Germans from Russia.

And, by June, 1944, the Allies, comprising the United States, the United Kingdom and Russia had managed to invade Europe particularly France against Germany, Italy and Japan which had also moved in for an easy catch as both Italy had done earlier after seeing and being impressed with Hitler's successive easy victories after victories in the Rhineland, Austria, Czechoslovakia, Poland, France, Belgium, Luxembourg, The Netherlands, Denmark and Norway.

And, finally, as early as April, 1945 the Allies had already entered Berlin and humbled Hitler's Germany that finally forced Germany to surrender on 9th May, 1945.

A Balance Sheet of World War II Cost

Whereas national leaders and ordinary peoples of today may indulge in solemn commemoration services as it has just happened this year (2005) marking the 60th anniversary of the Hitler's Nazi Germany's defeat on the one hand and also of the Allies' victory on the other and also marking the end of the World's most devastating war particularly to Europe continent and her peoples, a statistical data on the actual cost of that War with reference to the loss of human life as concerned is definitely a noble act for a noble cause.

In this regard, the following table shows that more than 52 million people lost their lives during that War which should not have actually been allowed to take place had sanity been hearkened to and used by the leaders of the time:-

Table: World War II-Human Cost

COUNTRY FATALITIES

Name	Military	Civilian	Total
1. Soviet Union	14,500,000	7,000,000	21,500,000
2. Republic of China	1,324,000	10,000,000	11,324,000
3. Poland	850,000	5,000,000	6,628,000
4. Germany	2,850,000	2,300,000	5,150,000
5. Japan	1,506,000	300,000	1,806,000
6. Yugoslavia	305,000	1,200,000	1,505,000

7. Romania	519,822	165,000	684,822
8. Austria	380,000	145,000	525,000
9. Hungary	200,000	290,000	490,000
10. United States	405,399	9,000	414,699
11. France	210,671	173,260	383,931
12. Italy	279,820	93,000	372,820
13. United Kingdom	271,311	60,000	331,906
14. Others (16 Nations)	306,202	914,800	1,221,002
TOTALS	23,908,225	28,428,955	52,337,180

Source: Harper Collins Atlas of The Second World War; Encyclopeadia Britannica; American Battle Monuments Commission Picture; Associated Press; and The Daily Nation, Nairobi, May 9, 2005, p.12.

NB: These figures show only fatalities (thus, only those who were killed); but they do not show those who were maimed by the War; psychologically driven to insanity; and loss of property in monetary terms.

II: THE IMPACT OF THE THIRTY YEARS' WAR (1618-1648) ON HITLER'S GERMANY ROLE IN WORLD WAR II (A 1ST TEST)

In order for one to gain more insight into the actual root-cause of the role of Hitler and his Country's involvement in World War II, the following additional findings gained from a clinical diagnosis of the dynamics of the Thirty Years' War of 1618-1648 that devastated the entire Europe leading to the destruction of The Roman Empire as the aim of the war, is, therefore, very much necessary. In this regard such a diagnosis with a view of establishing any possible roots that this War may have left behind in Germany for future leaders such as Adolf Hitler, but which have always evaded recognition by former research.

(A) Back Ground

This Thirty Years' War was fought in Europe in general but Germany in particular. It began in 1618 and ended in 1648 by the Treaty of Westphalia.

It arose from the revolt of the Calvinists, the followers of John Calvin (1509-1564).— who together with both Martin Luther (1483-1546) a German Church Reformation Leader, and Ulrich Zwingli, (1484-1531), a Swiss humanist and theologian—against the existing intolerable harsh Hasburg Catholic rule under Ferdinand II of Austria who, on becoming Emperor of The Holy Roman Empire arrogantly and brutally sought:

To alter the existing peaceful balance of power (or status quo) between the Lutherans and the Catholics concluded by the Peace of Augsburg of 1555 which had declared that the two were to mutually co-exist in Germany from then henceforth;

To not only disrupt this existing peaceful co-existence but also totally eradicate Protestantism from Germany;

And, to then revive the already declining life of The Holy Roman Empire in Germany.

In the first 10 years of the War, Ferdinand II was very sure of victory after noting that he had an advantage over the Calvinists' efforts. On the strength of this hope, he issued an Edict of Restitution in 1629 in which he returned to the Catholic Church all properties formerly seized and nationalized by the State effective 1552.

But, unfortunately, no sooner had his Edict of Restitution taken root than the tables were suddenly turned upside down against him by a surprising entry into the War of the Sweden's Lutheran King Gustavus Adolphus. This sudden change of wind was further worsened by an overwhelming support of the Germanic Catholic princes who were also eager to be freed from subjection of the Roman Empire's dictatorship in Rome.

But that was not all against Emperor Ferdinand II and his anti-Protestantism goal in Germany.

Also, his arch-enemy (the Calvinists) received an over-whelming additional support from France's Catholic Cardinal Richelieu, who did not only support them but also, and in a biggest way, financed the Lutheran King in Sweden not because of any other sinister reason other than because such victory by Ferdinand II was going to make the Habsburg supremacy too powerful and thus upset the existing balance of power in Europe of the time.

But on the King's death, the Catholics once again regained superiority over their arch-enemy.

This drastic change of events forced France to also join the War in support of the Calvinists and the deceased Swedish King's supporters.

And, with a reinforcement from both the German Protestants Princes and the Dutch Republic to the Calvinists against the Hasburg Catholic dictatorial rule under Ferdinand II of Austria.cum Emperor of The Holy Roman Empire, the unfortunate Germany increasingly became a bloody battle field between the Catholics and the protestants led by the Calvinists.

The impact of this War disaster on Germany soil and people was, in fact, further worsened by the rise of mercenaries coupled by the plague, butchery and starvation that collectively led to over 40% of the Germany's population dead.

The Peace of Westphalia (1648) And Its Impact on The German Leadership & People.

The Peace of Westphalia was the pill that brought this famous Europe's Thirty years' war to an end in 1648. Because of the religious nature and character of its root-cause, it was categorically christened "The War of Reformation" in the sense that in as much as its cause was to reform the Christian Church management in Rome, so did the Reformation achieved for those who fought and bravely shed blood for it!!

The Peace process began in the mid-1640's and ended in 1648. But, throughout its process till its conclusion, the whole deliberation lacked enough power and the will to bring an end to a continued blood-shed on the Germany population. Consequently, by the time the process ended in 1648, Germany had already suffered terribly. She had lost uncountable lives and encountered uncountable non-fatal injuries to her population, some of whom became permanently maimed!!

Its signing set a significant land mark in intra-European politics. For example:-

France now emerged as a super power of the time in Europe, as compared to the poor Germany, which had actually suffered the most from the War.

More than300 German states were to remain intact (I.e., unaltered) sovereign states.

France was allowed to acquire Alsace, the most economically wealthy district because of its abundant coal deposits.

The Holy Roman Empire was allowed to exist only in theory but not in practice.

The Austrian Habsburgs lost all territory they had acquired in Germany due to Ferdinand II's arrogant leadership in favour of the Catholics at the demise of the protestants.

Church territories in Germany which the Catholic Ferdinand II of Austria had, by the Edict of Restitution of 1629, ordered to be returned back to the Catholic Church were restored back to their original owner(s) as at 1624 before the Edict.

The Dutch Republic and the Swiss Confederation were now formally recognized as district sovereign political entities in intra-European politics.

The Dutch received:-

Trading rights in Brazil and also Indonesia from Portugal;

And, the territory it had conquered along the Scheldt River in Western European flowing from North France through Belgium into the North Sea in The Netherlands.

Sweden, as a result of its significant role it had played in support of the Protestants, gained territories on the Baltic Sea.

Significance of Thirty Years' War in Europe in General and Germany in Particular

The War now established a New Order in Europe with an explicit understanding that neither Catholicism nor Protestantism or any other faith or force had any absolute right or power or dominion over the other's right to life (existence) through coercion.

The peace of Westphalia redrew a new political map of Europe and set in motion the reality that every one's national interest must now be based on one's recognition and appreciation of the concept of equal sovereignty, failure of which would automatically lead one to suicide as so demonstrated by the experience from the just ended Thirty years War.

On the Strength of this Treaty, Europe now emerged as a continent of no more feudal states dominated and dictated by a colonial mother entity such as Rome but now as a continent of sovereign political entities with equal political and territorial independence that Europe had never experienced before 1648.

France's entry into the War in support of the Swedish King Caustorus Adolphus against his own Catholicism in Rome,

Was a flabbergasting diplomacy to the Catholics who had, in principle, expected such support to come to them since France was predominantly Catholic;

Added unexpected oil on fire by energizing the Protestants' efforts against the Catholics;

And, thus enhanced Europe to bring down and tame the Habsburgs' dictatorial tendencies and the self-seeking superiority complex over others in intra-European politics.

And, The Netherlands, also displaced Spain from the latter's status as a master of The Seas.

Nations of the time were now able to learn, understand and appreciate the bloody danger of dictatorial leadership and war as instruments of power and territorial acquisition and kind of painful risks and humiliations they entailed as in the case of the Habsburg Catholic regime and their godfather Ferdinand II of Austria who, in the final analysis, not only lost the war but also suffered a terrible humiliation and various other painful losses.

III: BUT WHY THIS WORLD WAR II DISASTER?: A Retrospective Analysis of Hitler's Leadership Roots Using A Psychiatric Approach (A 2nd Test)

(1) Introduction

The wisdom and knowledge gained so far from the preceding coverage about Hitler's leadership obviously leaves one in a messy jam of the most complex and complicated confusion and anxieties about this leadership particularly with regard to reasons for Hilter's personal role as the principal architect of both World War II and the most flabbergasting genocide drama of millions of his fellow Jewish Germans, Gypsies and all others of non-pure German blood a dramatic act which suddenly began immediately after the death of the Country's democratically elected President Paul von Hindenburg in 1934, that also led to the death of his own democratic government of Second Weimar Republic leaving behind a power vacuum that Hitler now grabbed and assumed absolute power as Germany's overall leader (The Fuehrer) for fulfillment of his wild goals.

In this regard, a retrospective analysis of this most complex and complicated situation using a psychiatric approach is very much in order so as to expose to the surface those hidden microscopic factors which might have unfortunately evaded recognition of previous research on the issues of the resurgence of World War II and also the Genocide.

With the aid of this approach, we will clinically and meticulously examine and answer various pertinent questions in order to expose those microscopic factors and then use them to establish who Hitler actually was; reasons why he had to subject the victims of Genocide to this act; what might have been hidden in the German history that became so special to him that he had to accomplish by all means; and whether or not all this that he was after in history was also known and desired by his German people? If so, or not, what empirical evidence can one glean from German history?

(2) A Meticulous Search for Hidden Microscopic Factors Responsible for Leading Adolf Hitler Into a Ruthless Militaristic Leadership

A ruthless militaristic leadership of Adolf Hitler's Germany did not come or arise from nothingness. It arose from its ancestral ruthless militaristic leadership manifested in the following empirical roots:-

Clovis I, who reigned from King of the Salian Franks, reigned over only one of the petty Germanic Kingdoms within Gaul. He was an eccentric personality who used cleverness, military skills, treachery and dishonesty, to conquer and extend his rule over all Gaul (now called France) and to establish his Capital at what is today called Paris. He did so after having first ruthlessly terrorized and conquered the Gallo-Romans at Soissons in 486 AD, and eliminating all remnants of the Roman Empire in Gaul. As a result of his conquest and occupation of Gaul with the aid of what he believed to be Christ's Divine intervention, Clovis I first converted himself to Roman Catholic through baptism and then forced entire Gaul to become Roman

Catholic—thus, setting up a granite foundation of Roman Catholicism as France's national religious faith till today.

Pepin of Heristal who ruled as mayor in France from 680-714 AD and who, upon his death in 714, was succeed by a ruthless Charles Martel (whose character is detailed in 3 below).

Charles Martel was an illegitimate son of Pepin of Heristal, whose name meant the "Hammer" in English language; and whose name also meant "Carolus" in Latin. The name later gave rise to the name "the Carolingian" dynasty during his reign from 714 to 741 AD.

Using his land grabbed from the Church to bribe his mounted warriors as a pay-off for their loyalty to him, Charles Martel succeeded in promoting France's political prestige noted in Europe today. Also, he had an advantage over his counterparts in Europe of two inventions of the stirrup and the horseshoe whereby the former reduced the fatigue of riding and permitted a mounted worrier to remain firmly seated while striking his enemy with his weapons, the latter enabled the horses to travel long rough terrain quickly and securely than horses without them.

These two inventions placed Charles Martel's Calvary army too superior above his enemy's infantry army in battle. His superiority always led him to an assured victory, e.g his victory over the Moslems near Tours in 732 AD—a victory which led him to be christened Charles Martel "The Hammer", i.e, a conqueror of the most impossible.

After his death in 741, Charles Martel the Hammer was succeeded by his two sons, Carloman and Pepin The Short.

But, because of being pious in spirit, Carloman chose to retreat to a monastery and live a monk's life. This, in turn, gave a full green light for his brother, Pepin The Short, to assume all political leadership of his Carolingian dynasty left behind by his father, Charles Martel the hammer in 741 AD.

Pepin The Short, ruled from 741 to 768, as both mayor and figurehead King but his latter status was later recognized through anointment by Archbishop Boniface in 751. When asked by Pope Stephen II in Rome for a military aid against external aggression by another Germanic group of barbarian warriors, The Lombards, who had invaded and already captured Rovenna, Pepin battled with the aggressor between 754 and 756 with a view to forcing them to surrender all Church lands they had usurped from the Pope extending from middle Italy to Ravenna.

In 756, Pepin the Short defeated the Lombards repossessed the lands and restored it back to the Pope—an act which pleased the Pope so much that he christened it as the "Donation of Pepin" and also became an added asset to the affinity between France and Pope in Rome throughout the medieval political life; and a legacy that Pepin The Short now left behind for his successor Charles The Great popularly known as Charlemagne to use in French Empire building in Europe as empirically noted in (5) below.

Charlemagne who reigned from 768 till 814 was as fierce and ruthless leader akin to his father Pepin The Short. Through this ruthlessness and militarism, Charlemagne conquered and extended the already existing dominion of the Carolingian dynasty left behind by his grandfather, Charles Martel the Hammer, on the latter's death in 741 AD by not just getting what he wanted on a platter but by ruthlessly conquering most Continental Europe except the Muslim Spain, Scandinavia, Southern Italy, and Sicily. He was the first monarch to stubbornly proclaim himself emperor and a guardian of the Church. Empowered with the love for wisdom knowledge, and military conquests, Charlemagne stunned Europe of the time with his zeal for a Carolingian Renaissance and equating his conquests with extension of Christianity by forcing every territory he conquered to convert to Roman Catholic faith and by punishing every one who resisted with a death penalty. Although Charlemagne was unable to convert all Muslim Spain to Christianity, he successfully managed to convert a small portion of Spain using a military force, a portion which came to be called "Spanish March" (i.e a military buffer zone). After conquering Western Europe militarily, Charlemagne advanced into Eastern Europe creating Marches, e.g, "East March" occupying the land south of Denube River Region which later became Austria. After that, Charlemagne further advanced, Eastwards into other additional new territories belonging to the Slavs and Avars and turned them into a new world for possession by German missionaries and settlers who began laying claims to these lands at the expense of their original owners (the Slavs and Avars). To make the matter worse, when Rome was besieged by rioting hostile groups aimed at deposing the newly elected Pope Leo III, the latter secretly fled to Germany for Charlemagne's emergency assistance. Desirous to capitalize on this emergency request, Charlemagne hurriedly travelled to Rome with Pope Leo III and swiftly suppressed the riot. In return, Pope cheerfully reciprocated by coronating Charlemagne "Emperor of the Romans" thus empowering the Carolingian dynasty's dominion over Rome and all Rome's former provinces in the West; Germany South of the Elbe; and most of Eastern Europe that had never been in the domain of the Roman Empire. But, although the Carolingian dynasty's dominion was later vehemently challenged by the invasion of the Northmen called "Vikings" descending down from Scandinavian Countries to invade and ransack monasteries in to England and Northern parts of mainland Europe, the German Empire had, by the conquests of Charlemagne, grown too powerful after having taken over all that had been under the Roman Empire. And by the time Charlemagne died in 814, Germany had already earned an undisputable title as "The Master of The Heartland" and "Master of the European World" that later became a lesson of admiration by geopolitics classical scholars such as Niccolo Machiavelli, (1469-1527), Charles Robert Darwin (1809-1882), Alfred Thayer Mahan (1840-1914), Sir Halford John Mackinder (1861-1947) and many others who used it as a point of reference in their advice to policy makers and statesmen of the 19th and 20th Century Europe, if they were to succeed over others.

Louis The Pious, a single heir of Charlemagne, who, on his father's death in 814, assumed a leadership responsibility over a vast conquered empire that their father (Charlemagne) had left behind.

Throughout his reign which lasted from his father's death year in 814 till 840, Louis The Pious, proved a less talented leader.

Because of this deficiency in him, Charlemagne's empire security deteriorated so much that he was deposed by his own eldest son, Lothair, though he was lucky to be restored back to the throne by his two younger sons, Louis the German and Charles The Bald in 841.

And in 842, the two younger sons met at Strasbourg and entered into an alliance by the famous swearing-in-ceremony of "Strasbourg Oaths" whereby the two swore to continue their collective opposition to their eldest brother's arrogance. But since their collective army was not that capable enough to eliminate their brother's, all three now decided to enter into a mutual tripartite Treaty of Verdum in 843 by dividing their father's Empire into three equal portions by which Charles The Bald received the

Western portion which is today called France; Louis the German received the Eastern portion which is today called Germany; and Lothair received the middle portion laying between the two portions extending from the North Sea to Central Italy.

Whereas both Western and Eastern portions of Charles the Bald and Louis the German possessed some distinct geographical, cultural and linguistic character, with a potential continuity, the Lothair's portion did not. Lack of this distinct character led the Lothair's portion to split into three distinct cultures of Alsace, Lorraine, Burgundy and Italy.

Hence the genesis of continued scramble and war between Germany and France for possession of Alsace Lorraine; and also the reason why France orchestrated Napoleonic War under her ruthless leader Napoleon Bonaparte (1769-1821), noted in (7) below.

Napoleon I (1769) popularly called Napoleon Bonaparte, was a very short French military genius of all leaders of his time. Obsessed with his ruthless appetite for military conquests motto "When I see an empty throne, I feel the urge to sit on it", he ruthlessly crowned himself Emperor of the French and created an Empire through ruthless militaristic conquests covering most Western and Central Europe. After having crushed one enemy after another, he entrenched himself so much over all other European leaders that, until he was also crushed at the Battle of Waterloo in 1815 AD, he was always feared as a totally impossible power for any other leader to reckon with throughout Europe.

Because of his short stature that came with his amazing enormous courage and zeal that France had never experienced before in European political life, he was popularly nicknamed "Le Petit Caporal" meaning the "Little Corporal" in English.

Guided by his ruthless appetite for military conquests after conquests, Napoleon personally commanded all formal activities of France and pioneered new military strategies totally unknown to other countries and leaders in Europe. He, for example, personally supervised formulation of a system of new laws called "Code Napoleon"; and conquered and expanded the French Empire beyond the imagination of every French and other European of his time until this might was finally brought to a dramatic and surprising end at the Battle of Waterloo in 1815 by combined forces of the British and the allies under the command of the Duke of Wellington and Marshall Gebhard ven Blucher.

Essentially, Napoleon Bonaparte's military success was none other than a function of his emulation of the military ruthless tactics of his late grandfather, the Carolingian leader, Charlemagne; whose foot-steps, he meticulously followed step-by-step in his quest to challenge the existing map of Europe left behind by Charlemagne, with his eyes focused on Alsace and Lorraine.

Psychologically controlled by his militaristic ruthless belief that "the object of war is victory"; that "the object of victory is conquest"; and finally that "the object of conquest is occupation", Napoleon Bonaparte ruthlessly swept most of Europe using military conquests and occupation.

He strengthened his victories by putting his brother, Joseph, as King of Naples; his other brother Louis as king of Holland; and even his sisters as queens of Naples and Tuscany.

He then chopped Germany and Italy into provinces and awarded them to his favourite Generals and Marshals. And, on 14th October, 1806, he brutally and courageously marched into Berlin and issued a Berlin Decree barring all British goods from Europe to Britain.

After conquering Germany and the rest of the Western Europe save Britain, Napoleon ruthlessly dominated most of Europe. Had it not been his defeat by the British and Allied forces at the Battle of Waterloo in 1815, France had already now proved, through her Charlemagne-like-ruthless minded Napoleon's conquests and occupation, a de facto new Master of The Heartland in the 18th Century European biopolitics.

But, whereas France and her militaristic ruthlessness, manifested in Napoleon's leadership, had indeed been the actual root-cause of Napoleonic wars and the disasters the latter had now cause in Europe, the already victim and sufferer (i.e, France) still again found herself being the real victim and sufferer of the harsh terms of the Congress of Vienna of 1814-1815 which, contrary to what was expected of its decision, forced Germany to surrender much of her territory to France!—A painful decision indeed to Germany!!

However, in spite of all this unfairness to Germany, the Country's military capability left behind by Charlemagne remained intact; unshaken; and, therefore, still very vibrant indeed. With this resurgence potential, Germany quickly rose up once again in the name of The German League to succeed the Holy Roman Empire in keeping with the Congress' terms. Thus, by virtue of the terms of The Congress of Vienna of 1814-1815, Germany was to inherit what the Holy Roman Empire had left behind.

The League consisted of 39 states; 5 substantial kingdoms; and the Germany parts of the Austrian empire. Prussia was one of the said 5 kingdoms led by Fredrick The Great, who in the mid-18th century, had led a series of successful wars of conquests over all other Germanic States thus placing Prussia to a political prominence above all others in Europe of the time. And, after defeating also France in the Franco-Prussian War of 1870-71, Prussia now categorically and majestically declared a formation of the German Empire. And, as will further be noted below from an account about Chancellor Otto von Bismark and his added militaristic contribution to German rise to prominence in Europe after Frederick The Great, under him (Bismark), Germany now became a de facto major European power for one to reckon with in the late 19th Century inter-European politics because of its booming industrial economy, agriculture, colonial empire and military might.

Chancellor Otto von Bismack who lived from 1815 to 1898, was also officially known as Prince Bismarck-Schonhansen, or Otto Eduard Leopold von Bismarck.

He was a Prussian statesman with an extra-ordinary ingenuity by which he managed to unite the warring militaristic German states into one German Empire.

Like his predecessors, he vowed that the great political problems in Europe had to be settled by use of one's "blood and iron" (i.e., war weaponry) instead of relying on useless rhetoric speeches and conferences and treaty resolutions.

Armed with this ruthless militaristic attitude, Bismark fought three wars to unify the warring militaristic German states into one Empire. These included the war with Denmark in 1864, the Seven Weeks' War against Austria in 1866, and the Franco-Prussian War of 1870-71—the latter being Bismarck's landmark military victory for Germany against France under Napoleon III (or Louis Bonaparte, King of Holland and brother to Napoleon I) who had secretly sought to annex the Rhineland, Luxembourg, or Belgium, leading to Napoleon's overthrow at home by revolutionists disgusted with Napoleonistic militarism and his flight to Chislehurst in England, where he died on 4th September, 1870 (only two days after his defeat by Otto von Bismark and surrender at Sedan on 2nd September, 1870.

After this decisive victory against Napoleon III, Chancellor Otto von Bismark was elevated to a post of "Reichschancellor (or Arch-Chancellor) of the now new German Empire; and was now popularly addressed as the "Iron Chancellor", (i.e., The Gun-man Chancellor who never believed in rhetorics but in "blood and iron".

But unlike his predecessors, von Bismark did not rely entirely on military diplomacy. He also used peaceful diplomacy where it was deemed necessary. Consequently, his success in uniting the warring Germanic states into one Empire was a function of a mixture of his love for a ruthless and military conquest policy, extra-ordinary political wits and cunning, and diplomatic ingenuity above all leaders of his time in Europe.

Using this mixture as strategic means, von Bismark did not only unite the warring German states into one Empire but also cultivated and achieved numerous treaties with other European leaders he had not conquered with a view to fortifying his German Empire's security against other militaristically ruthless European leaders.

For instance, he achieved Triple Alliance with Austria and also Italy that lived up to the outbreak of World War I in 1914. Also, he achieved another treaty of peaceful co-existence with Russia in which Germany chose neutrality in event of any attack on Russia, with a sole view that he had also to use such bilateral peaceful agreements as an added weapon for his Empire's Security.

Thereafter, von Bismarck chose to retire in 1888 upon King Wilhelm II's ascension to the throne with an anti-Bismark attitude due to von Bismark reputation.

Wilhelm II (1859-1941) who took over from his grandfather (Wilhem I) in 1888, was the last emperor of the German Empire. Consequently, he was the Emperor of German Empire during World War I.

From his lineage, Wilhelm II was a close cousin of both King George V of England and Nicholas II of Russia with whom he fought in World War I

As a student of military education which he actually specialized in during his studies, Wilhelm II relied heavily on military conquest as leadership to rational means. Consequently, he expanded the German Empire by encouraging manufacturing, foreign markets for trade and commerce; by militarily gaining foreign countries as colonies in Africa and the Pacific Ocean; and by building up a huge powerful army and navy to the extent that they became the greatest military power of the World of the time.

Having gained such superiority for his German Empire through those strategies, Wilhelm II now turned to von-Bismark's diplomatic legacy which he did not now see any more need of, consequently, in 1890, he immediately terminated the old Russian alliance with Russia thereby giving rise to a loss of security of his German Empire from the East and also from the West a loss of World War I in 1918 and the German navy's revolt against him.

Because of this leadership blunder, Wilhelm II was forced out of office by his Prime Minister; and Wilhelm II fled to Doom in The Netherlands where he lived in exile for over twenty years.

On the other hand, through Kaiser (Emperor) Wilhelm II, German Empire had reached its peak of greatness before World War I in 1914.

But as a result of the Kaiser's leadership poverty due to its marginalization of Otto von Bismark's leadership strategy that was a blend of both militarism diplomacy and peaceful co-existence diplomacy, Germany did not lose the war. Also, Germany was forced to swallow the most bitter pill she had ever dreamt of. She was forced to accept harsh terms of The Treaty of Versailles of 1919 that stripped her people of their most indispensable possessions viz:

Their colonial empire by taking and giving away all their African colonies of Rwanda-Urundi (now divided into independent states of Rwanda and Burundi) to Belgium, and also Tanganyika (now called independent Tanzania) and South West Africa (now called independent Namibia) to the United Kingdom who were to act as Mandate Administrators of such colonies on behalf of The League of Nations Mandate System.

Part of their Schleswig was returned back to Denmark.

Their most rich coal-deposit districts of Alsace and Lorraine were given away to France.

And, part of their Prussian territory was given away to Poland.

In this regard, Germany's defeat in World War I that resulted into all this painful loss and the loss of the glory she had already achieved before the War must have been a terrible nauseating epidemic to her, her people and her new leadership, Weimar Republic that was formed in 1919.

This diabolic situation caused by a reckless militaristic leadership of the now exiled Kaiser Wilhelm II, was further compounded by the rise of the labour strife coupled with domestic political fragmentation; armed rebellion from both the armed forces and the civil society accusing Kaiser Wilhelm II's reckless military leadership that had now plunged the innocent population into a sea of irrelevant agonies, and the economic depression of 1929. All this now complicated the situation so much in the Country that it easily led to the creation of an enabling environment for Adolf Hitler's National Socialist German Workers' Party (NSDAP) also called the Nazis, to gain a full support and power momentum over all other political parties in Germany that were seen to be having no vision of a good solution to the Country's emergency plight.

Hence, Hitler's easy political victory over the mind of most Germans and all opposition parties leading to his being called by President Hinderburg on 30th January, 1933 to form a new government, which, in turn, put an end to the Weimar Republic upon the President's death in August, 1934.

IV: A COMPARATIVE ANALYSIS: The Resurrection of German Traditional Warrior Tendencies in Hitler.

Since the advent of World War II to the present (2013), the name Adolf Hitler has always meant World War II and the agonies of the holocaust of millions of Jewish Germans and Gypsies who had to suffer because of having no Aryan German blood. Thus his name and the two have always been so synonymous in that any reference to one automatically triggers a remembrance of the other as in the case of the Jewish Exodus from Egypt automatically rings the bell to the name Moses, albeit in a totally good omen way to the Jews as opposed to Hitler which is in a totally bad omen way to the same people.

But, if an ancient leader such as the Pharaoh(s) was able to sustain the same Jews in order to use them to help him to build Egypt beyond recognition of other Countries of the time by building amazing pyramids and means of food security, and Adolf Hitler could not learn from such a lesson but instead killed most of them using gas chambers thereby robbing his Country a valuable source of human manpower resource that would have helped him to build a super power Germany beyond the reach and recognition of other Countries of his time as they had so done to Egypt, what could have forced him or blocked his wisdom so as to resort to such heinous/abnormal act? What could have been the root-cause? Was the root-cause of this a bad omen to the Jews in Hitler unique to Hitler as an individual or was it anchored in Hitler's ancestral blood (heritage)? If not, was he a drunkard or a madman suffering from a schizophrenia disease that could have consequently triggered him to behave in such a flabbergasting manner leading to the advent of World War II and the holocaust?

In search for a succinct answer to this nagging puzzle, the following Autopsy, using a psychiatric approach (which is, of course, not a treatment of a mental disorder as so conventionally understood in traditional, social and Behavioral Science but essentially in a Neo-Social and Behavioral Science context meaning unearthing hidden secret roots of one's behavior) is in order. An Autopsy of both World War II and The Holocaust clearly shows the following striking findings leading to a possible understanding of the roots of Hitler's leadership behavior:

From the behavior of the first ever recorded leadership in the leadership history of the Germanic peoples, (the Franks, Anglo-Saxons, etc), Clovis I, who reigned the Salian Franks within Gaul (now known as France) from 481 to 511 AD behaved just like Hitler in that he was also an eccentric personality who like Hitler, used cleverness, militarism, militarization, treachery and dishonesty to conquer, occupy and expand his rule over all France; and also to eliminate the Gallo-Romans in 486 AD as well as roots of the Roman Empire in France. Like Clovis I, Hitler sought to do the same by exterminating all non-Aryan Germans without a pure Aryan blood.

(2) The same militaristic ruthlessness in Hitler's leadership blood is also borne out in most of all other leaders after Clovis I. For example,

(a) Although much is not documented about Pepin of Heristal who, later also ruled France from 680-714 AD, the fact is that Pepin also used the same mode of ruthless leadership manifested in Hitler's ruthless leadership that led Pepin to also conquer occupy and dominate over almost all Frankish Kingdom, before he was succeeded by his illegitimate son, Charles Martel, upon his death in 714 AD.

However, a very vivid understanding of Hitler's eccentric leadership behavior also mirrors or comes to the surface in the leadership of Charles Martel who was popularly referred to in jubilation and public euphoria as "The Hammer"(in English) or "Carolus" in Latin leading to the rise of the Carolingian dynasty, during his reign from 714 to 741 AD. Like Hitler,

Charles Martel was such a ruthless militaristic leader who loved Victory after Victory as a source of his joy. And, in as much as this joy in Charles Martel was much reminiscent/evident his victory over the Moslems near Tours in 732 AD thus leading him to be christened "The Hammer" meaning the conqueror of the most impossible, so was the same euphoria of joy in Hitler's leadership victories also evident in (Hitler's) victory over France on 22nd June, 1940. The victory pleased both Hitler and his German people so much that Hitler had to suddenly jump into a Happy Jig Dance on receiving the Formal Surrender Word from a French Delegation in the Compiegne forest near Paris on 22nd June, 1940.

And, in the same way Hitler was so interested in discovery and inventions of new technologies totally unknown to other leaders and countries in Europe that this led him to gain superiority over all Europe (except the United Kingdom and Russia) by inventing new machines such as a Volkswagen (cheap vehicle and easier to use in both muddy and rugged roads without any trouble than expensive ones only affordable by the rich but unable to maneuver in both muddy and rugged roads and which, unlike the Volkswagen, must use a water cooling system in order to function), so was Charles Martel. Like Hitler, Charles Martel was also very much interested in scientific and technological discoveries and inventions. And, like Hitler, he invented the stirrup and the horseshoe, which individually and collectively aided him so much that they empowered Charles Martel's Calvary army to become too superior above his all enemies' infantry army in battle. And in the same way Hitler's love for technological discoveries and inventories in weaponry enabled him to gain victories after victories in Europe before he was silenced by the United States' entry into the War in support of the Allies against Germany, so did Charle Martel's love for technological discoveries and inventions in weaponry also enable him to gain victory after victory as also manifested in his victory over the Muslims in 732 AD.

And finally, but not least, in as much as Hitler was fond of using bribery and lies to influence his followers to support his policies and goals and to enhance Germany's fame and superiority over all other Countries in Europe through a series of military victories, so was Charles Martel also in love with the same strategy by grabbing land from the Church and using it to bribe his mounted warriors in order to gain their maximum/total loyalty needed to promote France's political fame and superiority in Europe.

Also with regard to the relationship between Pepin The Short's leadership style and Adolf Hitler's,

Whereas the former reigned in a focused leadership status as both mayor and King of France from 741 to 768, the latter also reigned in a fused leadership status of Fuehrer which was a combination of both Chancellorship and the Presidency after the death of The Weimar's President Paul von Hindenburg in August, 1934.

(ii) And, like Hitler who reigned with an iron hand of ruthless militarism manifested in a flabbergasting series of military conquests after conquests in The Rhineland in 1936 in a total violation of the Versailles Treaty of 1919, and then Austria, Czechoslovakia, Poland, France, etc; with an ultimate aim of making Germany absolute Master of Europe and Total World and protector of his Aryan German blood purity, so did Pepin The Short also did exactly the same particularly in the Pyrenees region with an ultimate aim of making his Frankish Kingdom supreme in Europe and also as a reliable protector and ally of The Church in Rome by driving the Lombards out of Rome, repossessing the Church land from these Lombards, and then returning the same to The Church—an adorable assistance that pleased The Pope so much that the latter decided to Christen it as a "Donation of Pepin"

Like Hitler and al his predecessors such as Pepin The Short, Charles Martel, Pepin the Heristal and finally Clovis I, Charlemagne who reigned from 768 till 814 was equally a fierce and ruthless leader who lived a belief of military conquests as his leadership delicacy. For instance,

Like Hitler, he conquered almost entire Continental Europe.

(ii) Like Hitler who proclaimed himself Fuehrer (meaning absolute leader) of Germany by abolishing the Presidency after President Paul Von Hindenburg's death in August, 1934, Charlemagne proclaimed himself Emperor and a guardian of the Church.

(iii) And, like Hitler who flabbergasted Europe and the Total World of the 20th Century with his zeal for a German Empire Renaissance and for gnating his conquests with his desire to extend a *Lebenstraum* (i.e, a living space) for the already overcrowded Germans by conquering and occupying such space in Europe thus leading to World War II catastrophe, so did Charlemagne also flabbergast Europe of the 8th Century with his zeal for a Carolingian Renaissance and for equating his conquests with his desire to extend Christianity by forcing every territory and people he conquered to convert to Roman Catholicism.

(iv) And, other most striking evidences justifying similarity between the two is that, whereas Charlemagne used a penalty death to every one that did not accept his conversion to Christianity declaration, Hitler also used the same coercive means against his opponents by using his Hitler Youth, and the SPD (intelligence organizations to report every dissident for punishment) in as much as Charlemagne was obsessed in military conquests in Eastern Europe in search for marches i.e, military buffers) for his Empire by conquering and occupying as much land as he could conquer in both Western Europe such as Austria and territories in the Eastern Europe belonging to the Slavs and Avars, so was Hilter also obsessed with the same idea of territorial conquest after conquests as a resurrection of his Germanic warrior tradition; and in as much as Charlemagne was closely friendly to Rome as also manifested in his alliance with Pope Leo III against those rioting hostile groups aimed at deposing the newly elected Pope, thus leading the Pope to crown him (Charlemagne) Emperor of the Romans" thus empowering Germany to the status of "Master of The Heartland and Total European World", in the 8th Century World Politics, so was Hitler also very much closely friendly to Rome as also manifested in his mutual relations with Italy's fascist leader, Benito Mussolini, although this relations later became strained because of the Jewish Question. In all, Hitler and Mussolini were but two sides of the same coin. For instance, as far back as May 1933, when the newly inaugurated United States President Franklin D. Roosevelt called for a World Disarmament of dangerous and offensive weapons, Hitler promptly and readily agreed with the idea with a good hope that the rest of the World Leaders were also going to do the same. Due to his feeling at that time that "war was madness", Hitler first and foremost visited his friend Mussolini in Rome and begged Mussolini to come out with a European Peace Plan that would lead Europe to a lasting peace and justice and also save Germany from the on-going bitter terms of The Versailles Treaty against Germany.

As a good friend also manifested in Hitler's assessment of Mussolini "With Mussolini, I am in the clear, my ties of friendship are close", Mussolini gladly agreed to do so. He quickly invited, and briefed the British Prime Minister and the latter's Foreign Minister, Sir John Simon, in Rome who also collectively got impressed with the idea and then successfully called and persuaded their French counterpart to come over to Rome on the issue. But when the four nation-states (Britain, France, Germany and Italy) met in Rome, with Mussolini chairing, France unfortunately rejected Mussolini's Peace Plan, which also had an element of recognition of the principle of each people's right to self-determinations, that if accepted by the Four, Hitler's Germany could have, by virtue of this Principle, been sympathized and possibly relieved from the existing painful Versailles Treaty terms, particularly the reparation debt agony of 6,000,000,000 British Sterling Pounds.

As a result, Hitler retaliated with Germany's withdrawal from her obligations to those harsh terms; and decided to revert back to his original revolutionary motto of The Beer Hall Putsch speech of 8th November, 1923 that "We need a revolutionary to lead a March on Berlin" and his militaristic belief that "Conquest, is not only a right but also a duty for the protection of the people and the state", just as Charlemagne also believed in his series of militaristic ruthless victories after victories during his reign (768-814) leading him to be crowned as Emperor of The Romans by Pope Leo III.

(e) A lesson gleaned from the conflict among three sons of Louis The Pious, viz: Lothair, Louis The German and Charles The Bald leading the three to the famous Swearing-In-Ceremony of The "Strasbourg Oaths" embodied in the tripartite drama of the Verdun Treaty of 843, is another indispensable fertile ground for an explanation of Hitler's leadership behaviour, and also the behaviour of his counterparts in intra-European conflicts of 1870/71, World War I and finally World War II.

Whereas by The Vendun Treaty, the three sons vowed not to physically eliminate each other, and since they were all equal in military strength in such a manner that neither one could easily be eliminated by the other, such a mutual memorandum of understanding was necessary and beneficial to each. In this regard, Charles The Bald received a Western portion of their father's empire which is now called France; Louis the German received an Eastern portions which is now called Germany; and finally Lothair, the eldest and troublemaker of the three brothers received the Middle portion laying between France and Germany which now constitutes Alsace and Lorraine districts which has, since that time (843 AD), remained a perennial bone of contention in European politics, in the succeeding account.

(f) Hitler's military conquest obsessions must also have originated from his grandfather, Napoleon I also known by most people as Napoleon Bonaparte as evidenced by the latter's horrifying lessons of military conquests after conquests coupled with the human agonies Europe had to encounter. Because of his ruthlessness evidenced by his notorious motto that "the object of war is victory"; "the object of victory is conquest; and "the object of conquest is occupation", Napoleon crushed most of Europe in emulation of a lesson of conquests from his grandfather Charlemagne that had stunned Europe so much including Pope Leo III that the latter had, on his own volition, based on what he had observed so far in Charlemagne, to crown him (Charlemagne) as "Emperor of The Romans", though Charlemagne, was not a Roman but a German.

And further that these two (Napoleon and Charlemagne) and Hitler had some significant thing in common in their leadership blood, a psychiatric diagnosis of their belief systems shows that all three of them had a common unique abnormal love for military conquest and occupation as their ultimate object of war. This striking commonality of their thinking, beliefs and goal is clearly manifested in their military conquest records. Charlemagne's stunning record of his military conquests and occupation of the countries and peoples he conquered is significantly congruent to Napoleon Bonaparte's and Hitler's military conquest records in that the end result of military victory of both Hitler and Napoleon Bonaparte was also succinctly "occupation" of every conquered country and people(s).

Another significant source of the roots of Hitler militaristic ruthlessness is definitely Charles Otto Von Bismarck's leadership. Like Bismarck whose view was that great political problems in Europe could only be settled using "blood and iron (guns)" and that he therefore, had no time to waste on listening to empty speeches and arguments and counter-arguments, Hitler had the same view. This is the reason why Bismarck earned the title of "Iron Chancellor", (meaning, The Gun-man Chancellor who had no time for rhetorics) Also, this is the fundamental reason why Hitler had to earn the title of "The Iron Cross" which led him to be promoted to the rank of a "Lace Corporal" in 1917 during his military service in the Baverian government before he became Chancellor in The Second Reign of President Paul von Hindenburg in 1933.

But, that is not all. In addition to the above documented hidden subcutaneous microscopic sources responsible for the development of Hitler's militaristic ruthless leadership character which this autopsy has been able to unearth using a psychiatric approach, in its marathon research expedition through those unvisited scary dark landscapes, this autopsy also further establishes that the complex conduct of Hitler's immediate predecessor, Wilhelm II (who succeeded Chancellor von Bismarck) is reminiscent as another significant source. It is reminiscence in that his conduct is very similar in character to that of Hitler. It is reminiscent to Hitler's in that like Hitler's, it was characterized by ruthless militarism and militarization manifested in Wilhelm II's huge military build-up of both army and the navy; expansion of the Germany Empire at all costs and place such as Africa where Wilhelm II brutally did so by not only conquering but also occupying and converting conquered territories into colonies as in the case of Tanganyika (now known as Tanzania), South West Africa (now known as Namibia) and Rwanda-Urundi (now known as separate sovereign countries of Rwanda and Burundi). And, also like Hitler who turned to The Treaty of Versailles and abrogated it by terminating Germany's obligation to its terms of Reparation re-payments as soon as he noticed in Rome that France was not interested in Mussolini's proposed European Peace Plan and immediately begin his militaristic conquest missions, so did Wilhelm II also do the same by imprudently terminating the von Bismarck's Prussian Alliance with Russia of 1890 which gradually led to Germany's security on both East and West and therefore, made Germany to easily lose in World War I of 1914-1918, and to be subjected to humiliating and painful terms of Reparation repayments to the Allies—a punishment which could have been prudently avoided, at the outset had Wilhelm II not abrogated the Alliance with Russia and plunged Germany to militarism and militarization against her neighbours; and also a punishment that turned out to be very much similar to the conduct, and consequences of Hitler's militarism and militarization that led to the same Germany (a victim of world War I) to be again also a victim of World War II to face another painful punishment for World War II by The Treaty of San Francisco of 1945. And as History repeated itself this way so did it also repeat itself at the same end time of World War II when Hitler like his predicessor Wilhelm II at the end-time of World War I in 1919, also abdicated his leadership over Germany and fled into a hidden self-exile in the bunker of the Reich Chancellery in Berlin where he decided to quickly commit suicide on 30th April, 1945 in order to escape the already advancing fierce World anger and internal dissatisfaction for his reckless militaristic leadership blunder which had consequently plunged Germany and her innocent people on into the most costly World War II disaster exactly in the same way his predecessor, Wilhelm II, had also done in World War I. Like Hitler, Wilhelm II also abdicated his leadership over Germany and fled to hide in exile in The Netherlands on 9th November, 1918 in order to escape the already advancing fierce World anger including internal revolt from both civil society and the German Navy for his reckless militaristic leadership blunder which had consequently plunged Germany and her innocent people into the most costly World War I disaster. Hence the congruency of the two leadership behaviour and disasters. And thus, the resurrection of German traditional warrior personality and behaviour in Hitler.

A RECAPTULATION OF HITLER AND WORLD WAR II ISSUE

(A) ON HITLER'S STANCE ON WORLD WAR 1 REPARATION ISSUE

Hitler was extremely bitter about the harsh reparation burden imposed on his Germany and German People by the Treaty of Versailles terms at the end of World War 1, and, therefore, harshly complained against *inter alia* the £6,000,000,000 (Six Billion British Sterling Pounds) reparation debt imposed on Germany in 1919 by the said Treaty for World War 1 damages to France, Great Britain, Belgium, etc.

He, however, did so only after Germany having already honoured and paid the debt for one full year but because of now having found it extremely extenuating and difficult to continue any further as Germany was now too economically weak and fragile to be able to survive as a nation in post-World War 1 with such a huge and unbearable debt burden.

But whereas Britain showed some positive signs of sympathy and accordingly accepted Germany's appeal, unfortunately France and Belgium, being the main sufferers of World War 1, refused.

Because of such refusal, Germany continued with the repayment but, at this time, now using scheduled deliveries of timber and coal in lieu of cash money since she had no more cash for the reparations.

Though supported by Italy and Belgium, France became furious and consequently invaded Germany's industrial region called *"Ruh"* in order to tell Germany that the new mode of debt repayment was not acceptable to France.

(B) ON HITLER'S PAN-GERMAN NATION AND LEBENSTRAUM ISSUE (OR SUFFICIENT LIVING SPACE)

But because of his hyper love and adoration for his German state and anger for its poor state as also manifested in his two books, Mein Kampf (1960) and Table Talk (1953), Hitler, obviously, did not want to see his impoverished German people suffer to death because of the now existing high inflation caused by France's pressure for reparation repayments.

Hitler believed that the debt in question was too punitive and a humiliation that it must, therefore, to be over-turned and the Prussian Germany's lost territories (Alsace, Lorraine and parts of Poland inhabited by German speaking people) restored to Germany since Germany's sole aim in World War I was to restore the same.

Believed that France would not be willing to surrender Alsace and Lorraine peacefully to Germany unless militarily coerced to do so.

Wanted a re-creation of boundaries of Otto Von Bismarck's Germany created after the Prussian-Germany military victories of 1866 and 1871.

Wanted a pan-Germany that would include and cater for all ethnic Germans in one people and one empire (*ein Volk, ein Reich*)

Was bitterly furious with the Treaty of Versailles because contrary to US President Woodrow Wilson's emphasis of Allies' Spirit of commitment to the right of self-determination of peoples, Germany was denied this virtue (right) by post-World War 1's World Leadership regarding populous Germans living and being treated as a minority without a formidable voice in Danzig, Poland and The Polish Corridor and in Sudetenland, Czechoslovakia, in East Prussia which was physically cut off from its mainland German Body and thus reducing Germany's geographical size (or area), population power and total national power.

Believed that his populous German people in Europe were being forced to live in a too squeezed territorial area space that was so overcrowded and, therefore, too congested that was not able to meet their needs.

Argued that such various diabolic circumstances led Germans to humiliation, desperation and other agonies in Europe simply because of the conditions of The Versailles Treaty against his German people.

Consequently argued that Germany definitely needed a sufficient living space (Lebenstraum) which, according to history, Germans had already had before in Europe ever since the Old days of their supremacy over the Roman Empire in the 4th and 5th centuries under their King Odovacar (while in the service of Rome) and later King Theodoric (King of the Ostrogoths) who inherited Odovacar's reign over the Western Roman Empire effective 493 AD.

Argued that such space could not be met by being allowed to re-possess Germany's lost colonies since such colonies lacked an assured good security to be defended as they could be easily cut off from the Fatherland by naval action as it had already been witnessed between 1914 and 1918 in the Allies' action against Germany in World War 1.

Therefore, argued that such a demand by Germany could again prove another futile and costly mistake that the Imperial Germany Leadership under Wilhelm II had made before World War I thus subjecting Germany to an irreparable disaster of reputations and loss of Germany's territorial possessions in both Europe and in her colonial empire, e.g Africa.

Argued that because of these obvious obstacles, and that in order to avoid, them, a Lebenstraum (a clear and safe living space) for his Pan-German Nation was very necessary in the Eastern Europe and Russia in particular where valuable foodstuffs and raw materials were also abundantly available and well guaranteed.

(C) ON HITLER GERMANY'S STANCE ON EUROPEAN PEACE

Germany's long standing demands prior to World War I that there would never be any lasting peace in Europe short of the answers to those demands which in the process led Europe to World War I in 1914, repeated themselves in post-World War I (or prior to World War II) thus leading to World War II in 1939.

Also although being a culprit of World War I planning and atrocities, Germany became incensed on Anglo-American refusal to France's proposal for a creation of a League of Nations with a Standing Peace Keeping Force under the League, which Germany felt could have an essential peace keeping asset.

Further, Germany also became incensed by Britain's refusal of the American proposal calling for a principle of an all-round reduction of 1/3 (one third) of each nation-state's existing armed forces and armaments (Britain's refusal was a function of her belief that this action would reduce her power in the number of British Cruise Missiles).

Germany argued that all other powers must either disarm down to the Versailles Treaty of 1919 or else the same powers also recognize Germany's right to arm. She argued that this was very logical since Europe was already a known habitual battle field for militarism and militarization ever since the Antiquity before and after the dissolution of the Roman Empire in the Eastern and the Western Europe beginning with the Huns, the Visigoths, the Vandals, the Burgundians, the Franks, the Alemanni, the Angles, the Saxons, the Jutes, the Lombards and other most earliest European ruthless barbarians who were responsible in bringing The Roman Empire to its knees through terrorism, vandalization and military occupation of every part of that Empire that they ever conquered, most particularly the Huns who because of food insecurity, abandoned their native land of domicile in the Central Asia in the early 370's and swiftly began migrating Westwards on horse back right up to the Volga River area where they met and destroyed the Germanic Goths around the Black Sea, the Alans, and the Ostragoths in the Eastern Roman Empire in 372 AD whom they terrorized over the years under their terribly fierce leader, Attila the Hun, who, because of his most dangerous militarism and militarization earned himself the name of "The Scourge of God", during the reign of Pope Leo I in Rome, ways back before other terrible Germanic leaders such as Clovis I's reign in 481-511 AD; Pepin's reign in

680-714 AD; and the most flabbergasting ruthless leaders in Europe such as Charles The Great or Charlemagne who reigned from 768 to 814 and then Napoleon Bonaparte, who, through military ruthlessness crushed both Democracy and The Monarchy in France and concentrated all powers in himself as an absolute leader of France, on 5th October, 1795 a striking phenomenon that came to be also repeated once again by Adolf Hitler in the 20th Century Europe death of his President Paul von Hindenburg of The Second Reich in August, 1934.

Because of this security reason, Germany made an offer:

- to accept any limit on her army acceptable to either French, Italian or Polish armies; and

- to fix one German air force at 30% of combined capabilities of Air Forces of her neighbours.

- But, again France rejected this Germany's new offer, thus leading;

- to the demise of the Disarmament Conference in 1934; and

- to Germany's rationale of beginning to think twice as to what she should now do given the existing history of inter-European ethnic militaristic terrorism.

IV: ON THE OUTCOME OF THE DEATH OF DISARMAMENT CONFERENCE

This death of Disarmament Conference

Marked the transition of Europe's drift into World War II

Failure of Allied Powers to carry out their noble promise to disarm themselves automatically not only justified but also explained vividly Germany's right and rationale of rearmament.

This green light to Germany's rearmament became a vicious circle in that it gave birth to other green lights for the Allied Powers' further re-armament and for Germany's counter re-armament, and vice versa.

The Four Power Pact involving Italy, Britain, France and Germany agreed during the Conference that:

If disarmament Conference failed to find a solution to a disarmament call, then the Members would recognize Germany's right to re-arm by stages.

The Establishment of the League of Nations would henceforth be limited to persuasion and various levels of moral and economic sanctions that the Members deemed fit to execute against violating League Members.

The Washington Conference of 1921-1922 for the Principal Naval Powers agreed to limit their navies according to a fixed ratio.

The Locano Conference of 1925 produced a treaty guaranteeing German-French boundary and an arbitration agreement between Germany and Poland.

Paris Peace Pact of 1928 also known as The Briand-Kellogg Pact involving 63 nation-states which included great powers save The Union of Soviet Socialist Republic (USSR):-

Renounced war as an instrument of national policy;

Pledged to resolve disputes by peaceful means;

But exempted SELF-DEFENCE as reason for one's resort to war as an instrument for dispute settlement

(E) ON HITLER'S STRATEGY

Employed a social Darwinism strategy using every means (struggle) necessary including use of war between people(s) based on and governed by a survival of the fittest mentality.

Consequently, decided to appeal to his all German people (population) for their total participation in defence of their motherland's national dignity and superiority as they had always had ever since Antiquity after the fall of The Roman Empire, that left a vacuum for Prussia Germany.

Because to achieve this total support he needed a total national cohesion, he banned all oppositions and imposed dictatorship measures through censorship of the press; strict Nazi control over education; abolition of trade unions; use of secret police, etc in order to gain a firm grip on national unity and strength, etc.

Dismissed use of Pacifism strategy calling it a Jewish invention coined to aid a Jewish international imperialism

Regarded a war against the Soviet Union (Russia) as a necessary holy crusade against the Bolsheviks that were occupying a holy land needed by his Prussia German.

Took such a war as a necessity as it was aimed at implementing a racial hygiene to root out non-Aryan German blooded Jews and Gypsies from contaminating a pure Aryan German blood (Hitler's blood).

Was against Democracy because this divided Germans into different waiving Germans against each other.

Called for all Germans and their popular will as a German Community (Volks-germeinschaft) into a united nation as a people's community behind their one strong leader, a Fuehrer the only one to recognize and defend their united will in the outside world.

Called for this racial purity because Germans were a culture creating people who created things for others to enjoy at their expenses leading Germans to lose their creation later to parasites, the Jews, whom he called rats, vermin, disease, a plaque, germs and bacilli ready to destroy other's culture for their own good.

Because of such destructive aim, the Jews were regarded intolerable and so inhabitable that it was suggested that they be exported to Madagascar—a far away small Island on the East Coast of Africa.

In defence of his dislike of the Jews, Hitler argued that Christians had accused also them of being the murderers of Jesus Christ.

Argued that once a Jew became a Christian he/she ceased to be a Jew in public law of Jewish international law.

Argued that a Jew lacked a homeland and for this reason, he lacked a sense or interest in sacrificing for a greater, communal good such as a German or any other state.

And, because of this lack of a communal interest, a Jew was basically materialistic and more engaged in international finance (capitalism) and international Marxism against nationalism.

Because of this, all Jews are a contagious disease aimed at destroying every non-Jewish nation such as Aryan Germany by using its parasitism to finish off its host (the Aryan Germany).

(F) ON HITLER'S ACTUAL ACTION IN WORLD WAR II

On 5th November, 1937, Hitler addressed his Germany military leaders warning them on the growing economic difficulties, e.g., that the Navy was faced with a problem of acute shortage of raw materials that had to be overcome right away; that there was a growing fear that the existing military advantage that Germany now enjoyed at that very moment should no longer wait beyond 1940 since such a delay could lead to Germany losing this advantage; and that an aggressive action, was now very necessary and should therefore, start with Austria and Czechoslovakia and then force them to unite with Germany against other Germany's enemies.

INVASIONS

On 13th March, 1938, Hitler defied the Versailles Treaty of 1919 and with a green light from the Austrian Chancellor Kurt Von Schussnigg calling for a plebiscite on the issue of Austria's unification with Germany, Germany marched into Linz, amid a huge enthusiastic welcome from local Austrians, and annexed it to Germany; and also prepared to do the same with Czechoslovakia due to the pending burning issue of the densely populated Germans in Sudetenland, but the Czechs strongly appealed to both Britain and France for assistance against Germany.

On 29th march, 1939, Britain, France and Italy signed a Munich Agreement with Germany aimed at restraining Germany from annexing Czechoslovakia.

On 1st September, 1939, Hitler defied the Munich Agreement and sought to reunite the Reich (mainland Germany) and Danzing (a city plus its suburbs in North Poland which had been taken from German by the League of Nations Versailles Treaty and declared a Free zone under the League's administration)

But since Hitler could not that easily unite the two without Poland's complaint and physical retaliation, because of Danzing's strategic significance to Poland as Poland's main outlet port to the Sea, Hitler now resolved to use military coercion to invade and occupy total Poland thus igniting World War II.

But what could have triggered Hitler to do so to Austria, Czechoslovakia and Poland but not to others?

Hitler did so solely because he sought to regain Germany people's lost eastern land which had been forcefully taken from Prussia-Germany particularly by Poland in the late 18th Century through the partitions between Poland and Prussia, eg. Silessia.

Also, Hitler sought to recover from France her lost most economically endowed districts containing abundant coal mines viz: Alsace, Lorraine, Malmedy and Eupen (in the East Belgium formerly a Germany district but forcefully given to Belgium in 1919 together with Malmedy by The League of nations Versailles Treaty); and also

From Czechoslovakia Germany's Sudetenland inhabited by Germans.

To achieve these most complex and complicated goals Hitler occupied the Rhineland which he used to build up his German massive army base from which to retaliate against the Versailles Treaty's harsh conditions imposed on his German people.

To do so, Hitler also reinforced Germany against the enemy by creating the following numerous treaties:-

The Rome-Berlin Axis (1939) with Mussolini's Italy, to which Britain, Turkey and France promptly responded by also creating their own and by including Russia in their alliance against the Axis.

Berlin-Moscow Pact in August, 1939 of friendship, between Germany and Russia restraining Russia from challenging Germany's attack on Poland.

Pact of steel the Rome-Berlin Axis into a fast military alliance against enemy.

Rome-Berlin-Tokyo Axis (19.) by reinforcing the Rome-Berlin Axis to also include Japan against enemy.

Rome-Berlin-Tokyo-Spain-Hungary-Yugoslavia by intending the Axis to also include Yugoslovia, Spain and Hungary.

<u>Berlin-Moscow</u>

But on Franco-Britain's failure to promptly honour their defence pact with Poland when the latter was invaded by Hitler's Germany, Hitler exploited this loophole to also invade and occupy Austria and to re-possess the German populated region in Czechoslovakia's German populated Sudentenland area and the entire Czechoslovakia in March, 1939.

And on 1st September, 1939 he invaded Poland.

Britain and France issues an ultimatum to Germany to withdraw from Poland or else, Britain and France enter the War.

Germany refused. And, in response, Britain and France declared War on Germany on 3rd September, 1939.

And, on 27th September, 1939, Russia, also followed suit by entering the War against German through Eastern Poland.

In response, Hitler occupied Poland's capital, Warsau

And in Spring, 1940, Hitler also invaded and occupied Denmark, Norway, Belgium, Luxembourg, and the Netherlands in order to safeguard his Germany's iron-ore supplies from Scandinavia without British interference.

(G) ON HITLER'S HATRED AGAINST TO THE JEWS AND COMMUNISTS

According to Adolf Hitler's history and his own confessions contained in his book, *Mien Kampf,* a psycho-autopsy of him reveals these striking phenomena:-

His actual biological father, Aloys Hitler, who was half Jew and drunkard, habitually proved to be such a terror to the little boy, (Adolf Hitler), and the boy's mother (by also raping his mother, Klera, in the presence of the boy) *that the little boy automatically and naturally developed a hyper-hatred attitude against his father to such an extent that he now began also transferring the same hate to every Jew he saw, thought of, heard of, and met since for assuming that his father was doing so to him and his mother because he had some Jewish blood in him but not his mother, Klera.*

He compounded this scenario further by his other nasty experience with his mother's Jewish doctor, George Bloch, under whose professional care the boy's mother had died during operation of the breast cancer thus leading the little boy to bitterly accuse the doctor with an assumption that his mother had just been killed by the Jewish doctor because of her not being of a Jewish blood.

And, since his mother was the only parent he loved, adored and belonged to above his drunkard and morally deficient father, because of her soberness, helplessness and unjust maltreatment by the little boy's father, the little boy Hitler's mother's death was obviously a terrible shock to him tearing him with an unquenched desperation and anger against a Jewish doctor who, like his drunkard half-Jew father, had now been rendered him (the little boy) naked of a sense of belonging.

And also since both the doctor and his drunkard father were from the same Jewish blood, obviously, Hitler now took every Jew as his archi-enemy because of the maltreatment and the death of his helpless mother. C'est la vie deficille for the poor and defenseless little Adolf Hitler now sighing for any source of a safe haven!

After his dearest mother's death, Hitler again ran into a head-on collusion with another honderous dimension of mental torture as he could not find any employment from those who owned the means of production who, according to him, were by and large Jews.

Accordingly, Hitler simply resorted to the simple Arithmetic and calculated his all nasty past and present experiences, beginning with his half Jew father, Aloys Hitler; his mother's Jewish physician, George Bloch; and then the selfish owners of the means of production who, to him, were also predominantly Jews and then used the product as his reliable and valid answer and justification of his conclusion that all Jews were of no good to non-Jews and must, therefore, not be allowed to be seen around. Hence, the most logical source of the root-cause and green light to his Gas Chambers policy in World War II resulting into the Holocaust.

His hatred against Communists and Communism also arose from his understanding that Communism was a brain—child of Karl Marx who, to Hitler, was also a Jew who should, therefore, not be acceptable to him at all notwithstanding his impressive discovery of useful theories to Humanity and his Germans in particular. Hence his hatred to the Communists as well. Otherwise, there seems to be no any other sound and convincing root-cause that must have compelled such a sharp thinker with such extraordinary photographic memory that needed no notes for reference during his electrifying public speeches, etc.—unusual qualities not usually common to many.

(H) CONCLUSION

(1) A Preamble

It is submitted that Adolf Hitler left behind him to the 20th Century Civilization such a nalty and inerasable bloody stain which scholars after scholars have examined over and over again and piled up volumes and volumes of publications on him and the atrocities that he, together with his Nazi Germany, inflicted on Humanity of a totally uncountable loss of life and unquantifiable loss of property globally, though some researchers have attempted to give rough estimates as is in the case of the figures reflected in the Table I above attempting to show that the total global fatalities were 52, 337, 180 of which 23, 908, 225 being Military fatalities and 28, 428, 955 being Civilian Fatalities.

Using his U-boat submarines, bombers, artilleries, spies and saboteurs, science and technology and other means of warfare to enhance Germany's victory, Hitler, like his predecessors most particularly Charlemagne and Napoleon, caused panic to every living soul throughout the World particularly in Europe where he invaded, terrorized and occupied whichever Country he conquered, eg. Austria, Czechoslovakia, Poland, France, Denmark, Norway, etc. And, most particularly to the Russians where he sought a living space for his crowded Germans, he sent them an army of 3,000,000 men to humble them to submission thus subjecting them to the highest fatalities of 21,500,000 of which 14,500,000 were military and 7,000,000 civilians.

But, inspite of all this impressive data contributed to wisdom and knowledge by previous research efforts on the agonies of world War II and its architects such as Adolf Hitler, one pending nagging question persists. For example, why did Hitler do this? Was he a mad man suffering from schizophrenia or what type or kind of mental disease that led him to do this? But if so, how could he, being mad, have managed to overpower and lead all German population to this bloody mess without their resistance? Were they so blind and so deaf or foolish that they were unable to discern the out-come of the War and then refuse to go along with Hitler? But, apart from other German leaders and the civil society, where were World Leaders and Civil Society of the time? Were they also so blind and deaf or foolish that they could not discern from World War I and the existing Briand-Kellogg Pact of 1928 Protocols prohibiting every nation-state and its leaders from use of War as means of settling disputes?

(2.) A Resurrection of a German Traditional Warrior

The History of Germany shows that Germans of today are an offspring of the ancient Germanic barbarians beginning with the Huns of 371 AD, the Ostrogoths and Visigoths of 378 AD, the Vandals of 406-455 AD, the Franks, Angles, the Saxons, the Burgundians, the Alemanni etc (though the Franks, the Angles and Saxons) are now the ones one finds in France and England respectively. And, that these were a habitually war Germanic tribes who lived on terrorism as a source of their living.

Because of their military terrorism, they were responsible for the death of the Roman Empire both in the Eastern and Western Europe. And, because of that, they did not only bring down the Roman Empire but they also toppled and replaced it with their own by the military conquest of Charlemagne and thereafter Napoleon.

But, whereas their terrorism and occupation was not the only objective, the easily discoverable by researchers, the militaristic ruthlessness culture they left behind for their offspring to pass it over from one generation to another constitutes the most hidden secret that most researchers to date have not been able to unearth, so that they may use it to understand and succinctly explain with a high degree of precision, parsimony and confidence for one's satisfactory understanding and appreciation.

In this regard, it is therefore, hereby submitted that Adolf Hitler's leadership character was not a function of his own self. He did not make or deliberately design to make it so for the sake of his own madness as some researchers have unfortunately attempted to allude. His militaristic ruthlessness is embedded in his blood and arising from the militaristic ruthlessness blood of his forefathers named above. What Napoleon did by crowning himself as Emperor of France and instituting total dictatorship in France is the bold base from which Hitler also crowned himself as the Fuerher of the German People; destroyed both Democracy and individual rights; and replaced these virtues with dictatorship. And, in the same manner Napoleon practiced the same leadership style of Charlemagne which later also came to be a reminiscence in Hitler's leadership style, it is self-evident that Hitler's mode of leadership was neither an accident nor his own making but essentially a product of his ancestral ruthless militaristic leadership embedded in their blood. His leadership of ruthless militarism, militarization, military conquests, and terrorism leading to Abnormal Crime against Humanity as so manifested in World War II and The Holocaust of genocide against non-Aryan blooded Germans during his time was succinctly a function of his ancesterial past and thus qualifying him and his leadership as a Resurrection of German Traditional Worrior.

His extra-ordinary magnetic power over the mind of all his German leaders and general public in Europe that led Germany to become the architect of World War II was solely a resurgence of the German traditional warrior mentality. Hence his status as none other than a resurrection of the German tradition warrior akin to Napoleon Bonaparte, Charlemagne, Charles Martel and right up to the terrorist blood of the Huns, the Ostrogoths, the Lombards, the Visigoths, the Vandals, the Burgundians, the Alemanni, etc of his ancient Germanic barbarian ancestors envisaged in details above in this research.

3. <u>A Comparative Analysis of Legacy Fame Between Hitler and Other Leaders Globally</u>

Of all the leaders of extra-ordinary fame whether positive or negative from Antiquity to the Present Times, Adolf Hitler's name is undoubtedly one of them. A tabulation of them in terms of their categories of fame based on their leadership performance relative to Hitler's performance shows the following sides of the same coin:-

Each Pharaoh of Ancient Egypt was so concerned about his Egyptian people's needs such as food, security, health security, and other hierarchy of needs that he steered his Egyptian people into such amazing scientific and technological discoveries, inventions and innovations that Egypt did not only achieve those needs in abundance such as food security thus attracting the foreign attention of the hungry Patriarch Abraham and his wife Sarah and later on Patriarch Jacob and his Family to flee their famine-besieged home lands in Canaan to Egypt for food security, but also excelled Egypt to a flabbergasting positive fame over all other Countries and Peoples of the time. But unlike the Pharaohs who achieved this fame using positive means, Hitler who, of course, also loved his German people so much that he sought to do everything necessary to gain fame for them, did so using negative means.

Ur-Nammu of the Sumerians and the latter's Sumerian City in 2060 BC was so in love of his Sumerians that he made his people so famous in protection of social justice especially the defenseless poor that becoming King of his people of Mesopotamia, Hammurabi (1792-1750 BC, immediately turned to Ur-Nammu's rules of social justice as his salvation and consequently codified them into the famous "Hammurabi Code" that, in turn, placed his name to an ever-lasting fame as The Founder of The Code which also became the granite foundation of the Islamic Sheria Law of "an eye for an eye", and "tooth for tooth", today. But, whereas like Ur-Nammu and Hammurabi's love for their respective people leading them to develop for them moral principles to protect their social justice and unity as a people as also vividly reflected in The Code of Hammurabi, Hitler also did more less the same by developing The New Order with succinct austerity measures (or law) for the protection of the people and the state", and also set up the *Hitler Youth* organization, the secret police, the *Gestape*, etc to dispense these measures towards Germany's national unity. However, the contradiction between Hitler's goal and the goal of Ur-Nammu and also Hammurabi was totally clear. Hitler's goal led his Germans into World War II while the goals of his counterparts (Ur-Nammu and Hammurabi) did not lead their respective countries of Summeria and Mesopotamia to war(s), though their goals led each of them to a World Fame!

Patriarch Abraham the Founder of the Hebrew nation and Canaan in 1800 BC earned his fame using positive means for a positive course but not like Hitler who did so using negative means for a course that a mixture of both negativity and positivety by subjecting the whole World to War, thus plunging even the innocent peoples who had no part in the inter-European quarrel to suffer also.

Israel King Saul (reigned 1020-1010 BC), who was succeeded by King David (reigned 1010-960 BC) who was also succeeded by King Solomon (reigned 960-922 BC) are, like Hitler, World renown leaders: Saul as the first King of the United Israel Kingdom; David as the most obedient servant and friend of God; and Solomon for his most amazing wisdom, and also as the last King of the United Kingdom of Israel. However, the context through which Kings Saul, David and Solomon are famous is totally different from the context through which Hitler is known to be famous. The former context is positive while the latter is negative (hostility).

King Herod (37BC-4 BC) who was also known as Herod The Great, was the Tetrarch of Judea during the Birth of Jesus Christ. He earned his fame in a negative context because of his untold sorrows he inflicted death to the totally innocent little infants on mad intention that through this infanticide, he would also eliminate the Infant Jesus Christ. Hence, the congruency of his means and aim with Hitler's means and aim which also led to a blood-letting of millions of totally innocent peoples world-wide.

Vladimir Ilyich Lenin originally known as Vladimir Ilyich Ulyanov but later dropped his surname "Ulyanov" and adopted "Lenin" for reason(s) strictly known to himself who like Hitler, earned a reputation as an extra-ordinary revolutionary leader of abundant courage and pity for terribly oppressed (suffering) minority underdog Russian people at the merciless greedy survival of the fittest minded minority Russian rich, protected by an autocratic leadership of Czar Alexander III (who had come to power after the murder of his father, Alexander II in 1881); and, therefore, having liberated these oppressed Russian people using Karl Marx's theories of social and economic justice that called for the destruction of free enterprise (privately owned and misused enterprises against the majority poor) and creation and replacement of the former with a classless society with a view to creating a new Russian state without rich or poor—a phenomenon that rapidly engulfed the entire World turning it into a Marxism-Leninism tsunami against Capitalism, Colonialism and Imperialism globally.

Joseph Stalin, like Hitler, earned his fame in Russia and Europe as a whole, not only because of his reign as Head of State of the Union of the Soviet Socialist Republics (USSR) from 1929 to 1953 and his active co-operation with other Allied Powers (USA, Great Britain, France, China and Belgium) leading to military victory against Hitler's Germany and the latter's allied Powers (Japan and Italy) in World War II, but also for his Hitleristic policy of militarism and militarization that resulted into his occupation of Poland with a view to secretly dividing Poland between USSR and German in 1939, and also occupied and forced the Baltic countries of Estonia, Latvia, and Lithuania to join his Soviet Union, and finally for his secret decision to detach from his co-Allied Powers immediately after the defeat of Hitler's Germany, Italy and Japan and grab the eastern portion Berlin city and eastern region of Germany as essentially a USSR's share from World War II thus leading to the genesis of The Cold War, Stalin's blockade for the linkage between East Germany and Western Germany forcing other Allied Powers to resort to an airlift of food and other supplies to besieged population in Eastern Germany and Eastern portion of Berlin.

Karl Marx who during his life time (1818-1883) earned a positive fame not only as a German philosopher, social scientist and professional revolutionary but indeed as a man whose greatest and most lasting influence has had on Mankind in his capacity as Chief Founder of the two most powerful and highly related movements in history viz: Democratic Socialism and Revolutionary Communism aimed at emancipating the socio-economically under-dog individual from the evil goal of capitalism, Colonialism and Imperialism as also evidenced by its empirical success in Africa, Asia and Latin America using the following most attractive and efficacious publications to the minds of nationalists in those Colonial Continents seeking liberation, The German Ideology (1845-1846), The Communist Manifesto (1848), and Das Kapital (Capital) published in 1867, each armed with an etiological Tsunami air ready to destroy what he considered as the most evil and enemy of Mankind especially the poor.

Charles De Gaulle who, unlike Hitler, earned a positive fame not only in France and total Europe alone but also globally as a true and courageous defender of World Peace and Democracy against Hitleristic militarism and militarization, and who also like Hitler's extraordinary hyper-possessiveness and love for his Mother/Fatherland (Germany) and German People, he was equally so hyper-patriotistic to his Mother/Fatherland (France) and French People that he defied orders of his superior, the Regiment Commander Marshal Petain in defence of his Motherland and French People by refusing to accept France's surrender to Germany's military victory on 22 January 1940 calling it bull rubbish), and who, after his famous earnest appeal to all "soldiers of France, wherever you may be, arise!" while in exile in London where he had fled in order to escape a death sentence already imposed on him for such refusal, joined the Allied Forces' march into France and triumphed against fierce German Forces leading him to a recognition by the Allied Powers as the unquestionable leader of the "Fighting French" and the "Free France" effective September 1944 till his resignation in January 1946 and also a recall in 1958 to become France's President, a capacity in which he diligently and boldly served until his second resignation from politics in April 1969.

Sir Winston Churchill, who earned a positive fame not only in European political life as twice Prime Minister of Great Britain from1940 to 1945 but also as one of the greatest statesmen of Modern Civilization in his capacity as a hero of world War II by offering his British People he reigned as Prime Minister only "blood, toil, tears, and sweat" in order for them to keep themelves from Hitler's Germany's Colonization and Imperialism—and more so, a man who did not only make history but also wrote it for generations and generations to come by telling Hitler and his Nazi Germany that the days of militarism and militarization had already fallen on evil days and days of Democracy and The rule of Law and Justice had risen up to take the place of the days of militarism and militarization.

The Persian King Cyrus who was also known as Cyrus The Great reigned from 559 to 525 BC and earned that title for no positive aim and means as he, like Hitler, earned it by terrorizing and occupying all countries of his generation in Asia minor and North Africa and for capturing Babylon and making it his capital. And, like Hitler who became so happy upon hearing that France had surrendered so did he (Cyrus) also feel the same on noting that Babylon had fallen to him.

Also, in Asia, the name "Hitler' automatically rings a bell to the fame of many leaders who are, up to today, adored and revered, such as Mohandas Karamchand Gandhi (lived 1869-1948). a leader who is still not only adored by his people as the liberator and father of their (India) nation but also globally adored and admired as a mentor and exemplary model of Good Leadership to the many who used his model for their own liberation from colonialism and imperialism. Such as Kwame Nkrumah of Ghana who, consequently became a leading torch bearer of Freedom in Africa like Gandhi in India. Hence his fame as Mahatma meaning "Great Soul". Further, Gandhi earned this fame for his righteous life governed by none other than his own granite belief in Truth as his Road Map. His book, *My Experiments with Truth,* explains and confirms this fact. Thus, the similarity and dissimilarity between Gandhi's fame and Hitler's fame manifested in Hitler's book, *Mien Kampf* and Gandhi's book respectively.

Another leader in Asia whose name automatically comes to the surface whenever a switch button of fame is further activated is of course Mao Tse Tung who earned the fame for not only being a leader of the Communist China World but who also earned the fame for being one of the most powerful leaders of the 20th Century, and more so, as being the architect of a revolutionary guerrilla warfare using peasants as soldiers, that conventional means of warfare could hardly understand and manage. Hence the resemblance of his leadership fame and that of Hitler.

Also in Asia again, the name and fame of Ho Chi Minh who lived from 1890 to 1964 also comes to surface whenever a button of fame is touched. Like Mao Tse Tung in China, Ho-Chi Minh earned his fame for being the architect of the defeat of the French Colonial Leadership in Vietnam using Communism as his means; and for using the same means to bring the most powerful American military mighty's intervention in Vietnam to a humiliating defeat on the battle field and for forcing American military might's immediately withdrawal from Saigon as soon as America's military stronghold, Saigon, fell to Ho Chi Minh's North Vietnamese-Vietcong offensives on 30th April, 1975, thus leading to hundreds of thousands of Vietnamese refugees called "boat people" fleeing the Country for a safe haven mainly in USA and Canada. But although Ho Chi Minh earned his fame through blood shed, Hitler and his forefathers such as Charlemagne and Napoleon did so beyond the horizons of Sanity and Natural Justice in that whereas Ho chi Minh's aim was defence of his Vietnamese people from a foreign (French and American) aggression, Hitler and his forefathers primarily aimed at not defence but at conquests, and occupation as a meaning of victory.

And, finally in Africa, the names of Kwame Nkrumah, Nelson Mandela, Patrice Lumumba, Julius K. Nyerere, Samora Machel, Sekou Toure, Leopold Sedar Senghor, Nnamdi Azikiwe, Sir Abubakar Rafawa Balewa, Hastings Kamuzu Banda, Jomo Kenyatta, Kenneth Kaunda, Oginga Odinga, Tom Mboya, et al also readily come to surface whenever an electronic button of Names of Fame is touched or switched on.

However, unlike the names of Hitler, Herod The Great, Cyrus The Great, Napoleon Bonaparte, Charlemagne, and other names of blood who earned their fame by shedding blood of innocent people for no sane cause, all the above indicated leaders earned their fame for a sane cause vizv: <u>To drive out undemocratic ruthless Colonial Leadership which they believed to be naked of the virtues of Democracy and Humanism</u>—an amazing political phenomenon which has come to repeat itself in Kenya in 2002 after 40 years of a similar mode of misrule particularly during the reign of Daniel Toroitich arap Moi of Kenya who earned a very negative fame nationally and internationally throughout his reign from 1978 to 2002 thus subjecting African leadership and Africa's image to ridicule not for militarism and militarization like Hitler in Germany, but essentially for turning his KANU party Government into a den of flabbergasting secretly manufactured scandals of massive corruption, dictatorship, lies, dishonesty and inter-leader and inter-tribal incitement leading to untold agonies of irreparable national shame, poverty, bloodshed and fatalities during his tenure as President of The Republic of Kenya after President Jomo Kenyatta's death in 1978 till he was forced out of office in December, 2002 Election by the new Government of National Alliance Rainbow Coalition (NARC) under the President-elect Mwai Kibaki bitterly accusing him (Moi) for pocketing most of the nation's revenue realized from both Kenyan tax payers and foreign Donor Community as so empirically substantiated by the revelation of the most shocking scandal of the Goldenberg International; rampant cases of tribal clashes and deaths; and secret false promises to different individual leaders for the attractive post of the Vice President in order for him to gain political support from them. This mode of leadership proved so deceitful and nasty that on being discovered so, forced the deceived and undeceived to divorce him (Moi) and his ruling KANU party Government en mass for the Kibaki Opposition (NARC) party thus leading the latter to an overwhelming election victory against Moi's KANU party and bribed candidates in the December 2002 General Election. And, was such a man who feared the intellectuals and the like so much that he decided to shield his unlearned image (being only a Primary School drop-out) who then ended up as a Primary One School teacher) by manufacturing a Nyayo cult of himself through the so-called Nyayo philosophy of peace, love and unity through which he magnified himself as an indisputable everlasting cult personality in the Kenyan politics, whose "No" or "Yes" word was to be readily swallowed as it was without any iota of doubt by even his most learned ministers to the tune of a professor who were psychologically forced to lunch and sup on the such a horrendous terror of Moiphobia that they helplessly and hopelessly went around shockingly looking ridiculous and ludicrous by a habit of bursting into a madness for him "Nyayo", "Nyayo", "Nyayo" chorus whenever they saw him approaching them in his Presidential Security Escort convoy psychologically leading him into a false euphoria life of cult worship personality and reason for him to open for them the main gate of Kenya's treasury and other national resources to plunder as they so wished as is now so revealed by the Goldenberg International and other most painful scandals.

Also, turning our observatory devices from Asia and the African Continents to the Americas for names of fame, a number of them also come to the screen like Hitler's name among the names of fame in the European continent, e.g. the name of the

First President of The United States of America, George Washington (1789-1797) who unlike Hitler earned his fame in a positive way as The Founding Father of that Nation after successfully commanding his Thirteen North American Colonies to a War of Independence against what they considered as King George III's Great Britain's Colonial and Imperialistic unjust and illegal acts of terrorism against them in the 18th Century leading them to their Independence victory on 4th July, 1776 as The United States of America; the name of Abraham Lincoln who like Washington, also gained his name during his reign as President of The United States of America from 1861 to 1865 for vigorously enforcing his stern policy of anti-Slavery and Slave Trade through out the United States of America (USA) and for saving the latter's Union from being broken apart by what he perceived as pro-slavery and slave Trade Confederate rebels of the Southern States led by Alabama, Mississippi, George Tennessee, South Carolina, North Carolina, Maryland, Virginia, etc who viewed Lincoln as an essentially bad guy and an intruder tampering with their source of free labour, and, therefore, decided to organize and initiate a Civil War in order for them to secede from Lincoln's Union and his Northern States, who supported his policy, whom they derogatively referred to as "Yankees";

Theodore Roosevelt who, like Hitler, also earned an admirable (positive) fame for his charming affectionate leadership policy when he just took over the Presidency from President William McKinley upon the latter's assassination in September, 1901 leading millions of his American people to affectionately addressing him as "Teddy" or as simply "T. R.", but who, like Hitler, also later earned a most disgusting (negative) fame as a bully guy because of his hard line leadership by trying to jump the Constitution and run for a Third Term for The Presidency in 1912 thus forcing himself to be nick-named as a "Bull Moose" party candidate, and to lose the election to Woodrow Wilson, and more so by trying to militarily place his Country and American People above all other Countries and Peoples as a World Leader using his militaristic ruthless policy of "SPEAK SOFTLY AND CARRY A BIG STICK" which was significantly congruent to Hitler's German policy of militarism and militarization above all other European Countries and Peoples that, in the end, led Germany into World War II; Woodrow Wilson who like Hitler first earned a positive fame as an adored leader during his reign as President of The United States of America from 1912 to 1921 for first keeping his American People out of War until the War became so threatening to World Peace and Democracy that he then resolved to lead his Nation into the War against the aggressor (Germany) in order to save the World for Democracy, but who also like Hitler, later earned a very negative fame as a loser of the League because of his failure to win his American People's acceptance to join The League of Nations and Ratify It's Covenant, a situation that Wilson found to be so embarrassing, annoying and this agonizing that made him collapse at Pueblo, Colorado, on 4th September, 1919 and to his final death in his sleep on 3rd February, 1924, after having won The Nobel Price For Peace on 10th December, 1920 for his profound efforts in founding The League, of Nations and for seeking a fair Peace Agreement after World War I in 1919; Franklin D. Roosevelt, who earned a positive fame as a good leader during his reign as President of the United States of America from 1933 to 1945 because of his efforts to lead his Nation and American People into World War II in order to reinforce the Allies' efforts against Hitler's Germany and the latter's Tripartite Alliance (Benito Mussolini's Italy and Japan Under Showa Emperor, Hirohito), and also because of his admirable New Deal policy magic by which he boldly resuscitated the already dying America's socio-economy with an encouragement of Good Hope that to his American People that there is "Nothing to fear but fear itself" alone; Harry S. Truman who earned his fame as a bold leader during his reign as President of The United States from 1945 to 1953 due to his flabbergasting damnest chest decision of dropping a newly invented atomic bomb to Japan's cities of Hiroshima and Nagasaki in August 1945 thus forcing Japan to a formal surrender on 2nd September, 1945 after Nazi Germany had already surrendered four months earlier to the Allies on 8th May, 1945; John F. Kennedy who earned his fame for terrifying the World by confronting the S. Kruschev Soviet Union over the presence of their missiles in Cuba during his tenure as President of the United States of America from 1961 till his assassination in Dallas town, Texas on 22nd November, 1963, for visiting the Berlin Wall under the USSR's fierce surveillance, for the first time in the history of World Politics, set up the Washington-Moscow Hot-Line, and also for signing the first Nuclear Ban Treaty with the USSR in 1963, before his assassination; Richard M. Nixon who earned his fame during his reign as President of the United States of America from 1969 to 1974 because of being the only President of America to resign from office and also for the Apollo moon landing in 1969 during his Administration, his path-breaking visit to China in 1972 that no any American President had ever done, his first ever Strategic Arms Limitation Treaty with the Union of The Soviet Socialist Union (USSR) and his involvement in the famous American Water Gate Scandal in early 1973 that led him to his political demise in a television resignation on 9th August, 1974; Dr. Martin Luther

King who also earned his fame as an Arch-Hero and Matyr of Civil Rights in USA during his life from 1929 till his assassination on 4th April, 1968 in Mephis town Tennessee,—most particularly for his most electrifying unique throng "I HAVE A DREAM THAT ONE DAY, THIS NATION WILL RISE UP AND LIVE OUT THE TRUE MEANING OF ITS CREED: 'WE HOLD THESE TRUTHS TO BE SELF-EVIDENT; THAT ALL MEN ARE CREATED EQUAL'"!; Malcolm X who, also during his life in the United States of America (1925-1965) earned his fame as a hero of the Black Revolution in that Country in his capacity as a fearless leader of the movement aimed at uniting all Black People of the World before his assassination in New York City on 21st February, 1965 thereby adding oil on fire leading the movement to demand for creation of a New Republic of Africa by seizing some space in the Country for that very purpose; George Corley Wallace, who, like Hitler also earned his fame as an arch-racist who wanted only his own white race but bitterly hated the Black race during his reign as Governor of Alabama in USA from 1962 till his attempted assassination in May, 1972 during his campaign for the 1972 Democratic Presidential Nomination in Laurel town, Maryland; in the West Indies, Marcus Garvey earned his fame as The Founding Father of "BACK TO AFRICA" movement in both America and West Indies during his life time from 1887 till his death in Jamaica in 1940, and as is also documented in his own book, *Philosophy and Opinions of Marcus Garvey*, edited by Army Marcus-Garvey, his movement became one of the most phenomenal social movements in Modern History, and his name, one of the most globally renown because of his sterling philosophy to liberate the seeds of previously enslaved Africans in West Indies and The Americas from their darkness of ignorance of who they actually were to what they were to create The Universal Negro Improvement Association (UNIA) being a Provincial Government of Africa outside Africa in readiness to return and take up its mandate in Africa, and above all to procure a number of "The Black Star Line" ships for task of ferrying back these seeds of former African Slaves back to Africa, in both America and Europe, the name of Dr. William Edward Burghardt Du Bois popularly known as Dr. W. E. B. Du Bois, earned his fame as the leading spokesman for the Afro-Americans against their racial discrimination agonies in the United States of America throughout his life from 1868 to 1963, as both a historian and sociologist whose research work on Black-American Communist still, attracts modern researchers attention, and also as The Founding Father of the famous Black Americans National Association for the Advancement of Colored People popularly referred to as NAACP which was founded to achieve a goal clothed by the organization's name; and finally also in the United States of America the name of Booker T. Washington who also earned his fame in the United States as a noted Black-American educator who earned his fame during his life-time from 1856-1915 as the best known Black American educator in the United States of America by virtue of his role as advisor to Presidents Theodore Roosevelt and William Howard Taft on racial problems, and therefore exerted great influence to these Presidents regarding appointments of Black Americans to Federal Government jobs, and also earned the fame of being anti-Civil Rights movement by arguing that Blacks should earn their way out through hard work but not through Civil Rights movements, and consequently created a Negro Business League to assist Black-Americans develop their own businesses, raised money for rural Negro Schools and published a number of books, the most famous of all being Up From Slavery (1901)—his own autobiography; Mohammad Ali formerly Cassius Clay, who earned his fame as World Heavyweight Boxing Champion in 1964; and finally Fidel Castro of Cuba who earned his fame for his long and fierce anti-American speeches and also for using the heavyweight missile capabilities of Nikita Kruschev's Soviet Union to repel of an American threat to Cuba in 1962 and to defeat American sponsored invasion of Cuba through the Bay of Pigs—actions which led Castro to an adorable fame throughout Cuba and the rest of the World contrary to nauseating fame of Hitler and his predecessor's such as Charlemagne and Napoleon Bonaparte, who earned theirs by conquests and shedding of innocent blood throughout Europe.

PARTIAL BIBLIOGRAPHY

Dick Geary, *Hitler and Nazism,* Routledge, II New Fetter Lane, London. E C4P 4EE, (1993).

Edleff H. Schwaab, *Hitler's Mind: A Plunge Into Madness.*

Edwin Hoyt, *Mussolini's Empire-The Rise and Fall of The Fascist Vision.*

Paulo Freire, *Pedagogy of the Oppressed.*

W. Maser, Hitler's Mein Kampf, London (1970).

_____, *Hitler,* London (1973).

Adolf Hitler, *Table Talk*, London (1953).

_____, *Mein Kampf* ed. By D.C. Watt, London (1960).

A. Bullock, *Hitler*, London (1952).

T. Abel, *The Nazi Movement*, NewYork (1966).

The World Book Encyclopedia

Diane W. Darst, *Western Civilization To 1648*, McGraw-Hill Publishing Co., New York, (1990).

The New York Times Almanac, (2002).

Alexander Ignatier, "V-Day Etched in Russia's Collective Memory", *The Daily Nation*, Nairobi, (May 9, 2005) p. 5.

Margraten (Netherlands), "World War II Victory Marked" *The Daily Nation*, Nairobi, (May 9, 2005), p. 12.

Michael Mertes "How The Allies Liberated Germany As Well", *The Daily Nation*, Nairobi, (9th May, 2005).

A. J. P. Taylor, The Origins of Second World War, (1961).

B.   A Comparative Analysis

1)   Analysis

As already noted above with respect to Leadership illness in France and Britain, and the appropriate actions that had to be taken there as a remedy to the illness, it is self-evident that leadership problem is universal horizontally and vertically. Horizontally, it is a chronic problem globally; and vertically, it is a perennial problem having lived with man since Antiquity.

And, as will also be noted further below, this is a human disgrace haunting every country globally but not only Kenya, France or Britain. It also holds true in the entire World Community.[4] And, in fact, this problem is nothing compared to what is happening in other countries in Africa, eg. Nigeria. In his own words, Maina Muiruri warns that "There is no corruption here in Kenya to talk about; this is just a joke compared to Nigeria. This is the time for Kenya to turn around and refuse to go the way Nigeria has gone. You people don't know what you are headed for if you don't become very aggressive now against [corruption in your country, Kenya]".[5]

As also noted recently by Maina Muiruri the seriousness of all this situation is that "The vice has by now so much sourced Kenya's relationship with donors, led to destruction of the infrastructure; and tainted the Judiciary, the police, the civil service and the private sector as well, that conventional scientific approach alone may not be able to provide us with a reliable medicine or remedy against this vice".

In order for us to further understand and appreciate the critical danger of this pathological professionalism globally, experience overtime shows that Kenya and Nigeria are not the only casualties. It includes also the most politically mature and powerful countries such as Germany and particularly the United States of America, which, unlike Kenya, is expected to be the most experienced and seasoned both in political and other walks of life because of its long tenure as an advocate of this spirit of Honesty (Transparency and Accountability) and all other essential ingredients of Good Leadership (or Governance), now over two centuries effective since its time of independence in 1776 to the present (1999). This reality is borne out by the following prima facie evidences:-

(1) Like Kenya, Nigeria and all other younger and socio-economically less powerful countries globally,

(a) German leadership is not an exemption. While, under Adolf Hitler, it committed such a flabbergasting genocide catastrophe in the history of mankind since the infant-genocide committed by King Herod in Israel in the beginning of the 1st century AD that the catastrophe drove Hitler to suicide. This case and the corruption case in the year 2002 against the former Chancellor Helmut Kohl are individually and collectively a prima facie acid test confirming that leadership decay is definitely a global serious cancer.

(b)   And, like Kenya, Nigeria and Germany, cases noted above, the United States of America (USA) is not at peace either. In fact, its leadership has neither escaped nor rested from recurrent admissions in Intensive Care Unit (ICU). For instance:

   (i)   Recurrently increasing critical questions are now emerging against the Honesty and Rationality level of President George Bush Jr's leadership with respect to its decision to mislead America into an unjustified war against Iraq's leadership under President Saddam Hussein on false allegation that the leadership had a store pile of Weapons of Mass Destruction thereby plunging both innocent American and Iraq men and women into a sea of agony created by Bush's leadership-poverty—a concern that first created serious strained relations with NATO allies and the UN, and is now increasingly becoming critical against President Bush's good chance of winning the soon-coming Election for his Second Term in America (2004).

   (ii)   Its immediate former Head of State Bill Clinton, narrowly survived a possible impeachment by Congress for perjury and obstruction of justice by using his most powerful office in USA to tamper with witnesses with a view to frustrating and paralysing the process of justice in that Country, which, in the final analysis, is also an obvious manifestation of leadership corruption and Bad Governance.[6]

   (iii)   The Clinton's leadership was ridiculed vehemently by many other leaders, e.g. the Texas billionaire and one of the 1992 Presidential Candidates, Ross Perot, at his Political Party rally held on 27/7/98 in Atlanta, Georgia,[7] most especially in his own home State of Arkansas where he was being haunted with a possible legislation of barring him from practising law in that State due to perjury and telling lies under-oath in the Jones' case in that state.

   (iv)   But this is not all as a significant symptom of leadership failure. The same American leadership under President Clinton was vehemently accused by other leaders as being the one who was actually fuelling global civil wars e.g. in Africa where he is accused to be squarely responsible for encouraging the on-going civil war in Sierra Leone with a view of accumulating diamond and other diamonds from that country. Obviously, this must be a very valuable acid test finding giving us an amazing revelation on the true colours of a leadership such as that of the USA which has always gone around the world preaching to other people and leaders the meaning and significance of Peace and Democracy ideals with a view to telling them the reasons why a country should have a leadership that respects and adheres to these ideals enshrined in our Civilization. On the strength of this revelation, it appears that the USA leadership is no better than a chameleon (an impostor) trying to preach to others what it cannot actually practice at all. And, that whenever it does so, it perhaps does so for its convenience only.

(v)   Also, assuming that such conclusions may not be valid and reliable, it is open to question why a politically mature leadership such as that of the USA which is expected to be so much grounded in Peace and Democracy ideals could be fuelling civil war in Sierra Leone, Afghanistan, Iraq, and elsewhere for mineral wealth inherent in those countries as the USA leadership is now being accused of; and the accusations which are now being exploited and capitalized on by the Democratic Party Presidential Nomination Candidates against President George Bush with a view to using them as their weapon with which to oust Bush from the White House.

(vi) And, on turning our telescope from both Kenya, Germany and the USA to the rest of the world, we are also stunned by the following similar leadership corrosion and decay documented in (2)-(5) cases below:

(2)   In the Intra-European Relations,

(a)   The European Union Commission is also reported to be in a serious trouble. It leadership was under a fierce accusation of "fraud", "corruption", "arrogance", among others, which are also a manifest of a global leadership failure.[8]

(b)   And, in Britain (during the week of 26-29 January 2004), the British Prime Minister Tony Blair's leadership narrowly survived a critical probe by The

House of Lords on the same Iraq issue which is now increasingly putting a lot of heat on the US President George Bush's leadership to the extent that its survival in the forthcoming Presidential Election (2004) for the Second Term is daily growing uncertain. Like, President Bush's leadership, Prime Minister Blair's leadership is faced with increasing strained relations and critical questions regarding the Honesty and Prudence of its decision to mislead Britain into an unjustified war against Iraq's leadership under President Saddam Hussein on a false claim that Iraq had a stoke-pile of Weapons of Mass Destruction, thereby plunging both the Innocent British and Iraq men and women into a sea of agony simply because of Blair's leadership poverty. Nevertheless, although Blair's leadership has just survived the probe, the issue remains an albatross cancer around its neck, which could be its serious liability in the 2005 Election.

(3) Globally, the International Olympic Body which is strictly a global enjoyment entity is equally in a similar trouble. Its committee's delegates and agents have been accused of having demanded and actually received lavish bribes. The bribes were disguised as gifts of luxurious vehicles, watches and cash money while in reality, they were meant to buy Committee votes for countries contesting for the privilege of becoming host nations of the year 2002 Winter Olympic Games; and for denying votes to those countries such as Sweden which either refused or were unable to afford such exorbitant prices for the votes.[10]

(4) The United Nations (UN), which is expected to be the World leading reputable organisation of all international organisations is not free either from this leadership pathological cancer. It has inherited the same cancer from its member-states, and could be requiring a major surgery so as to be liberated from the cancer. Contrary to its original core Spirit clearly spelt out in The Preamble and Principles of its Charter[11] by The Founding Fathers which was to save this and future generations from the scourge (agony) of further wars, the tragedy is that:

(a) This Spirit has never been realised ever since the UN was created at the end of the World War II in 1945. The Spirit is virtually dormant. It is thwarted by the same Founding Members States of the UN who are self-baptized as UN "Permanent Members!" for mysterious reasons only known to them.

(b) Arab-Israel war, for example, which erupted in 1948 followed by a series of similar wars thereafter such as the North South Korea war in 1950; the war in both Rwanda and Burundi in 1959; the war in Congo in 1960 and the war in Ireland in the 1960's, etc., remain unresolved, becoming a catalyst of numerous genocides such as the recent cases of Bosnia and Rwanda in the 1990's. The UN leadership has failed to settle them all; and nobody knows what is likely to happen next in those countries and elsewhere in view of this prevailing global pathological leadership cancer, hampering the UN from fulfilling its Original Mandate enshrined in its own charter.

The destructive Self-seeking and Self-Justification Spirit of the same UN Permanent and non-Permanent member-states manifested in their destructive habit of resorting to the Principles of Sovereign Equality and Domestic Jurisdiction enshrined in the Law of Nations under Article 2, paragraph 7 of the UN Charter, as their excuse[12], which has always disrupted the same World Body they willingly created themselves with which to maintain World Peace.

In spite of free professional advice often offered the UN leadership with the hope that this would serve as an essential remedy to this cancer by distinguished authority on this cancer such as Professors L. Oppenheim, L. Sohn, J. Brierly, M. Rajan, G. Schwarsenberger, H. Kelsen, H. Lauterpacht, et al., most of this advice has always fallen on deaf ears.[13]

Instead of this World Body to first and foremost take enough time to clinically diagnose this cancer as experts mentioned in (d) above have already done with a view to finding a desirable resolution or remedy to the said cancer, this Body has in practice ever since its establishment in 1945, paradoxically sacrificed this Original Core Spirit, to peripheral secondary spirits. By its own conduct over time, it is self evident that:

(i) The UN has surrendered its Global Peace mandate to parochial national sovereignty and selfishness of its self-seeking and self-justifying Member-States by bowing at all times to their wishes whether injurious or not to World Peace as in the cases of Korea, Vietnam, Rwanda, Burundi, Somalia, etc. thereby disowning its original Spirit and the defenceless Peoples it was mandated to defend under the Preamble of the UN Charter.

(ii) The UN has instead diverted and invested most of its valuable resources into non-political serendipities such as economic, social, cultural, etc. whose success and survival, in fact, depends totally on this <u>marginalized</u> or <u>forgotten</u> Original Core Spirit (which is global political peace and security) as a prerequisite.

(f) In the final analysis, this unfortunate diversion from the original goal to those peripheries is:

(i) The fundamental root-cause of the rampant cancer now haunting the whole world community manifested in widespread wars, refugee exodus, massive poverty, etc. which could have been easily avoided or eradicated had the UN wisely adhered to its Original Spirit clearly envisaged in The Preamble of its own Charter.[14]

(ii) And a significant acid test finding confirming to the International Community as a whole that something very serious is indeed wrong with this World Body Leadership. By taking an in-action stand in the 1960 Congo Crisis thereby causing the loss of lives of both Prime Minister Patrice Lumumba and its own Secretary General, Dag Hammarskjold, by unwisely withdrawing its 2000 peace keeping force officers out of 2500 from Rwanda in the 1994 civil war thereby causing a catastrophe of massive mutual genocide and refugee agony in that country, it is obviously self-evident that the World Body's concept of Theocentric Humanism Philosophy characterized by Perfection, Holiness and Godliness on the one hand, and The Doctrine of Summum Bonum characterized by the virtues of Justice, Wisdom, Temperance and Courage on the other is extremely questionable.

(5) With regard to the on-going increasing world-wide concerns and efforts by Government Leaders and private persons alike to stamp out the increasing menace of drug trafficking which is now becoming as equally dangerous to humanity security as the existing world-wide corruption, Aids, poverty, detentions, terrorism, civil wars, and refugee exodus, etc. are the recently

published research findings by Argwings Odera[15] jointly sponsored by the UN International Drug Control Programme (UNIDCP), the US Government and other authorities, <u>revealing</u> the following most flabbergasting revelations which is also an added devastating question against the World Leadership's seriousness of commitment to its Mandate enshrined in The Preamble and the Total Principles envisaged in the UN Charter on the one hand and to the Philosophy and Doctrine envisaged in concern 4(f)(ii) above:

That out of a total of 43,383 cases of illicit drug instituted between 1990 and 1997, none of them has ever been convicted;

And, that it is not private individuals or cartels who are actually the chief promoters of this illicit drug trafficking but the same leaders and governments who are pretending to be anti-this menace. Obviously, this is indeed another added revelation confirming further that something is indeed critically wrong with our World-wide Leadership and Governance that therefore warrants and legitimises this diagnosis!

(6) And, to confirm further that our critical concerns above in (1)-(5) are real and therefore that the Earth is indeed so much wretched that an immediate booster is extremely essential right now against this leadership confusion and failures as a prerequisite,

  (a) One may also need to pay heed to a flabbergasting report by the Nation Correspondent (Paul Redfern) based in London which appeared in Kenya in <u>The Daily</u> <u>Nation</u> issue of Saturday, 20 September, 1997, in Nairobi under this shocking title "BABIES GIVEN AIDS IN TESTS".

  (b) This report is not only flabbergasting but also a very significant prima facie evidence in support of the Call in this Book for a thorough Clinical Diagnosis and Prognosis of the prevailing pathological problem haunting our World Leadership.

(2) CONCLUSION

In view of these alarming findings, our conclusion in this Clinical Diagnosis is, therefore, that our Global Leadership is not only a hostage of the Honesty Deficiency

Syndrome (HDS) caused by a thick darkness prophesized by Prophet Isaiah 2500 years ago,[16] and, that the consequences of this could be very serious indeed to total Humanity unless an immediate rationale action is to promptly re-examine and renovate the culture of this leadership as a pre-requisite of containing these consequences.

This action is necessary because as also noted in his analysis of both American and British current leaderships with respect to their entry, role and consequences in the on-going crisis in Iraq, Kwendo Opanga[17] observed that world-wide leadership and the Innocent Humanity as a whole is at a critical risk if this leadership is not clinically re-examined and treated of dishonesty very immediately. And that it is because of this disease that both leaders are definitely war criminals as also evidenced by the following facts:

(1)   For having stubbornly raided Iraq on wrong premise accusing Iraq leadership of Saddam Hussein that the latter had a stockpile of Dangerous Weapons of Mass Destruction (DWMD) namely nuclear, chemical and biological weapons which, according to the British Prime Minister Tony Blair, Saddam Hussein had explicit enough capabilities of deploying in a matter of 45 minutes against any target.

(2)   But, after invading and occupying Iraq and finding Iraq empty of these DWMD, the two are now hurriedly putting up committees of inquiry to look into the merits of the intelligence reports on which Washington D.C. and London declared war on Iraq leadership.

(3)   Their cunning intention to dishonesty deny responsibility of their leadership failure by trying to dump the Iraq invasion, occupation and consequences thereof on their national intelligence fraternities for giving them wrong information on the DWMD.

(4)   Their declaration of war on Iraq in total disregard of the UN Security Council decision against the idea.

(5)   The US Deputy Secretary of State Paul Wolfwitz's revelation last year (2003) that it was not the question of DWMD but one of tailoring the intelligence

reports to suit the White House's interest and plan to attack Baghdad and remove Saddam Hussein from leadership in Iraq.

(6) Former US Secretary of Treasury, Paul O'Neill's additional revelation in January 2004 that the British Administration began plotting the removal of Saddam Hussein from power immediately Bush came to power as US President.

(7) Confirmation by former UN Arms Inspector David Kay who headed the 1,200 strong Iraq Survey-Group in January, 2004 that Saddam Hussein did not actually possess the said weapons.

(8) False eloquent speech by US Secretary of State Collin Powell before the UN Security Council producing satellite pictures of sites and laboratories for production of these weapons in Iraq which he then used as valid evidences justifying necessary invasion and occupation of Iraq so that the said weapons may be captured and destroyed before Saddam Hussein uses them to destroy mankind.

(9) Addition falsehood by US Vice President Dick Cheney to the World Community through media that Iraq had these dangerous weapons, which were consequently a justification, that Saddam Hussein leadership indeed posed an imminent danger to the World Community if not disarmed.

CHAPTER **VI**

THE RISE OF UNDEMOCRACY AND ITS EFFECTS TO THE INNOCENT PUBLIC

I.   INTRODUCTION

It IS NATURAL IN life that no single living sane organism (be it in fauna or flora) can or would attempt to do anything and succeed in achieving the objective sought from such undertaking without, first of all, having a clear understanding or picture of what it seeks to do, how to do it, when to do it, and most important of all, what to gain therefrom, when and how much.

Hence, the Purpose, Rationale and Method of this Study is:

1)   To understand what is "Democracy" and "undemocracy";

2)   To systematically and meticulously identify and analyse those real underlying root-causes of the existing perennial political VIRUS of Undemocracy against Democracy in Africa; and

3)   To prescribe a possible CURE to the virus for the betterment of the Peoples and Governments of Africa in conformity with our Professional Ethics and Responsibility to Humanity.

(A) "CONCEPTUALIZATION OF DEMOCRACY AND PRACTICE OF DEMOCRACY IN AFRICA FOR PRODUCTIVE NATIONAL DEVELOPMENT"

"Conceptualisation" of an idea or object *means knowing or understanding* that idea or object fairly well enough in terms of what it is in life, e.g., its characteristics, its use, its constraints in life; and also *being able to tell, explain or define properly that idea or object in the simplest meaning or words possible to those who may not be knowing what idea or object actually is or means in life. One may do so verbally e.g. in speeches; or in writing books or other forms of publications, e.g.,(1) Congo my Country by Patrice Lumumba, (2) Facing Mt. Kenya by Jomo Kenyatta, (3) I Speak of Freedom, by Dr. Kwame Nkrumah; (4) Julius K. Nyerere, The Inauguration Lectures of the University of Zambia; (5) Oginga Odinga, Not Yet Uhuru; (6) Benjamin Nnamdi Azikiwe, Zik: A Selection From the Speeches of Dr. Nnamdi Azikiwe; (7) Samora Machel, Establishing People's Power to Serve the Masses.* Therefore, by the term "Conceptualisation of Democracy in Africa", we mean the manner in which the idea of "Democracy" is understood by African leaders and their respective governments; and particularly how these leaders are able to use the meaning or "Good Governance". The word "Practice", on the other hand, means how this idea which one purports/claims to know is actually applied or used in one's activities in life. Therefore, by the term, "Practice of Democracy in Africa" we mean the manner in which this idea of "Democracy" is actually applied or used in African political life by political leaders in the policies and activities in terms of **who gets what, where, when, how and why** in one's body politique. In this regard, the term "Conceptualization and Practice of Democracy in Africa", we simply mean How the idea of "Democracy" is understood in Africa; and How it is applied or used by the African leaders, and their respective governments in Africa, in their efforts for National Development, for the good of their respective General Public whom they are expected to serve under their Constitutional Oath. Accordingly in this Study we will attempt to demonstrate what African leaders purport to know about Democracy and whether they actually apply its meaning in their leadership activities, in both scientific and ethical terms, for that fundamental purpose.

But what is "Democracy" and "Undemocracy?" What political features must a country have in order to be recognized as "Democratic" or "Undemocratic?" And most important of all, what is the most unique/intrinsic value of Democracy for National Development which cannot be found in any other modes of political leadership and governance?

(B) METHODOLOGY

Our approach in this Study will solely be retrospective. I believe that this would be the most cost-effective way of getting a simplest answer to what we anxiously wish to know regarding the extent to which Democracy is known and used in Africa for National Development. Accordingly, our strategy will be:

To first define the concept of "Democracy" in its simplest meaning possible in terms of what it is and what it is not in political life, as a way of also understanding what "Undemocracy" is or means in political life.

To follow through the trails of our major political leaders beginning with our first leaders at independence to the present and analyse and assess the similarity between their level of understanding what "Democracy" means and their actual policies and activities using the meaning of Democracy;

And,

To show the degree at which these leaders' political actions have been really in keeping with their own understanding of what "Democracy" actually means in political life;

To show significance of Democracy in political life for national development, and;

To give viable recommendations as therapeutic solution to these on-going perennial political maladies caused by undemocratic political leadership, which have always hampered productive national growth and development in Africa.

II. DEFINITION OF THE CONCEPT "DEMOCRACY"

Before we dive deep into the subterranean strata of this concept called "Democracy" in order to get its actual meaning, let us take note that in political life, this very concept has suffered the most of all concepts because of conflicting definitions and understandings attributed to its real meaning which in most cases are most particularly by dictatorial, autocratic and cannibalistic leaders who love to joyfully qualify themselves and all their policies and actions as also being democratic in order to fool the innocent general public they lead so as to perpetually remain in power at the expense of the less informed general public of what "Democracy" actually means or otherwise.

Because of these habitual absurdities globally caused by leadership dishonesty, the following definition is extremely essential so as to liberate the less informed general public from perennial leadership dishonesty and hooliganism.

In this regard, "Democracy" succinctly means a mode of governance which is created, formed or adopted by all people or their leaders for the good or benefit of all those people without any discrimination against any one individual, group, or community based on race, religion, ethnicity, gender, physical health, or any other criterion.

This definition also agrees very well with the definition contained in all dictionaries and encyclopaedia. In the words of Webster's Collegiate Dictionary, for example, "Democracy" also concurs that it is:

". . . a government by the people; a rule of the majority; a form of government in which the supreme power is vested in the people and exercised by them directly (as in ancient Greek city—states or the New England town meeting)—called also direct democracy; a form of government in which the supreme power is vested in the people and exercised by them indirectly through a system of representation and delegated authority in which the people choose their officials and representatives at periodically held free elections—called also representative democracy".

In the final analysis, a synthesis of the two definitions noted above, one from the Webster's Collegiate Dictionary and one from the author's own efforts leads us to this wisdom:

That in order for a country to qualify as a democratic country, it must first and foremost have or prove that its government is not of only a few bunch of individual citizens but of all citizens;

That its government is managed by all citizens through their representatives since not all of them (citizens) can manage to have room in their law-making house;

That its government is managed not for the few but for all citizens at large, all depending on the leader's rational and just judgement as who wants what, where and when;

That all such representatives must be governed by regularly periodic elections;

- That such elections must always be free and fair to and for all and at all times but not rigged as has always been the case in the election culture in Kenya and most African countries since Independence: where an honest winner is turned into an agonized loser by the Electoral Authority robbing his/her votes and giving the same to the dishonest loser; and

- Where use of colossal money to buy votes with a view to practically using bribery to buy one's election to become a people's representative in an august house.

That, that country must have a mode of governance which is truly mindful for the welfare of those people the government is expected to serve.

That, that government must therefore be a servant but not a boss of the people it leads.

That to qualify as a democratic government, that country must have no more and no less than the constitutionally agreed upon number of representatives.

That such representatives must be elected once but not appointed or nominated by the authority in power as this would be in total conflict with the spirit of Democracy and Democratic Elections.

That in as much as representatives must be elected by their own constituencies, their electors must therefore be the Centre of power in the sense that it must be them and them alone in whom sovereignty of their country is vested, founded and anchored.

That they must therefore be the Employers of their representatives, able to hire and fire.

That all of them must be well educated on this TRUTH so that each is aware of his/her role in government, and the meaning of his/her role in the country. Otherwise, most of them will not be able to know what Democracy means and his/her role vis a vis all others and the leaders.

(A) <u>Governments which are "Democratic" and their Habitual Characteristics, Behaviour and Strategy in Authority</u>

As already noted above, the term "Democracy" succinctly means a government which is formed by a people through a structured popular election for the purpose of assisting them in the management of their affairs for their own general good called "Welfare".

There are two types of Democracy. One is a government in which the supreme power is vested in the people and exercised by them directly as in the ancient Greek City—States. This form of government is called "Direct Democracy". However, there is another form of government in which the supreme power is vested in the people and exercised by them indirectly through a system of representation and delegated authority and in which the people choose their officials and representatives at periodically held free elections. This form of government is called "Representative Democracy", e.g. USA, UK, France and Germany.

Accordingly, in order for a country to be called or accepted as "Democratic" that country must prove that it has a government formed by its own people and managed by the same people, for their own welfare.

But, empirical and scientific evidences overtime from Natural, Physical and Behavioural Sciences research confirm that life naturally originates from a mutual co-existence and interaction of two parts of life, one positive and the other negative, and also that any absence of one of the two or any tendency of one of them to dominate the other naturally leads to certain abnormalities of the product of that interaction.

Accordingly, also in political life, democracy can thrive and blossom only in a country which is prepared to open its doors for a mutual co-existence and interaction of two political parts, a <u>governing party and the opposition</u>. Therefore, any country which lacks this political environment naturally breeds internal autocratic, dictatorial leadership and other political abnormalities (chaos) arising from that leadership's tendencies to usurp all state apparatus, e.g. security, funds, civil service, the press, etc, making them his personal property. Any officer working under that leadership is naturally forced to behave according to the <u>Nyayos</u> (dictates) of that leadership. Any failure by that officer to do so naturally results in summary dismissal, detention or even death if necessary, all depending on the wishes of that leadership. In a democracy, co-existence between the governing party and the opposition is naturally essential because the two provide checks and balances on each other, i.e., they police on each other's behaviour on behalf of the general public.

(B) <u>Governments which are not "Democratic" and their Habitual characteristics, Behaviour and Strategy in Authority</u>

For this reason, all colonial governments which were managed by foreigners for the good of those foreigners were not "Democratic". They failed to qualify as such because they lacked free local participation. Also, since a "Democratic" government in our political life today must be a representative government in which a constitutionally agreed upon number of leaders are periodically elected by their own local people called "grassroots", all elected leaders must be <u>neither</u> rigged in office directly appointed by a head of state or any body of persons as it often happens in various governments of Africa. They must be properly chosen by their own electorates who shall, in turn, be the <u>Centre</u> of power. Accordingly, any independent African Country whose government ministers and other members of parliament become rigged in office but not properly elected as required under Democratic principles is automatically not "Democratic" although that country may be free from a foreign rule. This includes all other countries which are under the military rule through a coup d'etat; and those which condone "life presidency" such as Malawi.

The most very intriguing (striking) behavioural characteristics of such undemocratic governments include the following:

1. Unlike a democratic leadership which respects and honours <u>peaceful co-existence and mutual interaction</u> between a Governing party and the Opposition in accordance with the natural behavioural law in political life, undemocratic leadership is habitually autocratic, dictatorial, unethical and chaotic. It is so harsh, disrespectful, insulting and humiliating to those who try to criticise or challenge its policies or acts that it is ETHICALLY and MORALLY NAKED.

2. In order for it to survive at all, it does not only expropriate the state's apparatus (funds, security, civil service, etc.) but also all major professional institutions and persons by <u>use of a bribe</u> and every other unlawful means necessary so that these institutions and persons may cordially, and comfortably serve this leadership's interests regardless of whether or not such interests may be injurious to the interests of the general public. Such bribes include public money, public plots, public residential premises, promotions, etc.

3. Professional institutions and persons exist by <u>name</u> only without any genuine professional ethics. For this reason,

The <u>degree</u> of professional ethics under such leadership is normally very poor as the ethic is regarded as a <u>nuisance</u>, <u>hindrance</u> or <u>interference</u> to one's chance of getting rich quickly from accepting such bribes from the leadership.

The <u>degree</u> of honour, excellence, accountability and all attributes of professional Ethics is equally very poor indeed.

Filling of vacant important key positions in the public sector and elsewhere is not carried out on the strength of professional ethics and merits. The positions are habitually filled through <u>nepotism</u>, <u>bribery</u> and other unprofessional tactics whether or not such persons are qualified for the positions. And also for this reason,

The degree of productivity is normally very poor.

The chances of survival of these institutions, which are headed by such unqualified persons, are normally very bleak. In most cases, many of them gradually dry up and finally collapse.

In event of a critical case or issue implicating that leadership, all available evidences which are considered highly devastating with a potential danger to the leadership's survival are summarily destroyed or concealed from the reach of the general public by those professional institutions and persons in order to protect and safeguard the leadership from a possible downfall. And because of doing this, they are paid (compensated) very highly by the leadership.

If any one, acting in defence of the interests of the general public, ever tries to criticise or report that leadership's illegal acts or intentions to the official security authorities or any other responsible or interested persons, he or she is either ignored, ridiculed or is instead held totally responsible for doing so. If he is a government officer, such person is summarily sacked and may either be detained without trial in court of law or simply killed through dubious means thereby rendering any future investigation of his death too cumbersome and difficult to be carried out.

Every professional officer who comes to be identified and strongly confirmed by the general public to have been involved in a case implicating the leadership is habitually defended at all costs by that leadership and is normally set free and the report on the issue is simply noted and ignored in order to impress, encourage and ensure continuous protection to the leadership from those professional institutions and persons who have been lured to do so by the leadership.

However, in the event that such an officer is detected to be associating with the opposition, such an officer is summarily disowned and thrown away by the leadership like a used toilet paper.

Most institutions and persons involved in defending such leadership's acts do so without any moral hesitation <u>no matter how injurious</u> such acts may be to the innocent general public's interests and the state's repute in world community. Such persons are normally very distinct and conspicuous in that:

They are found to have become filthy wealthy in a very short period.

They own and drive one or more very luxurious unique vehicles, normally Pajeros, Mercedes Benz, Range Rovers, etc.

They live in owner-occupied luxurious residences, and also own several of them including expensive plots.

They eat and feast lavishly in highly expensive recreational institutions which they could hardly have afforded before.

They are always very liquid and can, therefore, afford whatever they wish at any cost.

Consequently, they are always arrogant, paranoid and defensive of their acts even when they know that they are in the wrong.

Their life style is very expensive, in terms of what they own, the time they have taken to own this wealth, and their attitude to their critics.

In the final analysis, such <u>leadership is always so (insecure) that it habitually resorts to certain non-logical defensive tactics</u> e.g. "I AM ABOVE THE LAW," and "I AM LIFE PRESIDENT" as their only means of survival because they all know very well that all their duties, privileges and limitations are GOVERNED by THE CONSTITUTION. Therefore, they do resort to such bad tactics only as a <u>Containment</u> weapon with which to fool the general public; and to keep off the Critics from trying to question the legitimacy or legality of the leadership's undemocratic acts.

Obviously, all these Leadership conducts are not in harmony with the true Ethics of a Democratic Government.

III. DEMOCRACY IN AFRICA

(1) <u>During the colonial Era (up to the late 1950's)</u>

In his book, <u>Cause-Effects of Modern African Nationalism on the World Market</u>5, discovered the following:

(a) That absence of Democracy in Africa during the colonial era became a womb in which and from which modern Africa nationalism and nation-states were conceived and born;

(b) That it was not due to the colonial rulers' ignorance of the concept of Democracy that these rules failed to copy it in their leadership of African colonies; and

(c) That all of them were fully and properly conversant with the concept and the consequences of it from their political experiences back home (in Europe) and also from the American War of Independence in 1776. From Auma-Osolo's research on the four hundred years of the European political experience, for example, he also discovered that there were numerous political philosophers such as John Locke (an Englishman, 1632-1704), Jean Jacques Rousseau (French-man) to whom "Democracy" was that in the eyes of God, all men were created equal regardless of their colour, creed or nationality including sex!

He also discovered from the American history records that it was this view which also became the main cornerstone of the American colonies' argument and excuse of their war of independence with Britain. The American colonies managed to gain their independence on the 4th July, 1776 using this excuse as their main weapon. Accordingly, political turmoils in both European and American experiences of the time were not caused by any other factor other than by the carelessness and negligence of colonial masters who could not honour and practice Democracy in Europe and American colonies.

Further, he came to discover that it was the same factor which also caused the rise of communism and socialism in Europe which later also filtered into other continents, such as Africa. Otherwise, Karl Marx and his philosophy of Marxism and Vladmir Lenin and his philosophy of Leninism could not have emerged in Europe by chance alone, had there been true Democracy in Europe, although some of us who even do not know this would have the guts to abuse and criticise Marx and Lenin for advocating their respective philosophies.

This reality also holds true in Africa. All colonies in Africa could not have began a war with their respective colonial rulers had these colonial masters dared to pay heed to the principles and virtues of Democracy; and to treat those colonies with mutual respect and dignity along the lines of those Democratic principles and virtues.

Our Scientific evidences show clearly that the colonial masters neglected these principles and virtues. They instead chose to believe in and practice all sorts of most inhumane acts <u>against Africans</u>. The Africans were, for example, regarded as half human beings. Accordingly, Africans were always denied suffrage as they were considered by the colonial masters as not qualified enough to warrant representation or participation of any kind in the political process. The Africans' attempts to resist this resulted into their arbitrary arrests and detention without trial. Also Africans were denied to hold or apply for any white-colour jobs, or to use any better facilities such as restaurants, hotels, parks, swimming pools, buses, trains, schools, hospitals, churches, beaches as all these were restricted to <u>whites only</u>. In all, Africans were confined to a socio-economic and political helplessness and frustration. Obviously, such conduct by the colonial rule against Africans was totally incompatible with those principles and virtues of Democracy known to all colonial masters.

In the book mentioned above, Auma-Osolo also discovered that in the same manner the colonial rulers were kicked out of North America in 1776 by the colonies because of these colonial negligence to honour and respect the principles and virtues of Democracy so were all other colonial masters also of the 1960s, almost all colonies in Africa had achieved their freedom to have their suffrage and representation in the political process in accordance with the principles and virtues of Democracy.

(2) <u>During the Post-Colonial Era (after the late 1950's)</u>

    (A) Incongruence between Actual Leadership & Principles and Virtues of Democracy

<u>The arrival of independence in Africa was received with greatest joy and euphoria of celebrations</u>. In independent Africa, one would, <u>therefore, have hoped with this jubilation that the new African leaders would now do better for their fellow</u> Africans than the former colonial masters. For example, one would have hoped that there would be no more such arbitrary arrests without trial; no more interference in individual's freedom of expression, etc.

On the contrary, whenever one has a quick glance at what has been happening up to today in independent African politics, one is left with nothing to be desired at all. Although, apart from South African (Azania), all Africa is now free from the yoke of colonial leadership, it is possible to conclude that Africa has just changed hands from a foreign evil to a local one; in fact, to the worst one.

The empirical evidence of this includes the following:

<u>All African leaders who liberated African from the foreign evil with an aim of restoring Democracy in Africa summarily </u>became victims at the hands of their fellow Africans because of their beliefs and defence of Democracy.

According to our history records, the majority of them were all summarily eliminated through assassinations and other means by those who claimed to know better. These unfortunate victims included Patrice Lumumba of Congo (renamed later Zaire by his successor), Dr. Kwame Nkrumah of Ghana, Ahmed Ben Mbella of Algeria, Samora Machel of Mozambique and other persons who sacrificed all their time to fight for the African Freedom and dignity from the colonial masters and to sustain that freedom and dignity at all costs in the Community of Nations. But those who took over from these masters began doing the opposite; worse than the colonial masters. This biggest tragedy was brought about by Mobutu Sese Seko, Moise Tshombe, Charles Taylor, Daniel T. arap Moi, Felix Houphouet Boigny, Mwanasa Kipwepwe.

Recurrent arbitrary arrests and detentions without trial, which are totally unethical to Fundamental Human Rights, abound in Africa. In Kenya, for example, Joseph Martin Shikuku, Raila Odinga, Kenneth Matiba, Charles Rubia, Koigi wa Wamwere, George Anyona, and many others were victims of this evil. Harassments of the Freedom of the Press and Individual Rights to express one's beliefs freely are also rampant all over Africa.

General and other forms of elections are only elections by name but not in real practical terms. Those who purport to have been elected during the elections do not get elected by their respective people as is expected under the principles and virtues of Democracy. Rather, they are craftly selected by the head of state through rigging elections. Certain leaders normally do this in order to return their political assistants as partners in the looting of public funds and property. Such assistants are elevated to important government portfolios so that they may all again continue their habitual looting together as a team. As head of state in control of all state machinery funds, security, media, and personnel, his job is to do exactly this in order to remain in power. To achieve this goal, all presiding officers are either willingly or forcefully instructed by the head of state to exchange votes from the winning candidate to the losing one so that the losing one turns out to be the winner of the elections—a totally pathetic flabbergasting situation hardly conducive for National Peace & Development. Because of this obvious African independent country which honours, respects and, therefore, practices Democracy in the strictest sense of the Democratic principles—for the good of the General Public whom they are expected to assist under the Constitutional Oath.

In addition, the disease of massive corruption is rampant throughout Africa. The Goldenberg Scandal in Kenya is not the only one. It is just a tip of the ICEBERG. The disease is so grandiose, contagious, and unchecked that a public service employee is naturally on two pay-rolls. A written payroll by which one is openly paid monthly in the form of a bona fide or de jure monthly salary; and an unwritten one by which one is secretly paid either under the table, in toilet or corridor in the form of a bribe. This reality holds true in all public offices; and is extremely worse among traffic police officers on roads, streets and highways who have now made it their habit. In fact, what these officers collect in a week from motorists, most especially from commercial ones, is so attractive to them that they would most likely die with whoever tries to challenge such acts. This reality was also confirmed recently by President Daniel T. arap Moi of Kenya during his speech at Mbale, Kakamega, a speech which was also replayed by the Kenya Television Network (KTN) evening news on 22nd October 1992. The President confessed to the Kenyans about this undemocratic evil; but argued that after all, the on-going corruption in Kenya had neither started during his leadership nor was it limited to Kenya.

According to him, this evil in Kenya had began during Jomo Kenyatta's regime; it was rampant in all Africa; and that it began with Adam. The President, therefore, concluded by arguing that, his regime had therefore no case to answer with respect to the issue as this was a God given sin on earth. During the November 1992 General Elections in Kenya, the President boldly used this strategy to buy the entire country with colossal sums of money so that the voters may vote him in as President of Kenya.

Another extremely flabbergasting pathological problem facing Africa which is totally unethical to the principles and virtues of Democracy and which one would not have expected from such African leaders who had claimed that they were better than the abnormal massive self-aggrandizement by such African leaders. In a scrutiny of most current heads of state in Africa one notes with shock the overwhelming wealth each has accumulated during his tenure of office. The most striking top leaders include, for example, President Mobutu Sese Seko of Zaire, President Arap Moi of Kenya and President M. Said Barre of Somalia (before the latter was ousted). The Goldenberg issue and the looting of all financial parastatals and state proper institutions in Kenya today are classic flabbergasting examples in Kenyan political culture today.

The problem is not limited to them alone as heads of state. It is a contagion all way below from their deputies and ministers right down to permanent secretaries and managing directors or executive chairmen who are the bona fide accounting officers of their respective ministries and parastatal bodies respectively. Most of them are filthy wealthy through these abnormal unethical dealings, which are totally destructive to the growth and development of their countries' economy.

This behaviour by a head of state is obviously as abnormal as it is in not keeping with the cardinal philosophy of being mindful of other people's welfare coined and daily echoed by same President Moi. And given that he himself cannot also honour, and respect his own philosophy in his leadership in Kenya, one, therefore, wonders what our African leaders are really up to and why African nationalists such as Lumumba, Jomo Kenyatta, Nkrumah, Machel and Mwalimu Julius Nyerere had to kick out the white man's leadership from Africa. Many Africans are now obviously asking these questions with strongest regrets, and guilty consciences.

It is therefore, questionable why an evil should be substituted with a worst one. This does not make any sense at all. It is no wonder then that in one single country such as Kenya, several leaders such as the Bishop of Diocese of Eldoret (Rt. Rev. Alexander Muge), the Kenya Foreign Minister (Dr. Robert Ouko), and many Kenya legislators such as Tom Mboya, Pinto, Argwings Kodhek, Ronald Ngala, etc. were assassinated simply because of their beliefs and defence of Democracy in Kenya. Even when inquiries were lawfully instituted to bring the culprits to book, the heads of state of the time either threw out the findings or simply dismissed the Commission before the latter had completed its investigation, thereby rendering the original objective of the inquiry totally hopeless and useless.

Surpringly, on realizing that things were now becoming extremely hot from the Opposition and Church activities and statements in and outside Parliament against the evil of this strategy, the President became extremely worried. He summarily summoned all Permanent Secretaries (who are Chief Executive and Accounting Officers of their respective Ministries in the Civil Service) at the State House Nairobi on the 7th April 1993 and instructed them to promptly initiate an immediate "Anti-Corruption" measure in their respective Ministries and root-out all those Civil Servants who are found to be corrupt.

The President further stressed to them that from now on, this was to be taken as new Government priority, and that it must be implemented with immediate effect in order to save the ailing Kenyan economy from collapsing.

However, it is apparent from all these that any sane person would obviously see this Presidential directive as strange. It is questionable how on earth culprit "A" could instruct and expect culprit "B" to take appropriate measure or action on culprit "C" given the fact that there is no difference between "A", "B" and "C" in their character. Given the fact that the whole system from top-bottom is saturated with the same evil, it is self-evident that "A", "B" and "C" do speak the same language and have a common culture. It is, therefore, questionable as to who of the three would blame who. Accordingly, the directive is not rational at all. To call on Permanent Secretaries to initiate anti-corruption campaign policy and to possibly root out all corrupt Civil Servants from their respective Ministries is impractical since this would automatically mean asking them to commit suicide.

This directive must, therefore, be a big joke, a myth and CONTEMPT of true DEMOCRACY and JUSTICE. This is exactly where and how African leadership always goes wrong, even at the simplest problem possible. It is a tragedy for which Africa is bound to pay dearly unless we all wake up and agree seriously to rectify our leadership careless behaviour before everything falls apart completely.

(B) <u>Consequences of Such Incongruence between Theory and Practice of Democracy in Africa among African leaders</u>. The end-results of this incongruence between Africa Leaders' understanding or knowledge of democracy and how they actually use their understanding of Democracy in treating their fellow African followers in their respective political jurisdictions is very pathetic, and devastating to the socio-economic development in their own countries.

This is the major reason (1) <u>Why each African country has failed to maintain any steady growth in</u> G.N.P.; (2) Why each African country has kept on <u>undergoing recurrent domestic socio-economic recession</u>; (3) Why each African country continues to be <u>faced by recurrent domestic political unrest</u>; etc.

Also in an article, "Objective African Military Control: A New Paradigm in Civil Military Relations"[8] this author discovered that most African countries have experienced either a successful or abortive civilian or military coup d'etat; and that the causal factor of these coups was African Leaders' <u>own negligence to use the principles and virtues of Democracy in their treatment of those that they govern</u>.

In this respect it is important to conclude in this Study:

(1) That although all African political leaders may not be ignorant of what Democracy means, and although they may also know very well that it was the carelessness of European political leaders to apply Democracy in Europe and North American colonies that caused leadership take-over in Europe and North America, it is apparent that what they know and preach about Democracy in Africa remain at the meetings. They do not apply it at all in their leadership for the Good of the General Public whom they govern.

(2) That it is because of their own carelessness in political leadership that they fail to put what they know about Democracy into proper use. But when they find themselves caught up in fire, they begin claiming that Africa was not <u>yet politically ready enough for multi-party politics</u>.

(3) And that Africa has fallen on evil days partly because of OAU's docility. Although Act 3 of OAU Charter prohibits OAU from intervening in Member States' domestic crisis, OAU Leadership has proved too weak to intervene in critically affected areas such as Angola, Liberia and Somalia where bullet wounds and famine keep on claiming innocent lives in thousands daily. Otherwise, one is left to wonder why outsiders such as UN, USA, UK and other sympathisers and volunteers should have to come all way outside Africa to assist while OAU exists in Africa but is nowhere to be heard of. This is another indicator of African leadership poverty, and shame to Africa.

IV. ESSENCE OF DEMOCRACY IN POLITICAL LIFE AND ITS SIGNIFICANCE FOR CONTEMPORARY AFRICA FOR NATIONAL DEVELOPMENT

(A) <u>A Retrospective Analysis</u>

In the final analysis,

(1) Democracy is the only Reliable Powerful ENGINE of a Political Culture which is capable of encouraging and nurturing a rapid resuscitation and evolution and growth of a state in all walks of life for the socio-economic betterment of the General Public.

(2) It is the only form of government, which is able to effectively tame a state's activities and attitude, which may be against natural human and civil rights of an individual in political life.

(3) It is a political culture which does not agree with current leadership dictatorship and other autocratic tendencies in contemporary Africa which include assumptions that one must be a "Life President", or is "Above-the-Law", in disregard of the wishes and welfare of the individual and general natural human and civil rights which, in the end, often become the real root-cause of civil war against that type of Leadership. (a) <u>Such tendencies in contemporary Africa obviously do not respect the natural law. (b) According to the natural law, it is only God who is above the law.</u> But since even Jesus Christ, and all Prophets recognised themselves to be below the Law, it is therefore open to

question why and how any sane political leader or religious leader who is mere creature of God and who goes to sleep, to toilet, to eat, to drink, etc. on the dictates of the law, can claim to be above the law. It is also very unbelievable for a leader whose powers are drawn from and protected by the Constitution of his/her respective Country or State can claim to be above the law as though his powers, duties and responsibilities came from air but not from the Constitution.

(4) Unlike autocratic dictatorial leadership, which is very rampant throughout Africa, Democratic Leadership is always sober, tolerant and accommodative to every criticism. (a) It encourages competitiveness, pluralism and plurastic undertakings so long as these undertakings are not injurious to society or to individual rights. (b) Most importantly, it encourages creative science and technology because unlike autocratic dictatorial leadership, it is the only type of political leadership which is capable of controlling the state's apparatus which include security forces and all other civil servants from arrogant and corruptive attitude and other forms of malpractices at the expense of the general public. (c) North America, Europe and Japan accepted to adopt this Democratic Path of Leadership because they had always failed in their socio-economic development through an autocratic dictatorial leadership. (d) Because of this attitude and character of an autocratic dictatorial leadership, North America and Europe had often been a hostage of recurrent political turmoils. (e) The only solution to such turmoils in Europe and North America was for them to FIRST search in their hearts a better form of government to adopt in order to put an end to this turmoil. (f) The two Continents accepted to follow a Democratic path. And as soon as they did so, their political turmoil ended. (g) The end of this political turmoil in Europe and North America became a major blessing to those two Continents. (h) This end of the turmoil became a fertile soil for their socio-economic development. FIRST, science and Technology began to flourish and blossom to their highest level. And, SECOND it was this growth in Science and Technology which in turn, generated a dynamic beginning of Accelerated productive socio-economic development in both Europe and North America. (i) This is exactly the way North America and Europe became super power on the World Market. The

two continents have since then continued to control and dictate prices on the World Market simply because of their socio-economic power monopoly, which they achieved through a Democratic leadership path.

(5) Unfortunately Democracy in Africa has not yet taken root properly. (a) Most African leadership is against Democracy in favour of autocratic and dictatorial tendencies, which have, in turn, continued to breed political unrest at home. (b) This is exactly the reason why Africa remains stagnant in socio-economic development on the World Market. (c) So, if contemporary Africa wishes to grow also and become recognized and respected as a credible and formidable socio-economic power on the World Market on an equal footing with North America, Europe and Japan, Africa would also need to accept to follow the same Democratic Path.

(6) In order to follow the same Democratic Path for National Development, Africa must, first and foremost, be willing to accept to disentangle herself from her present autocratic dictatorial nepotistic attitude and behaviour in political leadership. (a) Africa must reconcile with herself on this issue and be ready to build and sustain a democratic culture of openness, tolerance, integrity, honour and excellence in all her institutions. (b) Contemporary Africa has to realize that this is the only path to socio-economic salvation and power on the World Market, if Africa also wishes to have this power on the World Market. (c) Otherwise, Africa is subject to stagnate herself indefinitely in all walks of life, and to remain a perpetual minor actor on the Market for easier manipulation by North America and Europe who have accepted this salvation.

(7) The unfortunate corroded assumption by the current minority white political leadership in South Africa which purports that ANC Leadership including all other political leadership in Africa is not yet mature and experienced enough to be given the chance to rule and that if African Leadership were given such chance the latter would not respect, honour and follow the Democratic path is false. The fact that even in North America and Europe, Democracy was accepted though hard-work Democracy in Africa is most likely to take roots deeply only if African Leadership comes to understand Democracy properly and to also realize:

(a) That it was because of the presence of Democracy in North America and Europe that the two continents became socio-economic super powers on the World Market today, and

(b) That Japan has become another super power in that Market because of Japan's recognition and acceptance of the Democratic Path in her political process. Otherwise, Japan would still be as stagnant socio-economically as Africa is today.

V CONCLUSION

A Synthesis

From the evidences in Sections II-III above, on the absence of Democracy in Africa and empirical consequences thereof, it is self-evident that whereas Conceptualization of Democracy in Africa has been an easy task; putting these principles of Democracy in practice has been a very difficult task for the African leadership. This difficulty has risen from nowhere other than from African Leaders' own negligence. What they preach about Democracy has not been what they actually do in their respective leadership for and on behalf of their Citizenry (those they govern).

Like their colonial counterparts, African leaders still do not seem to have good foresight on the consequences of their own negligence. But unlike their colonial counterparts, they have proved to be more inhuman in their leadership. What they do to their own fellow Africans is worse than what the colonial masters used to do. Unlike them, colonial rulers would not condone corruption although they supported segregation or apartheid, as was the case in South Africa. During the colonial time, EFFICIENCY, TRANSPARENCY and ACCOUNTABILITY were extremely respected and honoured at all times in both public and private sectors. Almost every undertaking was guided by these three cardinal principles. Quality in terms of HONOUR and EXCELLENCE was another cardinal principle in the colonial Leadership. This held true in all public sectors, e.g. health, education, roads and in private sectors.

No matter how little a service was, it was a MUST according to the Colonial Leadership Ethics that it had to be Excellent. This is also the reason why an African student who had to go through various rigorous educational stages of examinations, etc. was always superior to a white student. This used to be vividly supported during English Competitive Examinations in the entire British Empire. Most Excellent marks such as "Distinctions" and "Credits" were scored by Africans. Therefore, one wonders why we should not do better in political leadership too. I am sure this is possible only if our political leaders meant it and directed their efforts and attention to the WELFARE OF THEIR PEOPLE whom they govern instead of their personal SELF-SEEKING PASSIONS as they are now doing. I believe this is the REAL ROOT-CAUSE of their FAILURES in Leadership.

Experience shows that every time professional advices have been offered to African political leaders free of charge by good Samaritan African Scholars such as Professor Ali Mazrui, and other Distinguished African Scholars, such advices often have unfortunately been overlooked with lame excuses that these African political leaders either have enough information on the issue or have their own way of getting the information needed.

For example The 2nd Congress of Africanists meeting held in November 1973 in Addis Ababa, in which this author was a participant, advised Emporer Haile Selassie of Ethiopia on the consequences of his undemocratic autocratic leadership; but he ignored!! Because of his own negligence, he was toppled from leadership in April 1974 in a military coup. Also throughout 1992, several appeals entered the State House in Kenya calling on President Moi to pay heed to professional advice from specialists on Peace and Conflict Reconciliation Research and from churches regarding the serious consequences of the new Era of Multi-Party Democracy in Kenya if proper arrangements of peaceful co-existence were not promptly made available between the Government and the Opposition by these two sides. But all these efforts were not accepted by the KANU Government. In short, numerous empirical evidences abound confirming that it is the African leadership's arrogance, dishonesty and over-pride in themselves that is the root-cause of this discrepancy between theory and practice of Democracy in Africa; and the root-causes of national socio-economic and political decay in contemporary Africa.

It is essential to reiterate here once again that most of our Leaders in Africa can hardly be advised. Most of them are anti-scholarship, anti-science and anti-professionalism. They would rather work without them than seek professional advice.

Similarly, they cannot accept peaceful co-existence with the Opposition and the Clergy as all of them consider the latter as arch-enemies and therefore, undesirable evils. This is the main obstacle to Democracy in the African leadership from the independence till today; and the main root-cause of on-going poverty in Africa. Otherwise, I strongly believe Africa would already be booming in socio-economic development.

Although the ruling parties in Africa appear to gladly accept the repeal of their respective constitutions in order to change their countries from One-Party to Multi-Party politics, this is just gimmicks. Their true stand, and attitude is that they are all against multi-party idea as each is unable to sleep soundly in the presence of this multi-party idea. They believe that in the absence of this idea, they are able to remain lords of everything. For them to accept Democracy, it appears to mean yielding to the principle of "majority rule" and "minority rights". And, by so doing they think that they would be supporting the principle of checks and balances which calls for a Balance of Power or Sharing of Power between the Presidency, Legislature and the Judiciary on the one hand; and the Opposition Party, the Press and the Peoples on the other,—ideas they definitely hate to hear at all at any time in their tenure.

African leaders hate this mode of power sharing which Democracy advocates because they seem to think that this would interfere with their selfish styles and habit of accumulating wealth by use of dictatorship. This is exactly why advocates of Democracy such as Bishop Alexander Muge, the Kenyan Foreign Minister Robert Ouko and many others had to become victims of their defence of Democracy. This list is neither new, nor strange. It dates as far back as the time of Independence. In Congo, we have a vivid case Prime Minister Patrice Lumumba; in Ghana, we have another vivid case of Dr. Kwame Nkrumah; in Kenya, we have vivid cases of J.M. Kariuki and Billdad Kaggia; in Guinea, we have a vivid case of Sekou Toure; etc. This malady is of course not limited to Africa. In the United Kingdom, the case of St. Thomas More (The British Chancellor of Exchaque) in 1478 to 1535 who had to be executed for his innocent dedication to the Rule of Professional Ethics and whose case has now become a Classic Exemplary Model for Emulation by all students of Jurisprudence. This case also holds true with respect to the case of the most objective English Judge and Scholar of the 18th Century, Sir Godfrey Higgins of Skellow Grange, near Doncaster, England, 1833 and the Father of Philosophy, Socrates, before Christ was born.

In the final analysis, this is the picture of the nature and degree of Conceptualization and Practice of Democracy in Africa; and the tragedy between the two. In view of these evidences, it is most possible that unless changed, African leadership is unlikely to improve on Democracy. Africa has a long way to go in Democracy. Also, this is the reason why the claim by most people that the recent general elections would be free and fair turned out to be false in Kenya. The elections became a myth because it was saturated with the use of colossal money by the ruling KANU political party. Several candidates from the Opposition parties were bribed left and right by KANU so that they may defect from their parties and rejoin KANU. These anti-Democratic tactics continued throughout the General Elections and thereafter leaving the Opposition with several casualties of defections to KANU. Hence, the perennial danger to Democracy and GOOD GOVERNANCE all over Africa.

VI RECOMMENDATIONS

In view of these numerous evidences adduced above in chapters II to IV, a possible solution to this disease against Democracy and Good Governance in Africa can include the following:

(i) Both the Ruling Party and the Opposition Parties should first and foremost be prepared to recognize each other as bona fide equal counterparts for GOOD GOVERNANCE. They should agree to agree and also to disagree whenever the situation demands in their capacities as mutual partners in and for Nation-Building.

(ii) Both sides should be prepared to accept the reality that both need each other in various ways; and that Peace and Security of their entire Nation depend solely on their conduct and the manner in which they relate to each other.

(iii) Immediately a country decides to accept a multi-party Democracy, and before a multi-party General Election is called, the Government and the Opposition must immediately agree to meet together in face-to-face dialogue and work out: (a) mutually agreed upon NEW MULTI-PARTY ORIENTED NATIONAL CONSTITUTION and (b) their MODUS OPERANDI, i.e. the Mode of their conduct during this New Difficult Era of Multi-Party Democracy. This work must not be seen as responsibility of the ruling party alone.

(iv) Both sides should also sit together and formulate the manner in which their entire Nation should be re-educated on the Principles, Virtues and Values of Multi-Party Democracy.

(v) All evil leadership mannerism and tactics such as use of money as a means of influencing voters must be prohibited with immediate effect. Otherwise, such practice cannot co-exist with Democracy. The two are mutual permanent arch-enemies.

THE GOALS, CAPABILITIES, PROBLEMS AND STRATEGIES OF THE EASTERN AFRICAN NATION-STATES ON THE WORLD MARKET

I. INTRODUCTION

1. Problem:

IN EVERY COMMUNITY OF living organisms, each organism is naturally duty bound to sustain itself in one way or another.[1] Thus survival is the fundamental goal of every organism. While by acting so, every organism also helps its community to sustain itself,[2] naturally, survival of the community results from the spillovers only. The community's goal is secondary as far as each organism's goal is concerned. The primary goal of every organism is to sustain itself.[3] Thus, the "self" concept is always the first priority of every organism in its community because the resources constantly sought by each are too scarce to meet its total demands. Because every organism seeks the same resource(s), and since these goal(s) are too scarce to find or get easily and cheaply from the community, competition and conflict for these resources among the members of the community are significantly high,[4] forcing each entity to indulge in various activities with which to remove that unpleasant situation from oneself. Similar limitations and situations also exist in our International Community. However, knowing (a) what these goals are, (b) where they are, (c) when to find them, (d) how to find them, (e) from whom a nation-state can possibly get them for its national survival and, (f) with what capability (ies) collectively constitute the most fundamental problems, concerns and worries of every nation-State.

In search for these goals on the World-Market, nation-States consequently interact with each other across their national boundaries. But, these goals are too scarce to meet every nation-State's demands. Therefore, they are too difficult to find and get that cheaply.

Also, because nation-states are composed of individuals, every nation-state is a human being. But, all individuals differ in their attitudes, temperaments, bargaining styles and other behavioural styles. They also differ in the ways they conceptualise reality, and perceive one another. Therefore, nation-states differ in their attitude, temperament, concept of reality, inter-perception, bargaining styles and behavioural strategy on the World Market.

Because of these universal significant intellectual and attitudinal variances among nation-states and the scarcity of the goals nation-states always seek on the World Market mixed with the amorphous and acephelous problem of that Market, which, in turn, makes it impossible for the Market to strictly regulate and police over the conduct of each nation-state in the same manner each nation-state strictly does over the conduct of each of its nationals at home and to even punish that national for any violation of the law of the land using its juridical and other law enforcement machineries, reckless competition and conflict among Nation-States for these goals on the World Market are also high. It is due to this very reason that nation-states' interaction on the Market is highly political and anarchical collectively posing a critical pathological problem of concern to each nation-state.

And, since nation-states significantly differ in their attitudes, temperaments, inter-perceptions and concepts of reality, they also differ in their bargaining strength,[5] and strategies towards the goals they always seek on the World Market. They may use pacific,[6] coercive[7] or both strategies, all depending on each actor's strength and the magnitude of the conflict.

Those who opt for coercive to pacific strategy, always rationalize that strategy. They justify it as another inevitable, rational means of achieving the goal(s) that they would not otherwise attain unless they use such strategy(ies). Consequently, todate, pacific and coercive strategies are the two integral parts of the World Politics that each nation-State is naturally expected to use in pursuit of its milieu goal and in defence of its possessional goal, all depending on each nation-State's capacity vis-à-vis the capabilities of other nation-States who are competing for the same milieu goal or defending their possessional goal.

But, in view of this complex pathological problem on the World Market, do the East African nation-States (herein after referred to as African nation-States) have necessary capacity with which to pursue what they seek from the World Market and to protect their dignity and heritage? Do they have a requisite leadership for this most competitive adventure on The World Market?

Further, in his article "Babies Given Aids in Tests" which appeared in the <u>Daily Nation</u>, Nairobi, on 20th September, 1979, the Nation Correspondent based in London, by Paul Redfern, reveals that African Nation-States are the easiest prey of such tests and all other politically, socio-economically and military too weak nation-States.

In his own words, Redfern shows that: "About 1,000 children in Kenya, Uganda and seven other sub-Saharan African countries may have been unnecessarily infected with the HIV virus because of unethical medical experiments conducted by the United States, Belgium, France, Denmark and South Africa.

This is because of experiments involving around 12,000 women in 15 different trials over the past two years. As well as the nine African countries, research was also carried out in Thailand and the Dominican Republic.

Some of the women involved with the trial were given AZT drug, which is known to cut the risk of transmission on the virus between mother and baby by two thirds, while others were only given placebo pills.

The Guardian newspaper, which led on the story today following publication of the research in the New England Journal of Medicine, said that even some US scientist had condemned the experiments as "unethical," adding that the way the research was conducted "appears to contradict global guidelines which say that medical research in developing countries should always be conducted according to ethical standards 'no less exacting' than in the developed worked, where placebo tests are strictly regulated."

An estimated six million women in the developing world will be infected with Aids by the turn of the century, researchers predict. The Independent said that he researchers n the trials were "knowingly condemning some of the yet-to-be-born infants to death by Aids."

In view of these serious facts, the nagging questions are: Are these African nation-states able to defend their possessional and milieu goals against their most aggressive and powerful counterpart on the World Market? Their inability to resist against such tests is a valid evidence of their inability to defend their national Dignity and Human Rights enshrined in the Universal Declaration of Human Rights of the UN Charter Principles and Articles. Because of this serious revelation against their strength to effectively defend their dignity and total survival on the World Market which is composed of Nation-States and Leaders of different attitude and morals, the following long quotation from Paul Redfern, is, therefore, very necessary in order for the reader to capture fully the criticality of this danger now facing the capabilities of the African Nation-States and their leadership on the World Market today:

But, this is not all. Although this HIV case may be a very devastating challenge to the competence of the African leadership to protect the health security and other goals of Africa and her African Peoples on the World Market which is in fact, Goal Number One of every African Leader and Nation-State on that Market, this case is just a tip of the iceberg. More serious cases abound between the Cold War Era (effective 1945) and the present Post-Cold War Era (2001). Prima facie empirical evidences of this reality include, for instance, the following:

1.   Numerous assassinations carried out against African leaders identified as being too bright, competent and tough in defence of the goals of Africa and her people and who are therefore perceived as being too difficult to be easily manipulated and used as puppets to advance the interests (goals) of the Super Powers on The World Market. From the Cold War Era to the present Post-War Era, these leaders are exceedingly many. The list is endless as of now (2013). However, for the purpose of clarity, a few of these leaders include Prime Minister Patrice Lumumba who was unjustly put to an ignominious death on 17 January, 1961 by the enemy of Justice, Truth and Righteousness without any cause against him, apart from being falsely assumed to be a pro-Communism and therefore a threat to the mineral interests of Belgium and the USA Led anti-Communism Camp in the mineral-rich Katanga Province of Congo Republic (now called The Democratic Republic of Congo); President

Gamel Nassar of Egypt who was also unjustly murdered in 1958 for no any substantive genuine cause against him other than for being assumed to be leaning too much on the side on the Communist Camp against the interests of the Capitalist Camp in Egypt particularly in the Suez Canal; President Samora Machel of Mozambique who was also unjustly put to a similar ignominious deathn in 1986 for falsely being perceived as Enemy Number One of the apartheid policy of the Minority White Regime in South Africa and also for his goal to assist Nelson Mandela and the latter's African National Congress (ANC) whose goal was to dismantly that policy and the culture of Bad Governance of that regime from South Afrca; Steve Bikko, another most brilliant and dreadful Human Rights and Civil Rights African leader who was similarly murdered simply because of his aim to achieve liberty and dignity of not only his Black People but also for both Whites and the Mixed Race Peoples of that Country in his capacity as an advocate of Good Governance and Summum Bonum (i.e. the Greatest Good or Happiness for all characterised by the virtues of Justice, Wisdom, Temperance and Courage); President Melchior Ndadaye of Burundi who was murdered in October 1993 together with several members of his newly constituted Cabinet shortly after winning the Presidential Elections of the August 1993 in that country; and Presidents Juvenal Habyarimana of Rwanda and Cyprian Ntaryamira of Burundi who were both murdered together with all Cabinet Members of Ntaryamira's Burundian Government on 6 April 1994, while landing at Kigali airport to drop off President Habyarimana from their last and final Peace Talks meeting in Dar es Salaam without any substantive act of intervention by the African Leadership to find out who actually killed them and for what reason(s) as a first step of identifying the actual root-cause(s) and remedy of the perennial catastrophe which has always devastated both Rwanda and Burundi ever since the 1950's, instead of leaving the matter to non-rightful persons who chose to cover up their convicting those who do not have any genuine cause for which to convict them and leaving out the actual criminals and evil-bearers. Although the UN did intervene, it too failed and could not provide a solution to this catastrophe due to its negligence on the question of why those heinous murders had to be carried out at all against those three innocent Heads of State of Rwanda and Burundi and members of their Governments, and most serious of all, why the Arusha Peace Accord of August 1993 chaired by the Organization of African Unity in Tanzania had been and rendered totally useless and meaningless by those who were signatories of the Peace Accord and the shooting down of the plane in Kigali for the purpose of killing President Habyarimana, President Ntaryamira and his Burundian Cabinet Members, and all those on board the plane.

2. Numerous Coups d'etat, e.g. the military coup d'etat of 1972 against President Kwame Nkrumah who had paradoxically emerged as the first and foremost Founding Father of African Nationalism, Freedom, Liberty and Independence on the one hand, and also as The Founding Father of Pan-Africanism and African Unity on the other, simply because of his global goal to enhance and promote those Africa's Goals on the World Market, particularly with a view to achieving Global Recognition of Africa's Dignity and Sovereign Equality on the World Market from ex-Colonial Masters such as Britain and France and non-Colonial Masters such as the USA and Japan in accordance with the Principles of The Universal Declaration of Human Rights and Sovereign Equality enshrined in the UN Charter—Masters who, because of their overly pride and self-seeking Darwinism, could hardly stomach that at all; and the most recent coup d'etat in the UN Organization against UN Secretary General Dr. Boutros Boutros Ghali in 1998, who was unjustly toppled from his post as a UN Secretarial Chief simply because of being supportive to the goals and wishes of African Nation States and for refusing to be susceptible to the influence and manipulation of the same Masters who, by virtue of their superior power, arbitrarily control The UN Security Council and its decisions on all issues affecting their interests such as the Rwanda, Burundi, Somalia, Sudan and Democratic Republic of Congo issues where current empirical evidence in those countries show that the socio-economic dynamics or behaviour is now drifting away from the old Francophone market to a new Anglo-phone market in favour of the USA and other Anglo-phone manufacturers and manufactured goods to suit the interests of those dominant Super Powers who were against Boutros Ghali's continuation as UN Secretary General.

3. Numerous Detentions during the colonial Era against African liberation leaders such as the African National Congress (ANC) Leader, Nelson Mandela, who was detained and jailed for a painful period of twenty seven (27) years

in an isolated remote Robin Island Prison in the Indian Ocean till 1987 simply because of his ambitious goal to liberate his endangered Country and People of South Africa and for organizing and leading ANC with which to dismantle apartheid policy and all other viruses of Bad Governance of Minority White Regime in Country—a goal which both that Minority White Regime and its associates in the socio-economic activities particularly from the Capitalist World who had been heavily interested immensely in the gold, diamond and other mineral wealth of that country could not afford to accept to yield to without use of coercion by ANC and its Military Wing; the Kenya African Union (KAU) leader, Jomo Kenyatta, who was arrested and detained by the British Colonial Regime for a period of seven (&) years till 1961 for organizing and leading an anti-British Colonial Rule rebellion called "Mau Mau" in Kenya aimed at dismantling that colonial Rule and restoring Freedom to the people of Kenya which according to Kenyatta and his Kenyan People, had been stolen or usurped from them by a foreign Colonial Rule which, at the same time, neither respected them nor was of any substantial use to their Human Rights and civil Rights enshrined in the UN Charter; and finally the Tanganyika African National Union (TANU) leader, Julius K. Nyerere, who was also arrested and sentenced to jail in 1958 for his rebellious goal against the security of the British Colonial Rule using TANU jail but who agree to pay a fine in lieu of a jail sentence.

4. Numerous Detentions during the post-Colonial Era against every advocate of Democracy against all modes of Undemocracy in Africa. In Kenya, for example, the Dententions of Jaramogi Oginga odinga by President Jomo Kenyatta simply because Odinga had criticized Kenyatta's adoption of "Undemocratic" mode of leadership in Kenya against his own Democratic principles which he stood for and for which he was detained for seven years by the British Colonialists (1957 to 1963). He also detained Joseph Martin Shikuku. After Kenyatta, President Daniel T. arap Moi detained Kenneth Matiba, Charles Rubia, Koigi wa Wamwere, Willy Mutunga, Raila Odinga.

5. Numerous Bribery acts also called "Carrot Diplomacy" by foreign mastmers to earmarked African Leaders with a view to luring and using them to enhance and promote the goals of these foreign masters in Africa at the expense of the

goals of the Nation-States of Africa. Prima facie evidences include, for example, Joseph Kasavubu, Moise Tshombe and Mobutu Sese Seko of the Republic of Congo, who because of such bribery that they were easy to be foolishly used by this source as a tool against their own national goal and leadership which often resulted into the assassination of their own Prime Minister, Patrice Lumumba, in 1961 for having been perceived by that source of such bribery as being a communist and therefore a real threat to socio-economic and political security of that source particularly the Union Minere based in Katanga Province in the Eastern Region of that Country which belonged to the Belgium settlers; and Mobutu Sese Seko who, after the fall of both Kasavubu and Tshombe through natural death, became so much rich from such bribery coming from the same source due to the latter's acute Cold War with the Communist Camp in Africa and Total World that his wealth overwhelmingly exceeded the Gross Nation Product (GNP) of his own Country (Zaire) that he ruled—a fact which also raises other serious questions against the competence and honesty of the African leadership to effectively defend Africa's goal today though the Cold War Era has now ended. It is this source which is the actual root-cause of bribery of the present culture of corruption and Bad Governance in entire Africa. It is this massive bribery by this source during the Cold War Era that planted corruption in Africa's Ecosystem. This bribery, in turn, bred lies, stealing, dishonesty, leadership mediocracy, intolerance and conflict throughout Africa. All this collectively generated a Culture of a Bad Governannce which is now already a permanent virus in the attitude (theory) and behaviour (practice) of every African Civil Servant which is another serious concern against the competence of both the Security and Law Enforcement Forces of every African Nation-state to defend Africa's security and Sovereign Equality enshrined in the UN Charter.

6. Numerous Wide Spread Dumping cases on the African Markets and total African Ecosystem against the health security of the Peoples of Africa, the dignity of African National Leaders, and sovereign equality of African Nation-States on the World Market which, under International Law, constitute a serious World Market Delinquency against African Nation-States. These acts of delinquency include, for example, the Dumping on the African Markets reject, substandard and obsolete manufactured goods such as bicycles,

razor blades, vehicles, TVs, electrical items, medicines and many other manufactured items especially from non-European Countries which have already been proved unfit for the markets of their manufacturing countries lacking a reliable life expectancy worth to one's effort of procuring them; Dumping of unsafe food stuffs such as corn, powdered milk, etc. which have been already declared expired or unfit for human consumption in their own countries of manufacture, but which come to be dumped on the African Market or offered to African national leaders with false pretence as "Food Aid," "Food for Peace", "Food for Freedom", "Food for Partnership" while the donor country knows very well that this food is not safe for human health security; Dumping on the African markets dangerous manufactured chemicals such as DDT, etc. which has already been scientifically tested and proven too dangerous to the Ecosystem by the country of manufacture; Dumping of obsolete medicines such as the famously dreadful Depo Provera and other contraceptives which have already been scientifically proven dangerous to the human use and therefore legally banned by the Court of Law in the manufacturing country but which have always secretly found ways to enter African markets and Total African Ecosystem to make huge profits from the African Nation-States, and irreparable injuries on their nationals without any protection from these dangers by their respective Political Leaders; the Dumping of contaminated foods on the African Markets with false labelling as in the on-going case of falsely labelling of the mad cow meats whose carcasses have already been banned on all markets throughout the European Union (UE) hemisphere but which are paradoxically allowed to enter into the African market without any due regard to the health security of Africa and her Peoples a fact which therefore also raises another challenge to the ability of African leadership to effectively defend Africa's health security and other goals; etc.

7. A One-Sided Restoration policy against Africa's goals e.g. the recent banning of the importation of the African fresh water fish particularly from East Africa (Kenya, Tanzania and Uganda) by the markets of the European Union (EU) hemisphere on the grounds that the fish was a health hazard to human consumption in Europe due to the chemical fishing means that was being used at that time by the fishing industry on Lake Victoria. To defend their policy, the EU markets argue that this is a kin to the same manner that the same EU

had banned its mad cow meats on its markets. While this was a noble action on the EU's part, it is therefore open to question why the same EU could, at the same time, turn around and export the same banned mad cow meat carcasses to Africa markets with a deliberate view to selling them on these markets without any concern, sympathy or compassion for the health security of Africa and her Peoples! What a pity!! Is this not tantamount to murder? How different is it from the Nazi policy's goal that the Allies fought against in World War II who are now the same key architects of the EU. And, worse of all, while all this World Market Delinquency was paradoxically allowed to go on by the unscrupulous EU Leadership and Peoples, the affected African Leadership and Peoples equally did a zero work by keeping quiet! What a pity to Africa's glory ad dignity! How can they successfully claim for Sovereign Equality while they cannot have the courage to effectively defend their possessional goal and rights for mileu goal!

8. Alarming increase in Brain Drain of African Expertise from Africa into foreign Countries particularly Developed Countries e.g. USA, UK, France, etc. looking for green pastures because of the negligence of the African Leadership which marginalizes and ignores the rare strategic national importance of these expertiese in preference of foreign expertise whose renummeration is paradoxically too exorbitant for a poor African country to afford. Another paradox is that whereas they are too expensive, they are not professionally competent and also fully sympathetic and supportive to the goal of Africa and her Peoples as African expertise are on the questions of Africa's Health Security, Leadership Security, Science and Technology Security, Economic Security, Population Security, Political Security, Sovereign Equality Security, National Dignity Security, Professionalism Security, etc. Obviously, this Brain Drainage poses a serious nagging question against the competence and wisdom of African leadership who have always failed to recognize this problem as a real threat to their own national security and dignity.

9. Recurrent Widespread of Student Riots and Rampage throughout Africa is another serious challenge to the African Leadership's ability and competence to maintain peace and stability at home as Africa's Goal Number One that every African Leader must seek and pursue at all costs in order for that

leadership to attract foreign investors and investment into Africa to boost Socio-Economic Recovery and Development in the Continent. Obviously, no foreign investor can afford to invest in a chaotic country in which the investment is likely to collapse due to this instability.

10. An absence of a Hybrid Culture in Africa which could have been ideal and instrumental to them for Socio-Economic Development and Recovery from Under-development legacy left to them by Colonial Rule by virtue of being a culture that is free from and resistant, resilient and robust to bribery, dishonesty and all acts of corruption and other symptoms of Bad Governance because of its firm belief in Theocentric Humanism Philosophy characterized by Holiness, Perfection (or Excellence) and Godliness and the Doctrine of Summum Bonum characterized by a belief in Justice, Wisdom, Temperance (or Compassion), Courage, Dignity (or Self-Love and Self-Respect) and Tolerance by every one in a Society which Africa is totally lacking and which she should have as pre-requisite in order for her to not only achieve a needed enabling environment for a rapid socio-economic recovery and development, but also to attract foreign investors into the Continent to boost her socio-economic recovery and development.

11. Abject Poverty which has for years, tormented and terrorized the overwhelming majority of the Peoples of Kenya and Total Africa and is now on an increase. Its impact is manifested in various ways, e.g. their miserable per capital income of less than US$.400 p.a.; poor health care; poor diet; poor housing (shelter); and unaffordable inflated costs of child education; foodstudffs; medicines; etc. By virtue of this miserable poverty, most Africans cannot afford to live a decent life like their minority filthy-wealthy counterpart, in the same Continent. This is exactly the reason why these most poor are always psychologically forced to indulge into heinous illegal and health-hazard socio-economic activities such as brewing and drinking of poisonous brew called "Kumi Kumi" in Kiswahili language (meaning cheap and affordable to drink to the poor). They are forced to do so with a view to inoculating themselves with such brews so that it may give them a possible relief from their day and night agonizing memories of acute poverty nightmares. Although this act has already proved to be too dangerous in

Kenya in 2000 for having resulted into a total of over 137 Kenyans dead and over 500 in critical condition in hospital in a single week from drinking such brew, the fact is that most Kenyans are too poor to do without it. Most of them cannot afford the inflated cost of the legalized and safe drinks such as beer, whisky, gin, vodka, wine, etc., whose cost has been deliberately inflated by the establishment (regime) on false excuse of socio-economic liberalization in Kenya and Total Africa as so demanded by the Donor countries who are also the same Super Powers who control the economy on the World Market and the Balance of Payment that all African countries do not have and must, therefore, seek at all costs in order for them to survive.

12. Super Power Industrial Mafia terrorism and unruliness on the World Market by which the socio-economically and militarily powerful Nation-States of the Industrialized World ruthlessly expropriate this leverage to hoard their economic advantage and discourage all attempts of both African Nation-States and other socio-economically and militarily poor (weak) Nation-States aimed at creating their own industrial capability on the contention that such attempts could energize Africa and enable her to become equal to them and then begin to not only complete but also to interfere with their super industrial Mafia monopoly on the World Market.

13. Numerous shocking cases of International Terrorism against the security of the leadership and peoples of Africa such as the recent cases of Bomb blasts in both Nairobi and Dar es Salaam cities in 1998 causing untold havoc and sorrows not only to Kenya and Tanzania but also to the entire African continent—a situation which could again happen to Africa at will in future due to the strategic weaknesses of not only Kenya and Tanzania but also most African Countries which are still strategically too weak to protect themselves against such acts of terrorism as effectively as strategically powerful countries such as USA, UK, etc. are each able to protect themselves and their destiny (goals) as recently witnessed by the USA devastating response to terrorism in New York and Washington DC on September 11, 2001. No single African country has the capacity to take such a measure.

14. Their inability to uphold their <u>pacta</u> <u>sunt</u> <u>servanda</u> enshrined in the normal functioning of the International System with respect to the <u>Original</u> and

Vicarious Responsibilities which each sovereign nation-state is expected by that System under International Law to recognize and carry out at all times on the World Market. Numerous prima facie evidences of this problem abound. These include, for instance, the recent bomb explosions in Nairobi, Kenya and Dar es Salaam, Tanzania in 1998, which according to the International Law, Kenya and Tanzania each had the rights and obligations to prevent from happening. Otherwise, each was liable for or supposed to be charged for the offence of an Original Responsibility if it ever had a prior knowledge of the act and did collaborate with the actor(s); or to be charged for a Vicarious Responsibility if at all each neither had any prior knowledge nor collaborated with the actor(s). But the fact is that like all other African nation-states, both Kenya and Tanzania are so poor and too weak socio-economically, politically and militarily that they could hardly have had the necessary means by which to know in advance the intentions of those internationally sophisticated terrorists in the same manner the most highly sophisticated Super Powers such as the USA, UK, etc. could have done. This is exactly another serious prima facie evidence against the security of all African nation-states on The World Market. Although they are entitled to the privileges and rights of Sovereign Equality on the World Market, the litmus paper tests listed above totally disqualify that theory.

15. Acute Intra-and Inter-African Leadership Schism, Assassinations and Detentions which have been rocking and tormenting the entire African Continent from the Colonial Era to the post-Colonial Era—a situation which has had nothing to do with the Super Powers' political influence at all but which was solely an African leadership's creation influenced by the obsolete pseudo-scientists' geopolitical colonial theory of Survival of the Fittest adopted from Charles Darrwin and Niccolo Machiavelli and which has often foolishly misled certain African leaders into a vain assumption that whoever is able to successfully influence the masses using every means necessary including use of terror and murder of one's opponent(s) wherever necessary is automatically qualified to control the Political Scene of leadership for life. This is exactly the crazy and most suicidal theory which has, over the years, fooled most African leaders into numerous heinous assassinations, detentions and imprisonment of their own African colleagues. Vivid recent examples include, for instance,

Paul Tembo of Zambia who had been President Chiluba's former Campaign Manager, and Vice President but expelled from Chiluba's Ruling Party in June 2001, and then foolishly murdered on Friday, 6th July 2001, using such theory simply because of his resentment against President Chiluba's bid for a Third Term tenure as Zambian President (Sunday Nation, July 8, 2001, p.7); Dr. Robert Ouko of Kenya who had been the Kenyan Foreign Minister in the President Daniel Toroitich arap Moi Government during his heinous assassination in 1988 for the same contagious virus of Acute Intra- and Inter-African Leadership Schism, Assassinations and Detentions tormenting the continent ever since the Colonial Era. Vivid cases of detention of Oginga Odinga include that which was totally antithetical to the Original Goal of Uhuru (Freedom) struggle in Kenya against the British Colonial Rule; and that of Kenneth Matiba who was detained due to his opposition to the Single Party Mode of Democracy in Kenya. Other vivid cases include self-exile foreign countries because of fear of their life they dared to return to their own Mother countries.

16. Inter-African Nation-State War of Aggression continues to be another devastating virus against the security goal of not only the African Nation-States in the Eastern Africa Region but also in the Total African Continent since the continent began to achieve her freedom from the Colonial Masters in the 1950's and 1960's. Vivid prima facie cases of this virus include, for instance, the on-going military invasion of the Democratic Republic of Congo (DRC) by the combined forces of Uganda, Rwanda and Burundi on pretext that they have a duty to do so for their own security reasons against their rebels alleged by the three countries to be hiding in the DRC between the said three invading forces and the combined forces of the DRC and the DRC's allies viz: Zimbabwe, Angola, Namibia, Chad and Mozambique. Another symptom of this virus is the invasion of Rwanda effective 1st October, 1990 by the combined forces of Uganda and the forces of the Rwanda Patriotic Front (RPF) called the Rwanda Patriotic Army (RPA) on Uganda's pretext that she had the duty to do so with a view to aiding the RPF and RPA to liberate Rwanda from the unwanted Hutu Leadership of President Jevenal Habyarimana—an ill-conceived act which has so far resulted into more than two million Rwandese dead and a loss of property of unquantifiable value in Rwanda effective the

day President Habyarimana's place was shot down by the same invading forces while the said plane was landing at Kigali airport in the evening of 6th April, 1994 to the present (July 2001).

17. An intesifying widespread of Neo-Viking Thuggery manifested in various forms of viruses akin to the old Northmen or Viking robbery of 8th-10th century characterized by armed robbery mainly of the banking and other commercial institutions, residences, vehicles, etc. and the Highway Mafia robbery characterized by corruptive demand for commissions from the goods and passenger transporters by both traffic police officers and touts popularly known in Kenya as "Manambas" and found at every Kenyan highway bus stop. Both viruses are now so much institutionalised and entrenched in the African political culture that socio-economic and political security in the continent is already in the Intensive Care Unit (ICU) requiring a major surgery to remove the viruses from the culture.

18. An increasing widespread of Unemployment throughout the Eastern Africa and the Total Continent arising mainly from the on-going ill-conceived policy of employee Retrenchment which is consequently not doing the Region and Total Continent any good other than taking the matter from the frying pan and putting it into the fire. In fact, a Clinical Diagnosis of the virus of the on-going Widespread Thuggery indicated in Problem No.16 above shows that this virus is a function of this on-going feeble-minded policy of Employee Retrenchment, which has now increased and intensified both armed robbery and cunning robbery in the Region and Total Continent.

19. Prevalent institutionalised culture of corruption manifested in massive looting of public property in the form of cash money and fixed assets such as land, plots, buildings, forms, etc. for personal use paradoxically by the same Government Officials who are expected under oath to be the custodians of these property—a fact which, is therefore, a serious acid test against the competence and legitimacy of Good Governance in Africa on the one hand; and also an acid test against Africa's rightful claim or demand for Sovereign Equality on the World Market in view of this decaying culture. A further Clinical Diagnosis of this looting mania in Africa shows the following striking revelation: Because of this mania, most African Government coffers

are virtually dry. <u>Most</u> revenues from all forms of taxes and the Donor Aid have already mysteriously disappeared. They cannot be easily traced. Even if they have to be traced, the law enforcement organ which is expected to sniff and apprehend the culprit for this crime is also a culprit of the same crime. Its rational option is to remain cool and pretend to be doing something good instead of trying to chase its own shadow and blood. This is precisely the reason why the Goldenberg case and similar cases all over Africa are simply mirages. They cannot be pursued. It is for this reason that on-going ill-conceived policy of Employee Retrenchment was hatched out as the only rational choice by which to cut down national recurrent expenditures on personnel emoluments since the national coffer already lacks enough funds due to such left and right lootings by its own guardians. In the final analysis, the policy is not for the greatest good of Africa as it has been so alleged by its architects and builders. The truth is that it is a two edged sword: First, it is to protect the coffer guardians by using the defenceless employee as a scapegoat and shield of these guardians against a potential public outcry and other acts of retortion against them demanding to know where the looted public assets went and also for an immediate return of these assets to the public coffer if these guardians prove unable to pay public staff salaries due to lack of funds. And second, it is to enable these guardians to sustain their tenure against the Opposition who are already another government in the waiting and very hungry for the takeover and a possible prosecution of the outgoing coffer guardians. This is precisely the main root-cause of the on-going pathological climate now haunting and terrorizing almost every African nation-State leadership not only in the Eastern Africa Region but also in the entire Continent. And, it is also the same reason why most African Government which are now in power are proving too difficult in handing over power through a free and fair elections; and the reason why assassinations, detentions, and coups d'etat continue to also haunt and terrorize the continent thereby making it virtually impossible for the continent to effectively defend its possessional goals and to pursue its competitive goals on the World Market.

In view of all these eighteen acid tests militating against strategic capabilities of African Nation-States to defend their people's Human Rights such as their rights to good health sovereign equality and dignity in the International Community, the nagging question is thus: Do East African Nation-States actually have necessary capability to do so? And do they have enough or reliable bargaining capacity to effectively compete with such most powerful and aggressive Nation-States such as USA, UK, Japan, France, Germany, etc. on the World Market for the possessional and milieu goals they believe to be definitely theirs and most essential for their national survival and dignity in the International Community? If so, how can we explain this phenomenon with a high degree of parsimony, precision and satisfaction in our scientific World? And, through what behavioural law(s) or body of knowledge can this dynamics be explained, predicted and understood better than it had been done before by other research on the same subject?

2. Purpose:

In the view of these nagging questions noted above, the purpose of this Chapter is to clinically identify and then examine very meticulously the goals, problems and strategies of the National Leaders of the East and the rest of the African nation-states on the World Market in terms of (a) what these goals are (b) similarities between their goals and the goals of other nation-states; (c) what strategies they use to defend or acquire such goals and why; (d) problems facing them in pursuit or defence of these goals; (e) strategies they use to manipulate or adapt themselves to such problems; and (f) political implications from the interaction between these two major variables viz: the East African Nation-States on the one hand; and their goals, problems and strategies on the World Market on the other. Succinctly, this Chapter seeks to show how relatively weaker Nation-States actually behave on a scarce Market amid most powerful Nation-States such as USA, UK, Germany, Russia, Japan, France, etc.

3. Methodology:

This Chapter is divided into six parts. Part 1 examines contending theories in the Normal Social Sciences literature on the subject matter. Part II gives a critique of such theories, and systematically re-examines the problem using an inter-disciplinary approach, which shall include Anatomy, Physiology and Ontology of The International System as a container of The World Market. It shall use this new and unique approach, in order to illuminate the reasons why and how nation-states behave as they habitually do on the world market vis-à-vis certain goals. Part III examines the relative strength of East African nation-states (hereafter referred to as the African Nation-States) on the World Market in order to determine whether they also really have any significant basis of bargaining power with their competitors. Part IV examines the problems facing African nation-states on the World Market resulting from their relative strength as compared to other members of that Market. Also, it gleans from such experiences some useful behavioural laws which constantly govern the political atmosphere between African nation-states and other nation states. Part V clinically diagnoses certain fundamental strategies which these African nation-states have always employed against anti-bodies internally.

Finally, Part VI systematically synthesizes these findings into some parsimonious body of knowledge called Behavioural Laws through which the conduct of African nation-states in the East African Region and the Total Continent on the World Market for their survival may be properly understood with a high degree of precision and confidence.

II. CONTENDING THEORIES ON NATIONAL GOALS ON THE WORLD MARKET RE-EXAMINED

A. First Observation: A Historical Reality of National Goals in World Politics:

Under the Charter of the United Nations,9 individual and collective maintenance of international peace and security; belief in and respect of <u>pacta</u> <u>sunt</u> <u>servanda</u>; promotion of international co-operation and fundamental principles of human rights; respect for the principles of sovereign equality, self-determination and territorial integrity among nation-states; and the like, collectively constitute the basic goals which every member of the International Community not only ought to respect, uphold and pursue at all times but is naturally expected by all others to do in keeping with the protocols, principles and rules of International Law. While nation-states may pursue other goals, they have to do so within the spirits of these rules.

Their rules are expected to contribute to peace, but not to conflict with others or undermine these goals. Thus, every nation-state is bound to defend these goals at all times and at all cost. Failure to do so constitutes a potential threat to the principles and purposes for which the United Nations was created after World War II on the one hand and also a potential threat to the principles and purposes for which that nation-state exists among others in the International System in general and World Market in particular.

A similar idea is mirrored directly and indirectly in 100% of bilateral and multilateral agreements and treaties in international political life, free of <u>spatio temporal</u> context. It exists in the Charters e.g. the East African Community (1999), Inter-Government Authority on Development (IGDA, 1987) the Organization of African Unity (OAU 1963), and the newly created African Union (AU, 2001); the North Atlantic Treaty Organization (NATO, 1949), and the Warsaw Pact (1951); and, in the Treaty of Versailles or the League of Nations Convent (1919), the Treaty of Westphalia (1648), the Treaty of Toresillas (1494), the Treaty of the first phase of the Peloponnesian War (421 B.C.)10 and the Egyptian-Hittite Treaty of Non-Aggression (1284 B.C.).

Whereas apart from a record on Egyptian-Hitite bilateral relations of 1284 BC in which each party was duty-bound to legally recognize and live with each other in mutual peace and to aid each other during emergencies, we may lack any other accurate record on International Politics before the Hellenic Civilization; and whereas, although our modern nation-states originated from the Peace of Westphalia in 1648 AD, it is self-evident that based on our own empirical experiences of International Politics since the Treaty of Westphalia of 1648, these goals are perennial and extremely crucial for the survival of every nation-state. And, they are likely to remain the fundamental universal basis of our future International Politics beyond the year 2001. Hence, the discovery and significance of this Research not only for Political Science but also for Science in total.

B.   <u>Second Observation: Contending Theories in the Normal Social Sciences Literature regarding National Goals in World Politics</u>

In the Normal Social Sciences Literature, numerous contending theories abound about national goals and strategies designed to help attain such goals and constraints against such strategies. For instance, Arnold Wolfer11 notes (1) that nation-states pursue <u>milieu goals</u>, i.e. those values which they do not have and must, therefore get from the World Market by trading with other nation-states, e.g. equal trading rights and opportunities and other economic benefits. And (2) that nation-states strive to protect their <u>possessional goals</u>, i.e. values which nation states already have (e.g. territory, sovereignty, self-love and self-respect, and the like) at all times and cost. Talcott Parsons, David Easton and other system theorists contend that every living entity performs four cardinal functions which constitute the basic goals of every political or social system: Pattern Maintenance, Adaptation, Goal attainment, and integration.[12]

A similar finding but with a different approach is also held by Gabriel A. almond and other structural functionalists.[13] To them, all political systems are similar in their input, output, functions and goals. Inputs consist of political socialization and recruitment, interest articulation, interest aggregation, and political communication; and output consists of rule making, rule application, and rule adjudication. In order to achieve these goals effectively, every political system has some capabilities with which it pursues such goals. Each political system has also administrative capabilities (regulative, extractive and distributive), conversion capabilities (interest articulation, interest aggregation, rule making, rule application, rule adjudication and political communication), and system maintenance and adaptation capabilities (political socialization and recruitment). Also Abraham Maslow[14] adds that all living organisms have common aspirations; they all seek similar basic needs. These needs include security, self actualisation, food, shelter, love, and the like.

But, each nation-state has constraints (financial, intellectual or prudence, military, manpower, etc), which collectively militate against the effectiveness and efficacy of each nation-state's capabilities. Hence the purpose of Part III of this Paper below.

III. A CRITIQUE VIS-À-VIS THOSE CONTENDING THEORIES

It is reasonable to assume, based on the argument in Part II, that the common, fundamental goal of every nation-state is to defend and nourish itself at all costs. Also, it is plausible that nation-states are <u>rational</u> beings in that they prudently analyze their past experiences as means of acquiring their perceived goal or of protecting their possessional goals.

By doing so, nation-states avoid risks and maximize their net gains. Also they have a concept of <u>pacta sunt servanda</u>, i.e. the ability to respect and uphold their mutual contract, agreement or treaty.

However, as fully documented in The Problem Statement in this Chapter, which, in turn, is the Justification of this Clinical Diagnosis, it is essential to note that although every nation-state's basic goal is survival and, in spite of the fact that every nation-state will do anything possible in order to survive, <u>it is doubtful that all nation-states particularly the relatively poor and therefore very weak African nation-states also use similar strategies vis-à-vis their possessional and milieu goals</u>. Any assumption which purports that due to their enherent sovereign equality spirit, all nation-states are identical in their aspirations for goals fails to take into cognizance the fact that nation-states are essentially human beings. And, that because of this reality, they naturally differ in their geopolitical, economic, military, social demographic, scientific and technological, and information gathering and deciphering capabilities.[16] And, their most serious of all mistakes, is that they fail to realize that due to the existing amorphous and acephelous nature of the World Market, the latter is too anarchical to ensure a high degree of Hobbes' <u>pacta sunt servanda</u>.[17]

Consequently, all African national leaders have a rough time and headache to pursue their milieu goals on this Market and to protect their possessional goals at home from foreign aggression.

****

Numerous empirical evidences shows that due to the anarchical nature of the World Market, certain nation-states have a tendency to exploit their national capabilities their national capabilities for their own egocentric/self goals without regard to international law under Chapter 1 of the UN Charter.[18] To these nation-states, ultimo ratio (War) is also diplomacy by other means. Consequently, those Nation—States which are relatively weak on the world market find it difficult to either acquire most of those milieu goals they need for their own nations or defend their processional goals from external aggretion by other bully nation-states.

The weak find it difficult to resist that strength of other actors and are often pressed to act in ways which economically and politically benefit only those other bully nation-states. They feed the cow but do not milk it. It is milked by and for the benefits of those Nation-state which are relatively strong on the world market.[19] In the final analysis, from the Anthropocentric Humanism it is the fittest that enjoys the fruits of the weaker's labour.[20] The fittest decides who gets what, when, how and why. And above all, it determines the fate of the weak members of the World Market.

It is plausible that such arguments could be spurious. However, this anarchical behavior is neither unique to nation-states, nor does it apply only to those species that Charles Darwin studied. It is common to every species of the Animal Kingdom.

For instance, in every given species, the strength of each member of that species determines the status and power location of each member relative to other members.

Thus, it is strength which determines who is who in the system, and the power configuration of, the System. Within a group of every species, the survival of weaker members is always at the mercy of the stronger ones. Among the fish species, the powerful ones, such as sharks, dolphins, mud fish, trout, white fish, in turn, feed on little and less powerful fish, such as melt, and the like. The little fish, in turn, feed on less powerful species, such as worms, fungi and the like. In the like manner, the most powerful animals, such as lions, cheetahs, leopards, hyenas and the like feed on the less powerful ones such as rabbits, deer, monkeys, squirrels, wild pigs and the like.

Furthermore it is plausible that stronger animals are often carnivores; they have no other choice but to feed on other animals because their biological constitution conditions them to do so in order to survive. But, carnivores do not bother elephants. If carnivores must exist at the expense of the lives of other animals, why do they not feed on elephant? Carnivores never attack elephant, even when carnivores are very hungry, due to elephants' enormous physical strength, greater than every carnivores power. The obvious law therefore is succinctly that carnivores exclude elephant from their menu, not because elephants are not delicious; only because of the elephants' enormous deterrent power.

Another striking behavioral pattern among animal which resembles the behavioral patterns of Nation-States in that a species never seeks to act foolishly. If A is to exploit B, A's success in doing so will be highly dependent on A's knowledge of the relative capabilities of A and B. Thus, unless A is physically stronger than B, it is likely tha A will dare to exploit B or make B act for the benefit of A. Another prerequisite is that, in order for A to attempt to exploit B, there must exist certain goals which A considers essential for its survival. A can use B as a means to achieve its goals only if he knows that by doing so A would benefit.

In other words, A would use B only if such exploitation was A's efficient way of achieving A's goals. On the World Market, these three fundamental patterns of exploitation behaviour may be explained in the following three behavioural models:-

Model I: A may use B to acquire certain goals (x), possessed by a third party (C) as Israel used Kenya to rescue Israeli hostages in Uganda since Israel could not successfully do it alone without the aid of one of Uganda's neighbors (Fig.I).

Fig. I   A   ⟶   B   ⟶   X

         e.g. Israeli   e.g., Kenya   e.g.,   Israeli
hostages   in   C
(Uganda)

Model II: A may use B to acquire goals (X) in B's possession, as industrialized nation-States use African and other raw material non-States to acquire material cheaply (Fig.II).

Fig. II   A   ⟶   B   ⟶   X

         e.g., the U.S.   e.g., Zaire   e.g.,
Uranium in B's

       Democratic Republic   (Congo's Jurisdiction)

                              of Congo.

Model III: A may use B to acquire certain goals (X) that are in A's possession, but A, for one reason or another, is unable or unwilling to expend the effort to make use of its own resources (Fig.III).

Fig. III: A   ⟶   B   ⟶

          e.g., a slave master   e.g., a slave

                                                            X

e.g. economic value in the job output.

Source: Author's work-product (Dec.2000)

Although non-human species do not often exploit each other along these indicated behavioral line, they also engage in exploitation. For example, carnivore exploit the lives of other animals which they use as their food. Also the dominant member(s) of that species. However, in most species, the strongest male normally tries to usurp and monopolize all the females. Among the lions for example, it is normally the lioness which hunts. But once she has killed her prey, she does not get to enjoy the fruits of her labors. The lion often takes the prey from the owner. Because of her inferior strength, the lioness always gives in to the lion. It is until the stronger (the lion) has finished eating and is ell satisfied that he will allow the weak lioness and the young ones to eat the left-overs.

Similarly, in the same Animal Kingdom, with regard to sex, the strongest male has no more sexual desires than weaker males have. However, the strongest of all always monopolizes the females. This reality holds true among dogs, cats, cattle, goats, birds and other species. Empirical evidence overtime shows that a bully male will always hoard females, and chase away other males in order to satisfy its greedy lust.

This behavioural law permeates and governs almost all members of the Animals below the Human Beings but mildly does so also among the Human Beings.

It is plausible that human behaviour can neither be equated with animal behaviour, nor be understood, explained or predicted with a high degree of parsimony, precision and confidence from an ethological context.

However, human behaviour is little different from other species' behaviour in the Animal Kingdom. [21] Empirical evidences drawn from the international System effective the Treaty of Westphalia in 1648 shows that all Nation-States and all other species have a tendency to feel frustrated when either mentally of physically disturbed by others, hunger, thirst, sexual desires and so on. They all respond to threats; they all have the propensity to defend their pride, their territory, love, prestige, young ones and other posessional goals; and, they all are likely to seek and pursue certain perceived milieu goals such as food, territory, prestige, water and love.

In this regard, it is one's strategies which determines one's position among other members of any given species. But, Nation-States are living human entities.[22] Therefore, among Nation-States it is also national strength which determines a Nation-State's status on the World Market. The fittest Nation-States decides who gets what, when, how and why. They determine the fate of all weaker Nation-States. Consequently, not all Nation-States behave equally on the World market, and not all successfully attain what they believe are their rightful goals. Weaker Nation-States are often the losers because of their inadequate bargaining power on the World Market. Weaker Nation-States such as African countries do not have the chance to defend the possessional goals or acquire those milieu goals which they seek as the fitter nations do. Like Congo in 1960 and Uganda in 1976 when those African Nation-States were easily invaded by Belgium and Israel respectively without any sufficient degree of resistance from both Congo and Uganda due to their knowledge that African Nation-States are automatic victims of not only the capability superiority of the stronger Nation-States but also of their own weakness and lack of the zeal to eradicate alleviate that liability in the International System due to their mismanagement of their own resources through corruption and civil strife. This is the fundamental constraint and reason why their goals and concerns on the World Market are not usually matters of much concern to the stronger parties [23].

However, since African Nation-States are also living organisms, it is possible that they also hold their own survival at the top of their list of objectives and will use whatever necessary to attain that goal, as any entity always does. Hence, our purpose in the following Part III of this paper.

IV BASIC DOMESTIC GOALS, PROBLEMS AND STRATEGIES ON THE WORLD MARKET RE-EXAMINED.

To understand the goals, problems and strategies of the East African nation-States, we must first conceptualize the latter as living human entities composed of a net work of interactions and an interdependence of parts, defined in terms of individuals. Also, we must perceive these individuals as a configuration of both formal political sub-systems (political parties, legislatures, cabinets, judiciaries, and the bureaucracy) and informal political sub-systems have their various functions, roles, norms, goals and strategies, all rooted into, and determined by the civic culture of the main system, the Nation-State. And, since as David Easton notes "every political system . . . is a set of interactions, abstracted from the totality of social behaviour, through which goods and services are authoritatively allocated for society, [24] it is equally self-evident that the individuals' behaviour in such a network are necessary to their Nation-States, in that they articulate their support for and their demands on the system.

But, if so, how do African political systems, in turn, aggregate, accommodate and satisfy these inputs?[25] In other words, compared to the most politically and socio-economically powerful Nation-States today such as the United States, Russian, the peoples Republic of China, the United Kingdom, France, Japan and others due to their most amazing level of socio-economic development, per capita income, life expectancy military capability and science and technology, do African Nation-States have the capacity to make binding decisions and the ability to implement those decisions on the World Market?

Compared to highly developed Nation-States, how much loyalty and economic support do African nation-States receives from within and without their domestic jurisdictions sustain themselves? What support do they, in turn, offer their citizens from the world Market? What are their common problems (constraints) and strategies against such problems?

It is generally accepted that the central concern of a polity is to mobilize its societal resources into goals (goods and services) for the members of its systems. However, it would be presumptuous for anyone to analyze the political behaviour[26] of any given African Nation-State in the World Politics without fully comprehending its unique political history, on the one hand, and its relative bargaining strength on the World Market, on the other.[27]

Geographically, Africa is an amazing land mass of approximately 11,700,000 square miles situated in a winger problem-free zone. Because of this amazing God-given climatically advantage, it is ever-green all year round. However, in spite of these natural advantages which are totally non-existent in North America and Europe which dominate the monopoly of socio-economic and military superiority in the International System as of today (2013), Africa has very little arable land. The north is almost covered by the Sahara Desert, except only a small arable strip along the southern coast of the Mediterranean Sea, which is favoured by. In the South, the Kalahari (Namibia) Desert occupies almost the whole of southwest Africa. Agronomically most of Africa is barren.

Where the land is arable at all, it has poor, red soil; it is infested with carriers of malaria, sleeping sickness, billihazia, and other tropical diseases; its science and technology are underdeveloped and other means essential for abundant socio-economic growth are lacking.[28] Because of these deficiencies and other symptoms of constraints in African Nation-States, most African Nation-States are frequently caught in a cobweb of socio-economic and hygienic problems. Some lack treated or safe drinking water, living instead on water from ponds, rivers or lakes. Some Nation-States, such as Senegal, must import their treated drinking water from as far away as France. Politically, contemporary African Nation-States are significantly young compared to Britain, France, the United States, Japan and the Soviet Union (see Table I). Between 1900 and 1947, there were only two African Nation-States, Ethiopia and Liberia.[29] It was not until the 1950's and 1960's that African Nation-States began to form. Even though many of them are now independent, they have not yet reached a political maturation, i.e., a significant national integration and patriotism as is found in the Untied States, the United Kingdom, France, Japan the Soviet Union and the longer-established Nation-States. Consequently, the African Nation-States' foreign policy and status on the World Market still lack significant internal and external support by comparison.

Table 1: Frequency Distribution of African Colonies Achieving Freedom from their Respective Colonial Rulers (1900-1978) +

<u>Ex-Colonial States</u>

Year	Belgian	British	French	Portuguese	Spanish	Total
1900-04	0	0	0	0	0	0
1905-09	0	0	0	0	0	0
1910-14	0	0	0	0	0	0
1915-19	0	0	0	0	0	0
1920-24	0	0	0	0	0	0
1925-29	0	0	0	0	0	0
1930-34	0	0	0	0	0	0
1935-39	0	0	0	0	0	0
1940-44	0	0	0	0	0	0
1945-49	0	0	0	0	0	0
1950-54	0	1	0	0	0	1
1955-59	0	2	3	0	0	5
1960-64	3	9	15	0	0	27
1965-69	0	4	1	0	1	6
1970-74	0	0	0	0	0	0
1975-78	0	0	0	0	3	3
x	3	16	19	3	1	42
y	3	20*	21	5	5m	54**
Proportion (%)	100.00	80.00	90.48	60.00	20.00	77.78

X = Total number of colonies which are now independent

Y = Total number of African countries which were occupied as "colonies".

* = Three of which are Namibian (or South Africa), South Africa (as Universally perceived by Africans) and Zimbabwe (or Rhodesia).

+ = Table excludes both Germany and Italy because the colonies they had occupied were removed from them by the Allies after World War I.

** = For details on frequency distribution of these countries among European Colonial powers, see the tables Appendix I—below, and the General Appendices. The tables show exactly which country was occupied by whom before independence. On the other hand, Chapters II-VIII show how these countries revolted against their respective colonial rulers. The Chapters also show how group formation (political parties) became essential to African nationalists in the course of their interest articulation against the colonial rule.

M   Two of the (infix and Spanish Sahara) were ceded to Morocco in 1969 and to Morocco and Mauritania in 1976 respectively.

Source: Author's work-product. Data computed from Appendix 1-1, of my book <u>Course-effects of African Nationalism in World Politics.</u> University Press of America, 1983.

Socio-economically, Contemporary Africa I inchoate compared to highly developed nation-States such as the United States, the United Kingdom and France (See Table 2, below). The average income per person in developed countries; the mobility rate per African is lower than that in the developed countries by 63.24%; the average literacy rate in Africa is lower than the literacy rate in the developed countries by 75.76%; and the average life expectancy in Africa is 54.72% lower than that in the more developed countries.

Due to these weaknesses, African average mortality rate is significantly higher than that of the developed countries by 83.81% per 1,000 births and by 58.33% per 1,000 population. And, between 1979 and today (2013), the situation is now extremely critical due to the emergence of Aids epidemic and sporadic Ebola and other infections diseases.

Young and weak as they are on the World market, how do African nation-States cope with stresses imposed on them from within and outside of their domestic jurisdictions? Can they really satisfy the needs of their citizens? Since the modern, highly informed African is likely to demand improved goods and services (education, housing, medical or health care, proper diet, etc.), is it not possible that every African national leader is faced with heavier obligation than the decision-makers in the more highly developed Nation-States? Faced with this rough leadership situation, are African decision-makers competent enough to comprehend, analyze, and accommodate the demands imposed upon them? Can the essential consumer goods be obtained for their citizens or will the elites have to resort to repression of their critical nationals in order to deter those demands? Even if the source of the disturbance were eliminated, is there any guarantee that those elites will be willing to satisfy the needs of their docile citizens.? But, according to the data in Tables 1 and 2 above, there is no doubt that African Nation-States are still too poor and weak to compete effectively and with dignity on the World Market. Then, how do they successfully compete with the most powerful Nation-States for scarce goods on the World Market? How do they avoid risks and troubles with those fitter nation-States?

In search for the answers to these nagging questions, let us now turn to Part IV here below.

Table 2: <u>Approximate x-s of African and Outside World Socio-Economic Differences</u>

Least Developed countries	Per Capita Income*	Mobility Rate*	Literacy Rate%	Life Expectancy		
AFRICA	$	%	%	Years	Per 1,000 Births	Per 1,000 Population
Algeria (North	660.00	37	28	53	86	15
Ethiopia (N.E)	100.00	4	7	38	84	30
Senegal (N.W.	315.00	5	10	44	93	24
Ghana (West)	394.00	42	25	48	156	22
Kenya (West)	209.00	42	25	50	54	16
Zaire (Congo)	172.00	12	12	45	104	21
Lesotho (South)	115.00	22	50	51	114	39
Swaziland (S.E)	<u>382.00</u>	<u>35</u>	<u>36</u>	<u>44</u>	<u>149</u>	<u>22</u>
$-\mu_x$ $X =$	293.00	25	24	47	105	24

Highly Developed Countries	$	%	%	Years		
Canada	5,680.00	80	99	73	15	8
United States	7,863,00	81	99	73	16	9
Soviet Union (Russia)	3,386.00	55	99	70	28	9
United Kingdom	3,871.00	65	99	72	16	18
France	6,512.00	52	99	72	12	9
Japan	5,117,00	70	99	73	10	6
West Germany	7,336.00	75	99	71	21	12
$X^{-\mu}$ $X =$	5,681.00	68	99	72	17	10

Means computed from Reader's Digest Almanac, The World Almanac, UNESCO, Statistical Yearbook, and Official Associated Press Almanac, in combination. Because every source gives different data, this method was used deliberately to eliminate this in congruency.

X^{-u}

X = Unweighted mean of the mean. This method was the only method I could use with maximum net gains because most African countries still lack complete census figures and emigration that always evade accurate census.

V   BASIC EXTERNAL GOALS AND PROBLEMS FACING AFRICAN NATION-STATES ON THE WORLD MARKET.

(1)   Their Socio-Economic and military Weakness as a critical Factor.

Although African Nation-States, like every Nation-State in the World Community, enjoy equal sovereignty under Chapter 1, Article (4-6), of the United States Nations Charter, their inchoate status on the World Market automatically weakens their rights to enjoy equal sovereign status with the others. Their socio-economic and military weaknesses automatically are their serious constraints. This forces them to depend on powerful nation-states which automatically are their serious constraints. This forces them to depend on powerful (industrialized) nation-States for economic and military aid. For instance, when Kenya wanted to deter Idi Amin Dada's Uganda in 1976 from what Kenya called "Uganda's provocation against Kenya" had to rely on assistance from the United States and Israel albeit the public humiliation Kenya had to suffer before other African Nation-States for having collaborated with foreigner(s) against her own sister African Nation-State, Uganda.

(2)   Their Parasitism as a Critical Factor

It is, therefore, evident that although African Nation-State is independent, they are inevitable victims of their own weakness on the World Market. They are independent in theory only; but in practice, they are parasites. Consequently, they are susceptible to the whims of stronger nations (to foreign subversion and to exploitation), i.e., they are potential victims of "neo-colonialism" and the prevailing tensions between the Capitalist and Communist camps. They do not only occupy an extremely delicate position in the World Market; also, they lack any insurance against potential external vultures. This scientific realism is supported or attested by these prima facie empirical evidences. In 1990, Belgium easily invaded Patrice Lumumba's Congo (re-named Zaire); in 1975, Portugal easily invaded Sekou Toure's Guinea; in 1976, South Africa and Some Western powers easily invaded Angola; in 1976, Israel easily invaded Idi Amin's Uganda; and in 1976,1977, and 1978 "Rhodesia" frequently invaded Mozambique.

In view of this scientific behavioural truth, it is therefore explicit that without adequate defense power from within African Nation-States, the latter are helpless against powerful aggressors. Their only recource may be the United Nations.

(3)   Their Judgment Poverty as a Critical Factor

A further clinical diagnosis of this UN resource also shows another scaring constraints. Ever since the UN was formed in 1945, the only aid Africa has ever received from the United Nations is formal condolences and informal condemnations of the aggressor since no victim African nation-States, or on its own. Even now, majority African nation States are as totally impotent on Sierra Leone, Sudan, Rwanda, Burundi, Congo etc as they were on the "Congo Apartheid and Rhodesian Questions" in the 1960s-1980s. In the Rhodesian Question, for example, they pleaded to Britain for a military action against the "Rhodesia Regime" without using their prudent judgment to realize that due to cultural ties between the Rhodesians and the British, Britain could hardly do what they expected other than giving them verbal support only as under no circumstances could Britain take up arms against the Rhodesians, except in cases where such action could be of crucial importance for Britain's national interest. But, the Rhodesian issue was not a Britain's highest priority. Britain had very little and almost nothing to gain from African majority rule in Rhodesia. Therefore, it was of utter nonsense for African Nation-States to assume that Britain would militarily intervene in a situation whose optimum net-gains for Britain was absent or non-existent.

A similar poor judgment on the part of African leadership also held true in the Namibia and apartheid question in South Africa. While all African Nation-States supported African majority in both Namibia and South Africa, their actions were limited to talk. They lacked a coercive capability to effect their wishes. Just as they expected Britain to take up arms against Ian Smith's Unilateral Declaration of Independence in Rhodesia, they also assumed that some other members of the World Community would take up arms against the apartheid regime of Southern African for them.

In the final analysis, due to their Judgment poverty, an African Nation-State's chances of successfully defending its possessional goals and achieving its perceived milieu goals without external help are still very slim.

(4)   Their Self-Confidence Deficiency as a Critical Factor

The same problem also holds true in African Nation-States' internal affairs. In 1964 and 1969, Kenya had to appeal to Britain for military assistance against internal upheavals against Kenyatta's regime. In 1964, Tanzania also called upon Britain for a similar assistance. Gabon and the Congo (Brazzaville) called up on France for Military aid during their internal troubles; and in 1976, Kenya called upon the United States for military assistance against Uganda.

Although, under Article 3 of the Charter of the Organization of African Unity, every African Nation-States, most of them still maintain bilateral military alignments with foreigners. Nigeria maintained such a treaty with Britain until the Mohamed regime terminated it in the 1970's. With the exception of Guinea, most ex-French African colonies such as Ivory Coast, Gabon and Chad, maintained bilateral military defense treaties with Britain. Liberia has maintained a bilateral defense treaty with the United States for more than century. Although under the OAU Charter, no African

Nation-State was supposed to transact business with the apartheid regime in South African, many African Nation-States such as Gabon, Kenya, Malawi, Lesotho, Ivory Coast and others did so.

And, although under the same OAU Charter, no African Nation-State is supposed to shy away from another African Nation-State whenever the latter is under foreign aggression, no single African Nation-State ever came to the aid of Mozambique and Zambia against the Rhodesian frequent military raids.

Their inability to promptly Discern a True Enemy and a

True Friend as a Critical Factor.

Another crucial problem facing African Nation-States is that, because of their parasitic relationships with foreign Nation-States, they are unable to discern quickly and easily between a true enemy and a true friend. Because of this deficiency, they are automatically susceptible to external penetration and manipulation. The more easily penetrated and manipulated by external influences they are, the more they are susceptible to high levels of internal political instability, e.g., coups d'etat, assassination, schisms, revolts, demonstrations and kickbacks as in the pathetic cases of Congo (1960) Mozambique, Angola, South Africa during apartheid, and Rwanda, Burundi, Democratic Republic of Congo, Somalia where peace solution has failed to firmly take root.

As of now, November 2013, approximately 100% of African Nation-States are now no longer miniature international systems as they used to be in the Cold War Era. During the Cold War, each African nation-State was characterized by two ideological camps, Capitalism and Communism. Because of this dynamics, most African Nation-States experienced at least one or more attempted coup d'etat, assassination, schism, revolt etc. While such symptoms of political instability very rarely occurred in more highly developed nation-states, the fact that such problems are common in African and other developing Nation-States (e.g., in South America) A further Clinical Diagnosis reveals that the internal political instability of weaker Nation-States is a function of their dependence on foreign economic and military aids (see Figure 1). As also indicated in Figure 1, every contemporary African Nation-State existed and functioned within a conflicting, ideological, international environment. They were caught between

Externality A (Communism) and Externality B (Capitalism). Each Externality was heavily engaged/in cultivating alliances on the World Market in order for it to consolidate its strength against the adversary.

Internally, every contemporary African Nation-State existed and functioned within the conflicting ideological problems that existed between an Internality x (a pro-elite faction which liked and supported the elite's domestic and foreign policies) and an Internality Y the anti-elite, e.g., Kwame Nkrumah, Patrice Lumumba, Idi Amin and others, in power. All those tough African leadership who could not prove as "Yes men to the Western Powers had to be eliminated as the cases of Lumumba, Nkrumah, Samora Machel etc.

Figure 1: Channels Through Which African nation-States
Became Manipulated on the World Market by Communism-Capitalism Race for Allies
during the Cold War.

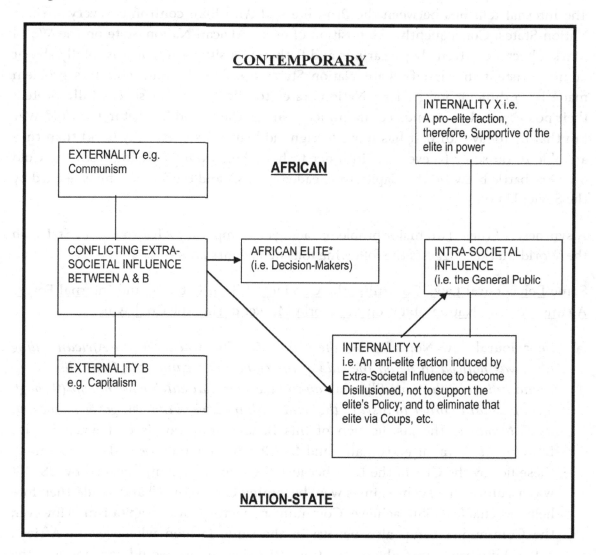

Where: Channels of Extra-Societal Influence and Impact on the African foreign policy decision maker.

Permeable Membrane of the Nation-State

* The elite may start out as either a Communist, Capitalist or Anti-both ideologies. However, due to the increasing Communism Capitalism race for allies, that Elite becomes an automatic target and,

therefore, innocent victim of that race on the World Market as in the case of Congo (1960), Korea (1950), Chile (1974), Vietnam (1954-1975), Angola and Mozambique (1976), etc.

Source: Author's work product—model synthesized form the entire paper.

The internal tensions between the Pro-Elite and Anti-Elite confronted every African Nation-States. Consequently, the position of every African Nation-State on the World Market became extremely precarious and Pathetic—a situation that was totally absent or non-existent in all self-reliant Nation States e.g., U.S, U.SS.R., etc. This problem made it so difficult for African Nation-States to effectively and successfully protect their possessional goals and acquire milieu goals on the World Market in the Cold War Era that by today (2013), it has more foreign aid loans to service (pay back) than they are able to do so or to even use in order to heal their wounds arising from the Cold War Era battle between the Capitalists headed by USA and the Communists headed by the Soviet Union.

A synthesis of these two major problems facing contemporary African nation-States on the World Market suggests the following four behaviours laws:-

<u>Some Behavioural Laws Governing the Conduct of Both External and Internal Forces Against African Nation-States on the World Market during the Cold War.</u>

(a)   Behavioural Law No.1: *During the Cold War Era, whenever, an African ruling Elite was noticed to be on the side of the communist camp, the Capitalist camp would influence the Anti-Elite faction to take over that elite's government (through a coup d'etat in order to disrupt the relationship between the new government and its Externality.* The justification of this Behaviourial Law is that when Patrice Lumumba's, Kwame Nkrumah's and S. Allende's regimes were destroyed along these lies by the CIA of the USA because the Capitalist camp (headed by USA) it was assumed that such regimes were becoming Communist[31] and would therefore help or enable USSR achieve Communism victory over Capitalism. However, the Communist camp also behave in the same fashion whenever an African ruling Elite was seen to be on the Capitalist side, as this would contribute to the downfall of Communism.[32]

(b)   Behavioural Law No. 2: *From the Colonial Era up to today, whenever a socio-economically powerful nation-state notices that its monopoly in an industry is likely to be threatened by the introduction of World Market in Africa by a far-sighted African Elite which might increase African productivity, employment, and, hence, independence, that Nation-State is likely to influence the Anti-Elite faction to uproot the existing Elite who is advocating that change.* For example, Nkrumah's extraordinary idea to create a United States of Africa with a Supreme Command and a domestic industry and Market, so that Africa would (1) no longer depend on the outside world and (2) minimize Africa's vulnerability to foreign influence, was summarily destroyed through the Capitalist camps influence on the late Ex-Emperor Haile Selassie 1 of Ethiopia, William Vacanarat Shadrack Tubman of Liberia, Mnadi Azikiwe of Nigeria and Felix Houphouet-Biology of the Ivory Coast. These leaders were persuaded and hoodwinked to disagree with Nkrumah at the Addis Ababa Conference in 1968[33] by warnings issued by the Western powers that Nkurumah's ulterior motive was to become the eventual, sole ruler of Africa.[34]

Also, when Patrice Lumumba was fond to be one of those able African elite members who desired to drive Africa into a mighty power and conceivably, had the ability to do so by virtue of his eloquence and his ability to reach people better than Moise Tshombe and Joseph Kasavubu, Tshombe and Seko turned against Lumumba.

When arrested and detained in Algeria in July, 1968, Tshombe uttered, "I am a victim of my popularity and the CIA," a statement that the U.S. Department of State strongly denounces.[35]

Similarly, on realizing that the cooperative aim of Tanzania and Zambia to build a railway between the two countries in 1968 would become another gigantic step towards industrial development in Africa and a reduction of Africa's dependency on the Capitalist camp, the latter denied the Tanzo-Zambian request for a loan to build the Tanzo-Zambian railway. Even when the two countries later decided to appeal to the people's Republic of China for the loan. The Capitalist camp continued to discourage them claiming that the plan was still inappropriate. [36]

Also, in 1956 President Gamal Abdul Nasser's request to the Capitalist camp for a loan to build the Aswan Dam had to be denied for the same reason. Had Nasser's appeal to the Communist camp not been positively answered, the Aswan Dam could not have been built.

(c) Behavioural Law No.3: *In the absence of a strong Anti-Elite faction, a Capitalist of Communist Camp would maintain or establish its relationship directly with a ruling Elite. Each camp would influence the Elite directly. It would use technological aid, economic aid, military aid, or a compound of those aids. But, should the Elite refuse to accept this offer, that Elite would be publicly humiliated by that Externality*. Supporting Evidence: Having failed to influence Sekou Toure's regime in 1958, President Charles de Gaulle of France vehemently humiliated that regime publicly by removing all office equipments in Guinea. Telephone and electric lines were disrupted, offices were stripped and even the electric light bulbs were removed. Guinea's political machinery was unable to function normally until Ghana and the Soviet Union responded to Sekou Toure's appeal for help with massive financial aid and technicians.[37]

(d) Behavioural Law No.4: *In a nation-State where there is both a strong Anti-Elite faction and a strong Elite, each being supported by either Communist or Capitalist camp, the camp which lacked influence on the ruling Elite would always attempt to influence the Anti-Elite faction against the Elite. In spite of its failures against the Elite, that camp would then be formed to continue to do so until that Elite is either removed from office or lured to that camp's side*. Supporting Evidence: in spite of the enormous economic, military and technological aids Egypt has always received from the USSR from 1948 to 1977 against Israel, a U.S. protégé; and in spite of Egypt's prolonged hatred of the Capitalist camp due to that camp's Imperialism and Colonialism, the Capitalist camp continued to lure Egypt's ruling Elite until the Elite was finally drifted from the USSR to the Capitalist camp in 1977.[38]

(e) Behavioural Law No.5: *In a political situation whereby there is total absence of a cold war between hostile camps such as the communist camp on the one hand and the capitalist on the other in the International System during the Cold War, such hysterical antagonism between the said camps and the efforts to Elites of weaker States such as African Nation-States today to change alliances and the efforts to eliminate the stubborn Elite who does not want to be lured also ceases to exist.* Supporting Evidence: As at November 2000, no single African political Elite has been openly accused and castigated by his people or World Public Opinion that he was a puppet or stooge to the Capitalist or Communist Camp as the case used to be during the Cold War when numerous African leaders such as Moise Tsombe and Mobutu Sese Seko were vehemently accused by the entire World Public Opinion.

(f)   Behavioural Law No.6: *In a non-camp International System, the search for puppets is silently done and minimal.* <u>Supporting Evidence</u>: In the Rwanda and Burundi cases between the mutually hostile Hutu and Tutsi tribes, research evidences show that France which sought to safeguard her foreign markets in those two countries through continuity of Hutu leadership while the USA supported the Tutsi tribe to take over so that Tutsis may dismantle existing Franco-phone Market and replace it with an Anglo-phone one which could then be conducive to USA commerce. Hence, the root-cause of the Rwanda Catastrophe of 1994-5.

VI   BASIC STRATEGIES BY WHICH AFRICAN NATION-STATES WITHSTAND DISTURBANCES FROM BOTH INTERNAL AND EXTERNAL FORCES ON THE WORLD MARKET

Every animate object has some sort of ability with which to defend itself. It develops biological defensive chemicals within its body against the invasion of foreign bodies which are so microscopic that they cannot be observed with naked eye. It may develop observable defensive weapons (horns, thorns, a nasty odour as with skunks, sharp teeth, claws poison, and so on). Or it may develop strategies with which it can rationally eliminate or evade its adversary. Such natural and totally involuntary strategies include the ability of a living entity to change colour as a mean of camouflage, as in the case of a chameleon. Such strategies evolve through the ages because of necessity, or can be acquired biologically, physically, or socially. <u>Biologically</u>, an entity can develop immunity against certain viruses in its environment, e.g. the immunity developed by people who are native to certain areas in African countries that are infested by malaria-carrying mosquitoes. <u>Physically</u>, an entity can discover artificial chemical that successfully neutralize and paralyze certain anti-bodies in its system. One can receive an anti-malaria inoculation and thereby artificially develop the immunity.

But in more complicated situations such as the treatment of polio, one must receive a polio vaccine discovered by Dr. Jonas E. Salk of the University of Pittsburg in 1955, and Dr. Albert Sabin of the University of Cincinnati in 1961 in order to be able to develop a biological immunity within one's body against poliomyelitis. Short of this close or inut, paralysis or death is automatic

Similarly, in the International System, nationals of countries in Euro-America, where malaria-carriers are very rare, cannot easily survive many African nations unless they receive anti-malaria inoculations or use anti-malaria pills as medically prescribed. Euro-Americans must depend on man-made anti-malaria medicine in order to survive in the African world but most Africans do not. Even though they may have never been vaccinated, they normally co-exist with malaria carriers. Socially, an entity may either create or emulate a defensive method of another entity.

Survival of the living entity can be used as an analogy to explain better the survival phenomenon of Nation-States on the World Market. While African Nation-States are still very poor and therefore, too weak to successfully compete with wealthy and, therefore, powerful Nation-States, each African Nation-States definitely has its own sufficient means of getting by within and outside of its domestic jurisdiction. Thus, each is reasonably competent enough in its own right to defend its possessional goals and to pursue its milieu goals without foolishly causing unnecessary quarrels with other Nation-States and thus jeopardizing its image (i.e. dignity) sovereign equality, and chances of getting what it seeks from others on the World Market.

Whereas African Nation-States are also too weak militarily to combat other nations militarily; their most efficient strategies against the source of internal political instability are: (1) use of prostitutional diplomacy, i.e. oscillating from one powerful Nation-State to another for both economic and military benefits; (2) use of ideological diplomacy e.g. Pan-Africanism, Socialism, non-alignment, etc as a defensive weapon or mechanism; (3) use of ex-colonial bureaucracy with which to effectively convert the Intra-Societal demands into satisfactory consumer goods (goods and services to its citizens); and (4) use of River Elimination, i.e. eliminating individuals who prove a potential threat to the existing regimes. In all those four ways, they may use local, foreign, or both security and economic aids. In Kenyatta's Kenya,

In the years that followed, the likely candidates to succeed Kenyatta were eliminated. Oginga Odinga, Kenyatta's first Post-Independence Vice President (but then resigned because of his disillusionment with Kenyatta's policy) was jailed and his opposition party banned.

Tom Mboya, Kenyatta's most likely successor, was short dead in Nairobi by a Kikuyu (Kenyatta's tribe) gunman. Ronald Ngala, widely popular Cabinet Minister, died in a mysterious car accident. Finally, last year J.M. Kariuki, a politician with mass appeal and open presidential aspirations, was murdered.[39]

Similarly, in Daniel T. arap Moi's Kenya all the above strategies have been emulated. In Moi: The Making of African Statesman (1988). Andrew Morton's comprehensive study of Moi's leadership since Moi took over this leadership from Kenyatta on 10th October, 1978 after the latter's death in the same year (1978) seems to confirm this reality.

And, this is not all. A list of numerous evidences of this truth is endless. This criticism abound in every African nation-state, e.g. in Tanzania today whose conduct in the recent Elections in Zanzibar has been vehemently condemned and classified as a total shamble by the international observers; and in Ivory coast whose conduct in the most recent elections has been as equally bloody as Tanzanian Elections and could have possibly, proved too catastrophic had the Ivory Coast masses not gone out in the streets to use mob justice (peoples' power) or anarchy to drive out the ill-cultured military junta who had already staged a military coup d'etat with a view to nullifying the election so that he may remain in power by force against the will of the people of Ivory Coast and the International Community.

In the final analysis, in spite of their prevailing weak status on the World Market, African Nation-States have a way of co-existing with their antibodies (see Figure 2). Internally, each African Nation-State receives local tangible support (P) and intangible support (Q) from its citizens as a defense against the stress imposed upon the decision-make (DM). In return, its citizens receive goods and services (r^1) in response to their demands (d^1).

Internationally, each African Nation-States offers certain services to some of the members of the International Systems (E) in response to demands (d^2) imposed on its decision-maker (DM) by E. For example, when Kenya's assistance was requested during the Israeli rescue of the Entebbe hostages, Kenya had to comply in order to fulfill the demand imposed upon it by an important external influence. Had Kenya been militarily and economically independent, as the United States is now, Kenya would definitely not have agreed to such request. Therefore, by carrying out such functions inside and outside their domestic jurisdictions, African and other militarily weak

Nation-States establish and maintain a political atmosphere conducive for their own existence. This is precisely why they resort to bilateral military treaties with foreign Nation-States in contravention of the provisions under their own OAU Charter; they simply welcome every foreign aid; they collaborate with foreign Nation-States against their own neighbouring African nation-States; they quarrel and speak ill of each other at International Gatherings as did Zambia, under President Kenneth Kaunda, when it spoke against President Idi Amin's Uganda at the Commonwealth Summit Meetings in London in June, 1977; sometimes they dissolve their treaties because they cannot stand each other, as Kenya, Uganda and Tanzania did in 1977 regarding East African Common Market; some of them trade with illegitimate regimes as Malawi, the Ivory Coast, Zambia and Gabon did when they traded with the minority white South African regime against the will of other African nation-States and the OAU. They break their own <u>pacta sunt servanda</u> in these and many other ways for their own survival.

Figure 2: <u>Strategies of African Nation-States for Survival on the Anarchical World Market due to the latter's Amorphous and Acephelous Structure</u>

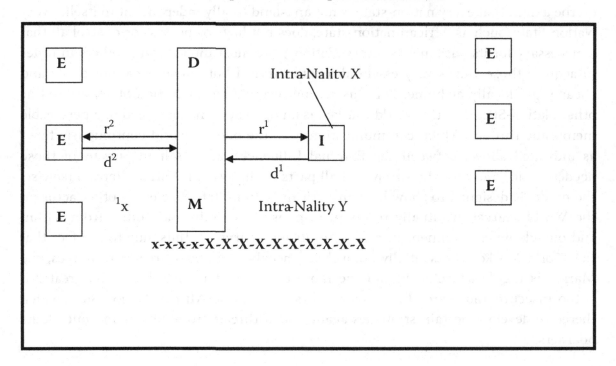

Key:

d^1 & d^2	=	demands
DM	=	Decision-Makers
E	=	Externality, i.e. foreign influence
I	=	Internality, i.e. domestic or internal Influence
P	=	Tangible support (i.e. taxes)
Q	=	Intangible support (i.e. loyalty)
r^1 & r^2	=	Response
. . . . .	=	Periodical group formation against the system
-x-x-	=	Permeable membrane of African nation-States because every nation-State is an open system in the International System.

Source: Author's work-product.

This is precisely an iconic model. Its objective is to depict communication flow between an African Nation-State(s) and the outside world on the World Market, based on the axiom that every nation-state is not an island totally independent to itself. Every Nation-State, such as African nation-state, does not have or possess or control all that is necessary for its basic needs. Every Nation-State must interact with others in order to acquire those values very essential for its survival but which it cannot easily and cheaply get locally at home. For this reason, every African Nation-State, as well as other Nation-States on the World Market, is an open system, contained in a permeable membrane through which communication with the outside world continuously flows as indicated above, between the External Influences' and itself in pursuit of those needed basic values for the survival of all parts of the system, Nation-States. Likewise, the model is designed to show how an African Nation-State, like every other actor on the World Market, habitually reacts in response to certain anti-bodies from within and outside its environment in defense of its own survival. Thus, due to the fact that the World Market is essentially amorphous, acephelous and scarce in resources, the Market is highly anarchical. And the more the Market is anarchical, the greater it is too insecure and scarey for weaker actors such as the African Nation-State which therefore develops certain strategies against such threats from within and outside its boarders.

VII CONCLUSION

The task of this Chapter has been a multi-dimensional one: (1) undertake a Clinical Diagnosis of The East African Nation-States as a representative of all African National-States with regard to their Habitual Goals; Problems; and Capabilities. Strategies they usually use on The World Market; and above all, (2) to bring forth Behavioural Laws synthesized from their conduct which govern their conduct on that Market which one may use in order to understand fairly well the actual dynamics of the Market and the International System as a whole. On the strength of numerous prima facie evidences adduced in this Paper from both The Problem Statement and Parts I to V above, it is self-evident that the East African and all other African nation-states are too weak politically, socially, economically and militarily to effectively compete on the World on the equal footing as their socio-economically and militarily most powerful counter part are on that Market. And, that because of this weakness, they are always easily susceptible and vulnerable to manipulation by their most socio-economically powerful counterpart on the World Market and are also faced with a host of difficulties that their counterparts do not have both at home and on The World Market.

But this is not and cannot be the end of the road for them. Like all other African nation-states, as well as all other Nation-States on the World Market, they are also living human beings. Although they are socio economically and militarily disadvantaged on the World Market than their socio-economically and militarily most powerful counterpart such as USA, Britain, France, Germany, etc are, for the sake of their own individual survival, they are also naturally duty-bound to respond to this behavioural law that governs and regulates all other living entities in life for one's own survival:-

In order for any living entity to live or survive in life, it has to seek identical hierarchy of goals namely milieu goals and possessional goals; to perform identical hierarchy of functions sacrosanct to these two categories of goals; to use similar hierarchy of strategies in pursuit and defence of these goals; and to ensure success in order to avoid dissonance i.e. self-blame and frustration in life.

Furthermore, the need to engage in Pattern Maintenance, Adaptation, Goal Attainment, and Integration does not mean that African and other social economically and politically weak National-States on the World Market use the identical strategy(ies) that relatively powerful Nation-States habitually use on that Market. Although African Nation-States are equally as interested in their national interest[40], nation building, [41] and socio-economic development[42] on the World market as all other Nation-States are, they are too weak to use war-by-proxy, kick-backs or other similar strategies which are commonly used by the most powerful Nation-States on the World Market.

Consequently, their chances of successfully defending their possessional goals and competing for milieu goals on the World Market with their most powerful counterpart are significantly <u>minimal</u>. Their inability to successfully defend their possessional goals and to compete for milieu goals is explicitly manifested in their easy propensity to be lured and subjected to <u>coups d'etat</u>, political assassination, schisms, terrorism, corruption (bribery) foreign sub-standard manufactured goods, and massive strikes and revolts in their own boundaries not easily found in the boundaries of those powerful nation-States such as the U.S., Russia, Britain, Germany, France and Japan by those other relatively powerful actors on the World Market for the socio-economic and political advantages of such actors.

In this regard, in order for them to maintain this equitable co-existence with their counter part on the Market, they do so only by relying on The Behavioural Law of Elimination Strategy and The Behavioural Law of Prostitutional Strategy which their counterpart neither use nor are governed by. <u>In the former</u>, most African Nation-States wipe out their internal political competitors and critics; and <u>in the latter</u>, they often cling on those powerful Nation-States like parasites and prostitutes behaviorally do for the purpose of getting foreign aid and other most essential goals which they do not have and cannot achieve on their own. In a nut-shell, African and other weaker Nation-States achieve their goals on the World Market by clinging to the most powerful Nation-States. Likewise, the latter achieve theirs by also doing the same to those weaker parties. In spite of its neo-colonialist and neo-imperialist effects, this symbiotic relationship between the two is <u>the most common rational strategy</u> used by all African Nation-States on the one hand and their socio-economically and militarily most powerful counter part on the other in their individual defense of possessional goals and in pursuit of milieu goals on the World Market[43].

These multi-goals and strategies are the key determinants[44] of the real dynamics of our International System not only between African Nation-States and their most powerful counterpart on the World Market today (2000). They are also the same determinants of the same International System throughout the life of the System ever since its inception during the time of the Egpyto-Hittie Treaty of Non-Aggression of 1284 BC up to the Treaty of Westaphalia in 1648 AD and right up to our own time today (2001). It is the same behavoural law that determines the eufunction of this system.

Therefore, although African Nation-States may be faced with various constraints such as other competing members on the market; demanding rules of International law a Scarce Market, and some other Aggressive Leaders competing for the same goals on the scarce Market, each African Nation-State is also an inter-subjective member of the System. It is <u>also governed by the same behavioural laws on the World Market</u> and <u>also honours them like every other Nation-State in the System</u> for its own national survival. Failure to abide with this strategic behavioural law is tartamount to a political suicide as the cases of Adolf Hilter Germany, Emperor Hirohito Japan, Mussolini Italy, Saddam Hussein Iraq, Idi Amin Uganda etc.—nation States which succumbed to their own political suicide because of their failure to recognize and abide with/by this strategic behavioural law on the World Market.

CHAPTER VIII

THE AMAZING INCREDIBLE HEAVENS AND THE LEADERSHIP PARADOXES IN THE KENYAN LAKE VICTORIA BASIN (KLVB) REGION

(A Resuscitation Action Plan)

I.   INTRODUCTION

ALL KENYANS LIVING IN the Lake Victoria (LVB) Region have an indisputable sound reason to be proud and to celebrate for being the only Africans to be blessed by the Creator with the most amazing incredible heavens in the Basin which, if prudently tapped by their Political Leadership would definitely:

1. <u>swiftly alleviate</u> the existing horrors of pathetic abject poverty in the Region and eradicate its roots from not only this Region but also from the latter's environs;

2. <u>be able to feed</u> not only all Kenyans but also our poverty stricken neighbours in Somalia, Ethiopia, Djibouti and Mozambieque;

3. <u>and, thus help Kenya</u> significantly in generating hard currency from a diversity of income generating socio-economic development initiatives in this Region.

However, a quick glance at these Region's heavens shows that whereas this hope sounds very attractive, lucrative and tempting, all these "heavens" are no more than ghosts and mirages albeit they are vividly visible to one's naked eye! They have never been exploited by the Leadership and only God knows <u>when</u> they will ever be exploited and by <u>whom</u>! C'est la problem! Hence, the ultimate object of this inquiry with a view to apprising the reader and the political leader alike of the existence of these amazing incredible potentials which are unfortunately still lying idol but which could be a reliable source of socio-economic safe haven for these poverty-stricken Kenyans in and outside the Region if these potentials would be exploited and developed into tangible benefits for them.

1.   Problem

But what are these potentials that make the Region a potential safe haven for these poor? What has the leadership done so far todate to realize this value for its poverty-stricken citizens who, by their daily appearances and standard of living, are no better than paupers living from hand-to-mouth daily? Why are they hostages of this poverty terrorism? Also why are they an easy prey to not only both preventive and curative diseases but also victims of simple and easily manageable problems such as malnutrition, illiteracy, unemployment, hunger, clean water, poor roads and shelter, child delinquency, drug addiction and trafficking, short life expectancy, etc and yet Kenya has all these abundant God-given heavens at her disposal which its leadership could have freely exploited and used against these problems?

2.   Purpose

In view of this pathetic problem stated in Part I(1) above, the purpose of this chapter is to carry out a clinical diagnosis of the said problem in the Kenyan Lake Victoria Basin Region (hereafter referred to as KLVB Region) in order to:

(a)   <u>Identify</u>, first and foremost, those amazing incredible heavens the KLVB Region is actually endowed with by the Creator;

(b)   <u>Examine</u> whether and how they have been or are being tapped (exploited) by our political machine (government) for the benefit of the Kenyans residing inside and outside this and the extent to which this action has been successfully done;

(c)   <u>Recommend</u> any viable action-plan which may be cost effectively and speedily used to alleviate the existing poverty terrorism in the KLVB Region and the entire republic;

(d) <u>and</u> to confirm that the ultimate goal of science is not only to understand, explain and predict phenomena but also to save humanity from every insecurity such as this poverty terrorism by providing the leadership with needed remedy against such terror. Jerome Bruner's contribution, see for example MP sadker and D M Sadker, <u>Teachers, School and Society</u> McGraw-Hill, Inc., NY 19.

3.   Hypothesis

In view of these amazing incredible natural potentials, our general working hypothesis shall be as follows:

1.   The LVB Region is endowed with an immense potential wealth second to none in the entire Republic of Kenya which, if well exploited could rapidly liberate Kenya from the existing poverty terrorism and thus alleviate or eradicate poverty in the Republic.

2.   The University is also well placed to assist the Kenyan leadership in this crusade against poverty terrorism by virtue of its inherent unique potentials as the centre of knowledge and wisdom needed by the leadership against poverty and all types of insecurity terrorizing humanity

3.   As also noted by Jerome Bruner (1915—in his contribution to cognitive psychology, that human needs affect and, therefore, determine one's perception and behaviour, it is also hoped heretofore that the Kenyan leadership whose mandate is to first and foremost satisfy its Kenyan people under Oath to defend and protect from all sorts of insecurities such as the on-going rampant abject poverty, unemployment, child malnutrition, etc in order to also protect its tenure of office, will be able to prudently hearken to this potentials and if necessary also seek co-operation from the University and elsewhere in its crusade against this common enemy called poverty.

4.   And, since man has the ability to not only train and transform handicapped and brain damaged children into capable persons and to also use the same method to train typical animals to behave as man may wish them to do—a reality which was also confirmed by Maria Montessori (1870-1952) and later

by Burrhus Frederick Skinner (1904-) in their laboratory tests, such effort would also assist a lot the Region and Kenya in particular with appropriate technology against poverty.

5.   Methodology:

The data shall be drawn from the author's personal experience in his capacity as a habitual resident of the Region by birth and also from his past professional experience during his tenure as a shepherd, a national and international civil servant and researcher in this region.

6.   Rationale

This enlightenment to the leadership and general public is extremely necessary because as also noted by Horace Mann (1796-1859) over a century ago, ignorance is a serious bondage to man most particularly to leader who is a servant of Humanity. It leads man to poverty terrorism which in turn also leads him to pathetic sorrows and eventful self-destruction. But since enlightenment is a reliable passport and visa to a promising future in as much as even mentally handicapped and brain damaged children can be developed by proper education into a socio-economic status beyond the reach of poverty terrorism, the same is also a necessity to the LVB Region if the latter is to be resuscitated. Leadership alone in absence of this enlightenment to the peoples (communities) of the Region would be futile.

II.   SYMPTOMS OF THE AMAZING INCREDIBLE HEAVENS OF THE KENYAN LAKE VICTORIA REGION

Any researcher, observer, tourist, wild game hunter or fund-raiser travelling all through the Kenyan side of the Lake Victoria Basin (KLVB) Region would be first and foremost struck, at a quick glance, by the amazing potential natural wealth this Region is actually blessed with by our Almighty Creator. Accordingly such a person would definitely agree that the Region is indeed endowed by the Grace of God with most amazing fertile masses of potential arable land including mass land and swamps all along the lake extending from our borders with Tanzania in the East and Uganda in the North West (an area encompassing Nyanza Province, Western Province and almost half of the Rift Valley Province). Further, the person would definitely be astonished by the fact most of these fertile arable lands still lie furrow and totally idle!!

But, is that all that one would be struck with? Such a person would also be flabbergasted by the following astonishing heavens:

1. The Region has an amazing spatial population distribution of the Region which is, therefore, a natural prima facie proof that the Region is definitely superior to most other Regions in Kenya as a reliable potential enabling environment for both large and small scale agriculture and livestock entrepreneurship; and as a reliable source of cash crop for both food and income security for the residents of this Region and also for our less privileged neighbouring sister countries such as Somalia, Djibouti, Ethiopia and Mozambique whose arable land is not sufficient enough as a reliable source of their food security.

2. Although most of this region's residents may be hostages of massive abject poverty terrorism characterized by poor shelter, roads, waterborne diseases, rampant malaria and cholera, etc, al of them are morphologically well built men and women with an amazing robust physical structure from their waist down and from their waist up! They are neither that thin nor weak as one may have expected them to be by virtue of their massive abject poverty.

3. Also the Region has an amazing burning interest in various types of entrepreurship such as fishing, mixed farming, brick making, etc. which is a clear ramification of the fact that, if assisted well by the leadership, its communities would definitely do very well to rapidly resuscitate and accelerate their socio-economic development.

4. The Region has an amazing unique good morality conducive for a rapid socio-economic recovery and development and eradication of existing poverty through successful mutual inter-community trade and commerce within the Region and also with those other communities outside the Region.

5. The Region has an amazing natural topography characterized by a wonderful phenomenon of the hilly landscape which, from the agricultural engineering

technology perspective is a clear manifestation of the fact that the region is indeed very favourable for both large and small scale irrigation. The Region is endowed with many chains of hills arranged in straight lines position which therefore make these:

(a) Strategically a good base or foundation for positioning water tank reservations for the water being pumped in from the lake for irrigation purpose;

(b) Strategically instrumental for facilitating the down flow of this water from these hill-top reservoirs into the targeted farms by way of GRAVITY in order to reduce costs to the farmer.

6. Also, the Region has an amazing natural phenomenon of the presence of an incredible abundant fresh water mass in Lake Victoria which is significantly very much suitable for irrigation due to its salt-free quality and abundance in quantity which is second to no other lake basins in the African Continent.

7. And, The Region has amazing beach potentials and many similar heavens along the lake Basin extremely conducive for tourism promotion if they were developed and maintained wisely so as to attract and stimulate Kenyan tourism industry for hard currency purpose. These beaches include Kaloba (located in Seme Location), Uhanya and Usenge (located in Yimbo), Mageta Island (a small island district located right in Lake Victoria waters), Rusinga Island (also in Lake Victoria waters), Mbita (located in South Nyanza), Bumbe (located in Busembe Sub-Location in Busia District), Marenga (a neighbour of Bumbe Beach), etc.

8. Also, the Region has an amazing all year-round excellent climate most favourable for cultivation various edible and non-edible cash crops. Non-edible ones include, for example, cotton, flowers, pyrethrum and sisal; and edible cash crops are sunflower, tea, pineapples, rice, maize, beans, simsim, bananas, groundnuts, pawpaws, oranges, sorghum, millet, green and cow peas, cassava, sugarcane, groundnuts and various types of vegetables such as tomatoes, cabbages, onions, etc—particularly cotton which had proved a chief source of income for every Kenyan in that region due to the booming cotton farming industry which had been initiated and encouraged by the colonial regime, but

which is now dead due to the present leadership poverty and low vision in this activity and its advantages to Kenyans!

III. THE AMAZING PARADOX OF THESE INCREDIBLE HEAVENS

(A) Paradoxes

Whereas everyone is bound to be amazed by all these incredible heavens enumerated in Part I of this paper (above), this is not all about the Region, most especially for a social scientist.

Any sane person would not miss to note the following paradoxes. For example, of the presence of all these God-given incredible heavens endowed to the KLVB Region:

1. Kenya still has millions of hungry mouths and stomachs which seriously need to be fed, and yet she is unable to even pick up these available manna from The Region for her children.

2. Kenya has millions of naked bodies needing to be clothed and yet she is also unable to recognize and exploit these God-given potentials as a reliable source of clothings for her naked children.

3. Kenya has millions of patients who are victims of various diseases ranging from simple curative and simple preventive diseases to most complicated ones, and who are therefore dying daily because of lack of proper attention and drugs, especially, among infant children amid all these God-given gold mines she is already sitting on.

4. Kenya has millions of her citizens under the yoke of malnutrition especially young children who therefore, badly need assistance from their mother Kenya (who is visibly able presently) but who is paradoxically not inclined or readily available to assist that much in spite of these available heavens!

5. Kenya has millions of children with good potentials to become her reliable source of sound manpower ranging from leadership to many other responsible positions who, therefore, urgently need sufficient subsidized facilities in education and professional training but who cannot get these facilities—a

situation which, in the end, consequently forces most of them into becoming unruly and to engage into various types of child and adult delinquencies such as armed robberies, drug trafficking, drug addicts, terrorism and a terminal cancer to the leadership.

6. Kenya has millions of potentially eager men and women who are ready to invest into various potentially income generating activities or undertakings such as fresh water fishing in Lake Victoria and mixed farming particularly rice, cotton, groundnuts, peanuts, sunflower, sugar cane, citrus fruits, vegetables and sunflower for edible oil processing. The astonishing paradox is that they cannot do so due to lack of seed money, encouragement, and other similar tangible resources from the government though they have relevant talents and interests for these initiatives.

7. The above enumerated list of *prima facie* symptoms of the paradox of our so-called "incredible heavens of the Kenyan Lake Victoria Basin Region" is not enough. The list is quite endless. For example,

   (a) Whereas the KLVB Region is equally blessed with an amazing incredible beach potentials which if wisely developed could attract and enhance much volume of tourism, the amazing paradox is that all these potentials have not been developed even since the independence in 1963.

   (b) Whereas Lake Victoria itself is the largest lake in the African continent with abundant source of varieties of fresh water fish species highly useful and needed as a basic source of nutrition and income for most KLVB Region, the other most amazing paradox is that these resources are now in jeopardy as the entire Lake is now in the Intensive Care Unit (ICU) due to the hyacinth menace. The whole lake is saturated by this menace who source and management is still yet a mystery to everyone.

   (c) Whereas the World Donor Community e.g. the European Union (EU), the Government of Italy, the British Overseas Development Administration (ODA) etc have todate poured lots of aid into the said Region in the form of free grants and soft loans especially through the Lake and the Lake Victoria Environment Management Project (LVEMP, Lake Basic Development

Authority (LBDA), the nauseating paradox is that no substantive tangible evidence of success against this menace has been realized!

Apart from the massive *Summum Malum* ie the Greatest Evil manifested in such failures plus numerous socio-economic ghosts such as the molasses in Kisumu and abject poverty terrorism in this KLVB Region, there exists no tangible evidence of successful utilization of these God-given heavens for the good of the residents of the Region.

As prima facie proof of such environment managerial inefficiency and mediocrity which has caused the KLVB Region and its residents an irreparable damage:

The hycine hazard on the Lake Victoria would not have emerged to frustrate the fishing industry and the petty fishermen whose daily survival totally depends on that industry, had the LBDA and other agencies charged with the KLVB Region management executed their work in conformity the concept of <u>Summum Bonum</u> (ie the Greatest Good or Happiness) for all Kenyans!

The old-time harbours initiated, developed and well managed by the colonial leadership along Lake Victoria eg. Kisumu, Sio Port, Homa Bay, Sondu Bay, Usenge, Port Victoria etc, connecting Kenya to other harbours in our neighbouring sister states bordering this Lake (namely Uganda and Tanzania) would not have died. They could still be functioning as actively as they used to do during the colonial rule. Their death is man-made. It is a murder case for which the LBDA and other agencies mandated to environmentally protect the amazing heavens of the KLVB Region for the well being of Kenyans is definitely responsible.

The infrastructure of the main commercial road in this Lake Victoria Region from Mayoni to Port Victoria and the infrastructure of another one road from Port Victoria to Siaya could not still be in the present most pathetic ragged condition that they are in today thereby making easier transportation of fish catches from the lake to the inland markets very difficult and dangerous due to potholes and other symptoms of impassibility of those roads most especially during the long heavy rains seasons.

Similar existing pathetic situation also holds true with regards to all other roads in Nyanza between the fishermen on the Lake and the markets eg. From Usenge, Osieko,

Homa Bay, Sondu Bay and from other points on this lake to the markets in Bondo, Ramula etc.

The cotton farming and processing industry in this Region which was a booming activity and a most reliable source of income for most residents of this Region would not also have died the slow death it encountered immediately after the end of the colonial rule and the beginning of Kenyan independent rule.

Today, all cotton receiving stores built by the colonial rule are now nowhere to be seen. And, the cotton processing plant in (Samia Busia District) called MULWANDA COTTON GINNERY is now dead and abandoned! It is now just a ghost in the district.

The edible oil farming and processing industry idea using sunflower seeds, ground nuts, cotton seeds, simsim and other seeds as a raw material source which had been conceived immediately after independence with a view to stimulating and promoting large scale farming of these sources of edible oils in order to reduce the foreign exchange burden on Kenya from imported foreign edible oils. This golden idea was mysteriously abandoned and forgotten by the political leadership.

Whereas during my tenure as head of the Kenya National Academy of Science Secretariat from January 1985 to June 1988, the Academy sought to revive this idea with the financial support of various donors such as the East African Industries with the hope that such effort would include development of semi-arid areas in our Republic particularly in Northern Eastern and Eastern Provinces for cultivation of other oil producing plants such as yoyoba, the amazing paradox is that this idea failed to receive the support of the political leadership immediately I left that Academy for my new post in Addis Ababa effective 1st July, 1988.

A Kenyan agro-economist of Busia District, Gabriel Mbinda, who had brilliantly and courageously another fantastic idea of initiating a cotton gauze plant called BUMBE COTTON GAUZE in Funyula Division of Busia District, with a view to: resuscitating the cotton industry in the KLVB

Region;reducing Kenya's hard currency burden in the balance of payment by reducing importation of gauze cotton by Kenya from foreign countries and generating employment opportunities to reduce unemployment and poverty terrorism in the Lake Victoria Region, Mr. Mbinda's plant is now one of Kenyan prominent ghosts in the Republic. Mr. Mbinda's bright idea failed to attract necessary political support from the very center of the republic's political machine which is mandated to encourage such ideas.

Also, in as much as Mr. Mbinda's brilliant idea failed to receive the support of our political machine, so has this author's idea of BUMAYENGA IRRIGATION SCHEME in the same Funyula Division of Busia District also failed to receive sufficient attention of the political machine from 1986 up to now. Though electric power supply for this scheme has already been installed and the Busia District Development (DDC) approved an allocation of Kshs. 6 Million for it in 1996 from the social dimensions source,

This Kshs, 6 million was neither received by the scheme for the work so intended, nor was there any indication received and

No water supply has, up to now, been provided to facilitate commencement of this scheme. Obviously, such prolonged delays are a killer-disease to public's motivation and what cause them to start ought to be checked and nipped in the bud at once and at all costs in order to protect and sustain the image and dignity of the political machine on the one hand and the general public's motivation on the other.

The Funyula fish ponds, the Odiado Fish Ponds, the River Sio fish farming and similar promising projects initiated and managed by the lake Basin Development Authority to provide nutrition and employment to the residents of the area are also all dead.

The Munana Water Supply in Samia Funyula Division of Busia district originally designed for the good treated water to all residents in Samia is also dead. Because of this, it is perceived as a betrayal of these residents and leaving them at the mercy of cholera, typhoid and similar water-borne diseases.

The Bulemia and Matayos forestry seedlings project (in Busia District) originally initiated to facilitate aforestation efforts in Busia District are also dead!

Well intended most polytechnics such as Nangina, Bumbe, Butula and other technical training institutions initiated in Busia District to provide appropriate technology in order to reduce unemployment and youth delinquency in KLVB Region are also virtually dead due to the same environment management poverty.

Almost all public agriculture and livestock managed farms have been butchered and the farmers training centers such as Maseno Farmers Training Centre, etc are either closed or now grinding to a halt. They are all in a comma in the Intensive care unit (ICU)!

B.   RETALIATIONS BY THE COMMUNITIES OF THE REGION.

Faced with such extenuating threat of object poverty, diseases, unemployment and various other socio-economic insecurities, and being fully cognizant that all these were preventable and also curable if only their government ever cared and came to their rescue with appropriate technology and other investments such as the Kisumu Molasses plant which miscarried due to leadership poverty and the resident communities deliberately and mercilessly retaliated by resorting to the following acts in defense of their socio-economic security since their leadership had now ignored them:-

(1)   They invaded these hills cutting down every tree they could go and hold of for the purpose of turning them into burning charcoal as a source of their income.

(2)   By so doing, they made all these hills so bare that, for the last thirty or so years, the Region's annual rainfall was reduced significantly due to the absence of these trees which are naturally very essential for sufficient amount of rainfall.

(3)   And, by so doing, they made massive soil erosion inevitable in the Region that has consequently butchered the Region so much that it will definitely take it a long time to recover from this natural tragedy.

(4)   Also, because of these charcoal burning acts, many cases of bush fires have been experienced in the Region which have also added another havoc of tragedy in the Region.

(5)   But to the shock of other residents of the Region, all their cries to their government for protection against these destructive self-seeking charcoal making activities always fell on the government's deaf ear.

(6)   And, the more the government continued to pay a deaf ear to their calls, the more anarchical tendencies of self-seeking survival for the fittest charcoal makers and arsonists continued with total impunity.

(7)   And the more the traditionally expected year—round good climate cultivation of the following various edible and non-edible cash crops in.

(8)   And, the more the good quality of traditionally expected year-round climate for cultivation of various edible and none edible cash crops in the Region was tampered with by these charcoal makers, the more.

A BALANCE SHEET

In the final analysis, various lucrative, socio-economic undertakings in the KLVB Region which could have significantly helped to enhance soci-economic development and thus reduce poverty terrorism in the Region at a very remarkably cost-effective rate are all dead but can still be revived. These include the Molasses Plant in Kisumu, Clay Bricksand Tiles; railway infrastructure from Mayoni to Port Victoria which is the mother or centre of all lake fishing point; small and large scale irrigation farming and fish pillating plants in Sio Port, Port Victoria, Usenge etc. Revival of all the above and the cotton industry; encouragement of practical training centers in order to increase appropriate practical skills (technology) and good understanding of the concept of Summum Bonum characterized by the virtues of justice, prudence, temperance and courage are very highly needed from the leadership if one is to realize any tangible and intangible fruits from the existing amazing incredible heavens endowed to the KLVB Region by the creator.

V.   A RESUSCITATION ACTION-PLAN

In the preceding sections I and IV of this study, the intended purpose was to take a critical clinical diagnosis of the Kenyan Region of Lake Victoria Basin with a view to examining its environment's socio-economic potentials and obstacles, as an a priori step towards our action plan policy recommendations on what the Kenyan political leadership should now do in order to alleviate those numerous environmental management obstacles which collectively constitute the primary source of the existing massive poverty terrorism in the Region.

In the final analysis, this diagnosis candidly confirms:

1. That Kenyan Lake Victoria Region is, by all means, very promising. It has lots of God-given socio-economic potentials next to none in the African Continent.

2. That the Region definitely has an amazing incredible heavens which if properly tapped by the leadership could prove an incredible source of multi-socio economic securities such as food security not only to Kenya but also to the neighbouring sister countries which often suffer from food shortages especially Somalia, Ethiopia and Djibouti due to floods such as Mozambique today.

3. That Kenya's long-term failure to tap these God-given blessings has not necessarily been due to the government's negligence but rather due to the obvious failure of the scientists to properly sensitize the political machine on what to actually do. This failure on the part of the university or academic in its capacity as the centre of intellect is very critical indeed. It must be responsible for the demise of creative lucrative projects in the KLVB Region as the THE BUMBE COTTON GAUZE, THE KISUMU MOLASSES, THE COTTON INDUSTRY AND THE RICE SCHEME, and many other ideas since the political machine lacked the necessary tools of knowing how to resuscitate them after the demise of the colonial regime in December 1963.

4. That in order to achieve what ought to be achieved for the Region from these potentials, the following socio-cultural engineering would be very necessary as an *a priori modus operandi*.

    (a) Elite Re-education, i.e. a systematic structure training programme restricted specifically for the political machine (leaders) at the TOP LEVEL including donor community with a view to:

        i) Sensitizing them on: (1) the concept, virtues and significance of Summum Bonum, (2) the above identified past mistakes, and (3) the RESUSCITATION ACTION PLAN, i.e. on needed or required remedies in order to alleviate those past mistakes or obstacles and resuscitate dead projects.

    ii)   <u>Enabling</u> them to re-educate and guide their public administrators in the ministries and parastatals on the same for the purpose of achieving this common goal (i.e. A resuscitation of their KLVB Region).

(b) <u>Mass Re-education</u>, i.e also a systematic structure training programme aimed not at the elite in (a) above but at all Kenyans (both elite and non-elite) on what has always been wrong in the Region and what the government now seriously wishes to do in order for it to enable all Kenyans: i) To realize what they have all along been missing from their God-given potentials of the Lake Victoria Region; ii) To appreciate and support fully the government's new initiative(s); iii) and to encourage or attract resumption of the stalled donor aid to our republic—a reality which is most likely to take place as a result of this new noble change of heart within the ruling elite in the KLVB Region. This innovation within the ruling elite would definitely resuscitate also the present lukewarm spirit of the donors due to the on-going culture of bad governance which had contributed to withholding of the donor aid needed by the Republic.

5.   And, finally that all political leaders ranging from the ancient Egyptian pharaohs to Alexander the Great whose leadership success always relied heavily on the intellectual inputs of their advisors such as the African Mysteries Systems of the Grand Lodge of Luxor on whom the ancient Egyptian pharaohs heavily depended on at all times and also Aristotle on whom Alexander the Great similarly depended on so much for his success in leadership and empire conquests:

(i)   It is self-evident that the university has an inherent mandate to arise above its classroom and theoretical research preoccupation and assist the political leadership (the political machine) with appropriate technology on how to solve environmental management and socio-economic issues and problems such as the poverty terrorism now facing the KLVB Region.

(ii)   It is also self-evident that the political leadership has a duty to recognize the significant role of the university as a centre of the intellect which every leader should always tap for his leadership success in the same manner the ancient Egyptian pharaohs and Alexander the Great also did for the same goal.

(iii) And, if the two (the political machine and the university) could now afford to <u>mutually agree</u> as good partners to recognize and employ environmental management needed for the KLVB Region, obviously (1) poverty alleviation crusade in this Region would be assured; (2) Kenya and the rest of Africa would no longer continue to live as a perpetual hostage to foreign donor aid or have any problem of the balance of payment on the world market.

V: OUTCOME

As already noted in chapters I-III of the Study, the fundamental aim of this intellectual safari was to cut through the jungles, deserts, swamps and wild game reserves from the east-end to the west-end of the Kenyan Lake Victoria Basin Region with a view to seek a viable Action-Plan that would successfully and rapidly resuscitate and promote <u>summum Bonum</u> the greatest good for happiness for all Kenyans and also our neighbours outside the Region who are often hostages of food insecurity caused by those factors noted in chapters I to IV above.

Accordingly, if this proposed Action-Plan were adopted and implemented, the following outcome for the Region would definitely be assured:

1.   Kenya would now be able to easily satisfy many existing hungry mouths and stomachs which are not able to do so on their own because of the rampant abject poverty situation in this Region.

2.   Kenya would now no longer be classified as an 8th poorest country in Africa as recently noted by Dr. Peter Okaalet, Director of Map International, East and Southern African Region, in his paper titled "Poverty in Africa" presented at a seminar in Nairobi sponsored by the World Bank etc.

3.   Amid all these abundant God-given heavens in the KLVB Region it is a shame that Siaya and Bungoma Districts which are full members of this Region, are some of the 17 poorest districts out of 60 Kenyan districts as discovered by Dr. Okaalet during his recent research efforts on "Poverty in Africa." However, <u>both Siaya and Bungoma would soon be no longer associated with such a list of poor countries in Africa, if this Action-Plan were seriously considered and adopted.</u>

4. All naked hills; the existing depleted road infrastructure; all dead cotton, fishing and other industries, all dead ports and harbours along the Kenyan Lake Victoria side, etc, would now be fully resuscitated to their full normal functioning and services to all Kenyans if this Action Plan were adopted.

5. Successful resuscitation of this Region would be an eye opener model, paradigm or lesson for a resuscitation of many other socio-economic development activities which already are also now ghosts not only in the KLVB Region but also in other regions of Kenya due to their present perennial environment management poverty.

6. This Action Plan could also be useful to other sister countries in Africa for their environmental management resuscitation, should it prove a success in Kenya.

7. And, this success would also serve as an exemplary justification essential for future leadership-university mutual partnership which is very necessary for every sustainable environment management that each country and leadership normally needs in order for that country to conquer poverty and all its agents against humanity.

ENDNOTES

CHAPTER I: INTRODUCTION

On Parable

The Sunday East African Standard, Nairobi, Sunday, 1st February, 2004, pp.1-2.

On Substantive Subject

[1] The Holy Bible, Genesis 1:26.

[2] Ibid., Genesis 2:17.

[3] The Lost Books of The Bible and The Forgotten Books of Eden, A. Meridian Book, New American Library, New York (1974).

[4] For details of this reality, also see for example, 1 Samuel, Chapter 18:1-30 of The Old Testament of The Holy Bible.

[5] The Daily Nation, Nairobi, Tuesday, 20 January, 2004, p.40.

CHAPTER II: LEADERSHIP IN FAUNA AND FLORA

[1] Is almost non-existent because of the fact that apart from the hermaphrodite species such as protozoa that have both sexes on one organism, all other Members of the Animal Kingdom do not.

FOOTNOTE I: As also used in detail in my previous research work with an immense results for one's in-depth understanding of the dynamics of behaviour in theory and practice, a Psychiatric approach is not a treatment of schizophrenia (mental disorder) as so used and understood in Normal Social Science/Conventional Research in Academic. Unlike the latter's Approach, this Approach is succinctly an in-depth Clinical Diagnosis of the actual root-causes of a behaviour in terms of one's decision(s) and execution of such decision(s). It drives deep into one's total life (historical experiences) from birth to the time of the decision(s) or act(s) in question with a view to unearthing contributing factors to the decision(s) or act(s) that a researcher seeks to find but which he/she could not have been able to discover using only those other Conventional Methods/Approach whose low power lens cannot allow or manage. For further details, see also Agola Auma-Osolo, <u>Cause-Effects of Modern African Nationalism on The World Market</u>, University Press of America, London (1983) chaters 7 and 8;—, "A Retrospective Analysis of the UN Activity in The Congo . . .", Vanderbilt Journal of Transnational Law (1975), Vol.8, No.2 pp.468-474; and—, <u>Psycho-Dynamics of African Nationalism: The Quest for National Self-Love and self-respect in The International Community</u>.

CHAPTER III: THEO-PSYCHIATRY OF LEADERSHIP

[1] (Copy from bottom of page 91)

[2] 2 Kings 16:7-22 of <u>The Holy Bible</u>.

[3] Proverbs 4:3-6 of <u>The Holy Bible</u>.

[4] Proverbs 3:5-18 of <u>The Holy Bible</u>.

[5] Again, "Psychiatry" concept as used here does not mean treatment of mental disorder as so used in traditional conventional scientific context. In here, it is used succinctly meaning an inquiry into those microscopic factors that make up one's whole being in terms of attitude, desires, and temperaments that always have a bearing on one's decisions and ways of actions to a situation at hand.

[6] 2nd Samuel 12:17, <u>The Holy Bible</u>.

[7] Ibid, 12:7-8, 10-14; <u>The Holy Bible</u>.

[8] Ibid 24:15, <u>The Holy Bible</u>.

[9] 1 Chronicles 17:1-2 and 22:6-10, <u>The Holy Bible</u>.

[10] For a detailed account of this truth see for example the following detailed study of the same by George G.M. James, <u>The Stolen Legacy: The Greeks were not the Authors of but the Peoples of North Africa commonly called the Egyptians</u>, New York: Philosophical

Library (1954); also the most recent study on the same phenomenon by Innocent C. Onyewuenyi, the African Origin of Greek Philosophy, University of Nigeria Press, Nsukka, Nigeria (1993); and Agola Auma-Osolo, "Africa is the Mother of World Civilization", Maseno University, Maseno (2003).

[11] David Reagan, The Master Plan, Harvest House Publishers, Eugene, Oregon, 97402 (1993).

[12] Daniel 3:1-30; 4:1-37; 5:1-30; and 6:1-28, The Holy Bible.

[13] Daniel 5:25-31, The Holy Bible.

[14] Under Genesis 1:1-31 and 2:1-25, The Holy Bible.

[15] See: George G.M. James, op. cit. note no.10.

[16] 1 Corinthians 5:13, In The Holy Bible.

[17] 1 Kings 15:9-15 of in The Holy Bible.

[18] 1 Kings 21:17-24 in The Holy Bible.

[19] 1 Kings 22:7-28 in The Holy Bible.

[20] Mathew 7:21 and 24 in The Holy Bible.

[21] Mark 16:16 in The Holy Bible.

[22] Haggai 2:9, in The Holy Bible.

[23] The Holy Bible

From Antiquity to the modern generations Mankind has experienced the following human intellect for the benefit of our Leadership:

A. During Antiquity, we have, for example:

(i) Imhotep (2980 BC) and several other priests/professors versed in various disciplines and who for security reasons permanently resided at The African Mysteries System of The Grand Lodge of Luxor (re-named Alexandria by Alexander The Great on conquering North Africa in the year 332 BC and where he preferred to be buried on his death in 323 BC because of its extraordinary intellectual legacy that amazed Alexander so much that he ordered his Tutor, Aristotle, to loot all its books and transfer their authorship to his name (Aristotle)).

(ii) Greece-Iionian neophytes who graduated from The African Mysteries System of The Grand Lodge of Luxor before the latter was occupied in 332 BC by Alexander the Great, e.g.
Thales (640 BC)
Anaximander (611-547 BC)
Phythagoras (580 BC)
Xenophanes (576 BC)
Zeno (3rd, 4th BC)
Melisus (3rd, 4th BC)
Herodotus (530 BC)
Anaximenes (530 BC)
Anaxagoras (500-428 BC)
Socrates (470-399 BC)
Post-Socrates
Plato (427-347 BC)
Aristotle (384-322 BC)

B. During the Classical Era, we have, e.g.
Niccolo Machiavelli (1469-1527)
Thomas Hobbes (1588-1679 AD)
John Locke (1632-1704 AD)
Jean Jacques Rousseau (1712-1778 AD)
Edmund Burke (1729-1792 AD)
Jeremy Bentham (1748-1832 AD)
James Mill (1773-1839 AD)
John Stuart Mill (1806-1873 AD)
Karl Marx (1818-1883 AD)
Friedrich Engels (1820-1895 AD)
Nikolai Vladmir Lenin (1870-1924 AD)
Victorian Novelists; e.g.
William Makepeace Thackery (1811-1863)
Charles Dickens (1812-1870)
Mathew Arnold (1822-1888)

Thomas Carlyle (1795-1881)
John Ruskin (1819-1900)

Victorian Poets, e.g.
 Alfred Tennyson (1809-1893)
 Robert Browning (1812-1898)

C. During Modern Era, we have e.g.
(i) Political Philosophers, e.g.
In African Continent
 Kwame Nkrumah (died 1973)
 Leopold Sedar Senghor (died 1990)
 Patrice Lumumba (died 1961)
 Julius K. Nyerere (died 1994)
 Jomo Kenyatta (died 1978)
 Oginga Odinga (died 1997)
 Samora Machel (died 1986)
 Ndabanigi Sithole (died 19.)
 Ali Mazrui

Outside African Continent
 Mao Tse-Tung (1893-1976)
 Ho Chi Minh (1890-1969)
 Rupert Emerson
 Max Weber

(ii) Novelists, e.g. In Africa
 Frantz Fanon
 Chinua Achebe
 Ngugi wa Thiongo
 Agola Auma-Osolo, <u>Cause-Effects of Modern African Nationalism on The World Market</u>, University Press of America, New York (1983).
 <u>Ibid</u>., pp.24-25.
 Ibid., P.25.
 <u>Idem</u>.
 George G.M. James, <u>op</u>. <u>cit</u>., note No.10.
 <u>The World Book Encyclopaedia</u>, vol.1, p.327.

Again, see George G.M. James, op. cit., note No.10.

To Walter Wallbank, Alastair M.Taylor and Nels M. Bailkey, Civilization; Past and Present, Chicago, Scott, Foresman and Co., 1962, p.491. Also, Agola Auma-Osolo, op. cit., note no.24, p.25.

The Holy Bible, John 12:42.

The Holy Bible, John 12:42.

Ibid, John 12:43.

Ibid, Mathew 13:51.

Ibid, 2 Chronicles 20; 15-33.

The Daily Nation, Nairobi, Saturday, 20 September, 1997.

CHAPTER IV

[1] "Jomo" means Both "Jomo" and "Kenyatta" names are derived from Kenyatta's Gikuyu language burning spear and "Kenyatta" was coined from the word "Kenyatta" meaning a beaded belt which his first wife, Grace Wahu, used to wear around her waist. Kenyatta later also began wearing a similar belt. On his return from Britain in 1946, due to his political activism against Colonialism in Kenya, most children began calling him by the "Kenyatta belt" he wore. Thus the reason why his original name, "Johnstone Kamau", gave room to the new name "Jomo Kenyatta".

[2] Note that nominology in African tradition, (especially among the "Bantus" in East Africa and traditional Egypt), places emphasis on one name only, though one could also be given two or more names by parents. Either way, each name had a special meaning in its own right/way.

[3] See Note 1, above.

[4] Jeremy Murray-Brown, Kenyatta (New York: E.P. Dutton and Company Inc., 1973), p.63.

[5] Jomo Kenyatta, Facing Mt. Kenya (London: Secker and Werburg, 1938).

[6] See Karl Marx, Das Kapital, trans. By S. Moore and E. aveling, ed., (London: D. Torro, 1957); and Marx, Contribution to the Critique of Political Economy, trans. By S.W. Ryanzanskaya, ed. (London: M. Dobb, 1971).

[7] Jomo Kenyatta, Harambee! The Prime Minister of Kenya's Speeches 1963-1964 (Nairobi: Oxford University Press, 1964), pp.8-9.

[8] Kenyatta's Speeches in Parliament in July 1963 and in June 1964. also see Kenyatta, Harambee, p.9.

[9] Idem.

[10] Kenyatta's Speeches in Mombasa Stadium (February, 1964), to Meru Co-operative Union (August, 1964); and to a political rally at Githunguri (September, 1964). Also see Kenyatta, Harambee, p.10.

[11] Kenyatta, Harambee, 1964, p.18.

[12] Idem.

[13] Ibid, p.18.

[14] Idem.

[15] Jomo Kenyatta, Suffering Without Bitterness (Nairobi: East African Publishing House, 1968).

[16] Psalms, Chapter 69, Paragraph 1, verse 2, in The Holy Bible.

[17] Bernard Crick, Political Theory and Practice (New York: Basic Books, Inc., 1973), p.19.

[18] Frantz Fanon, Black Skin, White Masks (New York: Grove Press, 1967).

[19] Robert Muema Mbato, "Identity", Nairobi, Vol.2, No.s, 1969, pp.31-34.

[20] Colin M. Turnbull, The Lonely African (New York: Grove Simon and Schuster, 1962).

[21] See Kenyatta, Harambee, p.15.

[22] Ibid, p.17.

[23] See Donald G. Morrison, Robert C. Mitchell, John N. Paden and Hugh M. Stevenson, Black Africa: A Comparative Handbook (New York: the Free Press, 1972).

[24] To the Point, January 12, 1974, p.23.

[25] A Working Party, Who Controls Industry in Kenya (Nairobi: East African Publishing House, 1968); W.A. Attwood, The Reds and the Blacks (New York: Harper and Row, 1967);

Colin Leys, <u>Under-Development in Kenya, The Political Economy of Neo-Colonialism</u>, 1964-1971 (California: University of California Press; 1975).

[26] Ali A. Mazrui, "The Monarchial Tendency in African Political Culture" in Marison Doro and Newell M. Stultz, <u>Governing in Black Africa</u> (Eaglewood Cliffs, N.J. Prentice-Hall, Inc., 1970), p.21.

[27] Jomo Kenyatta, <u>Facing Mt. Kenya</u> (London: Secker and Warbug, 1938); Kenyatta, <u>Kenya, The Land of Conflict</u> (Manchester: International African Service Bureau, Pana-Service, Ltd., 1944).

[28] From Ali A. Mazrui, <u>op</u>. <u>cit</u>., in Note 26 above. Also in <u>East African Standard</u>, Nairobi, April 12, 1965.

[29] Ngweno Osolo-Nasubo, <u>A Socio-Economic Study of the Kenya Highlands from 1900-1970: A Case Study of the Uhuru Government</u> (Washington, D.C.: University Press of America, 1977).

[30] See <u>Washington Post</u>, issues between March 21-30, 1977.

[31] See Note 32 below.

[32] Roger Mann, "Kenya Finds Succession as a Troublesome Issue", <u>The Washington Post</u>, October 24, 1976, p.A24.

[33] <u>The Toronto Star</u>, July 5-17, 1976. Also see Kenya Government Statement on the "Current Relations with the Republic of Uganda" (Washington, D.C.: Kenya Embassy, July 27, 1976).

[34] <u>The Washington Post</u>, March 31, 1977, P.A1, A27.

[35] Oginga Odinga, <u>Not Yet Uhuru</u> (London: Heinemann, 1967).

[36] Julius K. Nyerere, "The Rational Choice", in Paul E. Sigmund, Jr., <u>The Ideologies of the Developing Nations</u> (New York: Praeger, 1974), pp.111-128.

[37] See Roger Mann, <u>The Washington Post</u>, op. cit., Note 32 above. Mann's findings also hold in Kenyatta's recent cancellation of the 1977 election in Kenya in fear of Odinga's increasingly growing popularity and chances of winning the election.

38 Mao Tse-Tung, On New Democracy (Peking: Foreign Language Press, 1960); also, see Paul E. Sigmund, Jr., ed., The Ideologies of the Developing Nations (New York: Praeger, 1974), pp.44-50.

39 Agola Auma-Osolo, "Objective African Military Control: A New Paradigm in Civil-Military Relations", Peace Research, Vol.17 (1980).

40 Idem.

41 Mary P. Nicholas, "Aristotle's Defense of Rhetoric", The Journal of Politics Vol.49, No.3 (1987) pp.657-677.

42 The Herald, Vol.1 No.551, Dec. 13th, 19th December, 1998 article titled "Moi's Order to Debtors.

44 The Daily Nation, Nairobi, Friday, February 19, 1999, p.1.

45 The Sunday Standard, Nairobi, May 16, 1999, p.16.

46 The Daily Nation, Nairobi, Tuesday, February 25, 2003, pp.1-5.

47 Idem.

48 Ibid., Wednesday, December 17, 2003, pp.1-12.

49 The East African Standard, Nairobi, Friday, 23rd January, 2004, p.14.

50 The Daily Nation, Nairobi, Friday, January 23rd, 2004, p.13.

51 Ibid., pp.12-13.

52 Kivutha Kibwana, "Using to Paint Others Black", Sunday Nation, Nairobi, December 28, 2003.

53 Copy from Bottom of Page 272.

54 See Daily Nation, Nairobi, 1966 (? Ask Bajah) for exact date.

55 Kenya Sessional Paper on African Socialism (1966) and The Daily Nation, Nairobi, Wednesday, 9, 1966.

[56] Copy from Bottom of pg.279.

[57] Daily Nation, Nairobi, Thursday, February 5, 2004, pp.1-2.

[58] Copy from bottom of pg.289.

CHAPTER V

LEADERSHIP ILLNESS IN NON-KENYAN COUNTRIES

[1] The World Book Encyclopaedia, ol.14, p.14.

[2] Ibid., Vol.

[3] Ibid., Vol.

[4] Agola Auma-Osolo, "The Law Society of Kenya Committed Professional Suicide" in The Kenya Times, Nairobi, Wednesday, April 16, 1997, pp.6-7.

[5] Maina Muiruri, "BABIES GIVEN AIDS IN TESTS", in Business Review Column of The Sunday Standard, Nairobi, May 16, 1999, p.17.

[6] The Agencies in Washington, D.C., Sunday, September 13, 1998, p.11.

[7] The Daily Nation, Nairobi, September 28, 1998, p.11.

[8] Ibid., January 14, 1998, p.10.

[9] The Sunday Standard, Nairobi, January, 17, 1999, p.25.

[10] Idem.

[11] A full text of the UN Preamble reads as follows:

We the Peoples of the United Nations determined:-

- To save succeeding generations from the scourge of war, which twice in our lifetime has brought untold sorrow to mankind; and
- To reaffirm faith in fundamental human rights, in the dignity and worth of the human person in the equal rights of men and women and of nations large and small; and

- To establish conditions under which justice and respect for the obligations arising from treaties and other sources of international law can be maintained; and
- To promote social progress and better standards of life in larger freedom, and for these ends
- To practice tolerance and live together in peace with one another as a good neighbour, and
- To unite our strength to maintain international peace and security, and
- To ensure, by the acceptance of principles and the institution of methods, that armed force shall not be used, save in the common interest, and
- To employ international machinery for the promotion of the economic and social advancement of all peoples, have resolved to combine our efforts to accomplish these aims.

[12] Agola Auma-Osolo, <u>The Law of The United Nations as Applied To Intervention Within the Framework of Article 2 Paragraph 7 of the UN Charter, An comparative Analysis of Selected Cases</u>, An MA Degree Thesis, University of North Carolina at Chapel Idill, (1969).

[13] <u>Idem</u>; and particularly Auma-Osolo "UN Peace Keeping Policy: Some Basic Sources of Its Implementation Problems and Their Implications", <u>California Western International Law Journal</u>, Vol.6, No.2 Spring 1976, pp.323-359.

[14] <u>Ibid.</u>, n.11.

[15] Argwings Odera, <u>Expression Today: The Journal of Democracy, Human Rights and The Media</u>, Media Institute, P.O. Box 46356, Nairobi, February 11, 1999.

[16] Prophet Isaiah, 60:2 in <u>The Holy Bible</u>.

[17] Kwendo Opanga, "Bush and Blair as War Criminals", in <u>The Sunday Standard</u>, Nairobi, February 8, 2004, p.6.

CHAPTER VI

[1] Patrice Lumumba, <u>Congo my Country</u>, New York; Praeger, (1962).

[2] <u>Jomo Kenyatta</u>, London, Secker and Warburg (1938);—The <u>Land of Conflict</u>, Manchester, International Service Bureau, Pana-Service, Ltd. (1944);—<u>Harambee! The Prime Minister of Kenya's Speeches, 1963-1964</u>, Nairobi, Oxford University Press, (1964).

3 Kwame Nkrumah, I Speak of Freedom, London, William Heinemann. (1961);—, Africa Must Unite, New York, International Publishers, (1963);—Challenge of the Congo, New York, International Publishers, (1972);—, Revolutionary Path, New York, International Publishers (1973);—Autobiography of Kwame Nkrumah, London, Thomas Nelson Ltd. (1957); and—, Ghana, London, Thomas Nelson Ltd. (1957).

4 Julius K. Nyerere, The Inauguration Lectures of the University of Zambia, Manchester, Manchester University Press (1967);—, ujamaa, Essays on Socialism; Dar-es-Salaam, Oxford University Press, (1968);—, Uhuru Na Ujamaa; (Freedom and Socialism), Dar-es-Salaam, Oxford University Press (1968);—"The Arusha Declaration: Ten Years After", Embassy of The Republic of Tanzania, 2010 Massachusetts Ave. N.W. Washington, D.C., February 14, 1977; and—, Uhuru Na Maendeleo (Freedom and Development), A Selection of Writings and Speeches, 1968-1973, London, Oxford University Press (1973).

5 Oginga Odinga, Not Yet Uhuru, Heinemann, London (1967).

6 Benjamin Nnamdi Azikiwe, Zik: A Selection From the Speeches of Dr. Nnamdi Azikiwe, Cambridge, Cambridge University Press (1961);—, Development of Political Parties in Nigeria, London, Office of The Commissioner in the United Kingdom for the Eastern Region of Nigeria (1957);—, Liberia in World Politics, New York, The Negro University Press, (1934);—, The Evolution of Federal Government in Nigeria, Orlu, Freedom Printing Press (1956).

7 Samora Machel, Establishing People's Power to Serve the Masses, Toronto, Toronto Committee for the Liberation of Southern Africa Better Read Graphics (1976).

8 Agola Auma-Osolo, "Objective African Military Control: A New Paradigm in Civil-Military Relations", Peace, Journal, Norwegian Institute of Peace Research, Oslo, Norway, No.1, Vol.17, (1980).

CHAPTER VII

1 This conclusion is a result of my practical experience as a one-time shepherd and my direct observation on the conduct of both wild and domesticated species in the village of Ebumayenga (where I was born and raised) in Esamia, and also in the Kenyan national game reserves, such as the Seringiti, Eldoret, Rimuruti and others. My findings from such studies concur with findings seen on television shows, such as Wild Kingdom, presented by the Mutual of Omaha Insurance Company.

The search for survival is an empirical reality. It does not only hold true among poultry, goats, sheep, cattle, pigeons, dogs or worms and other members of the Animal World or Kingdom. It also holds true in the botanical world of The Plant Kingdom. One does not have to be a botanist, biologist, or a farmer to understand animal behaviour. Anyone who enjoys taking the time to observe the behaviour of any animals, birds or fish and insects even those that exist in the back yard, or who enjoys observing plants in the garden, will find that each species' major goal is to sustain itself. Inasmuchas Plants compete for sunlight and water, all mammals also compete for territory, food, mates and other goals they hold as necessary. Hence, the universal behavioural paradigm among all animate species.

2   This argument is similar to that of Earnest Hass, David Mitriny, and other functionalists, who argue that each nation-State's conduct on the World Market contributes to integration among all nation-States. It also resembles Adam Smith's concept of 'laissez-faire' see, Earnest B. Haas, International Organization, Vol.15 Autumn (1961) Haas, Beyond the Nation (1964); Haas, Tangle of Hopes: American Commitments and World Order (1969) Haas, The Web of Interdependence: The U.S. and International Organizations (1970); and David Mitriny, "The Functional Approach in Historical Perspective," International Affairs, July (1971), See also Adam Smith, The Wealth of Nations (1976).

3   See George Organiski, World Politics (1969), pp.282 and 299-300, where the author argues that there is no such thing as a balance of power, and that the ultimate goal of one's attempt to form a balance of power is one's maximization of one's own national interests, but not to maintain the stability of the International System. The same argument is also found in Hans Morgenthau's Politics Among Nations (1976), Chapter 3 where he argues that international politics, like all other politics is the struggle for power, and that all statesmen throughout the history of mankind have always sought to maximize their countries' national interests.

4   During my time as a shepherd, I found that the most striking phenomenon about animal behaviour is their conduct towards a goal. Whenever I took goats to the pond or river for a drink in the later part of the afternoon (as is the tradition), the animals always ran in competition for their drinking spots. The same thing happened whenever I took them out to graze. They all ran to the pastures as fast as their legs could carry them. For sex, the males often fought very bitterly against each other over females, though the latter did not fight over the males. In the final analysis, their conflicting demands made them compete with each other for perceived goals. Greed was also a contributing factor to their competition, their running, and their physical fighting. However, the most important thing was that they made their competition for a perceived goal significantly intense. Similar

behaviour is not unique to the Animal Kingdom. Among plants, competition for sunlight and water is highly significant. In the Congo Basin Region in Africa in which luxuriant forests grow, trees strain skyward in order to be in the best position to receive the sunlight. Any tree which is unable to grow as rapidly as others do is likely to be squeezed out of the community by those that are fast growers. Those which are squeezed out automatically begin to turn yellow and finally wither away as they cannot compete for those goals essential for their survival. The other heuristic or striking phenomenon I observed and found extremely extra-ordinarily amazing was their bankruptcy in the concept of the incest law. Whereas in human life, one is not allowed to indulge in sexual intercourse with immediate relations of one's family, e.g. mother, father, brothers and sisters, all other members of the Animal Kingdom do so. They do not know this. But whereas some members of Humanity disobey the homosexual prohibition law stipulated under Leviticus 18:22 and 20:13 by God's own Command, all other members of the Animal Kingdom strictly observe it. But mankind does not and yet he/she is commanded by God under Genesis 1:26-30 to be above all creatures on earth and have total dominion over them by making sense of them his/her food or to serve him/her as he/she so wishes.

[5] For further details about the role of bargaining in political life, also see the following: Thomas C. Schelling, Arms and Influence (1968) and Strategy of Conflict(1966); Thomas L. Payne, The American Thought, The Fear of War as an Instrument of Foreign Policy (1970); John C. Harsanyi, "Bargaining in Ignorance of the Opponent's Utility Function," The Journal of Conflict Resolution, Vol.6 (1962); Thomas W. Wolf, Soviet Strategy at the Crossroads (1965); Klaus Knorr, On the Uses of Military Power in the Nuclear Age (1966); Glenn H. Snyder, "Crisis Bargaining," in Charles F. Herman, ed., International Crisis (1972), Chapter 10, pp.215-256; Paul Gordon Lauren, "Ultimatum and Coercive Diplomacy, "International Studies Quarterly, Vol.16 (1972), pp.131-167; Oran Young, The Politics of Force (1968); and Alexander George, D. Hall, and W. Simons, The Limits of Coercive Diplomacy (1971).

[6] In pacific bargaining, nation-states soberly (i.e. calmly and cheerfully) interact and transact their businesses with each other, strictly on the basis of mutual equality and sovereignty. They are always mutually concerned about who should get what, from whom, for how much, and for how long. They always enter into negotiations (i.e. a formalized pattern of bargaining) in order to establish a certain perennial goal such as, a tariff agreement to facilitate trade and other communications between or among them who are parties to that negotiation.

For instance, during the 1977 conflict between Kenya on the one hand, and Tanzania, Uganda, Zambia, Somalia, Ethiopia, Sudan and Libya on the other hand, Kenya had to send a peaceful delegation, headed by President Jomo Kenyatta's son, Peter, to Arab nation-States in June 1977, seeking for an explicit long-term mutual trade agreements as an alternative. Also see Fred Charles Ikle, How Nations Negotiate (1964) for further details on the concept of negotiation among other forms of pacific bargaining, and the strategic role these forms have played in creating a long-overdue awaited in the recently concluded two marathon peace settlement of the Somali and Sudan conflicts with the aid of Kenyan Government as host and African Union (AU), Inter-Governmental Authority on Development (IGAD), and others from the International Community in 2004/5 which had been assumed as a right-off issues in Africa.

[7] In conercive bargaining, nation-States use whatever means each consider rational (i.e. efficient) and necessary. Such means range from warnings to threats and the use of military force against each other. In warning, nation-State X may caution nation-State Y if X does not appreciate what Y is doing or plans to do either against X or another nation-State(s). Also, X may warn Y of some unjurious acts which are essentially within the domestic jurisdiction of Y, as in the case of the warning issued by the United States during the Cold War to the Soviet Union concerning the latter's violation of the Fundamental Principles of Human Rights by mistreating the Soviet Union's dissidents in the Soviet Union—an act which made the Soviet Union also warn the United States to stop interfering with the Soviet Union's domestic business. In a threatening situation, X may inform Y that unless Y stops carrying out certain acts, X would use any means necessary against Y, whatever the costs, as in the case of U.S-Soviet Union Conflict, in which the former always threatened the latter that the U.S. would definitely use massive retaliatory efforts against the Soviet Union's cities and military installations with thermonuclear weapons unless the Soviet Union quitted spreading Communism at the expense of capitalist nations. In the case of using real force, X may decide to attack Y with military forces in order to stop Y from carrying out certain acts or acquiring certain goals, as Israel did against Uganda on the 4th July, 1977, when Israel assumed that Uganda was collaborating with the captors of the Israeli hostages.

For an in-depth explanation of coercive bargaining in International Politics in the Nuclear Age, see for example, Hermann Kahn, On Thermonuclear and Defense (1961) and On Escalation (1965); Glenn H. Snyder, Deterrence and Defense (1961); and Thomas C. Schelling, Arms and Influence (1968).

[***8] The concept, "Normal Social Sciences" in this Study science" in Thomas S. Kuhn's The Structure of Scientific Revolution (1970) where the author defines it as the prevailing conventional scientific idea(s).

[9] See the principle and Purposes of the United Nations, Chapter I of The UN Charter, beginning with The Preamble.

[10] See for example, T. Walter Wallbank, Alastair M. Taylor and Nels M. Balkey, Civilization, Past and Present (1962); Zdanek Cervenenka, The Organization of African Unity and Its Charter (1969); and other relevant document(s).

[11] Arnold Wolfers, Discord and Collaboration (1962).

[12] In Pattern Maintenance, each system habitually seeks to reproduce its own basic patterns of values and norms through socialization in order to establish and maintain its unique inter-subjective world. It may do so with or without the vanguard party. However, all its sub-systems exist and function under a continuous socialization process, directly and indirectly. In Adaptation, each system seeks to adjust itself to its mediological, economic, political, ideological and normative environments. In Goal Attainment, every system seeks to identify its goals on the market and the means by which it might safely and efficiently attain those goals.

Thus, in order to function effectively in this highly competitive market, each system rationally analyzes its past experiences, the prevailing situation, and calculates the cost and net gains involved as accurately as possible because the more a system is rational, the more it will maximize the net gains of its endeavours on the markets. In Integration, each system seeks to synchronize the activities and functions of its sub-systems towards common national goals. Thus, each system seeks to maximize its enfunctions (normal functions) over its dysfunctions (malfunctions). For further details, see, for instance, Talcott Parsons, The Social System (1951); David Easton, Systems Approach to Political Life (1966). A Framework of Political Analysis (1965) and A systems Analysis of Political Life (1965); Robert K. Merton, Social Theory and Social Structure (1965); Robert K. Merton, Social theory and Social Structure (1957); Parsons and Edward Shils, eds., Toward a General Theory of Action (1951); and Marion Levy, The Structure of Society (1952).

[13] Gabriel A. Almond, "A Functional Approach to Comparative Politics," in Almond and G. Bingham Powell, Jr., Comparative Politics: A Developmental Approach (1996); Samuel P. Huntington, Political Order in Changing Scoieties (1968) and A.R. Radcliff-Brown, Structure and Function in Primitive Society (1957).

[14] Abraham Maslow, "A Theory of Human Motivation," Psychological Review, Vol.50 (1943), pp.370-396.

[15] Thomas Hobbes, The Leviathan (1651). Ibid., Chapters 14 and 15. Also see Agola Auma-Osolo, "Rationality and Foreign Policy Process, "The Year Book of World Affairs, 1977, p.261.

[16] Geographical Capability may be measured in terms of area in square miles or kilometres of that nation-State; Economic Capability in terms of that nation-State's GNP, per capital income, level of industrialization, level of urbanization, magnitude of fixed property ownership, etc., Military Capability in terms of that nation-state's capacity to inflict a decisive damage on the adversary in either pre-emptive or retaliatory strike, and its annual expenditures on the military establishment; social capability in terms of that nation-State's literacy rate; Demographic capability in terms of that nation-State's level of scientific and technological advancement; and Information Gathering and Deciphering Capability in terms of that nation-State's ability to penetrate into the information networks of both its allies and enemies, collect and transmit the highly classified strategic information (data) it desperately needs from such ends back home to its foreign policy formulation apparatus secretly and quickly for the purpose of strategic overpowering or neutralization of the enemy's ill intentions. For other definitions of national capabilities, see David O. Wilkinson, Comparative Foreign Relations: A Framework and Methods (1969), Chapters 2 and 3-7, where the author defines national capabilities in terms of power (potential military, economic and geo-demographic factors), political leadership or will, political institutions, political culture and the style of political process. Also see Julius Emeka Okollo and Winston E. Langley, "The Changing of Nigerian Foreign Policy, "World Affairs, Vol.135 (1973), pp.309-325; and Agola Auma-Osolo, Cause-Effects of African Nationalism in World Politics, Chapter IX (1979).

[17] Fredrick L. Schuman, International Politics: Anarchy and Order in World Society (1969); Robert J. Art and Robert Jervis, War and Peace (1966); Robert Osgood and Robert Tucker, Force, Order and Justice (1967) and others.

[18] Agola Auma-Osolo, "UN Peace-Keeping Policy: Some basic Sources of Its Implementation Problems and Their Implications, "California Western International Law Journal, Vol.6 (1976), pp.323-359; Auma-Osolo, The Law of the United Nations as Applied to Interventions within the Framework of Article 2(7) of the UN Charter, A Comparative Analysis of Selected Cases (1969); and Auma-Osolo, "A Retrospective Analysis of the UN Activity in the Congo and Its Significance for Contemporary Africa, 'Vanderbilt Journal of Transnational Law, Vol.8 (1975), pp.451-474.

[19] Also, see John A. Hobson, Imperialism (1965); David Healy, U.S. Expansionism, The Imperialist Urge in the 1890's (1970); Pierre Jalee, (1973); Pillage of the Third World (1968);

Imperialism in the Seventy's (1973); William L. Langer, Diplomacy of Imperialism (1951); Lenin, Imperialism, The Highest Stage of Capitalism (1917); George Lichtheim, Imperialism, The Highest Stage of Capitalism (1971); James Petras and Morris Morley, The United States and Chile: Imperialism and the Overthrow of the Allende Government (1976); and Elizabeth Farnsworth, "Chile, What Was the United States' Role?" Foreign Policy (1974).

[20] Also see Charles Darwin, On the Origins of Species by Means of Natural Selections: Or, The Preservation of Favoured Races in the Struggle for Life (1859), whose biological studies findings seem to concur pretty well with my findings on Nation-State's behaviour on the World Market.

[21] Also see Quincy Wright, A Study of War (1965).

[22] Proved in Paragraph 2 of this paper.

[23] The same problem also holds true in Mozambique where "Rhodesia" recurrently invaded without Mozambique's equal ability to deter or retaliate against Rhodesia.

[24] David Easton, op. cit., in Note 12, above.

[25] The need to satisfy multiplicity of desires from within and without African nation-States remains the most cumbersome puzzle confronting both African national leaders and political scientists. See Karl W. Dutch, "Social Mobilization and Political Development" in APSR, LV, Sept. 3 (1961). Also in S.N. Eisenstadt, ed., Political Sociology (1971); Max Weber, "Representation" in Theory of Social and Economic Organization, ed. Talcott Parsons (1974), pp.416/423; Alex de Tocqueville, "Social Conditions of the Anglo-American" in de Tocqueville's Democracy Studies in Society and History, X No.2, January (1968), pp.1973-210; Raymond Aron, "Social Structure and the Ruling Class," in British Journal of Sociology, I, No.1, March (1950); Edward A. Shils, "The Intellectuals and the Powers . . . ," Some Perspectives for Comparative Studies in Society and History, VI, No.2, November (1960), pp.205-208; and especially Samuel Huntington, Political Order in Changing Societies (1968), "Political Development and Political Decay" and "The Change to Change," Comparative Politics, April (1971), pp.283-322.

[26] Behaviour is expressed in terms of the policy's ability to respond to either mutual or disrupting inputs in order to adapt to its various and changing environmental situations.

[27] Most of the existing theories on African nation-States' affairs are a product of distorted information about Africa because "what a man sees depends upon both what he looks at

and also, upon what his previous visual-conception experience has taught him to see." In corollary, "in the absence of such learning, there can only be," What William James calls, "a blooming," buzzin' confusion," in Thomas S. Kuhn, <u>The Structure of Scientific Revolutions</u>, Vol.II (1970). P. 113. Most of this problem is derived from the works of colonial and the Normal Social Sciences historians and anthropologist, dominated and guided by Psuedo Science.

An examination of African history books shows that most accounts on Africa have been deliberately distorted mainly by historians and anthropologists who keep on misnaming traditional African peoples and places with derogative terms such as 'Bushman" instead of Kung, "Pygmy" instead of Mbuti or Twa, Lake "Victoria" instead of Lake Mwanza; and, also by hopelessly claiming that some significant places in Africa were "discovered" by European explorers. They claim that Krapf "discovered Mt. Kenya (1848) and that Rebman "discovered" Mt. Kilimanjaro (1849), as though these places had never been seen before by any African! Given that the Akamba and the Gikuyu people had been living by Mt. Kenya and the Chaga by Mt. Kilimanjaro for many centuries, were these places unknown to Africans until European "explorers" came to Africa? What about those tribes living around the so-called Lake "Victoria"? Does it also mean that no single African saw this lake until Europeans came to reveal it to him? Since they lived by, drank, swam, bathed and even reprocreated on the Lake's beaches, they were definitely knowledgeable about the Lake before the white man knew it.

[28] Andrew Karmark, <u>The Economics of African Development</u> (1971), and his article, "Obstacles to Rapid Growth in Africa: The Environmental Problem," in Agola Auma-Osolo, and Mark Tessler, eds., <u>Contending Theories and Approaches in Contemporary African Studies</u> (in progress); Benjamin Higgins, <u>Economic Development</u> (1968); D.H.K. Lee, <u>Climate and Economic Developent in the Tropics</u> (1957); and M. Colbourne, <u>Malaria in Africa</u> (1966).

[29] Most authors fallaciously regarded Ethiopia and Liberia as the traditional nations of Africa without colonial influence. An examination of the complexion of the current Ethiopians reveals two types of people: the absolutely black type and the light skinned type. The latter have long and fluffy hair, completely eccentric to the African heritage.

The long and fluffy hair breed resulted from the Arabic and Persian slave trade and the Italian colonial influence. Since the emergence (imposition) of Islam into Africa and its motto, "you either become Moslem or be enslaved," which finally resulted in the Arab slave trade in Africa and the annihilation of most Coptics (traditional Egyptians) in Egypt, who could neither accept Islam nor submit to slavery, most north and northeast Africans were subjected to torture, rape and other bodily mutilations by the Arabs. In the North, most African land was usurped and turned into what is now Algeria, Egypt, Libya, Morocco, and Tunisia. Further South, many Arabs still occupy northern Sudan. In East Africa, where Arabs had occupied Zanzibar, Pemba, and Kilwa from 1800 until they were ejected in 1960, people are still engaged in the traditional petty trade. In a sub-section of the Port of old Mombasa, Kenya, Arab dhows are still used by arabs to travel between Saudi Arabia and Kenya. When the Italians began to drift into Abyssinia, the mixed birth rate significantly increased, although statistics cannot be found to prove this because nobody kept a record. In Liberia, President Tubman was installed in power by the U.S.A. In fact, the Liberian flag shows that Liberia is in an American sphere of influence. If not, why is it made of Stripes and One Star akin to the characters of the US flag?

Also, according to the New York Times, March 24, 1957 T.O King (the then Liberian Ambasssador to the United States) confirmed that Liberia was a colony of the United States.

[30] Kwame Nkrumah, Neo-Colonialism, The Last Stage of Imperialism (1965); see also Teresa Hayter, Aids as Imperialism (1971)whose fundings are equally collaborated by the conduct of Donor Community vis a vis Countries relying on Foreign Aid such as Libya which had to bow down to pay reparations as so demanded by USA for victims of Pan-American Airline 103 on Lockerbie, Scotland on 21 December 1988.

[31] The New York Times, February 14, 1996.

[32] Both Camp have been equally active in Africa, Europe, Asia and Latin America.

[33] The conference was the search for total African unity. The idea was introduced by the Casablanca Group, Headed by Kwame Nkrumah, calling for a United States of Africa, free from neo-colonialism.

The idea was vehemently opposed by the Monrovia-Lagos Group, headed by Tubman, Azikiwe, Houphouet-Boigny and Haile Selassie I. Also, see Nkrumah, Class Struggle in Africa, (1972) and his Revolutionary Path (1973). All these empirical evidences of Nkrumah's contributions to Africa's political self awareness on the World Market outweigh those empty allegations that have been often been raised against Nkrumah by most "Africanists" e.g. Christian P. Potholm, The Theory and Practice of African politics (1979), p.57. Where Pothlom calls Nkrumah "totalitarian," etc. But shortly after his retirement as President of Tanzania in 19—and shortly before his death the late Julius K. Nyerere bitterly lamented this opposition of his colleagues against Nkrumah's idea during his keynote address to African Heads of State meeting in Accra, Ghana repenting that he was very wrong in siding with his Opposition. Because of this new change of heart in Nyerere, President Gadaffi of Libya picked up the momentum and pushed the idea further when he took up the mantle as Chairman of the Organization of African Unity (OAU)in 19—abid finally influenced all other African Heads of State to drop the opposition stand and adopt Nkrumah's original idea. It was due to this new change of heart that the OAU name has metamorphosed into the present continental name "The African Unity (AU) effective—.

[34] The New York Times, April 30, 1968

[35] Also see The New York Times, July 2, 3 and 4, 1967. For further details on the Congo Question, see for example: Ian Scott, The Tumbled House: The Congo at Independence (1969); Cone Cruise O'brien, To Katanga and Back: A UN Case History (1963); Colin Legum in Patrice Lumumba's Congo, My Country (1962); and Agola Auma-Osolo, The Law of the United Nations as Applied to Interventions within the Framework of Article 2(7) of the United nations Charter, A Comparative Analysis of Selected Cases (1969); and Auma-Osolo, "A Retrospective Analysis of the U. N. Activity in the Congo", Vanderbilt Journal of Transnational Law, Vol.8 (1975), pp.451-474.

[36] African Report, October (1969)

[37] African Report, April (1965)

[38] As a result, in spite of the Capitalist camp's continuous military aid to Israel against Egypt and other Arab nation-States, Egypt became one of the most outstanding protégés of the Capitalist camp and critic against Communism. The same model held true in Chile and the People's Republic of China vis a vis Communism today (1978-1979).

[39] Roger Mann, The Washington Post Special Correspondent in Nairobi, "Kenya Finds Succession is a Troublesome Issue", The Washington Post, October 24, 1976, p.A4.

[40] The need of national freedom, security, economic and political independence, territorial integrity, sovereign equality, the rights of self-determination, and participatory rights on the World Market.

[41] The need to mobilize and integrate different ethnic groups in one's geopolitical jurisdictions into one Nation-State.

[42] The need to improve and increase one's nations' standard of living and life expectancy. Failure to a Nation-State to achieve any of these fundamental goals generates a diabolic situation in a nation characterized by frustrations among both leader and followers and is likely to make that nation-State vulnerable to open attack by its unfriendly members of the World Market. Consequently, every Nation-State always tries to defend its own rights vis-a vis the goals it needs to protect or compete for on the World Market.

If Nation-State Y is blocked by Nation-State X from defending or acquiring certain goals, Y is likely to retaliate at all costs. For example, although Kenya and Uganda are against each other because of their common national interest they do enjoy from their membership in The East African Community in the event that one tries to block the other's aspiration towards certain goals. Each is bound to go its way and do whatever it may deem necessary in self-defence as they negatively acted against each other because of the negative way in which they perceived one another as a result of the Entebbe tragedy on the 4th of July, 1976; and the dissolution of the East Africa Community in 1977. Similarly, Tanzania and Zambia are also likely to come into conflict under similar circumstance even though both parties have always perceived each other very positively as a result of their collaboration in the Tanzo-Zambian Railways and other economic activities, fundamentally important to their economic growth and their growth as nations. A similar reason caused the break between the Soviet Union and the People's Republic of China in 1961 and the two parties' military confrontation along the Amur-Issuri Rivers in 1969. Their common beliefs in the need for the triumph of Communism over Capitalism did not deter such incidents.

When defending its goals, each Nation-State may brand the other party as "aggressor" as Israel and Uganda did against each other in the Entebbe Question. Also, while Uganda bitterly accused Kenya of collaboration with Israel against Uganda's possessional goals (Entebbe Airport), Kenya accused Uganda of collaborating with the captors of Israel's possessional goals (Israeli nationals) at Entebbe and of trying to annex what Kenya regarded as Kenya's possessional goal (territory) along the Kenya-Uganda border. However, while Kenya's subjective goal was to get the Israel hostages released, Kenya's objective goals was to exploit the prevailing Uganda-Israel hostage situation for two specific reasons: (1) to protect Kenya's possessional goals and (2) to acquire certain milieu goals. With regards to the possessional goals, Kenya sought to use Israeli's military strength and sophisticated logistics not primarily to help Israel rescue the hostages or to subdue the terrorists. Its goals was to strike a heavy blow against Uganda—to deter Uganda from annexing the territorial strip along the Kenya-Uganda border, over which Kenya and Uganda had been quarrelling for several months before the Israel hostage situation arose; and to prevent

Uganda from carrying out other acts which Kenya characterized as "Uganda's provocations against the republic of Kenya". Secondly, with regards to milieu goals, Kenya sought to gain favour with pro-Israel Nation-States and to appear heroic on the World Market. Thus, Kenya's goal on the Market was to use the situation as a political ladder by which to receive economic, moral and military aid against U.S $67.2 million worth of military hardware and aid and both naval and air cover in case Uganda chose to retaliate against Kenya— evidences which Uganda used as a justification of "Kenya's collaboration with Israel against Uganda's Entebbe Airport" (data received by phone from Kenya Desk, with Mr. Thomas O'Keefe and Mr. Richard Baker, ARF/ESA, October 21, 1976). Although the United States rationalized its military aid to Kenya by arguing that such aid was strictly humanitarian to enable Kenya to defend its possessional goals against unpredictable Ugandan attacks in revenge of what Israel had destroyed at Entebbe Airport in July of 1976, the United States did so on Israel's behalf.

Empirical evidences show what when the state of Israel was created in 1948, the United States was the principal supporter of that state; and that ever since 1948, Israel has remained a perennial economic, political, religious and moral protégé of the United States. Whatever affects Israel automatically affects the United States.

[43] Also see Julius K. Nyerere, "The Rational Choice," in Nyerere's Uhuru Na Maendeleo: Freedom and Development (1974), pp 379-380; and Nyerere, "The Arusha Declaration: Ten Years Africa," The President's Office, Dar-es-Salaam, Tanzania February 14 (1977). This Official Document is available at every Tanzanian Embassy. Also, Julius K. Nyerere, "Stability and Change," in Nyerere's Uhuru Na Maendeleo: Freedom and development (1974), pp. 108-141, where that head of state indicates that, since his Nation-State lacks the capital essential for nation-building and socio-economic development, he has no other choice but to place Tanzanian at the mercy of the sources of capital. Also, see Jomo Kenyatta, Suffering Without Bitterness (1968).

Further, Samora Machel, Establishing People's Power to Serve the Masses (1976), Amilcar Cobral, "The Weapon of Theory" in Cobral's Revolution in Guinea (1971), pp.90-110; Sekou Toure, "African Emancipation" in Paul E. Sigmund, ed., The Ideologies of the Developing Nations (1972), pp. 225-240; The Cabinet of Kenya, African Socialism and Its Application to Planning (1965); Leopold Sedar Senghor, African Socialism (1959); and Julius Emeka Okollo and Winston E. Landley, "The Changing Nigerian Foreign Policy, "World Affairs, Vol. 125 (1973), pp.309-327, "Che" Guevarra, "Socialism and Man in Cuba," in Paul E. Sigmund, ed., The Ideologies of the Development Nations (1972), pp. 373-379; Ivor Seward Richard (British Ambassador to the UN) in the Christian Science Monitor (March 18, 1975).

[44] Also, for further explanation of the strategic role and measurement of determinants of a Nation-State's behaviour on the Intenational Market <u>cum</u> International Community for System, see also P. Godfrey Okoth, <u>United States of America's Foreign Policy Toward Kenya 1952-1969</u>. Gideon S. Were Press, Nairobi (1962); Agola Auma-Osolo, <u>Cause-Effects of Modern African Nationalism of The World Market</u>, University Press of America, Lanham (1980); Andrew Morton, <u>Moi: The Making of African States-man</u> (1998); Hans Morgenthan, <u>Politics Among Nations</u>, Alfred A. Knopf, New York (1966) and—, <u>In Defense of National Interest</u>, Alfred A. Knopf, New York (1951) and also Agola Auma-Osolo "<u>Rationality and Foreign Policy Press</u>" <u>The Year Book of World Affairs 1977</u> The London Institute of World Affairs, London, 1977.